Study Guide

for

Plotnik's

Introduction to Psychology

Seventh Edition

Study Guide

for

Plotnik's

Introduction to Psychology

Seventh Edition

Matthew Enos
Harold Washington College

Language Workout by
Eric Bohman
William Rainey Harper College

THOMSON

WADSWORTH

Australia • Canada • Mexico • Singapore • Spain • United Kingdom • United States

Printed in the United States of America
1 2 3 4 5 6 7 07 06 05 04

Printer: Globus Printing

0-534-63410-9

For more information about our products, contact us at:
Thomson Learning Academic Resource Center
1-800-423-0563

For permission to use material from this text or product, submit a request online at
http://www.thomsonrights.com
Any additional questions about permissions can be submitted at
thomsonrights@thomson.com

Thomson Wadsworth
10 Davis Drive
Belmont, CA 94002-3098
USA

Asia
Thomson Learning
5 Shenton Way #01-01
UIC Building
Singapore 068808

Australia/New Zealand
Thomson Learning
102 Dodds Street
Southbank, Victoria 3006
Australia

Canada
Nelson
1120 Birchmount Road
Toronto, Ontario M1K 5G4
Canada

Europe/Middle East/South Africa
Thomson Learning
High Holborn House
50/51 Bedford Row
London WC1R 4LR
United Kingdom

Latin America
Thomson Learning
Seneca, 53
Colonia Polanco
11560 Mexico D.F.
Mexico

Spain/Portugal
Paraninfo
Calle/Magallanes, 25
28015 Madrid, Spain

Contents

Introduction

Welcome to Psychology

You are taking a challenging course. I think you will enjoy it, because psychology is one of the most exciting and relevant fields of college study today. An explosion of new ideas and research in psychology is creating a vast accumulation of knowledge that is radically changing the way we understand other people and ourselves. To participate fully and effectively in today's world, we need a kind of psychological literacy, just as we need computer literacy, Internet literacy, and other new technological abilities. This course can help you acquire the skills and information you need to become psychologically literate.

Let's Work Together

Forgive me for using the personal pronoun "I" in this Study Guide. As a teacher, I can't help imagining you working your way through psychology and Rod Plotnik's exciting new textbook, and I'd like to help. I want to speak to you as directly as I can. Even though I don't know you personally, I am sure I have had a student very much like you in my own classes. Happily, we can get to know each other — through e-mail. Throughout the Study Guide, I invite you to e-mail me! **Profenos@aol.com**

Rod Plotnik's New "Introduction to Psychology" (7th Edition)

I predict that you are going to enjoy using your new psychology textbook. My own students often ask, "Why can't *all* textbooks be like this?" Dr. Rod Plotnik, a psychologist and professor at San Diego State University, is an experienced teacher and writer who sees examples of psychology's importance everywhere he looks and loves sharing his observations with us. You'll find Rod Plotnik's book as fresh as your morning newspaper or your favorite talk show. At the same time, you'll see that his book is a work of solid scholarship. He covers the relevant research and carefully explains the major theories. It's how Rod tells it that I think you will find especially rewarding.

Rod's book is different. An expert in learning psychology, Rod knows we *understand* what we can visualize in a picture and *remember* what we can organize into a story. That's why he has filled his book with attractive pictures and compelling stories.

Excellent as his book is, I wouldn't want you to passively agree with everything Rod says. Instead, try to become actively involved in a dialogue with the book. You'll notice how often Rod *asks you a question.* Argue with him. Write notes in the margins. Highlight the important stuff. Make reading and studying this new textbook an adventure.

What Is a Module?

You may have noticed that Dr. Plotnik calls his units "Modules" instead of "Chapters," and that there are more of them than in most textbooks. Rod Plotnik wants his book to be as flexible as possible, so instructors and students can adapt it to their own needs.

Each module tackles an important aspect of psychology. If you mastered everything in every module, you would have a near-perfect understanding of modern psychology (you also might flunk your other courses!). When you read a single module, you learn the main facts and ideas about one area of interest in psychology.

Please remember that there's no law against reading an unassigned module that interests you. Hint: if you do, tell your professor about it and you'll make a good impression.

How this Study Guide Works

The bottom line for this Study Guide is that it must help you earn the grade you want in your psychology course. I tried to include materials that have worked for my own students. Some information is highly specific, aimed straight at getting more questions right on the next exam. There are observations about the field of psychology, because, as I explain in my Study Guide introduction for Module 1, if you can't see the forest because of the trees, you're lost. Still other parts have the general goal of helping you become a more effective student (and where better than in a psychology course?). The Study Guide is organized as follows:

Module Introduction

Each module in the Study Guide begins with an observation I think may help you tackle the module in the textbook more successfully. These introductions are not summaries, but thoughts about how to orient yourself toward understanding what you are reading in the textbook.

Effective Student Tip

Next, you will find a specific tip on how to become a more effective student. Some Effective Student Tips tell you how to study better, but most are general ideas about the psychology of effectiveness. Please read Tip 1, which explains more about this feature of the Study Guide.

Learning Objectives

There are seven Learning Objectives for each module. These Learning Objectives should help you understand what is most important in the module. You will notice that the first one attempts to place the subject of the module into the broad sweep of psychology. I hope these first objectives will help you understand how the subject matter of that module fits into the story of psychology.

Key Terms

Rod Plotnik has carefully selected the words or phrases he believes are the most important for beginning psychology students to learn. He puts each Key Term in **boldface** type in the text and provides a brief, clear definition of the term. These terms are also listed at the end of each module and collected in a Glossary at the end of the textbook.

If you did nothing but memorize the definition for each of the Key Terms, you would pass most psychology exams and have a pretty decent command of the vocabulary of the discipline. Of course, it wouldn't be much fun that way, and you need the story to understand psychology in any depth. Still, I can't stress enough the importance of learning the basic vocabulary.

To help you focus on these Key Terms, I have placed them (in alphabetical order) in the Study Guide right before my Outline of the module. I have also included each Key Term in the Outline and placed it in **boldface** type so you won't miss it.

Outline

Each module in the Study Guide includes a topic outline of the module in the text. My Outlines stick very close to Rod Plotnik's organization. I think working with the Outline will help you read and master the textbook.

There is one thing wrong with my Outlines: I wrote them instead of you. Much of the benefit of an outline comes from the process of building it. Therefore, your job is to turn each Outline into your own product by writing all over it and revising it as you study. Make each Outline a personal set of notes that will help you prepare for your exams. If you add your own notes and details to my Outlines, you will have an excellent summary of each module.

Notice that throughout the Outlines I have scattered questions for you to think about and answer. Each is preceded by a check box, to draw your attention to it. Why not write your answers right on the Outline?

Language Workout

Following each Outline, there is a special Language Workout section prepared by my colleague Professor Eric Bohman of William Rainey Harper College. This section is intended not only for non-native speakers, but also for all students who wish to strengthen their skills with the English language. We hope every user of the Study Guide will try the Language Workout materials. Since English is such a powerful and complicated language, anyone who reads these pages will gain greater insight into the intricacies of our wonderful language.

Even if you are quite skilled in English, I can assure you that going through the special language exercises Eric Bohman has prepared will improve your skills and deepen your understanding of how the English language works. We hope every student will try them.

Eric has written a special introduction (see page 5) to help you make the best use of his exercises. Please read it. This material is too good to miss!

Self-Tests

In each module there are six sets of questions that will help you review and give you an idea of how well you are studying. These self-tests are the most immediate and practical part of this Study Guide. Be sure to use them.

- **The Big Picture**: This quiz is intended to test your overall understanding of the importance of the module. It presents you with five (well, four, really, as you will see!) general summary statements. Which statement best expresses the larger significance of the module? Circle the letter of your choice.

- **True-False**: Ten true-false questions are intended to indicate how well you understand the main ideas in the module.

- **Flashcards 1** and **Flashcards 2**: Two sets of ten matching questions each test your recall of the more important Key Terms in the module. I have quoted Rod Plotnik's definitions as closely as possible, so your results will be a good check on how well you know them. I call these questions "Flashcards" in the hope that you will study and test yourself on the Key Terms more than once.

- **Multiple-Choice**: Twenty-five multiple-choice questions explore the important facts, concepts, and theories presented in the module. The multiple-choice questions are especially important because many of you will be taking multiple-choice exams in the course. In fact, some of my questions will be included in the test bank from which your instructor may construct exams.

- **Short Essay:** Five short essay questions (designed for answers of about 75 words) will allow you to show your grasp of the material — or cruelly expose gaps in your learning. Short essay questions can be the toughest of all to answer — not much "wiggle" room. But don't chicken out! Give them a try.

- **"For Psych Majors Only..." and other special quizzes:** In several modules, you will find a special quiz. Some of these quizzes are serious, some not so serious. The purpose of these exercises is to go a bit beyond what your course will require. I hope psychology majors will be interested. As you may have guessed, I won't mind a bit if an English major or chemistry major tries these materials! I hope you enjoy them.

Answers Section

The last section of each module in the Study Guide is an unusual Answers section. It deserves special attention. The correct answers given, of course, but there is more. For *incorrect* answers you might have chosen, there is a brief indication why that alternative is not correct. Since textbook page numbers are given with the correct answers, you can go back to Plotnick's discussion to make sure you really understand the material.

I have a confession to make about the sample answers given for the Short Essay questions. I looked at the textbook while writing my answers! I had to make sure I was correctly representing the textbook. You shouldn't look, but you also shouldn't expect your own answers to be quite as neat as mine may appear to be.

Feedback Form

On the last page of the Study Guide you will find a special mail-in form by which you can let us know how well this Study Guide worked for you and what suggestions you have for helping us make it better. Please send it in at the end of the semester. We would love to hear from you. (And see below for how to give me more immediate feedback.)

Enjoy Your Study Guide

I hope you enjoy working with the Study Guide. Think about the Effective Student Tips as you write your responses to them. Make real flashcards for the Key Terms, if you have time. Add your own notes and comments to the Outlines.

By the way, if an occasional question or comment of mine makes you laugh, *I'll be delighted!* I don't believe learning has to be deadly serious all the time. So when I was writing and couldn't take it any longer, I sometimes indulged myself in what I hoped would be a bit of humor. The results may be too corny, but you be the judge.

"You've Got Mail!"

Music to my ears! I would love to have immediate feedback about the Study Guide. Use my e-mail address to ask questions, share your thoughts, make suggestions for improvements, and, darn it, tell me about those inevitable mistakes I know some of you will find. It will be fun to share ideas with you. My e-mail address is **Profenos@aol.com** and I am eager to hear from you!

Introduction to the Language Workout Sections (by Eric Bohman)

OK, you're probably wondering what a Language Workout is. Well, when you want to build muscles and strengthen your body, you would exercise or work out. So what would you do if you wanted to strengthen your English and build your vocabulary? You would probably need to exercise your English, so that is what the Language Workout can do for you. If English is your second language, or even your first language, this part of the Study Guide will you help with certain words and sentence structures that you may be unsure of. With the Language Workout, understanding English will be "no sweat" (easy)!

You will be encountering many new words in reading *Introduction to Psychology*, especially if English is not your first language. So to help you as you read, every module of the Language Workout starts with a section on these words, expressions, idioms, and references that you're unlikely to find in your dictionary. It's called **What's That?** As you are reading the text, you can follow along in the Study Guide, page by page, to help you understand. Since most words in English have several meanings, **What's That?** can tell you which meaning is being used if you're not sure from the sentence.

There are several sections in the Language Workout to help you build up your vocabulary. **Flex Your Word Power** helps you practice how certain words are used in English, while **Build Your Word Power** will show you the different parts of the word so you can quickly identify new words with similar parts. Since it's sometimes easier to learn a family of words that all have the same basic meaning, **Meet the Word Family** will show you different forms of a word. And because some words are often confused with other words, there is a section called **What's the Difference?** to assist you.

Language is not just vocabulary, but also how those words are connected together to create meaning. **Making Connections** is a section that will help you understand how the author uses punctuation and sentence structure to guide the reader. This section also gives you a chance to practice these structures so that you can use them in your own writing and impress your teacher with your new English "muscles."

Don't worry! Each module has only a couple of these sections, but they *all* have exercises for you to practice and an **Answers** section where you can check your work.

Feel free to contact us anytime with questions, suggestions, or just feedback to tell us how the Language Workout is working for you.

Have a great time strengthening your English with the Language Workout!

Discovering Psychology

An Explosion of Knowledge

One day I found a box of my old college textbooks. I was delighted to discover the textbook I used when I took my first psychology course, years ago. Would you believe I still remembered some of the pictures and lessons?

I was shocked, though, to see how slender a book it was. It had a chapter on the eye, another on the ear, and others on the rest of the senses. There was some material on Freud, but not much on anyone else. I was struck by how much less knowledge there was in the field of psychology back then.

The explosion of research and thinking in psychology has created a problem for teachers and students. Textbooks are four times as thick, and they apologize for leaving material out. In the newer textbooks, such as the one by Rod Plotnik that you are using, the writing is lively and the graphics are superb, but there still is much more material to cover. The problem is that colleges and universities, which change very slowly, still expect you to master it all in one semester!

How to Tell the Forest from the Trees

My experience as a teacher says the single greatest problem of introductory psychology is that the sheer mass of information thrown at students overwhelms them, no matter how diligently they study. What is really important? Where are the connections between all these facts and ideas and names? What must I remember for the exams? The study of introductory psychology presents a classic example of the old problem of not being able to see the forest because of the trees.

The solution is to develop a conceptual framework for understanding psychology. If you have an overview of what questions psychology attempts to answer, how it goes about seeking answers, and what the dominant themes in the answers have been, you will be able to fit any new fact, idea, or name into a coherent picture.

That's where Module 1 comes in. In addition to describing the kinds of work psychologists do, Rod Plotnik gives you an important tool: the six major theoretical approaches to psychology. As a student and consumer of psychology, you need to know how the major pioneers in the field have tried to answer our most important questions about human behavior. Module 1 is the road map for an exciting journey.

Effective Student Tip 1

Take a Tip from Me

I have been teaching psychology for many years, but that's not what makes me so smart (ahem!). I have learned from experience. The next tip, for example, owes a lot to my own checkered past. Have you ever heard of the "reformed drunk syndrome"? Guess who you call on if you want a really convincing lecture about the evils of Demon Rum? When I talk about the importance of good attendance, do as I say, not as I did!

But there's more to it. Not only does my experience as both a student and a teacher tell me that every student wants and needs to be effective (I tell you what the professor wants and needs in Tip 18), but I think the psychology of motivation says we all desire effectiveness in every aspect of our lives.

Meanwhile, I hope you will read all these Effective Student Tips, even the ones in the modules your professor does not assign. Some will touch you personally, others may give you something to think about, and some you may not agree with at all. Writing your answers to the "Your response..." questions should help you think about yourself as a student. *Write your answers in the boxes provided.*

Please read the *next* tip and the *last* one right now. Tip 2 is the simplest, and yet the most important. Tip 25 says more about the underlying theme of all these Effective Student Tips.

Your response...

Do you consider yourself an effective person? In what ways "yes" and in what ways "no"? *[Write answer here.]*

Learning Objectives

1. Understand the aims and contents of psychology as a distinct field of study within the social sciences.

2. Learn the *six approaches to understanding behavior* as the fundamental structure of this field and know them well enough to apply them to any aspect of psychology.

3. Explain how psychology as a scientific study has developed in the modern world.

4. Appreciate how psychology has reflected the prejudices and discrimination in our culture and how professional psychology has worked to overcome them.

5. Learn what research in psychology suggests about the best strategy for taking class notes.

6. Consider the career opportunities and research areas in psychology in relation to your own interests and possible career choices.

7. Apply psychology to your immediate learning task of mastering the material in this module and to the broader goal of planning for success in the course.

Key Terms

Forget how big the textbook seems. You are not starting at square one in psychology. So much of psychology is becoming general knowledge these days that you already know quite a bit about it. Rod Plotnik defined 26 terms in this module he thought were especially important to know. How many of the following terms mean something to you right now, even without intensive study of the module?

approaches to understanding behavior
autism
behavioral approach
biological approach
biological psychology (psychobiology)
clinical psychologist
cognitive approach
cognitive neuroscience

cognitive psychology
cross-cultural approach
developmental psychology
experimental psychology
functionalism
Gestalt approach
humanistic approach
introspection
personality psychology
procrastination

psychiatrist
psychoanalytic approach
psychologist
psychology
psychometrics
social psychology
structuralism
test anxiety

Outline

Reminder: Topic outline follows textbook closely. Key terms in boldface. Outline most useful for learning and review when you add your own notes and definitions. Try my questions, too (with checkbox).

- *Introduction*
  - ☐ Why do you think Rod Plotnik begins with one very rare and one quite common example?

   1. Growing up in a strange world (Donna Williams' **autism**)

   2. **Test anxiety** (Students like you)

A. *Definition & Goals*

   1. Definition of **psychology**

   2. Goals of psychology

     a. Describe

     b. Explain

     c. Predict

     d. Control

B. *Modern Approaches*

   ☐ Can you learn the six **approaches to understanding behavior**? Well enough to understand and remember them all through the course? If so, you will possess a master plan into which almost everything in psychology will fit.

   1. **Biological approach**

     a. Autism (Donna Williams)

     b. Test anxiety

   2. **Cognitive approach**

     a. Autism (Donna Williams)

     b. **Cognitive neuroscience**

     c. Test anxiety

   3. **Behavioral approach**

     a. Autism (Donna Williams)

     b. B. F. Skinner (strict behaviorism) and Albert Bandura (social cognitive approach)

     c. Test anxiety

   4. **Psychoanalytic approach**

     a. Autism (Donna Williams)

     b. Sigmund Freud

     c. Test anxiety: example of **procrastination**

   5. **Humanistic approach**

     a. Autism (Donna Williams)

     b. Abraham Maslow: dissatisfaction with both psychoanalysis and behaviorism

     c. Test anxiety

   6. **Cross-cultural approach**

     a. How is autism diagnosed in other cultures?

     b. Test anxiety

   7. Many approaches, many answers

C. Historical Approaches

☐ Have you noticed that there is some overlap between the modern approaches (above) and the historical approaches (following)? Do you see how it's all part of the same story?

1. **Structuralism**: elements of the mind

    a. Wilhelm Wundt

    b. **Introspection**

2. **Functionalism**: functions of the mind

    a. William James

    b. Purpose of mental activity

3. **Gestalt approach**: sensations versus perceptions

    a. Max Wertheimer, Wolfgang Köhler, Kurt Koffka

    b. Perception as more than the sum of its parts

    c. Apparent motion (phi phenomenon)

4. **Behavioral approach**: observable behaviors

    a. John B. Watson ["Give me a dozen healthy infants… and my own special world to bring them up in…"]

    b. Objective, scientific analysis of observable behaviors

    c. B. F. Skinner and modern behaviorism

5. Survival of approaches

D. Cultural Diversity: Early Discrimination

1. Women in psychology

    a. Mary Calkins

    b. Margaret Washburn

2. Minorities in psychology

    a. Ruth Howard

    b. George Sanchez

3. Righting the wrongs

    a. APA efforts to help minority students

    b. State laws banning affirmative action programs

E. Research Focus: Taking Class Notes

1. What's the best strategy for taking lecture notes?

2. A research study of three techniques (which also illustrates the four goals of psychology)

☐ Which technique worked best? Can you figure out why it was superior?

F. *Careers in Psychology*

    1. Psychologist versus psychiatrist

        a. **Psychologist**

        b. **Clinical psychologist**

        c. **Psychiatrist**

    2. Many career settings

G. *Research Areas*

    1. Areas of specialization

        a. **Social psychology** and **personality psychology**

        b. **Developmental psychology**

        c. **Experimental psychology**

        d. **Biological psychology** (psychobiology)

        e. **Cognitive psychology**

        f. **Psychometrics**

    2. Making decisions

H. *Application: Study Skills*

    1. Improving study habits

        a. Common complaint

        b. Poor judges

        c. Time management

    2. Setting goals

        a. Time goal

        b. General goal

        c. Specific performance goal

    3. Rewarding yourself (self-reinforcement)

    4. Taking notes

        a. In your own words

        b. Outline format [like this one]

        c. Associate new material with old

☐ Look at the Concept Review (p. 15) and Summary Test (pp. 22-23) in the textbook. Did you notice that Rod Plotnik repeated the same illustrations he placed in the text pages? Why is this a good learning strategy?

        d. Ask yourself questions as you study

    5. Stop procrastinating

        a. Stop thinking or worrying about final goal

        b. Break overall task down into smaller goals

        c. Write down a realistic schedule

Language Workout

What's That?

p. 3   involuntarily **anesthetized** = without feeling or sensations
such as **grave** problems in developing spoken language = serious
figuring out the day of the week = identifying
getting through an ordinary day = completing the work of

p. 4   if they were **reared** by parents who were cold = raised
if they were reared by parents who were **cold** = without showing caring or love
prevent **potential** abuse = possible in the future

p. 5   **rigid corpselike stance** = standing like a dead body, unmoving

p. 6   **process** human faces = organize information into clear identification
stressful thoughts **trigger** the emotional component = stimulate, start

p. 7   students who **channeled** their worry into studying = directed, redirected

p. 9   Psychologists know that **ingrained** personality characteristics = deeply rooted

p. 20   researchers have discovered a **startling** fact = surprising

p. 24   Dr. Rimland **downplayed** the finding = argued that it is not important

Flex Your Word Power

Potential means possible, or can be developed.

> Losing financial aid is a **potential** problem for some students.
> One **potential** grade in this course is _____.
> Luis wants to get married, so he's looking for a **potential** _____.
> I am studying for a **potential** career in _____.

Potential also means possible ability that can be developed in the future.

> All students should search for ways to reach their academic **potentials** (p. 10)
> Some children have **potential** in art or math, while others show **potential** for _____.
> Guo Ping likes to help his father work on car engines, so his family thinks he has good
>   **potential** for a career as a _____.
> A _____ is one way employers try to judge an applicant's **potential**.

Meet the Word Family: perceive, perceptive, perception

Perceive (verb)

> Maria perceived that her boyfriend was angry because she read a letter where he explained
>   his feelings.
> Maria perceived that her boyfriend was angry from the look on his face.
> Maria perceived that her boyfriend was angry because he told her so.

So, <u>perceive</u> means _____

   a) feel

   b) know

   c) understand

That's right: it means all of these, and more. See how it fits in the following sentences:

People who are color-blind can't _____ the difference between red and green.

He lost his glasses, so now he can only _____ the general outlines of big objects.

Dogs are able to _____ sounds and smells that humans cannot.

Perceptive (adjective)

A highly sensitive person who **perceives** more than the ordinary person is called **perceptive**.

Helen made a good police officer because she was especially _____ about people and how to help them.

An especially _____ lawyer can usually guess whether the client is guilty or not.

Jorge notices more than the average person. That's why his teachers believe he is a _____ student.

Perception (noun)

The information you **perceive** is your **perception**.

They had created the **perception** of movement (p. 13)

The senator hid his marriage problems well, so the public _____ was that he was a good family man.

A doctor needs good powers of _____ because patients don't always reveal their problems directly.

Two people can see the same traffic accident but have different _____ s about what happened.

Test Yourself

Read the following passage and choose the best word to fill the blank.

perceive / perceptive / perception / potential

Researchers have designed experiments to test perceptual differences between men and women. They wanted to establish whether men _____ colors differently from women. The popular _____ is that females can actually see smaller differences in color, so many people believe that women are more _____ in other areas as well. One theory is that both sexes have the same physical ability but that some cultures develop women's _____ to discriminate colors more than men's.

Answers

Researchers have designed experiments to test perceptual differences between men and women. They wanted to establish whether men **perceive** colors differently from women. The popular **perception** is that females can actually see smaller differences in color, so many people believe that women are more **perceptive** in other areas as well. One theory is that both sexes have the same physical ability but that some cultures develop women's **potential** to discriminate colors more than men's.

The Big Picture

Which statement below offers the best summary of the larger significance of this module?

A   Building on a long history that goes back to the ancient world, psychology today offers respect, honor, and financial security to those few who can complete medical school and post-doctoral training.

B   There is no single "true" psychology because it is still a young and hotly debated science. At this stage in its growth, six theoretical approaches offer quite different but still valuable answers to life's complex problems.

C   Psychology has not yet achieved the respect of the scientific community because there are so many answers and so many different specialties competing for our attention.

D   A civil war has raged within psychology for more than a century, but the Freudian system is gradually emerging as the most convincing overall answer.

E   How many psychologists does it take to change a light bulb, you ask? The answer is three: one to hold the ladder, one to change the bulb, and one to share the experience.

True-False

_____   1. The goals of psychology are to explain, describe, predict, and control behavior.

_____   2. There are as many different approaches to psychology as there are psychologists writing about psychology.

_____   3. The psychoanalytic approach to psychology is based on the belief that childhood experiences greatly influence the development of later personality traits and psychological problems.

_____   4. Abraham Maslow wanted humanistic psychology to be a new way of perceiving and thinking about the individual's capacity, freedom, and potential for growth.

_____   5. It is best to pick one of the general approaches to psychology and organize your thinking and work around it exclusively.

_____   6. Wilhelm Wundt attempted to accurately measure the conscious elements of the mind with his method of introspection.

_____   7. The Gestalt approach emphasized that perception is more than the sum of its parts and studied how sensations are assembled into meaningful perceptual experiences.

_____   8. There has been ethnic discrimination in psychology, but at least women have always been equally represented.

_____   9. Not only do you have several career choices in psychology — whichever one you choose, you are almost certain to make big bucks!

_____   10. There is no special program for overcoming procrastination: just get off your duff and get to work.

Flashcards 1

_____ 1. autism

_____ 2. behavioral approach

_____ 3. biological approach

_____ 4. cognitive approach

_____ 5. cross-cultural approach

_____ 6. humanistic approach

_____ 7. psychoanalytic approach

_____ 8. psychology

_____ 9. psychometrics

_____ 10. test anxiety

a. The systematic scientific study of behaviors and mental processes

b. rare problem with severe impairments in communication, motor systems, socialization

c. studies the influence of cultural and ethnic similarities and differences on functioning

d. physiological, emotional, cognitive problems in thinking and reasoning caused by stress of exams

e. emphasizes individual freedom, capacity for personal growth, potential for self-fulfillment

f. interested in how we process, store, and use information; how information influences us

g. focuses on measurement of abilities, skills, intelligence, personality, abnormal behaviors

h. focuses on influence of unconscious fears, desires, and motivations on thoughts, behavior

i. examines how genes, hormones, and nervous system interact with environments

j. analyzes how organisms learn new behaviors through reward, punishment from environment

Flashcards 2

_____ 1. clinical psychologist

_____ 2. cognitive neuroscience

_____ 3. developmental psychology

_____ 4. experimental psychology

_____ 5. functionalism

_____ 6. Gestalt approach

_____ 7. introspection

_____ 8. psychiatrist

_____ 9. psychologist

_____ 10. structuralism

a. study of basic elements like perception that make up conscious mental processes

b. emphasized that perception is more than sum of its parts; how sensation becomes perception

c. has completed 4-5 years of postgraduate education; has obtained Ph.D. in psychology

d. includes areas of sensation, perception, learning, human performance, motivation, and emotion

e. study of function rather than structure of consciousness; how mind adapts to change

f. taking pictures and identifying structures and functions of the living brain during performance of mental processes

g. medical doctor (MD) with additional years of clinical training in diagnosis, treatment

h. has Ph.D. plus specialization in clinical psychology and supervised work in therapy

i. method of exploring conscious mental processes by asking subjects to look inward

j. examines moral, social, emotional, cognitive development throughout a person's entire life

Multiple-Choice

_____ 1. Rod Plotnik tells the story of Donna's struggle with autism in order to make the point that psychology is
   a. the one science that has all the answers
   b. a rather grim science that involves lots of pain and suffering
   c. helpless when confronted with really severe human problems
   d. dedicated to answering questions about complex behaviors

_____ 2. One thing that was different about Donna in school was that
   a. when she made a friend, she tried to avoid getting a friendly hug
   b. when the teacher asked a question, she always had her hand up first
   c. when a student seemed sad, she was sympathetic and understanding
   d. when the school day ended, she always found a friend to walk home with

_____ 3. A small percentage of autistics are called "savants" because they
   a. believe they have been "saved" by religion
   b. have incredible artistic or memory skills
   c. probably will have to work in low paying jobs like being servants
   d. are extremely smooth-talking with other people

_____ 4. Which one of the following is _not_ one of the four goals of psychology?
   a. to explain the causes of behavior
   b. to predict behavior
   c. to judge behavior
   d. to control behavior

_____ 5. The biological approach to psychology focuses on
   a. the workings of our genes, hormones, and nervous system
   b. conscious processes like perception and memory
   c. the effects of reward and punishment on behavior
   d. unconscious processes

_____ 6. One of the most powerful new techniques in the biological approach is
   a. testing how people process, store, and use information
   b. discovering how individuals learn new behaviors or modify existing ones
   c. taking computerized photos of the activity of living brains
   d. studying how the first five years affect later personality development

_____ 7. The cognitive approach to psychology studies how we
   a. are motivated by unconscious processes
   b. are motivated by the need for self-fulfillment
   c. process, store, and use information
   d. program our behavior by seeking rewards and avoiding punishments

_____ 8. The major contributor to the behavioral approach to psychology was
   a. Sigmund Freud
   b. B. F. Skinner
   c. William James
   d. Abraham Maslow

_____ 9. Some behaviorists, such as Albert Bandura, disagree with strict behaviorism because
   a. there are mysteries in psychology we will never understand
   b. animals pressing levers are not the same as real people dealing with life
   c. our behaviors are also influenced by observation, imitation, and thought processes
   d. most psychologists like to take a position different from everyone else

_____ 10. The great importance of the unconscious is stressed in the _____ approach
   a. psychoanalytic
   b. cognitive
   c. behavioral
   d. biological

_____ 11. The psychoanalytic approach to understanding procrastination as a component of test anxiety would
   a. emphasize the role of habitual modes of thinking and problem solving
   b. study brain scans of procrastinators while they think about schoolwork
   c. compare school strategies used by students in different cultures
   d. look beneath the obvious reasons and try to identify unconscious personality problems

_____ 12. _____ was one of the major figures of the humanistic approach to psychology
   a. Sigmund Freud
   b. Abraham Maslow
   c. B. F. Skinner
   d. Donna Williams

_____ 13. The newest of the six approaches to psychology is the
   a. psychoanalytic
   b. humanistic
   c. cognitive
   d. cross-cultural

_____ 14. The cross-cultural approach to psychology studies the influence of _____ on psychological functioning
   a. brain chemistry
   b. information processing
   c. cultural and ethnic similarities and differences
   d. automatic behaviors and deeply ingrained habits

_____ 15. Once we understand the six approaches to psychology, Rod Plotnik advises us to
   a. make a personal decision about which approach is best
   b. combine and use information from all six approaches
   c. place our trust in the approaches that have stood the test of time
   d. judge each approach by the famous people who have supported it

_____ 16. The difference between "structuralism" and "functionalism" in the early years of psychology concerned a choice between
   a. British or American psychology
   b. Abraham Maslow or John B. Watson
   c. studying the brain or the cultural setting of behavior
   d. studying narrow sensations or general adaptations to our changing environment

_____ 17. the first textbook in psychology (1890) was written by
  a. William James
  b. John B. Watson
  c. Max Wertheimer
  d. Wilhelm Wundt

_____ 18. By explaining perceptual phenomena like the phi phenomenon [apparent motion], Gestalt researchers gave psychology the idea that
  a. the whole is more than the sum of its parts
  b. research results could be profitable when applied to advertising
  c. Wundt and the structuralists had been right about the importance of the individual parts
  d. individual parts are more significant than resulting wholes

_____ 19. The pioneering psychologist who offered the famous guarantee about being able to shape a baby into any type of specialist you might want was
  a. William James
  b. John B. Watson
  c. Max Wertheimer
  d. Wilhelm Wundt

_____ 20. The early behaviorist John B. Watson wanted psychology to be a/n
  a. introspective investigation of how people understood the workings of their minds
  b. objective, scientific study of observable behavior
  c. philosophical study of the continuous flow of mental activity
  d. religious program for "building" moral children

_____ 21. Despite an earlier history of discrimination, today women in psychology
  a. earn more money than men
  b. are still stuck in teaching jobs at women's colleges
  c. are still barred from the elite university training programs
  d. earn more Ph.D. degrees than men

_____ 22. As measured by membership in the American Psychological Association, minorities in psychology
  a. lag far behind other Americans
  b. are about the same as their proportion of the general population
  c. will soon exceed white Americans
  d. may have lagged earlier, but are now rapidly catching up

_____ 23. The efforts of American psychology to overcome discrimination may be threatened by
  a. state laws banning affirmative action programs
  b. a steady decline in the numbers of men going into psychology
  c. wide-spread African American and Latino disinterest in the subject of psychology
  d. a new policy of the American Psychological Association against affirmative action

_____ 24. After reading the material on careers and research areas, it would be reasonable to conclude that psychology
  a. requires so much education that few students should consider it
  b. will have fewer job opportunities in coming years
  c. offers a great variety of intellectual challenges and kinds of work
  d. is one of the best paid professions today

_____ 25. Which one of the following is *not* a good strategy for overcoming procrastination?
  a. stop thinking or worrying about the final goal
  b. break the final assignment down into a number of smaller goals
  c. write down a realistic schedule for reaching each of your smaller goals
  d. do not begin working until you have complete confidence that you will succeed

For Psych Majors Only...

Contributors to Psychology: A matching exercise based on important people in psychology.

_____

_____ 1. Albert Bandura	a. humanistic psychology movement
_____ 2. Mary Calkins	b. author of your psychology textbook
_____ 3. Ruth Howard	c. denied a doctorate in psychology by Harvard
_____ 4. William James	d. social learning theory
_____ 5. Abraham Maslow	e. founded Gestalt psychology movement
_____ 6. Rod Plotnik	f. strict behaviorism
_____ 7. B. F. Skinner	g. studied function of conscious activity
_____ 8. John B. Watson	h. first laboratory for psychological research
_____ 9. Max Wertheimer, Wolfgang Kohler, and Kurt Koffka	i. "Give me a dozen healthy infants… and my own special world to bring them up in…"
_____ 10. Willhelm Wundt	j. first African-American Ph.D. in psychology

Short Essay

All Short Essay questions are designed for answers of about 75 words.

1. Of the six approaches to understanding behavior, perhaps the *biological* and *cross-cultural* differ the most from each other. Explain, describing the key ideas and focus of study of each approach.

2. What point was John B. Watson making when he claimed that he could make a child into any kind of specialist if he could control the child's environment?

3. Summarize the history of discrimination against women and minorities in psychology.

4. How do the training and responsibilities of psychologists and psychiatrists differ?

5. What advice does psychology have to offer a student suffering from procrastination?

Answers to "Contributors to Psychology" quiz

| 1 d | 2 c | 3 j | 4 g | 5 a | 6 b | 7 f | 8 i | 9 e | 10 h |

Answers for Module 1

The Big Picture

A Neither medical school nor post-doctoral training is necessary for a career in psychology.
B Correct! You see the "big picture" for this Module.
C Science does not demand a single approach; there is controversy in all scientific fields.
D Just the opposite is true (Freud's theory is in decline today).
E It's just a joke!

True-False (explanations provided for False choices; page numbers given for all choices)

1	T	4	
2	F	5	There are six major approaches to psychology.
3	T	9	
4	T	10	
5	F	11	Each of the six approaches can be a valuable source of information.
6	T	12	
7	T	13	
8	F	14	There has been discrimination against women as well as minority groups.
9	F	17	Psychology is a varied field in which the pay is good but not spectacular.
10	F	21	There are three specific steps you can take to overcome procrastination.

Flashcards 1

1 b	2 j	3 i	4 f	5 c	6 e	7 h	8 a	9 g	10 d

Flashcards 2

1 h	2 f	3 j	4 d	5 e	6 b	7 i	8 g	9 c	10 a

Multiple-Choice (explanations provided for incorrect choices)

1 a Psychology does not claim to have all the answers.
   b Psychology studies all human behavior, not just painful events.
   c Like other sciences, psychology *in theory* can answer any question stated in operational terms.
   d Correct! See page 3.

2 *a Correct! See page 3.*
   b Autistics do not easily engage in social activities.
   c Empathy does not come easily to autistics.
   d Autistics would tend to avoid social situations.

3 a "Savant" refers to knowledge, not religion.
   b Correct! See page 3.
   c "Savant" refers to knowledge, not service.
   d This would not fit the typical autistic.

4 a Understanding and explaining behavior is one of the four goals of psychology.
   b Predicting behavior is one of the four goals of psychology.
   c Correct! See page 4.
   d Controlling behavior is one of the four goals of psychology.

5 *a Correct! See page 6.*
   b This would be true for the cognitive approach.
   c This would be true for the behavioral approach.
   d This would be true for the psychoanalytic approach.

6 a This would be true for the cognitive approach.
   b This would be true for the behavioral approach.
   c Correct! See page 6.
   d This would be true for the psychoanalytic approach.

7   a   The psychoanalytic approach studies unconscious processes.
     b   The humanistic approach studies the need for self-fulfillment.
     c   *Correct! See page 7.*
     d   The behavioral approach studies reward and punishment.

8   a   Sigmund Freud was the major contributor to the psychoanalytic approach.
     b   *Correct! See page 8.*
     c   William James was a major contributor to the cognitive approach.
     d   Abraham Maslow was a major contributor to the humanistic approach.

9   a   Most scientists would not rule out any aspect of human behavior from eventual explanation.
     b   Behaviorists believe animals and humans follow the same basic laws of behavior.
     c   *Correct! See page 8.*
     d   For any good scientist, finding the truth is more important than individual fame.

10   *a*   *Correct! See page 9.*
     b   The cognitive approach stresses conscious mental activity.
     c   The behavioral approach stresses learning through reinforcement.
     d   The biological approach stresses brain functioning and heredity.

11   a   This would be truer of the behavioral approach.
     b   This would be truer of the biological approach.
     c   This would be truer of the cross-cultural approach.
     d   *Correct! See page 9.*

12   a   Sigmund Freud was a major figure in the psychoanalytic approach.
     b   *Correct! See page 10.*
     c   B. F. Skinner was a major figure in the behavioral approach.
     d   Donna Williams is the autistic woman described in the textbook.

13   a   The psychoanalytic approach is a century old.
     b   The humanistic approach dates to the 1960s.
     c   The cognitive approach dates to the 1970s.
     d   *Correct! See page 11.*

14   a   Brain anatomy and chemistry are studied by the biological approach.
     b   Information processing and thinking are studied by the cognitive approach.
     c   *Correct! See page 11.*
     d   Automatic behaviors and deeply ingrained habits are studied by the behavioral approach.

15   a   Each approach to psychology offers unique insights — we need all of them.
     b   *Correct! See page 11.*
     c   Neither "trust" nor "the test of time" is an appropriate measure in evaluating the six approaches to psychology.
     d   The fame of persons associated with an approach is not relevant to its value.

16   a   The debate was not about national rivalry for leadership.
     b   Neither Maslow nor Watson was involved in the earlier debate between structuralism and functionalism.
     c   The debate was over specific or general mental activity, not brain or culture.
     d   *Correct! See page 12.*

17   *a*   *Correct! See page 12.*
     b   Watson was the first behavioral psychologist.
     c   Wertheimer argued that the whole is more than the sum of its parts.
     d   Wundt established the first laboratory in psychology.

18   *a*   *Correct! See page 13.*
     b   The Gestalt psychologists were motivated by science, not profit (too bad for them!).
     c   Just the opposite is true.
     d   Just the opposite is true.

19   a   James wrote the famous *Principles of Psychology*.
     b   *Correct! See page 13.*
     c   Wertheimer was a pioneer of Gestalt, not behaviorist, psychology.
     d   Wundt established the first laboratory in psychology.

20 a Watson argued against introspection and in favor of an objective psychology.
    b *Correct! See page 13.*
    c This would be true for William James and cognitive psychology.
    d This is a misreading of Watson's famous statement about shaping behavior.

21 a Women in psychology do not earn more than men.
    b That was true earlier, but not now.
    c That was true earlier, but not now.
    d *Correct! See page 14.*

22 *a* *Correct! See page 14.*
    b That is the goal, but psychology is still far from it.
    c A wild exaggeration.
    d That should be happening, but is not yet.

23 *a* *Correct! See page 14.*
    b There is no significant decline of men going into psychology.
    c There is no evidence that African Americans and Latinos are uninterested in psychology.
    d The APA continues to favor affirmative action.

24 a Most desirable professions today require significant investment in education.
    b Job opportunities in fields related to psychology are increasing.
    c *Correct! See page 19.*
    d Only a few specialties in psychology are especially well paid.

25 a Focusing on more immediate goals is a good way to overcome procrastination.
    b Breaking the task down into smaller goals is a good way to overcome procrastination.
    c Making a realistic schedule for reaching goals is a good way to overcome procrastination.
    d *Correct! See page 21.*

Short Essay (sample answers)

1. The biological and cross-cultural approaches to understanding behavior differ more than any other pair. The biological approach is based on physical characteristics like genes, hormones, and the nervous system. The cross-cultural approach, in contrast, is based on cultural and ethnic similarities and differences on psychological and social functioning. The differences between the two approaches involve biology vs. sociology, brain functions vs. human interaction, and a focus on individuals vs. a focus on groups.

2. Watson meant that the environment a person grows up in is more important than his or her inborn characteristics. He imagined that if he could control a child's environment he could shape that child into almost any kind of adult one might specify. Watson wanted psychology to be an objective, scientific analysis of observable behaviors. He believed that this approach, and only this approach, would provide the ability to predict and control behavior.

3. Psychology, as the scientific study of human behavior, should have rejected prejudice and discrimination from the beginning. But psychologists are also members of their culture, and they have reflected the prejudices and discriminatory practices of American society. Women and members of minority groups suffered the same discrimination in psychology as in the wider society. Today, psychology is trying hard to overcome this heritage, but women and minorities still lag significantly behind white males in the field.

4. Both psychologists and psychiatrists help people with mental health problems, although they differ in training and special focus. Psychologists usually have a Ph.D. in psychology, while psychiatrists have an M.D. and clinical training in psychiatry. Psychologists generally offer counseling and insight therapy, sometimes called "talk therapy," while psychiatrists consider physical and neurological causes of abnormal behavior and may prescribe drug therapy in addition to counseling.

5. Instead of panicking and freezing up, as overburdened students often do, psychology applies scientific analysis and an objective approach to the problem of procrastination. Three steps can help: (1) stop thinking about the final goal, (2) break the assignment down into smaller, easier to accomplish steps, and (3) write down a realistic schedule for reaching each of the smaller goals. Finally, use self-reinforcements or rewards to keep on schedule and accomplish the specific goals.

Module 2

Psychology & Science

Science and the Scientific Method

When we think of science, we imagine a person in a white lab coat working some kind of magic we can't understand. But that's not science. Science is a method of asking and answering questions about nature, including human nature. Science is only one of many ways of solving problems by answering questions through the analysis of gathered information. There are older and more widely used methods, such as reliance on tradition, custom, or authority. For much of our work, however, science is the most powerful intellectual tool yet invented.

Science offers a methodical procedure for the analysis of objective events. It is *not* simply the discoveries scientists make, or the techniques scientists use, or the beliefs that any scientists may hold. Instead, science is a way of approaching the task of gathering information and creating knowledge. It is a *method* of analysis.

Rules of Procedure and Basic Assumptions about Reality

Science consists of two related features: (1) a set of characteristics or rules of procedure, and (2) a set of basic assumptions about reality. The first feature constitutes the rules of the game that scientists follow in the laboratory. These rules require objectivity, freedom from bias, objective data collection, public procedures, precise definitions, careful measurements, logical reasoning, rigorous control of variables, systematic examination of relationships, and self-criticism. Through replication, scientists aim to create theories that allow prediction and control.

The second feature constitutes the starting point of science, what all scientists agree on about how nature works. These assumptions are that all events are naturally determined, that nature is orderly and regular, that truth is relative, and that knowledge is gained through empiricism, rationalism, and replication. Of course these basic assumptions about reality are assumptions rather than proven facts. Consequently, it is not necessary to believe that these assumptions are universally 'true' in order to use the scientific method.

Together these two features of the scientific method also serve as a checklist for the researcher. Any violation of or deviation from the rules of procedure or the basic assumptions about reality puts an investigation outside the realm of science and renders its results untrustworthy.

> Check it out! PowerStudy 2.0 includes a 40-50 minute presentation that uses animations, visuals, and interactive activities as well as quizzing to help you understand concepts in this module.

Effective Student Tip 2

Attend Every Class

I shudder when I hear about college teachers who advise, "Come to class if it helps, but attendance isn't required." That's such poor psychology and such destructive advice. Students should attend *every* class, even the dull ones, because regular attendance leads directly to involvement and commitment, the basic ingredients of effective college work.

We aren't talking morals here, we're talking the psychology of effectiveness. Here's why attendance is the basis of successful college work. (1) Good attendance makes you feel more confident, purposeful, and in control. (2) Attendance is the one feature of college that is completely under your control. (3) The reason for an absence usually reveals some area in which you feel ineffective. (4) Whether they make a big deal of it or not, your professors want and need your good attendance. What if no one came? (5) There is more to a class than the lecture. Other good things happen when you attend class regularly. Your professor gets to know you. You become better acquainted with your classmates. You learn from them and you learn by helping them. (6) Most students can achieve perfect attendance if they try, and their professors will admire them for it. You can help make a good class a great one.

Your response...

What is your attendance history? Do you have an attendance goal for this class?

Learning Objectives

1. Understand psychology as the scientific pursuit of knowledge about human behavior.

2. Know the main strengths and weaknesses of each of the three main methods of scientific research — the survey, the case study, and the experiment — and when each should be used.

3. Appreciate the concepts of bias, error, testimonials, correlation, and causation and explain why it is so important for educated citizens to understand them.

4. Apply the concept of a placebo to both research method and everyday human behavior.

5. Explain the logic of the scientific experiment, the seven rules it requires, and why only an experiment can reveal causation.

6. Appreciate how scientific research is attempting to resolve important controversies over ADHD.

7. Be aware of the controversies about science in psychology: the ethics of research, the role of deception, and problems with using both human and animal subjects.

Key Terms

The vocabulary of science has become essential for any educated person. How many of these key terms did you know something about already, even before you read the textbook?

animal model
attention-deficit/hyper-
   activity disorder (ADHD)
case study
control group
correlation
correlation coefficient
debriefing
dependent variable
double-blind procedure

experiment
experimental group
hypothesis
independent variable
interview
laboratory experiment
laboratory setting
naturalistic setting
placebo
placebo effect

questionnaire
random selection
scientific method
self-fulfilling prophecy
standardized test
statistical procedures
survey
testimonial

Outline

- *Introduction*
   1. **Attention-deficit/hyperactivity disorder (ADHD)** (Dusty)
   2. Rhino horn and magnets (Beliefs)

A. *Answering Questions*

    1. Why the controversies about ADHD?

    2. Three major research methods

        a. **Survey**

        b. **Case study**

        c. **Experiment**

B. *Surveys*

    1. Kind of information: hand washing, worries, ADHD

    2. Disadvantages

        a. How questions are worded

        b. Who asks the questions

    3. Advantages

    ☐ What are the main advantages and disadvantages of the survey method?

C. *Case Study*

    1. Kind of information in **case study**

    2. Personal case study: **testimonial**

    ☐ What are the main advantages and disadvantages of a testimonial?

    3. Error and bias in testimonials

        a. Personal beliefs

        b. **Self-fulfilling prophecy**

D. *Cultural Diversity: Use of Placebos*

    1. Examples of mind over body

        a. **Placebo**

        b. **Placebo effect**

    2. Common world-wide placebos

        a. Rhino horn

        b. Bear gallbladders

        c. Tiger bones

        d. Magnets

    ☐ What beliefs and practices in the United States might be thought of as our own "rhino horn?"

    3. Conclusion: testimonials and placebos

E. *Correlation*

    1. Definition

        a. **Correlation**

        b. **Correlation coefficient**

2. Correlation coefficients

   a. Perfect positive correlation coefficient (+1.00)

   b. Positive correlation coefficient (+0.01 to +0.99)

   c. Zero correlation (0.00)

   d. Negative correlation coefficient (-0.01 to -0.99)

   e. Perfect negative correlation coefficient (-1.00)

3. Correlation versus causation

4. Correlations as clues

5. Correlation and predictions

F. *Decisions about Doing Research*

1. Choosing research techniques

   a. **Questionnaire** and **interview**

   b. **Standardized test**

   c. **Laboratory experiment**

   d. **Animal model**

2. Choosing research settings

☐ What are the main advantages and disadvantages of each setting?

   a. **Naturalistic setting** (case study)

   b. **Laboratory setting**

G. *Scientific Method: Experiment*

1. Advantages of scientific method

   a. **Scientific method**

   b. **Experiment**

2. Conducting an experiment: seven rules

☐ Why is a control group needed in a scientific experiment?

☐ What makes the double-blind procedure superior to the typical experiment?

   a. Rule 1: ask (**hypothesis**)

   b. Rule 2: identify variables

     (1) **Independent variable** (treatment)

     (2) **Dependent variable** (resulting behavior)

   c. Rule 3: choose subjects (**random selection**)

   d. Rule 4: assign subjects randomly

     (1) **Experimental group**

     (2) **Control group**

  e. Rule 5: manipulate independent variable

   (1) administer treatment

   (2) **Double-blind procedure**

  f. Rule 6: measure resulting behavior (dependent variable)

  g. Rule 7: analyze data

   (1) Sample

   (2) **Statistical procedures** (see Appendix in textbook)

H. *Research Focus: ADHD Controversies*

   ☐ Do you know a child who is hyperactive? What is he or she like?

  1. Controversy: diagnosis

  2. Controversy: treatment

   a. Stimulants: advantages

   b. Stimulants: disadvantages

  3. Controversy: long-term effects

   ☐ Do you have an opinion concerning the controversies surrounding ADHD?

I. *Application: Research Concerns*

  1. Concerns about being a subject

   ☐ Would you volunteer to be a subject in a psychological experiment?

  2. Code of ethics

   a. American Psychological Association ethical guidelines

   b. **Debriefing**

  3. Role of deception

  4. Ethics of animal research

   ☐ Do you believe animals should be used in research?

   a. Pros, cons, and safeguards

   b. Striking a balance

College Study

The longer you are in college, the more you will appreciate the great overlap in all fields of study. The way we have them neatly arranged in the college catalog is artificial. Therefore, whether you are a business major or English major, congratulate yourself on having had the wisdom to enroll in psychology. You'll find that there are many connections and tie-ins between psychology and other fields of study.

Language Workout

What's That?

p. 27 **throwing a fit** = show uncontrolled anger
such as **fidgeting** = nervous moving
maladaptive development = growing in the wrong direction
children who are **rambunctious** = lively, full of energy

p. 28 a family **copes with** a child = manages problems of
my sons ate green **frosting** = sweet covering for cake

p. 30 observer has **preconceived notions** = ideas about something before it happens

p. 31 **poachers** had reduced the number of rhinos = illegal hunters
increase **flagging** libidos = decreasing, tired
increase flagging **libidos** [lih-BEE-dohz] = sexual drive or energy

p. 35 children **throw tantrums** = same as **throwing a fit**

p. 36 information can suggest but not **pinpoint** = identify precisely

p. 40 no **lingering** psychological worries = continuing

p. 41 may have seen a **disturbing** photo = makes you feel uncomfortable
isolated cases of **malpractice** = done in an unprofessional manner
I go through a **soul-searching** = thinking deeply about your values and beliefs
especially true **in light of** recent rules = considering

p. 44 names were **flagged** = highlighted, marked for special attention
the **epidemiological** study = recording spread of disease

Build Your Word Power

When you see **over** at the beginning of a word, it usually means "too much." Look at these examples from the text and see if you can guess the meanings.

> **Over**stimulation caused Donna to stare (p. 3)
> A tremendous sensory **over**load that makes her freeze up (p. 4)
> the use of Ritalin concerns whether it is being **over**prescribed (p. 27)

Another prefix (the beginning part of a word) that is similar is **hyper**. For example, **hyper**sensitive means too sensitive. Guess this word's meaning from the text: Dusty was diagnosed as being **hyper**active. (p. 27)

What's the Difference?

Affect? Effect? These words are often confused by native speakers of English.

Affect means to change or influence = Heat and cold **affect** water in different ways.
Effect means a result or to cause something = Steam is one **effect** of heating water.

Remember that only **effect** is used as a noun.

> A bad grade can **affect** a student in different ways.
> If the teacher can **effect** a change in Syed's attitude, he may do better.

Hard work will have a positive **effect** on his grade.

Each student's own personality will **affect** his or her own reaction.

Other variables, such as family problems, money problems, and physical health, can also _____ the student's response.

Parents worry about the _____ of violent movies on young children.

Drinking coffee can _____ both mind and body. Increased energy is one good _____, but trouble going to sleep is a bad _____.

TIP: Try substituting with the word "change." If it sounds correct, then use **affect**.

Flex Your Word Power

bias: (noun) means prejudice, a judgment distorted by personal feelings.

> Job applicants for the police department are tested for **bias** against particular races or groups.
> The chief of police has stated that racial **bias** and religious **bias** have no place in police work.
> Max's years of eating in school cafeterias developed his **bias** against macaroni-and-cheese.
> While guarding against error and **bias**. (p. 29)

biased: (adjective) means distorted by personal feelings, influenced by bias

> Hyun loves hiking in the woods, so she is **biased in favor of** strong controls to protect the environment.
> Alvaro complains that his parents are **biased against** rap music because they won't even listen to the songs.
> Surveys may be **biased**. (p. 29)
> case studies can also result in wrong or **biased** answers. (p. 30)

Bias can also be used as a verb. This means to influence or distort based on personal feelings.

> The misleading survey questions **biased** the answers.
> If we believe strongly in something, it may **bias** our perception. (p. 30)

Test Yourself

Read the following passage and choose the <u>three</u> best words to fill the blanks.

> **affect / effect / bias / biased**

Why did the dinosaurs disappear? One hypothesis is that a giant meteor hit the earth. What sort of _____ would such an event have on animal life? Certainly the disaster would _____ the weather and the food sources for all animals, possibly leading to widespread death. Of course, these critics want to push their own theories, so their arguments could be _____.

Answers

Other variables, such as family problems, money problems, and physical health, can also **affect** the student's response.

Parents worry about the **effect** of violent movies on young children.

Drinking coffee can **affect** both mind and body. Increased energy is one good **effect** but trouble going to sleep is a bad **effect**.

Why did the dinosaurs disappear? One hypothesis is that a giant meteor hit the earth. What sort of **effect** would such an event have on animal life? Certainly the disaster would **affect** the weather and the food sources for all animals, possibly leading to widespread death. Of course, these critics want to push their own theories, so their arguments could be **biased**

The Big Picture

Which statement below offers the best summary of the larger significance of this module?

A   The essence of scientific research in psychology necessarily is deception. Therefore, it probably would be wise not to volunteer to be a subject in a psychological experiment.

B   Psychology, because it sometimes uses the case study method and the survey method, is only partly a science. To be a true science, psychology would have to rely on the laboratory experiment alone.

C   When psychology at last becomes completely scientific, it will be able to answer any question we might have about the truth of our beliefs, the rightness of our behaviors, and the meanings of our lives.

D   Psychology uses several different research strategies and techniques. What makes psychology scientific, however, is that all of them have in common a devotion to *objectivity* (knowledge sought through the five senses).

E   On the other hand, some people would argue that it only takes one psychologist to change a light bulb — if the light bulb *really wants to change*.

True-False

_____   1. Rod Plotnik's definition of psychology (in Module 1) as the "scientific study of behaviors and mental processes" means that psychology is strongly linked to the power of the scientific method.

_____   2. The scientific technique with the lowest potential for error and bias is the survey method.

_____   3. The main disadvantage of gathering information through surveys is that it takes so long and is so hard to do.

_____   4. Testimonials have a high potential for error and bias.

_____   5. If it turns out that there is a *negative* correlation between studying the textbook and getting good grades, you just wasted a big chunk of money.

_____   6. If you can establish a significant correlation between two variables, you have also determined the causal relationship between them.

_____   7. Research in naturalistic settings has greater reality, but research in the laboratory has greater control.

_____   8. What the experimenter manipulates is called the dependent variable; how the subjects react is called the independent variable.

_____   9. Random selection is crucial in choosing subjects because you want them to accurately represent the larger population you are studying.

_____   10. There is no way to justify doing research using animals.

Flashcards 1

_____ 1. case study

_____ 2. control group

_____ 3. correlation

_____ 4. dependent variable

_____ 5. experiment

_____ 6. experimental group

_____ 7. independent variable

_____ 8. random selection

_____ 9. scientific method

_____ 10. survey

a. identifying cause and effect relationships by following a set of rules that minimize error, bias, and chance

b. composed of subjects who receive the experimental treatment

c. composed of subjects who undergo all the same procedures but who do not receive the treatment

d. an in-depth analysis of the thoughts, feelings, beliefs, experiences, behaviors, or problems of a single person

e. a general approach to gathering information and answering questions so error and bias are minimized

f. a treatment or something that the researcher controls or manipulates

g. one or more of the subjects' behaviors that are used to measure the potential effects of the treatment

h. a way to obtain information by asking many individuals to answer a fixed set of questions

i. each subject in a sample population has an equal chance of being selected to participate in experiment

j. an association or relationship between the occurrence of two or more events

Flashcards 2

_____ 1. correlation coefficient

_____ 2. debriefing

_____ 3. double-blind procedure

_____ 4. hypothesis

_____ 5. laboratory setting

_____ 6. naturalistic setting

_____ 7. placebo

_____ 8. questionnaire

_____ 9. self-fulfilling prophecy

_____ 10. testimonial

a. a relatively normal environment in which researchers observe behavior but don't change or control it

b. neither the subjects nor the researchers know which group is receiving which treatment

c. some intervention (pill, injection) that resembles medical therapy but has no actual medical effects

d. a statement in support of a particular viewpoint based on observations of our personal experiences

e. studying individuals under systematic and controlled conditions, with real-world influences eliminated

f. a technique for obtaining information by asking subjects to check answers on a list of questions

g. having a strong belief or making a statement about a future behavior then acting to carry out the behavior

h. explaining the purpose and method of the experiment to subjects, helping them deal with doubts or guilt

i. an educated guess about some phenomenon stated in precise, concrete language to rule out confusion

j. a number that indicates the strength of a relationship between two or more events

Multiple-Choice

_____ 1. Rod Plotnik begins this module with the example of Dusty, a hyperactive seven-year old, to show that
   a. often psychology must yield to medical science
   b. psychology needs accurate answers to highly complex problems
   c. science must recognize the problems for which it cannot find answers
   d. hyperactivity can be controlled by high doses of vitamin C

_____ 2. Like many other hyperactive children, Dusty is treated with a drug called
   a. ADHD
   b. Calmatin
   c. Ritalin
   d. Stimulantin

_____ 3. About 4–12 percent of children in the United States are diagnosed with ADHD; we know this and other information about ADHD from
   a. survey research
   b. blood tests required for admission to school
   c. articles and books written by veteran teachers
   d. laboratory experiments on schoolchildren

_____ 4. Among the disadvantages of the survey method is that
   a. many people won't go to the trouble of filling out the survey
   b. responses can be affected by how the questions are worded and who asks them
   c. it is difficult to survey enough subjects to make the results valid
   d. it takes so long to conduct a survey that the method is impractical for most purposes

_____ 5. When you encounter a testimonial, you know that it is
   a. true, if enough other people also report it
   b. false, because it is only a personal belief
   c. true, if the person conveying it has a good reputation for honesty
   d. possibly true, but not proven by science

_____ 6. According to the _____, if we strongly believe that something is going to happen, we may unknowingly behave in such a way as to make it happen
   a. wish fulfillment theory
   b. testimonial effect
   c. personal-belief problem
   d. self-fulfilling prophecy

_____ 7. A good example of a self-fulfilling prophecy is the belief that
   a. there's no use studying for multiple-choice exams because the questions are tricky
   b. psychology requires more study than literature
   c. if you do all your studying the night before the exam you'll do better
   d. you don't have to take notes in class if you listen carefully

_____ 8. Can a placebo administered in an experiment really cause change in a subject?
   a. no, because chemically the placebo is only a harmless sugar pill
   b. no, because subjects are aware that some of them are receiving placebos
   c. yes, because a few particles of the real drug often get on the placebo
   d. yes, but only if the subject believes a drug has been administered

_____ 9. A "correlation" is defined as
   a. an association or relationship between the occurrence of two or more events
   b. the connection between a cause and an effect
   c. the association of family members into the extended family
   d. an occurrence that can only be explained as random

_____ 10. You probably hope the correlation coefficient between using this Study Guide and getting an A in the course is
   a. +1.00
   b. -1.00
   c. 0.00
   d. +0.00

_____ 11. When she wears her lucky socks, Gail wins three golf matches out of four, a _____ correlation between wearing the socks and winning
   a. perfect negative
   b. negative
   c. positive
   d. perfect positive

_____ 12. Does this prove that the socks are the cause of Gail's winning?
   a. yes, because it cannot be just coincidence
   b. no, because correlation is not causation
   c. it would if she won _every_ time she wore the socks
   d. which socks Gail wears cannot possibly have anything to do with the outcome of the matches she plays

_____ 13. Whether to do research in a naturalistic or laboratory setting involves the issue of
   a. comprehensiveness versus cost
   b. testimonial versus science
   c. realism versus control
   d. objectivity versus subjectivity

_____ 14. Which one of the following has the _lowest_ potential for error or bias?
   a. case study
   b. survey
   c. experiment
   d. testimonial

_____ 15. The scientific method is defined as
   a. an approach to answering questions that minimizes errors and bias
   b. a faith that precise equipment will produce accurate information
   c. all of the findings of science in the modern era
   d. a set of guidelines published by the American Academy of Science

_____ 16. The special treatment given to the subjects in the experimental group is called the
    a. hypothesis
    b. independent variable
    c. dependent variable
    d. control variable

_____ 17. The reason why researchers choose their subjects by random selection is that
    a. in random selection, there is a positive correlation between subjects
    b. it is a tradition that goes back to the days of Wilhelm Wundt's psychology lab
    c. this method guarantees that the more motivated subjects will be selected
    d. only this method guarantees an equal chance of being selected for the experiment

_____ 18. Which one of the following is an example of random selection?
    a. winning numbers in the lottery
    b. National Football League player draft
    c. numbers people play in the lottery
    d. Miss America contest

_____ 19. The purpose of having a control group in an experiment is to
    a. show what results the opposite treatment would produce
    b. show how a different group would react to the treatment
    c. identify and rule out the behavior that results from simply participating in the experiment
    d. provide backup subjects in case any members of the experimental group drop out

_____ 20. A double-blind procedure means that
    a. the subjects are not informed that they are participating in an experiment
    b. the subjects are not allowed to interact with each other
    c. neither participants nor researchers know which group is receiving which treatment
    d. neither drug companies nor doctors know that research is going on

_____ 21. One of the main controversies about ADHD is
    a. how to find the precise dosage of Ritalin that works best
    b. whether behavioral treatment or drug treatment is most effective
    c. why girls are more likely than boys to exhibit ADHD
    d. whether it is worse at school or in the home

_____ 22. Should you volunteer to be a subject in a psychological experiment?
    a. no, because you are completely at the mercy of the researcher
    b. yes, because ethical guidelines protect subjects from danger or undue deception
    c. no, because they'll never tell you what the experiment was really about
    d. yes, because occasionally looking dumb or foolish makes us more humble

_____ 23. We know that Dr. Frankenstein's ghoulish research did not have American Psychological Association approval, because he
    a. did not submit a proposal for it to a university or federal research committee
    b. was only interested in building a body, not a brain
    c. did not plan what would happen to the monster after he threw the switch
    d. was stopped by an angry mob of torch-carrying psychologists

_____ 24. The basic justification for using animals in biomedical research is that
   a. it has not been proven that animals are harmed in research
   b. animals do not feel pain and suffering like humans do
   c. most religions place humans above animals in importance
   d. the potential human benefits outweigh the harm done to the animal subjects

_____ 25. The attitude of most psychologists toward the use of animals in research is that
   a. scientists must have complete freedom to conduct research however they see fit
   b. ethical concerns are involved in research on humans but not on animals
   c. animals have no rights
   d. the issue is complicated and calls for a balance between animal rights and research needs

Short Essay

1. What is attention-deficit/hyperactivity disorder (ADHD) and why is it controversial?

2. Describe the placebo effect and give examples of its power in everyday life.

3. Why is public confusion about correlation and causation a problem?

4. Why is the experiment the most powerful method for identifying cause-and-effect relationships?

5. Explain your own position on the controversy over animal research.

Are You Wired?

Rod Plotnik has an excellent page of Learning Activities for you to use at the end of each module in his textbook. Try them. But first, you have to be wired. If you own a computer and are connected to the Internet, you already know what I mean. If you do not yet own a computer, its time to report to the campus Computer Center. Ask about obtaining an account and learning how to crawl the Web. If you don't have these skills, you are really doing school (and life) with one hand tied behind your back. Get wired! P.S. When you do, you can contact me directly by e-mail. **Profenos@aol.com**

Answers for Module 2

The Big Picture

A Scientific research in psychology is governed by rules of ethics designed to protect subjects.
B Both the case study method and the survey method can be scientific.
C Science can only answer questions that can be stated in operational terms, not beliefs.
D *Correct! You see the "big picture" for this Module.*
E It's just a joke!

True-False (explanations provided for False choices; page numbers given for all choices)

1	T	28	
2	F	28	The controlled laboratory experiment has the lowest potential for error and bias.
3	F	29	Surveys based on random sampling and objective methods are scientific.
4	T	30	
5	T	32	
6	F	33	The fact that two variables are related does not mean that one is causing the other.
7	T	35	
8	F	36	Just the opposite is true.
9	T	36	
10	F	41	There are good arguments both for and against using animals in research.

Flashcards 1

1 d   2 c   3 j   4 g   5 a   6 b   7 f   8 i   9 e   10 h

Flashcards 2

1 j   2 h   3 b   4 i   5 e   6 a   7 c   8 f   9 g   10 d

Multiple-Choice (explanations provided for incorrect choices)

1 a Plotnik does not make this point.
   b *Correct! See page 27.*
   c Science is an appropriate strategy for any problem that can be stated in objective terms.
   d This is not one of the proposed treatments of hyperactivity.

2 a This is the name of the disorder, not the drug.
   b There is no drug by this name.
   c *Correct! See page 27.*
   d There is no drug by this name.

3 **a** *Correct! See page 29.*
   b There is no blood test for ADHD.
   c Such individual writings could not reveal current and precise statistical data.
   d How would a laboratory experiment reveal overall statistical data?

4 a Enough subjects complete surveys to make the results useful.
   b *Correct! See page 29.*
   c An advantage of the survey method is that it can be given to a large number of subjects.
   d An advantage of the survey method is that it is quick.

5 a Testimonials are individual statements, not demonstrated facts.
   b Testimonials, while not scientifically demonstrated facts, may be true.
   c Testimonials are individual statements, not demonstrated facts.
   d *Correct! See page 30.*

6 a This theory belongs to the psychoanalytic approach.
   b This is a fictitious term.
   c This is a fictitious term.
   d *Correct! See page 30.*

7   *a*   *Correct! See page 30.*
    b   Ask yourself, "Does believing this cause it to come true?"
    c   Ask yourself, "Does believing this cause it to come true?" (actually, just the opposite).
    d   Ask yourself, "Does believing this cause it to come true?" (actually, just the opposite).

8   a   The point is that change results from beliefs, not chemical elements.
    b   How would this prevent change?
    c   Not true.
    d   *Correct! See page 31.*

9   *a*   *Correct! See page 32.*
    b   Correlation different from causation.
    c   Correlation is a statistical, not a sociological term.
    d   Just the opposite is true.

10 *a*   *Correct! See page 32.*
    b   That would mean the more you use the Study Guide the worse your grade (I hope not!).
    c   That would mean using the Study Guide has no effect on your grade.
    d   Zero correlation is expressed as 0.00 [+0.00 is meaningless].

11 a   A perfect negative correlation would be losing every time she wears the socks.
    b   A negative correlation would be losing most of the times she wears the socks.
    c   *Correct! See page 32.*
    d   A perfect positive correlation would be winning every time she wears the socks.

12 a   Remember... *correlation is not causation!*
    b   *Correct! See page 33.*
    c   Remember... *correlation is not causation!*
    d   It could affect her state of mind, but remember... *correlation is not causation!*

13 a   Either setting could be comprehensive or not, costly or not.
    b   Neither setting would rely on testimonials.
    c   *Correct! See page 35.*
    d   Scientists would strive for objectivity in either setting.

14 a   The case study, with few controls, has high potential for error and bias.
    b   The survey has some controls, but also some potential for error and bias.
    c   *Correct! See page 36.*
    d   The testimonial is not a scientific research strategy.

15 *a*   *Correct! See page 36.*
    b   Faith is not a value in science.
    c   Do not confuse the method of science with the discoveries of science.
    d   The scientific method is much more than a set of guidelines.

16 a   The hypothesis is the presumed cause and effect relationship under investigation.
    b   *Correct! See page 36.*
    c   The dependent variable is how the subjects in the experiment respond.
    d   Control refers to elements in an experiment that are held constant.

17 a   Just the opposite is true.
    b   Wundt pioneered the laboratory experiment, not the survey.
    c   Just the opposite is true.
    d   *Correct! See page 36.*

18 *a*   *Correct! See page 36.*
    b   The NFL draft deliberately selects highly rated players, not all players.
    c   Lottery numbers people play are affected by many non-random factors.
    d   Miss America is not just any woman, but the most beautiful and talented woman in the country (isn't she?).

19 a   The control group does not get any special experimental treatment.
    b   The control group does not get the special experimental treatment.
    c   *Correct! See page 37.*
    d   Members of the control group stay in the control group.

20 a All subjects must give informed consent to participate in research.
    b Even if true in a given case, this is not what is "blind" in the experiment.
    c *Correct! See page 37.*
    d The two parties that are "blind" are the researchers and the participants.

21 a The dosage itself is not controversial.
    b *Correct! See page 39.*
    c Just the opposite is true.
    d The setting of the problem is not the basis of the controversy.

22 a Not true — there are ethical constraints on researchers and you always retain your freedom.
    b *Correct! See page 40.*
    c Research subjects must be debriefed after the experiment.
    d It's just a joke!

23 a *Correct! See page 40.*
    b Dr. Frankenstein was trying to create the whole package — body and brain.
    c He may not have planned exactly, but that wouldn't have mattered to the APA.
    d The participants in the angry mob carried torches, but were not members of the APA.

24 a Sadly, often animals are harmed, even killed.
    b Science now knows what any pet owner could have told them — animals do feel pain and suffering.
    c Some may, but few scientists would offer that as a justification for animal research.
    d *Correct! See page 41.*

25 a Scientists work under many ethical and supervisory restraints.
    b Ethical concerns of research apply to animals as well as to human subjects.
    c More and more scientists believe animals do have rights.
    d *Correct! See page 41.*

Short Essay (sample answers)

1. Attention-deficit/hyperactivity disorder (ADHD) is diagnosed in children who are inattentive, make careless mistakes in schoolwork, do not follow instructions, and are easily distracted. These children are also hyperactive, fidgeting, leaving their seats, running about, and talking excessively. A powerful stimulant called Ritalin is often prescribed. Diagnosis and treatment of ADHD are controversial because there are no objective tests to determine ADHD, and how Ritalin works and its safety are not fully understood.

2. The placebo effect is a change in the patient's illness that is attributable to an imagined treatment rather than to a medical treatment. In medical research, the placebo is often a sugar pill, not an actual medicine. In everyday life, the psychology of the placebo effect shows the power of the mind to affect the body. In other cultures, rhino horn, bear gallbladders, and tiger bones supposedly have curative effects. Magnets worn to cure pain may be an example from our own society.

3. The biggest mistake people make about correlations is assuming that they show cause and effect. When two things seem to go together it is difficult to resist the temptation to believe that one is causing the other. But instead of a causal linkage, all we have in correlation is systematic change. When one thing changes, the other also changes. The change itself does not indicate what is causing it. This common mistake can have serious consequences — just ask a rhinoceros or endangered tiger.

4. The superior ability of the laboratory experiment to identify cause-and-effect relationships comes from using the seven rules that reduce error and bias and from the ironclad logic of experimental procedure. If the subjects have been randomly selected and all variables are controlled, only the difference in treatment between the experimental group and the control group can explain any resulting differences in behavior between the two groups (everything else was held constant).

5. There is no one "right" answer to this question. You could argue in favor of animal research, against it, or take some position in between. But your answer should deal with the facts that animal research has contributed to significant medical advances, and is likely to aid in conquering more diseases, but also that there are some cases of animal mistreatment and even death. Many scientists are trying to strike the right balance between animal rights and research needs. But is such a balance possible, and how?

Module 3

Brain's Building Blocks

Psychology as a Spectrum of Approaches

In the first module we got acquainted with psychology and learned some of its history. In the second module we saw how psychologists pursue knowledge. It is all interesting and important, yet you could say that psychology itself really begins in Module 3.

Remember the six approaches to psychology discussed in the first module? I find it useful to think of them as forming a spectrum, a rainbow of ideas. At one end there is the biological approach — the brain and nervous system Rod Plotnik describes in this module and the next. At the other end is the cross-cultural approach — the social interactions he covers in the last module, which examines social psychology.

I put the brain and nervous system at the beginning of the spectrum because the brain seems like the most obvious, most elemental starting point in psychology. You could just as well put social interaction first, however, because we become experts about other people long before we know anything about the brain. It doesn't really matter; the point is that the biological and cross-cultural approaches are polar opposites in how we think about psychology.

The other four approaches (psychoanalytic, cognitive, behavioral, and humanistic) fall somewhere within the spectrum. How you arrange them only reveals your biases about their relative importance. (Which process, for example, do you consider more dominant — thinking or feeling?)

Our Starting Point, Deep in the Fields of Biology and Chemistry

At the far extreme we are studying now, psychology is almost pure biology and chemistry. But when Rod Plotnik discusses social psychology in the last module, or whenever he brings in the cross-cultural approach on one of his Cultural Diversity explorations, you will see just how deeply psychology also reaches into the fields of anthropology and sociology.

Now you can appreciate why this module is not an easy one to master (and probably wasn't an easy one to write, either). It involves a mini-course in biology. You could easily get lost just trying to remember the key terms. My advice is to concentrate on the *processes* involved. Try to appreciate how the brain and nervous system stand between us and the rest of the world, helping us understand it and make the best use of it. I suppose loyal Trekkies could compare the brain to the Starship Enterprise, going bravely where no man has gone before, in the name of peace and the orderly regulation of our affairs.

Check it out! PowerStudy 2.0 includes a 40-50 minute presentation that uses animations, visuals, and interactive activities as well as quizzing to help you understand concepts in this module.

Effective Student Tip 3

Meet Your New Friend, the Professor

Last semester it was Jason. Somewhat brash, but immediately likable, Jason came up to my desk after the first class and announced, "I'm getting an 'A' in your class!"

I like it when students make such pronouncements. For one thing, I learn their names right away. For another, we have the beginnings of a relationship. But most importantly, we have established a basis for working together. Now that I know Jason really wants an 'A,' I've got to pay attention to him and try to keep him on track. For his part, Jason has to make a genuine effort, unless he wants me to think he is just a blowhard. Some students may not have much of an investment in the class, but Jason and I know what we are doing. We're serious.

Meanwhile, that girl in the back who frowned all through the first lecture…, that guy who didn't take any notes…, and others who are just faces in the crowd for the first few weeks…, all these students could learn something useful from Jason.

Say hello to your professor right away. Let him or her get to know you. You need a friend in this new class, and what better person than the professor?

Your response...

What kind of relationship do you usually have with your teachers? Friendly? Formal? None at all?

Learning Objectives

1. Understand the brain as the electrical and chemical organ that initiates, organizes, and directs all thought, feeling, and behavior.

2. Learn the basic structures and functions of the parts of the brain.

3. Appreciate the differences between neurons and nerves and how they affect recovery from injuries.

4. Explain how the brain functions as an information system involving nerve impulses and neurotransmitters.

5. Explore the controversies and research surrounding the phenomenon of phantom limb pain for insight into the workings of the brain.

6. Appreciate the cultural differences in human attempts to affect brain functions and consciousness with different plants and drugs.

7. Consider your position on important controversies such as the philosophical debate over brain versus mind and the ethical problem of stem cell research.

Key Terms

Perhaps you know some of these terms from biology. Which will require the most study?

action potential	efferent (motor) neurons	neurotransmitters
afferent (sensory) neurons	end bulbs	Parkinson's disease
alcohol	genes	peripheral nervous system
all-or-none law	glial cell	phantom limb
Alzheimer's disease	interneuron	reflex
axon	ions	resting state
axon membrane	mescaline	reuptake
basal ganglia	mind-body question	sodium pump
cell body	myelin sheath	stem cells
central nervous system	nerve impulse	stereotaxic procedure
curare	nerves	synapse
dendrites	neuron	transmitter

Outline

- *Introduction*
    1. Losing one's mind: **Alzheimer's disease** (Ina)
    2. Diagnosis and causes (Research)
    ☐ How does Alzheimer's disease illustrate the importance of the building blocks of the brain?

A. *Overview: Human Brain*

   1. Development of the brain

      a. **Genes**

      b. Developmental stages

   2. Structure of the brain

      a. **Glial cell**

      b. **Neuron**

   3. Growth of new neurons

      a. Canary songs

      b. Primate brains

      c. Repairing the brain

   4. Brain versus mind

      a. **Mind-body question**

      b. How brain and mind influence each other

B. *Neurons: Structure & Function*

   1. Three basic structures of the neuron

      a. **Cell body**

      b. **Dendrites**

      c. **Axon**

         (1) **Myelin sheath**

         (2) **End bulbs**

         (3) **Synapse**

   2. Alzheimer's disease and neurons

C. *Neurons versus Nerves*

   1. Reattaching limbs

   2. **Peripheral nervous system**

      a. **Nerves**

      b. Ability to regrow

   3. **Central nervous system**

   ☐ How do the hopes for recovery of accident victims John Thomas and Christopher Reeve illustrate a key difference between nerves and neurons?

      a. Difference between nerves and neurons

      b. Regrowth or repair of neurons

D. Sending Information

1. Sequence: action potential

   a. Feeling a sharp object

   b. **Axon membrane**: chemical gates

   c. **Ions**: charged particles

   d. **Resting state**: charged battery

      (1) Chemical batteries in the brain

      (2) **Sodium pump**

   e. **Action potential**: sending information

2. Sequence: nerve impulse

   a. Sending information: **nerve impulse**

   b. **All-or-none law**

   c. Nerve impulse

      (1) Once begun, goes to end of the axon

      (2) Breaks in myelin sheath

   d. End bulbs and neurotransmitters

E. Transmitters

1. Excitatory and inhibitory

   a. **Transmitter**

   b. Chemical keys and chemical locks

   c. Excitatory transmitters and inhibitory transmitters

2. Neurotransmitters

   a. **Neurotransmitters**

   b. Chemical keys and chemical locks

   c. Excitatory neurotransmitters and inhibitory neurotransmitters

3. **Alcohol**

   a. GABA neurons

   b. GABA keys

4. New transmitters

   a. Endorphins

   b. Anandamide

   c. Nitric oxide

   d. Other chemicals

F. Reflex Responses

1. Definition and sequence of a **reflex**
2. Steps in a reflex
   a. Sensors
   b. **Afferent (sensory) neurons**
   c. **Interneuron**
   d. **Efferent (motor) neurons**
3. Functions of a reflex

G. Research Focus: What Is a Phantom Limb?

1. Case study
2. Definition and data
   (1) **Phantom limb**
   (2) Pain is real
3. Answers: old and new

H. Cultural Diversity: Plants and Drugs

☐   If it is true that all human societies seem to discover or invent psychoactive drugs, what does this say about our species? Is there a lesson for psychology?

1. Cocaine: blocking **reuptake**
2. **Curare**: blocking receptors
3. **Mescaline**: mimicking a neurotransmitter

I. Application: Experimental Treatments

1. **Parkinson's disease**
   a. Symptoms and treatment (L-dopa)
   b. **Basal ganglia**
2. Issues involving transplants
   a. Human cells
   b. **Stem cells**
3. Experimental treatments
   a. **Stereotaxic procedure**
   b. Results
   c. Another possibility
   d. Future

Language Workout

What's That?

p. 47   prepare a full dinner **from scratch** = from the beginning
her **late** husband = not living now
the number of patients is **projected** to rise = predicted, expected
the worst is **yet to come** = coming in the future
with these new **leads** = clues

p. 49   **breeding** song = making babies

p. 50   myelin **sheath** = covering, protection

p. 51   stringlike **bundles** = groups
By **suppressing** his or her own immune system = to hold back

p. 52   by using the **analogy** of a battery = comparison
segment by segment = part by part, piece by piece

p. 54   your heart **pounding** = beating
A transmitter is a chemical messenger that **transmits** information = carries

p. 55   alcohol has **been around** for 3,000 years = existed, been available
difficult to **pin down** = narrow to one
more likely to **pick a fight** = to start a fight

p. 56   after eating **tainted** food = bad, full of harmful substances

p. 58   What is a **phantom** limb? = cannot be seen, like a ghost
the brain **pieces together** a complete body image = organizes

p. 59   feelings of **euphoria** = great happiness

p. 60   in which **fetal** brain tissue = from an unborn baby

p. 61   he still has **ups and downs** = good times and bad times
sham operation = not real, fake
In the eyeballs of **cadavers** = dead bodies used for scientific study

Flex Your Word Power with Plurals

Language students know about irregular plurals of common words, like:

one **woman**, but many **women**

one **child**, but many **children**

one **mouse**, but many **mice**

Some formal words also have irregular plurals:

one **phenomenon**, but many **phenomena**

We'll discuss a very strange neural phenomenon that you may have heard of (p. 56)

Earthquakes and volcanoes are phenomena related to pressures within the earth.

one **datum**, but many **data**

To avoid lawsuits, a newspaper reporter must check every da**tum** in a story.

Computers are especially useful to store and analyze data from years of research.

one **stimulus,** but many **stimuli**

Some stimu**lus,** such as a tack, causes a change in physical energy. (p. 52)

Reward and punishment are both stimuli for actions, but which is more effective?

one **nucleus**, but many **nuclei**

In the center of the cell body is a small, oval shape representing the nucle**us**. (p. 50)

The scientist examined the nuclei of many cells to find a clue to unlock this disorder.

Test Yourself

All the dat___ from scientific experiments show that human activities are responsible for various phenomen___ like rising temperatures and more storms.

The promise of food is a good stimul___ to help an animal learn behavior. Humans use this phenomen___ to train dogs, horses, and elephants.

High blood pressure, the desire to fit in a new dress, and enjoyment are all stimul___ to start an exercise program.

With their tremendous shooting ability and rebounding skills, the twin brothers formed the nucle___ of a successful basketball team.

Answers

All the **data** from scientific experiments show that human activities are responsible for various **phenomena** like rising temperatures and more storms.

The promise of food is a good **stimulus** to help an animal learn behavior. Humans use this **phenomenon** to train dogs, horses, and elephants.

High blood pressure, the desire to fit in a new dress, and enjoyment are all **stimuli** to start an exercise program.

With their tremendous shooting ability and rebounding skills, the twin brothers formed the **nucleus** of a successful basketball team.

The Beauty of Linguistics

A subtle advantage of reading the Language Workout sections of the Study Guide is that while you are learning how the English language works, you are also learning much more. In a way, you are learning how *all* languages work. That's the subject of the exciting field called linguistics, which explores the foundations of our human ability to communicate. Eric Bohman, the author of the Language Workout materials, knows several languages and has taught English to students in other countries. You can learn a lot from him.

The Big Picture

Which statement below offers the best summary of the larger significance of this module?

A   No matter how much we discover about the structure and function of the brain, the workings of the mind will forever remain a mystery. Psychology should recognize that it must often yield to philosophy and religion.

B   The widespread human craving for alcohol and drugs shows that while the brain may be essential to human survival, it can also be our biggest enemy. The brain is an ancient evolutionary left-over, but we are stuck with it.

C   The brain could be described as an incredibly precise chemical and electrical information system. It is conceivable that brain science eventually will be able to decipher the composition and location of any single thought or idea.

D   Alzheimer's disease and phantom limb pain illustrate the fragile nature of the brain and its tendency to malfunction and wear down. The conclusion is simply that we have to hope for the best.

E   Having trouble learning all the terms in this module? Two words: brain transplant!

True-False

_____   1. Many people are worried about the effects of drug use on the brain — as well they should, in light of the fact that damaged neurons are not regrown or replaced.

_____   2. Science has determined that the mind is a separate entity from the brain.

_____   3. Most neurons have a cell body, dendrites, and an axon.

_____   4. Nerves are located in the central nervous system; neurons are in the peripheral nervous system.

_____   5. The "all-or-none law" refers to the fact that ions are either positively or negatively charged.

_____   6. Neurotransmitters are the keys that unlock the receptors of dendrites, cell bodies, muscles, and organs.

_____   7. Alcohol is a psychoactive drug that depresses the activity of the central nervous system.

_____   8. A reflex is an action you have learned to execute so fast you don't think about it.

_____   9. Drugs like cocaine and mescaline achieve their effects by interfering with the normal workings of neurotransmitters.

_____   10. The stereotaxic procedure is the treatment of Parkinson's disease with a drug called L-dopa.

Flashcards 1

_____ 1. action potential

_____ 2. all-or-none law

_____ 3. glial cells

_____ 4. ions

_____ 5. mind-body question

_____ 6. nerve impulse

_____ 7. neuron

_____ 8. neurotransmitters

_____ 9. phantom limb

_____ 10. reflex

a. brain cell with specialized extensions for receiving and transmitting electrical signals

b. chemical keys with a particular shape that only fits a similarly shaped chemical lock or receptor

c. series of separate action potentials that take place segment by segment down length of axon

d. brain cells that provide scaffolding, insulation, chemicals to protect and support neuron growth

e. an unlearned, involuntary reaction to some stimulus; prewired by genetic instructions

f. if an action potential starts at the beginning of an axon, it will continue to very end of axon

g. asks how complex mental activities can be generated by physical properties of the brain

h. chemical particles that have electrical charges; opposite charges attract and like charges repel

i. vivid experience of sensations and feelings coming from a limb that has been amputated

j. tiny electrical current that is generated when positive sodium ions rush inside the axon

Flashcards 2

_____ 1. Alzheimer's disease

_____ 2. curare

_____ 3. dendrites

_____ 4. end bulbs

_____ 5. mescaline

_____ 6. Parkinson's disease

_____ 7. reuptake

_____ 8. sodium pump

_____ 9. stereotaxic procedure

_____ 10. synapse

a. a chemical process responsible for keeping axon charged by returning sodium ions outside axon

b. incurable, fatal disease involving brain damage, with memory loss, deterioration of personality

c. miniature containers at extreme ends of axon branches; store chemicals called neurotransmitters

d. a drug that enters bloodstream and blocks receptors on muscles, causing paralysis

e. tremors, shakes, progressive slowing of voluntary movements with feelings of depression

f. fixing a patient's head in a holder and drilling a small hole through the skull; syringe guided to a brain area

g. process of removing neurotransmitters from synapse by reabsorbtion into terminal buttons

h. branchlike extensions that arise from cell body and receive and pass signals to cell body

i. a drug that causes arousal, visual hallucinations; acts like neurotransmitter norepinephrine

j. very small space between terminal button and adjacent dendrite, muscle fiber, or body organ

Multiple-Choice

_____ 1. Rod Plotnik begins with the example of Alzheimer's disease to illustrate the
   a. sad fact that the brain inevitably wears out
   b. hope offered by a new operation for those afflicted with the disease
   c. type of disease that could be prevented if people would take care of themselves
   d. key importance of the building blocks that make up the brain's informational network

_____ 2. The initial symptoms of Alzheimer's disease are
   a. profound memory loss
   b. deterioration in personality
   c. problems with memory, getting lost, and being mildly confused
   d. emotional outbursts

_____ 3. Believe it or not, your brain contains about _____ cells (neurons plus glial cells)
   a. one thousand
   b. 100 thousand
   c. 1 trillion
   d. a gad-zillion

_____ 4. The functions of the glial cells include
   a. sending messages within the brain
   b. providing chemical instructions for the development of the body and brain
   c. providing sugar to fuel the brain
   d. guiding the growth and functioning of neurons

_____ 5. A neuron is a brain cell that
   a. determines the sex of the individual
   b. receives and transmits electrical signals
   c. looks like a small wrinkled melon
   d. coats and protects the brain

_____ 6. Unlike nerves, neurons
   a. are not replaced or regrown
   b. have the ability to regrow or reattach
   c. are located outside the brain and spinal cord
   d. have no dendrites or axons

_____ 7. Recent research on animals suggests that the human brain
   a. is less evolved than most bird brains
   b. can develop new neurons each spring, as the canary does
   c. continues to grow and develop neurons all through life
   d. has only a limited capacity to repair or rewire itself after damage

_____ 8. Is the mind the same as the brain? Rod Plotnik says that the
   a. the mind must be separate — otherwise there would be no soul
   b. brain and mind are closely linked, and researchers are studying these links
   c. physical brain is the only thing — there is no actual "mind"
   d. questions like this are best left to philosophers

_____ 9. The _____ is a single threadlike structure that extends from, and carries signals away from the cell body to neighboring neurons, organs, or muscles
   a. axon
   b. dendrite
   c. myelin sheath
   d. synapse

_____ 10. The purpose of the myelin sheath is to
   a. receive signals from neurons, muscles, or sense organs
   b. wrap around and insulate an axon
   c. protect the nucleus of the cell body
   d. drain dangerous electricity away from the brain

_____ 11. John Thomas' arms could be reattached because
   a. neurons have the ability to regrow, regenerate, or reattach
   b. neurons are part of the central nervous system
   c. nerves have the ability to regrow, regenerate, or reattach
   d. nerves are part of the peripheral nervous system

_____ 12. The fact that John Thomas can use his arms but Christopher Reeve is unlikely to walk illustrates the difference between
   a. nerves vs. muscles
   b. the peripheral nervous system vs. the central nervous system
   c. receiving medical attention immediately vs. not for several hours
   d. neurons vs. fetal tissue

_____ 13. The purpose of the ions in the axon's membrane is to
   a. generate a miniature electrical current
   b. plug up the tiny holes in the membrane's semipermeable skin
   c. pump excess sodium out of the neuron
   d. dry up the watery fluid that collects in the membrane

_____ 14. The _____ says that if an action potential starts at the beginning of an axon, the action potential will continue at the same speed, segment by segment, to the very end of the axon
   a. unlocked-chemical-gate phenomenon
   b. nerve impulse principle
   c. all-or-none law
   d. opposite charges law

_____ 15. The "all-or-none law" explains what happens when
   a. positively and negatively charged ions meet
   b. an impulse starts at the beginning of an axon
   c. electrical impulses spread throughout the body
   d. your brain gets the idea of a six-pack

_____ 16. The effect of a neurotransmitter on an adjacent neuron, muscle, or organ is
   a. excitatory
   b. inhibitory
   c. either excitatory or inhibitory
   d. determined by the all-or-none law

_____ 17. If receptors in muscle fibers are thought of as locks, the keys are
   a. the action potential of the axon
   b. synapses
   c. the resting state of the axon
   d. neurotransmitters

_____ 18. On many nights you hear the cry "Let's party!" Odd, because actually alcohol
   a. increases tension and anxiety
   b. sharpens social judgment, therefore heightening inhibitions and self-doubt
   c. depresses activity of the central nervous system, dulling alertness
   d. improves memory, creating the ideal time to study

_____ 19. The brain produces a neurotransmitter called _____ to decrease the effects of pain during great bodily stress, such as an accident
   a. endorphin
   b. anandamide
   c. nitric oxide
   d. happy dust

_____ 20. An unlearned, involuntary reaction to a stimulus is called a/n
   a. explosion
   b. electrical burst
   c. conditioned reflex
   d. reflex

_____ 21. Donald, who had to amputate his own leg to survive an accident, now suffers from phantom limb pain. Researchers suspect that his pain comes from
   a. cut nerves in the stump
   b. a body image stored in the brain
   c. the spinal cord
   d. terrifying memories of the horrible ordeal

_____ 22. The use of cocaine, curare, and mescaline in different parts of the world shows that humans
   a. will use plants that imitate or affect actions of the brain
   b. will get high one way or another
   c. will never figure out how the brain really works
   d. do not pay sufficient attention to the effects of some plants

_____ 23. The newest hope for sufferers of Parkinson's disease is treating damaged cells with
   a. a new drug called L-dopa
   b. massive injections of dopamine
   c. genetically engineered cells grown in the laboratory
   d. transplanted human fetal brain tissue

_____ 24. The use of stem cells to treat Parkinson's disease is controversial because
   a. human embryos are destroyed when the stem cells are removed
   b. federal funding for stem cell research is limited
   c. long term use of L-dopa drug therapy is effective and safe
   d. stem cells can change into and become any one of the 220 cells that make up a human body

_____ 25. The stereotaxic procedure for treating Parkinson's disease involves
   a. deceiving the patient and relying on the placebo effect
   b. playing loud music into the patient's ear to block out symptoms
   c. removing the patient's adult brain and replacing it with a fetal brain
   d. fixing a patient's head in a holder and drilling a small hole through the skull

Short Essay

1. Why is Alzheimer's disease a good example to use in this module?

2. Describe the "mind-body question" in psychology and offer your own answer to the problem.

3. Explain why John Thomas and Christopher Reeve, both of whom suffered terrible accidents, are experiencing different recoveries.

4. Describe the central role of neurotransmitters in making your brain work.

5. What is the problem for scientists in explaining "phantom limb"?

The "Language Workout"

Have you tried Eric Bohman's "Language Workout" sections? Eric wrote this material especially for students new to English, but also for anyone who wants to use English more effectively.

  I went through all of Eric's exercises myself. I found that they helped me understand English more fully, even when I already "knew" the right answers. Eric explains the construction of English grammar so clearly that you can't help but gain a better understanding of our wonderful language, even if you are good at it to begin with. That's why I am urging you to try Eric lessons.

Please tell me how you like the Language Workout! **Profenos@aol.com**

Answers for Module 3

The Big Picture

A Many psychologists believe that mind and brain are actually the same thing.
B The brain is not our enemy; our evolution is largely the evolution of the human brain.
C *Correct! You see the "big picture" for this Module.*
D If the brain is exercised and the body is in good health, excellent brain function can be lifelong.
E It's just a joke!

True-False (explanations provided for False choices; page numbers given for all choices)

1	F	49	Mind (thinking) is one aspect of the brain.
2	T	49	
3	T	50	
4	F	51	Reflexes are inborn tendencies to act.
5	F	52	The all-or-none law refers to the firing of a nerve impulse through the axon.
6	T	54	
7	T	55	
8	F	56	Just the opposite is true.
9	T	59	
10	F	61	The stereotaxic procedure refers to surgically implanting fetal brain tissue.

Flashcards 1

1 j   2 f   3 d   4 h   5 g   6 c   7 a   8 b   9 i   10 e

Flashcards 2

1 b   2 d   3 h   4 c   5 i   6 e   7 g   8 a   9 f   10 j

Multiple-Choice (explanations provided for incorrect choices)

1 a The brain does not wear out.
   b There is no operation for Alzheimer's disease.
   c The potential for Alzheimer's disease is inherited.
   d Correct! See page 47.

2 a That comes later.
   b That comes later.
   c Correct! See page 47.
   d That may happen, but later in the course of the disease.

3 a If you think it is this few, re-read page 48.
   b If you think it is only this many, re-read page 48.
   c Correct! See page 48.
   d Just how much *is* a "gad-zillion" anyway?

4 a Messages are sent by neurotransmitters.
   b That is the function of the genes.
   c That would be more true of the cell body.
   d Correct! See page 48.

5 a That would be a chromosome.
   b Correct! See page 48.
   c That is a description of the cortex.
   d There is no single coating that protects the brain.

6 *a Correct! See page 49.*
   b This is true of nerves, but not neurons.
   c This is true of nerves, but not neurons.
   d Neurons do have dendrites and axons.

7   a   The human brain is *more* evolved (notice how you react when someone calls you a "birdbrain").
     b   Canaries may, but humans don't.
     c   This is true of nerves, but not neurons.
     d   *Correct! See page 49.*

8   a   Plotnik does not refer to the soul in this discussion.
     b   *Correct! See page 49.*
     c   Plotnik points out that some researchers, but not all, take this position.
     d   Plotnik says this is an important question for psychology to debate.

9   ***a***   *Correct! See page 50.*
     b   Dendrites receive and pass on signals.
     c   The myelin sheath protects the axon.
     d   A synapse is an infinitely small space between an end bulb and its adjacent body organ, muscle, or cell body.

10   a   This is the function of the dendrites.
     b   *Correct! See page 50.*
     c   The cell body keeps the nucleus in working order.
     d   Electricity is a key element in brain functioning.

11   a   Neurons cannot be regrown, regenerated, or reattached.
     b   True, but this feature of neurons is not related to the ability in question.
     c   *Correct! See page 51.*
     d   True, but this feature of nerves is not related to the ability in question.

12   a   The issue is what makes the muscles work.
     b   *Correct! See page 51.*
     c   Poor John Thomas did *not* receive immediate medical attention.
     d   The issue of fetal tissue is not involved in injuries to the body.

13   ***a***   *Correct! See page 52.*
     b   For the axon to work, the membrane must be semipermeable.
     c   Sodium is essential in the working of the axon.
     d   Fluid is essential in the working of the axon.

14   a   This is a fictitious term.
     b   This is a fictitious term.
     c   *Correct! See page 52.*
     d   This is a fictitious term.

15   a   This creates the action potential (the all-or-none law comes next).
     b   *Correct! See page 52.*
     c   The all-or-none law applies only to the axon.
     d   It's just a joke!

16   a   True, but this is only half the story.
     b   True, but this is only half the story.
     c   *Correct! See page 54.*
     d   The all-or-none law applies to electrical current before it reaches a neurotransmitter.

17   a   The action potential refers to the beginnings of an electrical current.
     b   Synapses separate neurons.
     c   In the resting state, the axon is ready but is not yet generating an electrical signal.
     d   *Correct! See page 54.*

18   a   Alcohol is a depressant.
     b   Alcohol causes loss of inhibitions and decreased self-control.
     c   *Correct! See page 55.*
     d   Alcohol decreases neural activity.

19   ***a***   *Correct! See page 55.*
     b   Close, since anandamide may help relieve stress, but endorphins are more related to bodily pain.
     c   Nitric oxide is a gas that functions like a neurotransmitter in the regulation of emotions.
     d   It's just a joke!

20   a   This is not a correct technical term in brain physiology.
       b   This is not a correct technical term in brain physiology.
       c   A conditioned reflex is a learned response to a stimulus.
       d   *Correct! See page 56.*

21   a   This early theory of phantom limb pain has been disproved.
       b   *Correct! See page 58.*
       c   This theory of phantom limb pain has been disproved.
       d   The pain is not due entirely to psychological sources.

22   *a*   *Correct! See page 59.*
       b   This may be true, but the point is *how* that effect is achieved.
       c   This is contradicted by abundant recent research.
       d   The trouble is that humans *do* pay attention to the effects.

23   a   L-dopa controls but does not cure the symptoms of Parkinson's disease.
       b   This is not a treatment for Parkinson's disease.
       c   This is not a treatment for Parkinson's disease.
       d   *Correct! See page 60.*

24   *a*   *Correct! See page 60.*
       b   Availability of funds is not the issue.
       c   Just the opposite is true.
       d   The power of stem cells is not the issue.

25   a   The placebo effect is not involved.
       b   That is not the treatment used in the stereotaxic procedure.
       c   Just think about this for a minute!
       d   *Correct! See page 61.*

Short Essay (sample answers)

1. The gradual deterioration and eventual death caused by Alzheimer's disease dramatically illustrates the central role of the brain in our physical, mental, and emotional functioning. Alzheimer's disease slowly destroys the building blocks that form the brain's informational network. The deterioration of brain cells and the inability of the chemical message system to start and stop information result in loss of the very processes on which life depends.

2. Is the mind separate from the brain? Or is "mind" simply an abstraction for explaining the workings of the brain? The question of how complex mental activities, such as feeling, thinking, and learning, can be explained by the physical, chemical, and electrical activities of the brain has challenged philosophers and scientists throughout the modern age, and is still a matter of serious debate. As yet, neither side can completely answer or refute the arguments of the other position. (What is your own answer?)

3. Both John Thomas and Christopher Reeve suffered accidents that caused serious impairment of their physical abilities. But there was a significant difference between the two accidents. Thomas suffered damage to his peripheral nervous system, Reeve to his central nervous system. Since nerves can be regrown, Thomas's reattached arms are slowly regaining their function. But the neurons in Reeve's spinal cord will not automatically regrow, so his heroic efforts to walk again are much less likely to be successful.

4. Neurotransmitters are at the heart of the brain's informational system. Comprised of about a dozen different chemicals (more are being discovered), neurotransmitters cross the infinitely small space between end bulbs and dendrites, carrying messages from one neuron to another. These messages command the physical and mental activities of life. Communication between the billions of neurons does not get mixed up because the neurotransmitters act as chemical keys that fit only into specific chemical locks.

5. The problem is that it can't be! How could sensations of pain come from a limb that (because of amputation) is no longer there? Researchers have generated several different theories in the attempt to answer the question. It was once thought that the sensations came from the nerves in the stump, or from the spinal cord, but research has discredited these answers. Today it is thought that the sensations come from the brain itself, perhaps from a mental body image that continues to function even when a body part is gone.

Module 4

Incredible Nervous System

A Golden Age of Biology

Not long ago a researcher commenting on a startling and provocative new idea about human functioning observed that we are living in "a Golden Age of biology." Hardly a week goes by without the media reporting a new breakthrough in genetics, evolutionary science, or human health. When early nineteenth-century scientists discovered the Rosetta stone, they suddenly had a blueprint that unlocked the secrets of ancient Egypt. Today's scientists are mapping the genes and discovering the blueprint for how we humans are constructed.

Progress in psychology has been no less dramatic. Neuroscientists, who study the brain and nervous system, are coming closer and closer to explaining human consciousness, perhaps the greatest mystery of all.

In the previous module, Rod Plotnik posed the question, are mind and brain two things, or the same thing? This is an old argument in psychology and philosophy. Plotnik gave you some of the reasoning on both sides. This debate is rapidly changing, however. For one thing, it is becoming less the province of philosophy and more the property of neuroscience. Philosophers continue to attempt to use logic and reason to find an answer, but for the first time neuroscientists are able to look into the functioning brain (Plotnik tells how) and conduct laboratory experiments on thinking in action.

The Biological Approach to Psychology

In the first module, Rod Plotnik carefully laid out six major approaches to psychology. It is hard to overstress the importance of becoming familiar with these six approaches. If you can learn them, and begin to see their reflections in all the facts and ideas you encounter in the textbook, you will be well on your way to having an overall view of the structure of the field of psychology and a real grasp of its organization.

The previous module, on the workings of the brain, and this one, on the functioning of the nervous system, contain the heart of the biological approach to psychology. Understand that the six approaches are not simply matters of the personal interests of researchers and practicing psychologists. They are bold claims to explain *everything* in psychology, and to have the best answers to our needs for specific health and therapeutic applications. Right now, the biological approach seems to be winning the debate. We live in an exciting time.

Check it out! PowerStudy 2.0 includes a 40-50 minute presentation that uses animations, visuals, and interactive activities as well as quizzing to help you understand concepts in this module.

Effective Student Tip 4

Why You Must Be Effective in College

Effectiveness comes into play in all our endeavors, the most trivial as well as the most crucial. Consider a systems analyst, triumphant in the solution of a tricky problem (effectiveness confirmed), who then wheels around and fires a paper ball in a perfect jump shot into the wastebasket across the room (effective again). The urge behind each effort was effectiveness, but realistically it's more important that our systems analyst solve the problem than make the imaginary buzzer-beating shot.

If we were only dealing with office wastebasketball, we could afford to ignore the psychological factor of effectiveness. The stakes aren't very high. College is a different matter — probably the highest stakes in your life so far.

College is an essential rite of passage in our society, a critical bridge over which you cross into adulthood. College is more important today than ever, with at least two outcomes of great consequence: (1) College may determine whether you gain admittance to a technologically sophisticated world of commerce, industry, and the professions. (2) College helps shape your self-esteem and psychological health.

That's why you must handle your college experience effectively. Your future depends on it.

Your response...

Realistically, and aside from your "official" goals, what do you hope to get out of going to college?

Learning Objectives

1. Understand the nervous system as an incredibly sophisticated integrated mechanism for building and maintaining a human being.

2. Learn the basic organization and functions of the brain, limbic system, and endocrine system and how they have evolved to serve us by helping us adapt, and yet sometimes fail us.

3. Explain how the brain, limbic system, and endocrine system function as an incredibly adaptive and powerful information system.

4. Understand the powerful influence of the limbic system on our emotions and the evolutionary significance of the "old brain."

5. Consider the research on possible sex differences in the brain and what practical significance such differences may have.

6. Examine a dark chapter in the history of psychology: the "research" into brain size and the accompanying racial myths.

7. Consider your position on the importance of the two hemispheres of the brain and their influence on human behavior.

Key Terms

There are more than the usual numbers of Key Terms in this module because it relies so heavily on biological concepts and ideas. If you have taken some biology, these terms will come fairly easily. If not, you will have to work harder on this module than on many others. Remind yourself that psychology is becoming an increasingly biological discipline. The work is difficult, but the rewards are great.

adrenal glands
amygdala
anencephaly
anterior pituitary
auditory association area
autonomic nervous system
Broca's area and Broca's aphasia
central nervous system
cerebellum
chromosome
cortex
endocrine system
fight-flight response
forebrain
fragile X syndrome
frontal lobe

frontal lobotomy
gene
gonads
hippocampus
homeostasis
hypothalamus
limbic system
medulla
midbrain
motor cortex
MRI scan (magnetic resonance imaging) and fMRI scan (*functional* magnetic resonance imaging)
neglect syndrome
occipital lobe
pancreas

parasympathetic division
parietal lobe
peripheral nervous system
PET scan (positron emission tomography)
pituitary gland
pons
posterior pituitary
primary auditory cortex
primary visual cortex
sex, or gender, differences [in the brain]
somatic nervous system
somatosensory cortex
split-brain operation
sympathetic division
temporal lobe

thalamus

theory of evolution

thyroid

visual agnosia

visual association area

Wernicke's area and

   Wernicke's aphasia

zygote

Outline

- *Introduction*
  - ☐ What do Rod Plotnik's wildly different examples of four unusual brains tell us about the development and functioning of our own brains?
  1. Lucy's brain: earliest ancestor (Evolution)
  2. Baby Theresa's brain: fatal flaw (Birth defect)
  3. Steve's brain: cruel fate (Brain damage)
  4. Scott's brain: Wrong instructions (Genetic defect)

A. *Genes & Evolution*
  1. Genetic instructions
     a. Fertilization
     b. **Zygote**
     c. **Chromosome**
     d. Chemical alphabet (DNA)
     e. **Genes** and proteins
     f. Genome
     g. **Fragile X syndrome**
  2. Evolution of the human brain
     a. **Theory of evolution**
     b. Increases in brain size

B. *Studying the Living Brain*
  1. Brain scans
     a. **MRI scan (magnetic resonance imaging)**
     b. **fMRI scan (*functional* magnetic resonance imaging)**
  2. Brain scans and cognitive neuroscience
     a. **PET scan (positron emission tomography)**
     b. Pictures of thinking
  3. Tools versus animals

C. *Organization of the Brain*
  1. Major divisions of the nervous system
     a. **Central nervous system** (CNS)
     b. **Peripheral nervous system** (PNS)

2. Subdivisions of the PNS

   a. **Somatic nervous system**

     (1) Afferent (sensory) fibers

     (2) Efferent (motor) fibers

   b. **Autonomic nervous system** (ANS)

3. Subdivisions of the ANS

   a. **Sympathetic division**

   b. **Parasympathetic division**

4. Major parts of the brain

   a. **Forebrain**

   b. **Midbrain**

   c. Hindbrain

     (1) **Pons**

     (2) **Medulla**

     (3) **Cerebellum**

D. *Control Centers: Four Lobes*

1. Overall view of the cortex

☐ What is the anatomical problem for which the cortex is a clever solution?

   a. Wrinkled **cortex**

   b. Four lobes

   c. Baby Theresa's brain: a fatal defect (**anencephaly**)

☐ Why did baby Theresa live only nine days?

2. **Frontal lobe**: functions

   a. A terrible accident (story of Phineas Gage)

   b. **Frontal lobotomy**

   c. Results of lobotomies

3. Frontal lobe: functions

   a. Location of **motor cortex**

   b. Organization and function of motor cortex

   c. Other functions of frontal lobe

4. **Parietal lobe**: functions

   a. Location of **somatosensory cortex**

   b. Organization of somatosensory cortex

   c. Other functions of parietal lobe

5. **Temporal lobe**: functions

   a. **Primary auditory cortex** and **auditory association area**

   b. **Broca's area** and **Broca's aphasia**

   c. **Wernicke's area** and **Wernicke's aphasia**

6. **Occipital lobe**: functions

   a. **Primary visual cortex** and **visual association area**

   b. **Visual agnosia**

   c. **Neglect syndrome**

E. *Limbic System: Old Brain*

1. Structures and functions of **limbic system**

   ☐ Why is the limbic system sometimes called our "old brain" or our "animal brain"?

   ☐ What is the function of each of its four parts?

   a. **Hypothalamus**

   b. **Amygdala**

   c. **Thalamus**

   d. **Hippocampus**

2. Autonomic nervous system

   a. Sympathetic nervous system

      (1) **Sympathetic division**

      (2) Increases physiological arousal

      (3) **Fight-flight response**

   b. Parasympathetic nervous system

      (1) **Parasympathetic division**

      (2) Decreases physiological arousal

   c. **Homeostasis**

F. *Endocrine System*

1. Hormonal system for sending information: **endocrine system**

   ☐ In what way is the endocrine system similar to the nervous system?

2. Endocrine system's glands and possible dysfunctions

   a. **Hypothalamus** (control center)

   b. **Pituitary gland**

   c. **Posterior pituitary**

   d. **Anterior pituitary**

   e. **Pancreas**

   f. **Thyroid**

g. **Adrenal glands**

h. **Gonads**

G. *Research Focus: Sex Differences in the Brain?*

1. Science and politics: **sex, or gender, differences**

2. Differences in solving problems

☐ What factors might explain the existence of sex differences in the brain?

3. Differences between female and male brains

☐ How important do you think these differences are in everyday life?

H. *Cultural Diversity: Brain Size & Racial Myths*

1. Skull size and intelligence

a. Results (Samuel George Morton)

b. Reanalyzed (Stephen Jay Gould)

2. Brain size and intelligence

a. Female brains

b. Correlations

I. *Application: Split Brain*

1. **Split-brain operation**

a. Seizures

b. Major breakthrough

c. Testing a patient

☐ What does the split-brain operation reveal about how the brain works?

2. Behaviors following split brain

3. Different functions

a. Left hemisphere

(1) Verbal

(2) Mathematical

(3) Analytical

b. Right hemisphere

(1) Nonverbal

(2) Spatial

(3) Holistic

4. Left-brained or right-brained?

a. Am I primarily "left-brained" or "right-brained"?

b. How is my brain organized?

Language Workout

What's That?

p. 67   a **protruding** jaw = sticks out
The **press** called her Baby Theresa = newspapers and TV news
He **babbled** = spoke nonsense sounds

p. 68   Each **rung** of the DNA ladder = step
as well as mild to **profound** levels = noticeable

p. 69   a **three-fold** increase = multiplied three times
three major **milestones** = important events

p. 75   he did no controlled or **follow-up** studies = later, to check results

p. 76   emotional **swings** = changes, from very happy to very unhappy

p. 77   you can easily **tell** a key from a nickel = feel the difference

p. 80   many kinds of **fleeting** memories = quickly disappearing

p. 85   had unknowingly **swayed** his scientific judgment = bias

p. 90   they sort of **bumbled** through life = moved in a clumsy way, without plans

Build Your Word Power

In Module 4, you read about the nervous system and encountered a series of words connected the nervous system. The word beginnings **neuro** or **neur** relate to nerves or the nervous system. Here are some examples of the prefix (word beginning) of **neuro**. Try to guess the meaning.

For example: maximum **neural** activity occurred in an area of the brain (p. 70)
neural means relating to the nervous system.

Now you try it:

a relatively new area, called cognitive **neuro**science, (p. 71)
What is this a study of?

Egas Moniz, a Portuguese **neuro**logist, used an untested surgical treatment. (p. 75)
What was Egas Moniz's job?

Imagine many billions of **neurons** laid on a sheet of paper (p. 74)
What's a **neuron**?

What's the Difference?

What's the difference between these two similar looking words?

Keep the body's arousal at an **optimum** level (p. 81)

Returns to a state of **optimal** functioning (p. 83)

It's a trick question. They both have the same meaning — the most favorable or the highest level possible. **Optimum** is most often used when writing about the highest level and can be used as a noun unlike **optimal**.

Flex Your Word Power

You have encountered the word **relatively** several times in Module 4.

> The above study is an example of a **relatively** new area. (p. 71)

> A larger body part indicates **relatively** more area on the motor cortex. (p. 76)

> All primates have a **relatively** poor sense of smell. (p. 79)

> The left hemisphere would recognize a face by analyzing piece by piece... a **relatively** slow process. (p. 87)

Relatively means in comparison. For example: let's describe the weather in Chicago.

> Compared to Arizona, the weather in Chicago is cold. Compared to the North Pole, the weather in Chicago is not so cold. So, we can say: The weather in Chicago is **relatively cold**. This means it is fairly cold, in relation to other places.

Let's try it:

> Plotnik's textbook is over 500 pages long. That's fairly long, but not as long as an encyclopedia. So, Plotnik's book is _____.

> A mouse looks small next to an elephant. Still, a mouse is not as small as a spider. So, a mouse is _____.

> It's fairly expensive to buy a computer. Compared to buying a car, a computer is not so expensive. Compared to buying a radio, a computer is quite expensive. So, a computer is _____.

> Most nurses earn less money than most doctors. Nurses earn less than many lawyers and engineers, too. Of course, nurses earn more than dishwashers.

> Therefore, nurses earn _____ money than other professionals.

Answers

What is this a study of? A study of the nervous system.
What was Egas Moniz's job? A doctor who specializes in problems of nervous system.
What's a **neuron**? They are cells in nervous system.
So, Plotnik's book is **relatively long.**
So, a mouse is **relatively small.**
So, a computer is **relatively expensive.**
Therefore, nurses earn **relatively less** money than other professionals.

The Big Picture

Which statement below offers the best summary of the larger significance of this module?

A   The "nervous system" is the name that is commonly given to a number of quite separate biological functions. It really should not be called a "system" at all.

B   The nervous system (including the brain) is an incredible regulatory arrangement that governs all the necessary functions and processes of human life. The nervous system makes us the most adaptable species on earth.

C   The finding that there are significant sex or gender differences in the brain suggests that there must be equally significant biological differences separating the various races and ethnic groups around the world.

D   The nervous system and the brain make up the two halves of the story of human biology: the brain gives the orders and the nervous system carries them out. We could live without a nervous system, but not without a brain.

E   The "nervous system" is the method by which psych students get ready for an exam.

True-False

_____   1. The brain and the spinal cord make up the central nervous system.

_____   2. The right and left hemispheres of the brain make up the peripheral nervous system.

_____   3. More than any other part, it is the operation of the hindbrain that makes you a person.

_____   4. When Igor hands Dr. Frankenstein a fresh brain, what we see quivering in his hands is the cortex.

_____   5. As human society evolves, the limbic system incorporates cooperative and positive tendencies and feelings into the brain.

_____   6. The general tendency of the autonomic nervous system is homeostasis.

_____   7. In the endocrine system, glands secrete hormones that affect many important bodily processes.

_____   8. Psychologists now know that human intelligence is determined by brain size.

_____   9. The need to perform split-brain operations for medical purposes gives science a rare look at the degree of specialization in the brain's two hemispheres.

_____   10. Science has finally explained why people are so different: each human being is either left-brained or right-brained.

Flashcards 1

_____ 1. autonomic nervous system

_____ 2. central nervous system

_____ 3. cortex

_____ 4. forebrain

_____ 5. frontal lobe

_____ 6. gene

_____ 7. MRI scan (magnetic resonance imaging)

_____ 8. peripheral nervous system

_____ 9. PET scan (positron emission tomography)

_____ 10. somatic nervous system

a. measuring a radioactive solution absorbed by brain cells; shows the activity of various neurons

b. regulates heart rate, breathing, blood pressure, other mainly involuntary movements

c. a thin layer of cells covering the entire surface of the forebrain; folds over on itself to form a large area

d. passing nonharmful radio frequencies through brain and measuring how signals interact with brain cells

e. a network of nerves that connect either to sensory receptors or to muscles you can move voluntarily

f. the largest part of the brain; has right and left sides (hemispheres) responsible for many functions

g. made up of the brain and spinal cord; carries information back and forth between brain and body

h. a relatively large cortical area at the front part of the brain; involved in many functions; like an executive

i. a specific segment on the strand of DNA that contains instructions for building the brain and body

j. all nerves that extend from the spinal cord and carry messages to and from muscles, glands, sense organs

Flashcards 2

_____ 1. amygdala

_____ 2. cerebellum

_____ 3. endocrine system

_____ 4. fight-flight response

_____ 5. gonads

_____ 6. homeostasis

_____ 7. limbic system

_____ 8. occipital lobe

_____ 9. parietal lobe

_____ 10. temporal lobe

a. involved in processing visual information, which includes seeing colors and recognizing objects

b. keeping the body's level of arousal in balance for optimum functioning

c. involved in hearing, speaking coherently, understanding verbal and written material

d. core of the forebrain; involved in many motivational behaviors and with organizing emotional behaviors

e. located directly behind the frontal lobe; its functions include the sense of touch, temperature, and pain

f. a system of glands which secrete hormones that affect organs, muscles, and other glands in the body

g. glands (ovaries in females, testes in males) that regulate sexual development and reproduction

h. involved in forming, recognizing, and remembering emotional experiences and facial expressions

i. a state of increased physiological arousal that helps body cope with and survive threatening situations

j. located at back of brain; involved in coordinating motor movements

Multiple-Choice

_____ 1. Rod Plotnik introduces us to four very different persons — Lucy, baby Theresa, Steve, and Scott — to show that
   a. one side of the brain controls most human behavior
   b. brain damage can strike almost anyone at any time
   c. humans have evolved an incredibly complex nervous system
   d. the brain will never be fully understood

_____ 2. Lucy, who may be the earliest ancestor of modern humans, lived about _____ years ago
   a. 3 million
   b. 3 thousand
   c. 10 million
   d. 10 thousand

_____ 3. The behavioral problems plaguing Scott, the child who had inherited fragile X syndrome, illustrate the role of _____ in human development
   a. evolution
   b. genetic instructions
   c. fertilization
   d. skull size

_____ 4. According to the theory of evolution, humans descended from
   a. one branch of the modern apes (it is not known which one)
   b. no other primate — they occupy a family tree of their own
   c. a creature that split off from apes millions of years ago
   d. chimpanzees, with whom they share almost 99 percent of their DNA

_____ 5. The new techniques of brain scans have a great advantage:
   a. the information they yield is more than worth the harm they do
   b. they permit a look inside the living, functioning brain
   c. it is no longer necessary to perform frontal lobotomies in mental hospitals
   d. it's so hard to find volunteers for experimental brain surgery

_____ 6. Today, through the use of _____ scans, neuroscientists are able to obtain "pictures" of cognitive activities
   a. fPET
   b. POS
   c. MRI
   d. PET

_____ 7. Which one of the following is _not_ included in the peripheral nervous system?
   a. somatic nervous system
   b. autonomic nervous system
   c. central nervous system
   d. sympathetic nervous system

_____   8. Which one of the following is *not* one of the three main parts of the human brain?
    a. forebrain
    b. midbrain
    c. hindbrain
    d. topbrain

_____   9. The cerebellum is an important part of the hindbrain that
    a. initiates voluntary movements
    b. influences social-emotional behavior
    c. coordinates motor movements
    d. makes humans distinct from all other animals

_____   10. The cortex is all folded and crinkled up because the human brain
    a. grows so fast during the first three years of life
    b. is divided into four separate lobes
    c. is protected by the skull
    d. evolved faster than the human skull that holds it

_____   11. Baby Theresa suffered from anencephaly, the condition of
    a. surgical removal of the frontal lobe of the brain
    b. the cortex being all wrinkled up
    c. being born with no brain
    d. having a metal rod blasted through the skull

_____   12. The incredible story of Phineas Gage's accident shows that
    a. the frontal lobe receives sensory information from the body
    b. a person lives at best in a vegetative state after a frontal lobotomy
    c. the frontal lobe is wired to the opposite side of the body
    d. the frontal lobe is critical to personality

_____   13. The motor cortex is located in the _____ lobe
    a. occipital
    b. parietal
    c. temporal
    d. frontal

_____   14. The somatosensory cortex is located in the _____ lobe
    a. frontal
    b. parietal
    c. temporal
    d. occipital

_____   15. Wernicke's aphasia and Broca's aphasia are evidence that
    a. language abilities are more inherited than acquired
    b. special areas of the lobes of the cortex control language abilities
    c. if one area is damaged, the other takes over for it
    d. human language is so complex that a number of things can go wrong with it

_____ 16. The failure of a patient to see objects or parts of the body on the side opposite the brain damage is called
   a. the neglect syndrome
   b. visual agnosia
   c. hysterical blindness
   d. visual association

_____ 17. When you understand the limbic system, you begin to see why
   a. modern humans are so far advanced over their prehistoric ancestors
   b. a human can do so much more than an alligator
   c. modern society is still plagued by so many primitive behaviors
   d. the social life of human beings is so much more complex than that of alligators

_____ 18. The limbic structure most involved in emotion is the
   a. amygdala
   b. hypothalamus
   c. hippocampus
   d. thalamus

_____ 19. If you see a snake crawling out from under your car, what happens next is an example of the
   a. arouse-or-die response
   b. homeostatic reaction
   c. parasympathetic push
   d. fight-flight response

_____ 20. The endocrine system and the nervous system are basically
   a. similar — they are both chemical systems
   b. similar — they both send information throughout the body
   c. different — the nervous system affects the brain and the endocrine system affects the body
   d. different — the nervous system causes positive functioning and the endocrine system causes dysfunctions

_____ 21. Me Tarzan, you Jane. Therefore, according to research on sex differences in the brain,
   a. me spatial, you verbal
   b. me verbal, you spatial
   c. me emotional, you logical
   d. me lusty, you cold

_____ 22. The sad history of research on the relationship between intelligence and skull and brain size shows that
   a. when a Nobel Prize is involved, some scientists will fudge their data
   b. science can be influenced by the prejudices of the times
   c. science is not always the best way to answer a question about human behavior
   d. sloppy measurement can undercut a sound hypothesis

_____ 23. Results of the split brain operation demonstrate that
   a. there is intense communication between the two hemispheres of the brain
   b. we would be better off with only the analytic left brain
   c. we miss a lot by neglecting the holistic right brain
   d. the body piercing movement has gotten _way_ out of hand

_____ 24. Which one of the following is *not* true about hemispheric specializations?
   a. left hemisphere – verbal
   b. right hemisphere – holistic
   c. left hemisphere – mathematical
   d. right hemisphere – analytic

_____ 25. Are you left-brained or right-brained? The best answer is that you are probably
   a. left-brained, since you are a college student
   b. constantly using both hemispheres
   c. right-brained if you are female and left-brained if you are male
   d. left-brained, since most people are

For Psych Majors Only...

The Brain and Nervous System: Match each system or structure to its main components or functions.

_____ 1. central nervous system
_____ 2. peripheral nervous system
_____ 3. somatic nervous system
_____ 4. autonomic nervous system
_____ 5. frontal lobe
_____ 6. parietal lobe
_____ 7. temporal lobe
_____ 8. occipital lobe
_____ 9. left hemisphere
_____ 10. right hemisphere

a. sympathetic and parasympathetic divisions
b. verbal, mathematical, analytical
c. motor cortex
d. brain and spinal cord
e. primary auditory cortex
f. primary visual cortex
g. somatic and autonomic nervous systems
h. afferent (sensory) and efferent (motor) fibers
i. nonverbal, spatial, holistic
j. somatosensory cortex

Short Essay

1. The module begins with Lucy, Baby Theresa, Steve, and Scott. How do their stories illustrate the basic forces that create the nervous system?

2. How do scientists study the brain?

3. What are the social implications of the evolution and function of the limbic system?

4. What is your take on the existence and importance of sex differences in the brain?

5. Do you consider yourself primarily left-brained or right-brained and why?

Answers to "The Brain and Nervous System" quiz

   1 d   2 g   3 h   4 a   5 c   6 j   7 e   8 f   9 b   10 i

Answers for Module 4

The Big Picture (explanations provided for incorrect choices)

A   The great strength of the nervous system is how beautifully all the parts work together
B   Correct! You see the "big picture" for this Module.
C   Sex and gender differences in the brain are not highly significant and do not point to this idea.
D   We could not live without either one; the brain is part of the nervous system.
E   It's just a joke!

True-False (explanations provided for False choices; page numbers given for all choices)

1	T	72	
2	F	72	The peripheral nervous system includes all the nerves in the body outside the brain and spinal cord.
3	F	73	It is the forebrain, not the hindbrain, that is most closely related to higher functions.
4	T	74	
5	F	80	The limbic system remains our older, more animalistic brain.
6	T	81	
7	T	82	
8	F	85	There is some correlation between brain size and intelligence, but it has little practical application.
9	T	86	
10	F	87	Humans probably use both sides of the brain almost equally.

Flashcards 1

1 b	2 g	3 c	4 f	5 h	6 i	7 d	8 j	9 a	10 e

Flashcards 2

1 h	2 j	3 f	4 i	5 g	6 b	7 d	8 a	9 e	10 c

Multiple-Choice (explanations provided for incorrect choices)

1   a   This is not true about brain functioning.
   b   Brain damage is rare and need not be feared.
   c   Correct! See page 67.
   d   Great progress is being made in understanding the brain.

2   *a   Correct! See page 67.*
   b   That would only be a thousand years before Christ.
   c   Modern humans don't go back nearly that far.
   d   That was about the beginning of the agricultural age.

3   a   This disease is not specifically related to evolution.
   b   Correct! See page 67.
   c   This disease is not related to fertilization.
   d   This disease is not related to skull size.

4   a   Humans and apes are both descended from an earlier ancestor.
   b   Some religions suggest this, but the theory of evolution does not.
   c   Correct! See page 69.
   d   Chimpanzees and humans are both descended from an earlier ancestor.

5   a   These scans are relatively safe, but not 100 percent harmless.
   b   Correct! See page 70.
   c   Brain scans are unrelated to frontal lobotomies.
   d   It's just a joke!

6   a   There is no fPET scan.
   b   There is no POS scan.
   c   MRI scans show static views of the structure of the brain.
   d   Correct! See page 71.

7 a The somatic nervous system is one of the two parts of the peripheral nervous system.
   b The autonomic nervous system is one of the two parts of the peripheral nervous system.
   c *Correct! See page 72.*
   d The sympathetic nervous system is one of the two parts of the autonomic nervous system.

8 a The forebrain is one of the divisions of the human brain.
   b The midbrain is one of the divisions of the human brain.
   c The hindbrain is one of the divisions of the human brain.
   d *Correct! See page 73.*

9 a The cerebellum does not initiate voluntary movement.
   b This is true of the frontal lobe, not the cerebellum.
   c *Correct! See page 73.*
   d Other animals also possess these faculties.

10 a True, but this does not explain why the cortex is folded.
   b True, but this does not explain why the cortex is folded.
   c True, but this does not explain why the cortex is folded.
   d *Correct! See page 74.*

11 a That would be the discredited frontal lobotomy operation.
   b That is an evolutionary adaptation to our small skull size.
   c *Correct! See page 74.*
   d That refers to Phineas Gage's accident.

12 a The parietal lobe receives sensory information from the body.
   b Phineas Gage was not in a vegetative state.
   c Phineas Gage's accident did not reveal the special wiring of each hemisphere to the opposite side of the body.
   d *Correct! See page 75.*

13 a The occipital lobe is the location of the primary visual cortex.
   b The parietal lobe is the location of the somatosensory cortex.
   c The temporal lobe is the location of the primary auditory cortex.
   d *Correct! See page 76.*

14 a The frontal lobe is the location of the motor cortex.
   b *Correct! See page 77.*
   c The temporal lobe is the location of the primary auditory cortex.
   d The occipital lobe is the location of the primary visual cortex.

15 a Learned factors in language abilities are at least as important as inherited factors.
   b *Correct! See page 78.*
   c Wernicke's area and Broca's area each control different language functions.
   d The two types of aphasia are relatively rare disorders.

16 **a** *Correct! See page 79.*
   b Visual agnosia is the failure to recognize the whole object even though the parts are recognized.
   c Hysterical blindness is a psychological problem not discussed in this module.
   d Not a real term for a visual problem.

17 a The limbic system reveals our similarities to our prehistoric ancestors.
   b It is not the limbic system that gives humans a cognitive advantage.
   c *Correct! See page 80.*
   d Other parts of the brain explain our greater social complexity.

18 **a** *Correct! See page 80.*
   b The hypothalamus is more involved in regulating many motivational behaviors.
   c The hippocampus is more involved in saving many kinds of fleeting memories.
   d The thalamus is more involved in receiving sensory information.

19 a This is not a correct technical term.
   b This is not a correct technical term.
   c This is not a correct technical term.
   d *Correct! See page 81.*

20 a The endocrine system is basically chemical but the nervous system is basically electrical
    b Correct! See page 82.
    c Both systems affect the brain and the body.
    d Both promote positive functioning, but both can also have dysfunctions.

21 *a Correct! See page 84.*
    b On some tests, men do better on spatial tasks and women better on verbal.
    c This is the reverse of a commonly held opinion.
    d It's just a joke! [And if you chose this answer, perhaps you should take some Women's Studies courses.]

22 a The Nobel Prize was not involved in this history.
    b Correct! See page 85.
    c Sometimes misused, science is still our most powerful method for answering questions about human behavior.
    d In this case, the hypothesis was wrong because it was based on personal bias.

23 *a Correct! See page 86.*
    b Would you want to live a life without feelings? Could you?
    c True enough, but the split brain operation does not negate the right hemisphere.
    d It's just a joke!

24 a The left hemisphere is thought to be more verbal than nonverbal.
    b The right hemisphere is thought to be more holistic than analytical.
    c The left hemisphere is thought to be more mathematical than spatial
    d Correct! See page 87.

25 a It is doubtful that any groups, or even many individuals, are truly "left-brained" or "right-brained."
    b Correct! See page 87.
    c It is doubtful that any groups, or even many individuals, are truly "left-brained" or "right-brained."
    d It is doubtful that any groups, or even many individuals, are truly "left-brained" or "right-brained."

Short Essay (sample answers)

1. Each of these four persons demonstrates an important aspect of the nervous system. Lucy shows the role evolution has played in developing modern humans. Baby Theresa shows that different parts of the brain control different aspects of life. Steve shows how brain damage both robs a person of basic functions and also points to specific links between parts of the brain and behavior. Scott shows how a complicated system of essential and interlocking genetic instructions underlies development.

2. Today scientists have powerful new tools with which to study the brain. MRI (magnetic resonance imaging) scans, in which radio waves are passed through the brain, reveal detailed images of the brain. The recently developed fMRI (functional magnetic resonance imaging) measures the activity of specific neurons that are functioning during cognitive tasks, showing the brain in action. PET (positron emission tomography), based on radiation in brain cells, shows where thoughts and feelings are occurring during mental activity.

3. The limbic system is involved in motivational behaviors, emotional behaviors, and storing memories. The limbic system in humans is similar to that of animals like alligators and represents a primitive stage in our evolution. If our most basic motivational and emotional systems are no more evolved than those of the alligator, no wonder we have so much trouble living peacefully and cooperatively with our fellow humans. The question for psychology is how accurate this picture is, and how much control the limbic system has.

4. Are there structural or functional differences in cognitive, behavioral, or brain processes that arise from being male or female? You could argue at one extreme that research has established fundamental differences. At the other extreme, you could argue that "differences" shown by cognitive tasks and brain scans are either inaccurate (like the skull size research) or unimportant (like hair color). In either case, you should offer your opinion on the possible social implications and practical consequences of such differences.

5. If you believe you are primarily left-brained, you should describe the verbal, mathematical, and analytic abilities you see as your main characteristics. If you believe you are primarily right-brained, you should describe the nonverbal, spatial, and holistic abilities you see as your main characteristics. In either case, you should acknowledge the opinion of experts that the whole left-brained/right-brained dichotomy is wrong. Is it possible that — in varying degrees — you possess all of these abilities?

Module **5**

Sensation

What is Real?

Back in the happy days before I studied psychology, I simply "knew" that there was a real world out there and that it came straight into my mind (I never thought to wonder what the "mind" is or how it works). When you study sensation (Module 5), perception (Module 6), and consciousness (Module 7), however, it gets confusing. If you don't watch out, you could find yourself in the predicament of poor Descartes, whose search for a proof of existence had him doubting his own existence, until he decided that just thinking about the problem must prove he was there to do it.

The story begins in this module, with the mechanisms of the sense organs (eye, ear, nose, tongue, and skin) and the processes by which they receive stimuli (light and sound waves, chemicals, and pressures) from the environment. But be prepared for a disappointment: it doesn't mean a thing.

How We Relate to the World

Suppose that right in the middle of writing a great paper your computer suddenly crashed and all you could recover was a data dump of everything it "knew" about your paper. You would experience a similar disappointment. All you would see on the printout would be a long succession of ones and zeros, the binary code in which computers work. It wouldn't mean a thing.

The processes of perception transform meaningless sensations into useful information. It's sort of like the word processing software that turns those ones and zeros in your paper into (hopefully) great prose. Now the raw sensations begin to take on meaning, as the perceptual processes involved interpret them.

Are we finally in contact with the real world? In a way, but notice that we are also one step removed from that world, apprehending it second-hand through the possibly distorted mechanisms of perception. Even then, exactly *what* do the perceptions mean? The researchers in neuroscience we mentioned in the previous module are trying to find out. We could guess that the answer will involve a complex interaction of cognition and emotion, each enriching the information and making it more useful to us.

We could say that at last we have the real world, but now it is at least three steps removed, as we experience it in our conscious (and unconscious?) mind. How real is it anymore? Perhaps psychology must leave the question of reality to philosophers and theologians. I still believe it's out there, but now I know that what is in my mind is constructed, not real.

Effective Student Tip 5

Go Ahead, Ask Me

I am always astounded when I review my class lists early in the new semester. There are more than a few students who have not yet said a word in class.

For some, it is politeness. Heaven knows, I am flying, and they hesitate to interrupt. For others, it is modesty. Maybe the point they would make isn't all that brilliant. For still others it is excruciating shyness. If they did speak up, they just know the class would turn as one and sneer, "You idiot!"

For each of these students, an effective strategy would be to ask a simple question. A good question can be just the thing to begin your involvement in the class.

As you prepare for the next class, find something in the textbook or your lecture notes that really interests you. What more would you like to know? Think how you could ask about it in a short, clear question. Pick a moment when your question is relevant, then ask away. (If you feel you can't do it, ask your first question either before or after class. It's a start.)

What do you get out of it? Aside from the information you wanted, you have made contact with the professor and your fellow students. You have demonstrated to yourself that you can talk in class. And the class is more fun now.

Your response...

How comfortable do you feel in class? Do you talk? Is talking something you enjoy, or dread?

Learning Objectives

1. Understand sensation as a process by which raw physical stimuli sent to the brain are changed into potentially useful experiences.

2. Learn the basic mechanisms of vision, audition, balance, taste and smell, touch, and pain.

3. For each of the basic sensations (vision, audition, balance, taste and smell, touch, and pain), explain how that sensation involves the interaction of stimuli, sensors, and the brain.

4. Appreciate the considerable impact of cultural differences on a simple experience like tasting a common food which is considered good in some cultures but disgusting in others.

5. Consider the implications of placebos and the placebo effect for human psychology.

6. Understand the complicated dimensions of pain, not as simple as you might think.

7. Learn about exciting new applications of artificial senses to correct age-old problems of vision and audition.

Key Terms

There are so many key terms in the module because it covers all the senses. The terms may be easier to learn if you organize them by the senses they help explain.

acupuncture	flavor	place theory
adaptation	frequency theory	placebo
afterimage	gate control theory of pain	placebo effect
auditory association area	hair cells	primary auditory cortex
auditory canal	iris	pupil
auditory nerve	lens	retina
basilar membrane	loudness	rods
cochlea	Meniere's disease	semicircular canals
cochlear implant	middle ear	sensations
color blindness	monochromats	somatosensory cortex
conduction deafness	motion sickness	sound waves
cones	nearsightedness	taste
cornea	neural deafness	taste buds
decibel	olfaction	touch
dichromats	olfactory cells	transduction
direction of a sound	opponent-process theory	trichromatic theory
disgust	ossicles	tympanic membrane
double-blind procedure	outer ear	vertigo
endorphins	pain	vestibular system
external ear	perceptions	visible spectrum
farsightedness	pitch	

Outline

- *Introduction*

    1. Electric billboard in the brain (Blind Katie)

    2. Three characteristics of all senses (Processes)

    ☐ Can you explain how the three characteristics of all senses produce the experiences of seeing, hearing, smelling, touching, tasting, and position?

        a. **Transduction**

        b. **Adaptation**

        c. **Sensations** versus **perceptions**

A. *Eye: Vision*

    1. Stimulus: light waves

        a. Invisible – too short

        b. Visible – just right (**visible spectrum**)

        c. Invisible – too long

    ☐ What is the visible spectrum and what makes it visible?

    2. Structure and function

    ☐ What happens when you look at something? Can you explain the process of looking?

        a. Image reversed

        b. Light waves

        c. **Cornea**

        d. **Pupil**

        e. **Iris**

        f. **Lens**

        g. **Retina**

        h. Eyeball's shape and laser eye surgery

            (1) Normal vision

            (2) **Nearsightedness**

            (3) **Farsightedness**

            (4) Eye surgery

    3. **Retina**: a miniature camera-computer

        a. Photoreceptors

        b. **Rods**

        c. **Cones**

        d. Transduction

        e. Nerve impulses, optic nerve and blind spot

4. Visual pathways: eye to brain

    a. Optic nerve

    b. Primary visual cortex

        (1) Specialized cells

        (2) Stimulation or blindness

    c. Visual association areas

    d. PET scans reveal visual activity

5. Color vision

    a. Making colors from wavelengths

    b. **Trichromatic theory**

    c. **Opponent-process theory**

        (1) **Afterimage**

        (2) Excited or inhibited

    d. Theories combined

    e. **Color blindness**

        (1) **Monochromats**

        (2) **Dichromats**

B. *Ear: Audition*

1. Stimulus: **sound waves**

    a. Amplitude and **loudness**

    b. Frequency and **pitch**

2. Measuring sound waves

    a. **Decibel**

    b. Decibels and deafness

3. Outer, middle, and inner ear

    a. **Outer ear**

        (1) **External ear**

        (2) **Auditory canal**

        (3) **Tympanic membrane**

    b. **Middle ear**

        (1) **Ossicles**

        (2) Hammer, anvil, and stirrup

        (3) Oval window

    c. Inner ear

        (1) **Cochlea**

        (2) **Hair cells** and **basilar membrane**

            (3) **Auditory nerve**

       d. Auditory brain areas

            (1) **Primary auditory cortex**

            (2) **Auditory association area**

    4. Auditory cues

       a. Calculating **direction of a sound**

       b. Calculating pitch

            (1) **Frequency theory**

            (2) **Place theory**

       c. Calculating **loudness**

 C. *Vestibular System: Balance*

    1. Position and balance: **vestibular system**

       a. **Semicircular canals**

       b. Sensing position of head, keeping head upright, maintaining balance

    2. **Motion sickness**

    3. **Meniere's disease** and **vertigo**

 D. *Chemical Senses*

    1. **Taste**

       a. Four basic tastes: sweet, salty, sour, and bitter (plus a possible new one, *umami*)

       b. Surface of the tongue

       c. **Taste buds**

       d. All tongues are not the same

       e. **Flavor**: taste and smell

    2. Smell, or **olfaction**

       a. Stimulus

       b. **Olfactory cells**

       c. Sensations and memories

       d. Functions of olfaction

    ☐ What is a recently discovered function of olfaction?

 E. *Touch*

    1. Sense of **touch**

       a. Skin

       b. Hair receptors

       c. Free nerve endings

       d. Pacinian corpuscle

    2. Brain areas: **somatosensory cortex**

F. *Cultural Diversity: Disgust*

1. Psychological factors

☐ Although most foods cause delight, some otherwise edible substances cause disgust. What explains this phenomenon and why is it automatically translated into a facial expression?

   a. **Disgust**

   b. Cultural influence

2. Cultural influences on disgust

G. *Research Focus: Mind over Body?*

1. Definitions and research methods

   a. **Placebo**

   b. **Placebo effect**

   c. **Double-blind procedure**

2. Placebo results

3. Conclusion: mind over body!

H. *Pain*

1. **Pain** sensations

   a. Tissue damage

   b. Social, psychological, and emotional factors

2. **Gate control theory of pain**

   a. Competing messages to the brain

   b. Pain: physical and psychological

3. **Endorphins**

   a. Pain reduction and addiction

   b. Adrenal cell transplants

4. **Acupuncture**

   a. Competing stimuli

   b. Psychological factors

I. *Application: Artificial Senses*

1. Artificial visual system

   a. Artificial photoreceptors

   b. Artificial eye and brain implant

   c. Functional vision

2. Kinds of deafness

   a. **Conduction deafness**

   b. **Neural deafness**

3. **Cochlear implant**

Language Workout

What's That?

p. 97   the ability to **tell** night from day = see the difference

p. 98   **opponent** = enemy, fighter against

p. 100   pitch is our **subjective** experience of a sound = personal
         a **cheerleader's** yell = a person who guides others in supportive messages to a team

p. 101   **jackhammer** = noisy machine to break rocks and cement
         firecracker = an exploding noise maker
         threshold of hearing = point where effect begins

p. 102   auditory canal may become **clogged** = to be completely filled

p. 105   you rarely forget to **duck** (head) = move head to avoid danger
         a sensory **mismatch** = wrong combination
         malfunctioning of the vestibular system = wrong operation
         feel a little **queasy** [KWEE-zee] = sick in the stomach

p. 106   an **innate** preference for sweet and salt = natural, inborn
         such as a **brownie** = chocolate cake squares

p. 107   or if a **blow** to the head = a strong hit
         that **elicit** pleasant memories = bring about

p. 112   This competition creates a **bottleneck** = obstacle, like a traffic jam

p. 113   scientists trained in the **rigorous** methods of the West = extremely careful

p. 115   The signals **trigger** impulses = activate, cause a series of actions or effects

p. 118   **take full advantage of** the Mozart effect = use fully
         have a **boost** in intelligence = an increase
         one **nursery** had positive proof = business that takes care of very young children

What's the Difference?

WHY A COMMA? (Part 1)

Commas are found in many languages, but how they are used can be quite different even by speakers of that same language.

One place where we find commas is when we have a series of three of more different nouns, verbs, or adjectives.

> Eye, ear, tongue, nose, and skin (p. 93)
> The continuous stimulation of glasses, jewelry, or clothes on your skin (p. 93)

Notice how the word "and" and "or" are used before the last word in the series.

Notice how a comma is used between each word. The comma before "and" and "or" is used commonly in American written English. This comma is not used in British written English.

TRY THIS: Many people don't realize that we use commas when we speak. A comma is like a pause in speaking. Read the following sentences out loud, and see where you take a little break between words:

Running as fast as possible the mouse ran into its hole.
From beginning to end the movie was very funny.
As a result of his broken leg Tom could not play football for months.

You probably put in a little breath after the words "possible," "end," and "leg." Now, if you put in a pause when you are reading the sentence aloud, you will probably need to put in a comma when you are writing the sentence. The pause helps the listener make sense of the sentence. In the same way, a comma helps the reader understand the meaning.

COMMAS AS SIGNPOSTS: Commas let the reader know what is important and what is not important. In any sentence, the most important action comes from the main subject and verb.

So, any information that we put *before* the main subject and verb needs to be separated by a comma. Look at the following sentences from the text:

Although your sense organs look so very different, they all share the three characteristics defined next. (p. 93)
In the second step, the brain quickly changes sensations. (p. 93)
After passing through the cornea and pupil, light waves reach the lens. (p. 95)
Unlike rods, cones are wired individually to neighboring cells. (p. 96)
Because rods are extremely light sensitive, they allow us to see in dim light. (p. 95)

In all these sentences, the comma tells us that the first part is *not* the main action of the sentence. When we see the comma, it tells us that the *next* words are the real action of the sentence.

So, the comma divides the introductory information from the main subject and verb. Try it yourself: read the following sentences. Each sentence needs one comma, so you decide where to put it:

Next to an elephant a mouse looks very small.
When she didn't see her mother the baby started crying.
After the war ended the soldiers all returned home.
With no warning at all to the students the teacher began to sing.

Now, what happens if we reverse these sentences? Do we still need to use commas? What do you think?

A mouse looks very small next to an elephant.
The baby started crying when she didn't see her mother.
The soldiers all returned home after the war ended.
The teacher began to sing with no warning at all to the students.

All these sentences are correct. In all of them, the important action — the main subject and verb — comes at the beginning of the sentence. This action is clear, so when the extra information comes at the end, we don't need to separate it with a comma.

Look at the next module for more on commas.

Answers

Next to an elephant, a mouse looks very small.
When she didn't see her mother, the baby started crying.
After the war ended, the soldiers all returned home.
With no warning at all to the students, the teacher began to sing.

The Big Picture

Which statement below offers the best summary of the larger significance of this module?

A   Sensation is the process by which the raw data we need for understanding the world around us comes into our brain. Perception is the process by which the brain makes the raw data meaningful.

B   Study of the eye, ear, nose, tongue, and skin are traditional subjects in psychology. Today, however, it is becoming clear that these biological functions do not have much to do with psychology.

C   Sensation is the collection of processes by which we understand what is happening in our world. For example, through vision we "make sense" out of what we see.

D   Perception is how we gather data about the world. Sensation is how we make sense of that data. Therefore, in human psychology, sensation is more important than perception.

E   Sensation is the excitement we feel when we see something really great, as in "I saw a sensational babe at the beach today."

True-False

_____   1. All of the senses share three characteristics: transduction, adaptation, and the experience of "sensing" something.

_____   2. The reason you can "see" a giraffe is that the animal emits light waves that humans can detect.

_____   3. The retina is a round opening at the front of your eye that allows light waves to pass into the eye's interior.

_____   4. The images you "see" are created by the primary visual cortex and related association area of the brain.

_____   5. Sound waves vary in amplitude and frequency.

_____   6. The vestibular system provides feedback on your body's position in space by interpreting sound waves from your environment

_____   7. Motion sickness, Meniere's disease, and vertigo are disorders of the outer ear.

_____   8. The tongue has receptors for four or five basic tastes.

_____   9. Humans won't eat just anything — we have biologically determined preferences for some foods and feelings of disgust at the thought of others.

_____   10. Acupuncture often produces pain relief — perhaps by causing secretion of endorphins in the brain.

Flashcards 1

_____	1. adaptation	a.	says rate at which nerve impulses reach brain determine how low a sound is
_____	2. frequency theory	b.	says color vision is due to eye and brain responding to either red-green or blue-yellow
_____	3. opponent-process theory	c.	a sense organ changes physical energy into electrical signals that become neural impulses
_____	4. place theory	d.	location of basilar membrane vibrations determines medium and higher sounds
_____	5. sensations	e.	stimulus activates sensory receptors, producing electrical signals that are processed by the brain
_____	6. sound waves	f.	stimuli for audition; resemble ripples on pond; have height (amplitude) and speed (frequency)
_____	7. transduction	g.	three semicircular canals in inner ear that determine our sense of balance and position
_____	8. trichromatic theory	h.	one particular segment of electromagnetic energy whose waves can be seen by human eye
_____	9. vestibular system	i.	says color vision is due to three kinds of cones in retina sensitive to blue, green, or red
_____	10. visible spectrum	j.	prolonged or continuous stimulation results in a decreased responding by the sense organs

Flashcards 2

_____	1. acupuncture	a.	smell receptors located in nasal passages; use mucus into which volatile molecules dissolve
_____	2. disgust	b.	dizziness and nausea resulting from malfunction of semicircular canals of vestibular system
_____	3. endorphins	c.	includes pressure, temperature, and pain; from miniature sensors beneath outer layer of skin
_____	4. gate control theory of pain	d.	a universal facial expression (eyes closed, lips curled downward) indicating rejection of foods
_____	5. nearsightedness	e.	chemicals produced by the brain and secreted in response to injury or stress cause reduced pain
_____	6. olfactory cells	f.	may result when eyeball is too long; result is that near objects are clear but distant are blurry
_____	7. placebo effect	g.	thin film with three layers of cells located at back of eyeball; includes photoreceptor cells
_____	8. retina	h.	inserting thin needles into various points on the body's surface and twirling them to relieve pain
_____	9. touch	i.	says rubbing an injured area or becoming involved in other activities blocks pain impulses
_____	10. vertigo	j.	change in patient's illness attributable to an imagined treatment rather than to a medical one

Multiple-Choice

_____ 1. Rod Plotnik says the experience of Katie, a blind woman who had tiny gold wires implanted into the back of her brain, raises the question
   a. are some cases of blindness actually hysterical?
   b. can blind persons regain their sight through intense practice?
   c. do you see with your eyes or with your brain?
   d. can science go too far in tampering with human capabilities?

_____ 2. The process by which a sense organ changes physical stimuli into impulses is termed
   a. adaptation
   b. experiencing
   c. sensing
   d. transduction

_____ 3. A decline in responding with prolonged or continuous stimulation is called
   a. transduction
   b. adaptation
   c. sensing
   d. experiencing

_____ 4. When you get that new road rocket for graduation, you may want a radar detector, too, because those things
   a. see the pulses of light that radar guns use
   b. hear the faint vibrations of radar guns
   c. see long wave lengths you can't
   d. make your car look cool

_____ 5. The function of the cornea is to
   a. add color to light waves entering the eye
   b. screen out irrelevant light waves
   c. prevent convergence from occurring too soon
   d. bend and focus light waves into a narrower beam of light

_____ 6. If you see close objects clearly but distant objects appear blurry, you are
   a. nearsighted
   b. farsighted
   c. normal
   d. abnormal

_____ 7. The work of the retina is to
   a. add sharp focus to what you are seeing
   b. transform light waves into electrical signals
   c. turn the inverted image we see right side up
   d. change impulses into light waves we can see

_____ 8. Which *one* of the following accurately describes the work of rods or cones in the retina?
   a. rods – allow us to see bright colors
   b. cones – allow us to see in dim light
   c. rods – allow us to see large objects
   d. cones – allow us to see fine details

_____ 9. According to the trichromatic theory, our color vision is based on
   a. three primary colors, which are mixed to produce all colors
   b. two opposite pairs of colors, red-green and blue-yellow
   c. an afterimage created by a bright original light stimulus
   d. a combination of the monochromat and dichromat theories

_____ 10. If a tree falls in an uninhabited forest, does it make any sound?
   a. obviously, it does
   b. not if there is no human there to "hear" it
   c. it depends on whether we define "sound" as the waves of air or the subjective experience of hearing
   d. I thought this was a class in psychology, not philosophy

_____ 11. How loud a sound seems is determined by the _____ of the sound waves
   a. frequency
   b. amplitude
   c. pitch
   d. cycle

_____ 12. The noise level near the speakers at a rock concert measures about
   a. 30 decibels, which is very loud
   b. 100 decibels, about the same as a chain saw
   c. 140 decibels, which can produce hearing loss
   d. 1,000 decibels, which is very loud

_____ 13. The tympanic membrane is the scientific name for what is commonly called the
   a. outer ear
   b. inner ear
   c. auditory canal
   d. eardrum

_____ 14. The function of the cochlea is to
   a. transform vibrations into nerve impulses
   b. move fluid forward toward the oval window
   c. house the hammer, anvil, and stirrup
   d. house the band of fibers called the auditory nerve

_____ 15. Our sense of movement and position in space is determined by the
   a. faint echoes from surrounding objects that the brain can decode
   b. movement of fluid in the three semicircular canals of the vestibular system
   c. primary visual cortex and related association areas
   d. movement of fluid in the eardrum

_____ 16. Motion sickness is probably caused by
   a. a sensory mismatch between the information from the vestibular system and the eyes
   b. the violent bouncing around of the head during a rough stretch of road
   c. individual personality factors
   d. drug use

_____ 17. Which one of the following is *not* one of the four or five basic tastes?
   a. sweet
   b. sharp
   c. salty
   d. sour

_____ 18. The experience of flavor results from the
   a. olfactory cells
   b. taste buds
   c. chemical sense called olfaction
   d. combination of sensations of taste and smell

_____ 19. Our sense of touch comes from
   a. a half-dozen miniature sensors located in the skin
   b. millions of tiny nerves on the surface of the skin
   c. special glands for pressure, temperature, and pain
   d. stimulation of the tiny hairs that cover the body

_____ 20. The experience of the sense of touch is produced by the
   a. auditory association area
   b. vestibular system
   c. somatosensory cortex
   d. visual association area

_____ 21. Why do some edible substances produce a feeling of disgust?
   a. our culture has taught us that these substances are not food
   b. our taste buds warn us that some substances are harmful
   c. the taste may be tolerable, but the smell is disgusting
   d. some food simply have no flavor

_____ 22. In the double-blind procedure,
   a. there are blinds (screens) separating the researchers from the subjects
   b. both researchers and subjects wear blindfolds in order to guarantee privacy
   c. subjects first receive the treatment, then later receive a placebo
   d. neither the researchers nor the subjects know who is receiving what treatment

_____ 23. "Let Momma kiss it and make it better," is an example of a wise mother applying
   a. her understanding of endorphins
   b. her knowledge that TLC is always more effective than medicine
   c. the gate control theory of pain
   d. the unspoken threat of using acupuncture

_____ 24. Can the ancient Oriental procedure called acupuncture actually relieve pain? Modern science says
   a. yes, because there are some mysteries Western science is not equipped to explain
   b. perhaps, because stimulation of certain points may cause the secretion of endorphins
   c. no, because there cannot be a relationship between twirling needles in the skin and pain caused by the nervous system
   d. no, because there is no research to date that supports acupuncture

_____ 25. Cochlear implants are effective
   a. in only a few cases, limiting their use to fewer than 1,000 persons worldwide
   b. in conduction deafness, but not in neural deafness
   c. because they are surgically planted deep inside the brain
   d. because a mechanical device does the work of damaged auditory receptors

Short Essay

1. Why is the process of transduction essential to human functioning?

2. Explain the basic workings of the sensation called vision.

3. Yes, there is a "sixth" sense, but it is not some form of intuition. What is the sixth sense and how does it work?

4. What does the feeling of disgust suggest about the interaction of psychology and culture?

5. Why is the double-blind procedure necessary in scientific research?

Wanted!

I pass out a corny "Wanted" poster urging my students to look for any errors I make in writing (spelling, grammar, formatting). I offer a payoff to the first student who finds the particular error. Have you found any mistakes? I can't ask your instructor to pay off (it's my mistake, after all), but I will send you an e-mail you can show your teacher. Might make a good impression! Please e-mail me if you find a mistake! **Profenos@aol.com**

Answers for Module 5

The Big Picture

A   *Correct! You see the "big picture" for this Module.*
B   The biological functions of sensation are the foundation of all psychological activity.
C   This is a definition of "perception" and a misunderstanding of the term "sensation."
D   This statement reverses the meanings of sensation and perception; both are necessary.
E   It's just a joke!

True-False (explanations provided for False choices; page numbers given for all choices)

1	T	93	
2	F	94	The animal does not emit light waves, it reflects them.
3	F	95	That is a description of the pupil.
4	T	97	
5	T	100	
6	F	105	The vestibular system relies on fluid in the inner ear, not on sound.
7	F	105	They are disorders of the inner ear.
8	T	106	
9	F	110	Food preferences and dislikes are determined more by culture than biology.
10	T	113	

Flashcards 1

1 j   2 a   3 b   4 d   5 e   6 f   7 c   8 i   9 g   10 h

Flashcards 2

1 h   2 d   3 e   4 i   5 f   6 a   7 j   8 g   9 c   10 b

Multiple-Choice (explanations provided for incorrect choices)

1   a   Plotnik does not suggest this rare possibility.
    b   Do you really think this is a possibility?
    c   Correct! See page 93.
    d   Plotnik does not raise this concern.

2   a   Adaptation is not the technical term for the process.
    c   Sensing is not the technical term for the process.
    b   Experiencing is not the technical term for the process.
    d   Correct! See page 93.

3   a   Transduction refers to the process of changing physical stimuli into impulses.
    b   Correct! See page 93.
    c   Sensing is not the technical term for the process.
    d   Experiencing is not the technical term for the process.

4   a   Radar is not based on pulses of light.
    b   Radar does not cause vibrations.
    c   Correct! See page 94.
    d   It's just a joke!

5   a   Color is not created in the cornea.
    b   No light waves are irrelevant in and of themselves.
    c   Convergence explains the operation of the rods and cones, not the cornea.
    d   Correct! See page 95.

6   *a   Correct! See page 95.*
    b   The opposite is true in farsightedness.
    c   Both near and far objects are clear in normal vision.
    d   This is a normal vision problem experienced by many people.

7   a   Focus is controlled by the shape of the eyeball.
    b   *Correct! See page 96.*
    c   This is a function of the primary visual cortex in the brain.
    d   The retina changes light waves into impulses.

8   a   Cones allow us to see color.
    b   Rods allow us to see in dim light.
    c   Both rods and cones are involved in seeing objects, large or small.
    d   *Correct! See page 96.*

9   ***a***   *Correct! See page 98.*
    b   This is the opponent-process theory.
    c   An afterimage is a visual sensation that continues after the original stimulus is removed.
    d   These are not theories, but two kinds of color blindness.

10   a   How would we know if we aren't there to hear it?
    b   What if a tape recorder had been placed there?
    c   *Correct! See page 100.*
    d   Here we see that a philosophical question has a psychological answer.

11   a   The frequency of sound waves determines the pitch of what we hear.
    b   *Correct! See page 100.*
    c   Pitch is related to frequency of sound waves.
    d   Cycles are a measure of the frequency of sound waves.

12   a   30 decibels is whisper quiet.
    b   100 decibels is loud, but not dangerous.
    c   *Correct! See page 101.*
    d   140 decibels is the upper threshold for human hearing.

13   a   It is at the inner end of the outer ear (see diagram).
    b   It is just before the middle ear (see diagram).
    c   The auditory canal comes just before the tympanic membrane (see diagram).
    d   *Correct! See page 102.*

14   ***a***   *Correct! See page 102.*
    b   The cochlea is further in than the oval window.
    c   The hammer, anvil, and stirrup are housed in the middle ear.
    d   The auditory nerves are further in than the cochlea.

15   a   True . . . for bats.
    b   *Correct! See page 105.*
    c   It is determined more by the ear than by the eye.
    d   Movement of fluid yes, but not in the eardrum.

16   ***a***   *Correct! See page 105.*
    b   It is not the bouncing but the mismatch with other information.
    c   Individual personality factors do not appear to cause motion sickness.
    d   Drug use does not appear to cause motion sickness.

17   a   Sweet is one of the basic tastes.
    b   *Correct! See page 106.*
    c   Salty is one of the basic tastes.
    d   Sour is one of the basic tastes.

18   a   Smell is only half the story.
    b   Taste is only half the story.
    c   Smell is only half the story.
    d   *Correct! See page 106.*

19   ***a***   *Correct! See page 108.*
    b   Nerves do not reside on the surface of the skin.
    c   Pressure, temperature, and pain are features of the sense of touch.
    d   What about the smooth, hairless skin where you also experience the sense of touch?

20   a   The auditory association area is involved in hearing.
        b   The vestibular system is involved in balance.
        c   *Correct! See page 108.*
        d   The visual association area is involved in vision.

21   *a*   *Correct! See page 110.*
        b   But that experience is not the same as disgust.
        c   But what would make the smell "disgusting"?
        d   Flavor is the result of smell plus taste.

22   a   In research, blind means not knowing the true nature of the treatment.
        b   Isn't this kind of silly?
        c   In research, subjects receive either the treatment or a placebo, not both.
        d   *Correct! See page 111.*

23   a   Endorphins might be involved, but not because of the mother's attention.
        b   If this is true, you better reconsider applying to med school.
        c   *Correct! See page 112.*
        d   It's just a joke!

24   a   Science does not accept the idea that there are mysteries it cannot explore.
        b   *Correct! See page 113.*
        c   What if it is not the twirling needles themselves but rather a byproduct of the needle stimulation?
        d   There is some evidence that acupuncture does relieve pain. The real question is how it works.

25   a   About 40,000 cochlear implants are done every year.
        b   Just the opposite is true.
        c   They are implanted in the ear, not in the brain.
        d   *Correct! See page 115.*

Short Essay (sample answers)

1. We are constantly bombarded by physical sensations gathered by the five basic senses. But in the form of physical energy this information is useless to us. It must be transformed into electrical signals that become neural impulses. In this form it can be sent to the brain for processing. That transformation is the process of transduction. Without transduction, the brain would be incapable of changing raw sensations into signals that can be used to interpret and understand the world that bombards us with its energy.

2. Vision begins with light waves of varying wavelength. In humans, the visible spectrum is the segment of electromagnetic energy we can see. The light waves enter the cornea, pass through the pupil in amounts controlled by the iris, are bent and focused by the lens, and absorbed by the retina. Rods and cones add detail and color and create nerve impulses that begin the process of transduction. The important quality of color probably results from a combination of the trichromatic theory and the opponent-process theory.

3. The "sixth" sense is balance, which is a product of the vestibular system of the inner ear. Three semicircular canals set at different angles contain fluid that moves in response to movements of your head. Tiny hair cells in the canals convey information about balance to the brain. If there is a mismatch between the information from the vestibular system and the eyes, you may experience motion sickness. Less well understood, and much more disturbing, are vertigo and Meniere's disease.

4. As any anthropologist or survivalist knows, we can eat many products of nature that normally we try hard to avoid. The physical products themselves are nourishing, and probably eaten by some peoples around the world. Yet our immediate reaction to them is disgust. Our faces register this emotion in a universally recognized expression that had clear survival value earlier in our evolution. Obviously this reaction is learned from our culture. Nothing is inherently disgusting. Hey guys, "Fear Factor" is on!

5. The laboratory experiment is the most powerful tool we have for determining cause and effect relationships in nature. If all other variables are held constant, any differences between control group and experimental group behavior should be due to the experimental treatment. But there is still a danger of bias from the knowledge of subjects and researchers. In the double-blind procedure, both subjects and researchers are "blind" to which group gets which, thus eliminating expectations about subject behaviors.

Module 6

Perception

How to Ruin a Professor's Day

When I took experimental psychology, years ago, our professor enjoyed bedeviling us with the same classic perceptual illusions that Rod Plotnik discusses in Module 6. The one that really got us was the famous Müller-Lyer illusion. It is so powerful that it fooled us every time, even after we already knew the lines were the same length. One day a troublemaker in the back row asked, "But *why* does it work?" Our professor hung his head and had to admit, "I don't know."

Today, cognitive psychology has an intriguing answer (it's in Module 6). Besides the fascination of discovering how sensing and perceiving work, understanding these processes can be personally liberating. Here's why.

The Task of Self-Management

Step on a rattlesnake and it whirls and strikes. Step on a human and... a hundred different things could happen. Instinct governs much of the snake's behavior, but almost none of the human's. That's why we humans constantly face the task of self-management, or self-regulation. We also face parallel tasks of managing physical objects and other people, but self-management is the most difficult because it's so subjective. As you will see in the modules on mental disorders, it's easy for things to get out of whack. Normally, the activity of self-management goes on so automatically it seems unconscious, but we are constantly working at it.

That's what I like about the module on perception. It helps us appreciate the incredibly complex processes of apprehending and interpreting reality, and in so doing can help us be more realistic about ourselves. There are many things in life to worry about and to fear. An important part of self-management is deciding which stimuli represent real threats and which do not. The disadvantage of our limitless freedom to create wonderful new things is our equally great ability to create fears where they are not appropriate. When we get a better handle on our processes of self-management, however, we begin to appreciate that some apparent perceptions are really glitches in the self-managing process, and we realize that we are scaring ourselves needlessly.

The modules on sensation and perception remind us that we are constantly creating our own reality. Just as illusions can fool us, we can torment ourselves with worries and fears about dangers that are illusory, not real.

Effective Student Tip 6

When You Participate, You Practice

My heart goes out to students who say "I would rather listen than talk...." They are invariably the quiet, supportive type of person the world needs a whole lot more of. (For a teacher, Hell would be a perpetual talk show, with everyone shouting at each other for all eternity and no one listening!) Yet I know that only listening is not really good for them.

Taking part in class discussion binds us to the group, satisfies deep social needs, and increases our sense of effectiveness. But it has a purely academic payoff as well. When you participate, you are practicing the facts and ideas of the course.

In class, you may have the strong feeling that you understand a point better than the student who is talking, maybe even better than the professor. When it's your turn to talk, you find out just how well you do understand it. As you struggle to put your ideas into words, you come to appreciate both what you have right and what you don't. The reactions of your professor and classmates further inform you how well you have grasped the material. Next time, you reword it, rework it, and begin to master it. The facts and ideas of the course are becoming more personal and more real. You aren't just sitting there waiting for the end of the period. You're really learning.

Your response...

Are you a talker or a listener in your classes? Is class discussion valuable, or a waste of time?

Learning Objectives

1. Understand perception as the psychological process of transforming physical stimuli into meaningful representations of reality.

2. Learn the basic differences between sensation and perception and how sensations are changed into perceptions.

3. Explain how the rules of organization, perceptual constancies, depth perception, and illusions work to create our perceptions.

4. Understand the research on subliminal perception, the controversy that led to that research, and the hopes and fears that the possibility of subliminal perception arouses.

5. Appreciate the influence of cultural diversity on the processes of perception and what that influence implies about the power of cultural learning.

6. Consider your position on the reality of extrasensory perception (ESP) and understand the arguments both for and against ESP.

7. Understand the procedures by which many perceptions are created artificially.

Key Terms

These key terms open up a whole new world. You'll never see things quite the same way after you learn the principles they explain. This module can be fun!

absolute threshold
Ames room
apparent motion
atmospheric perspective
binocular depth cues
brightness constancy
closure rule
color constancy
continuity rule
convergence
cultural influences
depth perception
extrasensory perception (ESP)
figure-ground rule
Ganzfeld procedure
Gestalt psychologists

illusion
impossible figure
interposition
just noticeable difference (JND)
light and shadow
linear perspective
monocular depth cues
motion parallax
perception
perceptual constancy
perceptual sets
phi movement
proximity rule
psi
real motion

relative size
retinal disparity
rules of organization
self-fulfilling prophecies
sensation
shape constancy
similarity rule
simplicity rule
size constancy
structuralists
subliminal messages
subliminal stimulus
texture gradient
threshold
virtual reality
Weber's law

Outline

- *Introduction*
    1. Silent messages (Maria's self-esteem tape)
    2. Nice dog, mean dog (Gabrielle's dog bite)
    3. White spot (Maria's mammogram)
    4. Perceiving things (Three questions)
    ☐ What are the three basic questions about perception Rod Plotnik says psychology tries to answer?

A. *Perceptual Thresholds*
    1. Becoming aware of a stimulus
        a. **Threshold** (Gustav Fechner)
        b. **Absolute threshold**
        c. **Subliminal stimulus**
        d. Accuracy problems
    2. Weber's law
        a. **Just noticeable difference (JND)** (E. H. Weber)
        b. **Weber's law**
    3. Just noticeable difference (JND) and soft towels

B. *Sensation versus Perception*
    1. Basic differences
        a. **Sensation**
        b. **Perception**
    2. Changing sensations into perceptions
        a. Stimulus
        b. Transduction
        c. Brain: primary areas
        d. Brain: association areas
        e. Personalized perceptions

C. *Rules of Organization*
    1. Structuralists versus Gestalt psychologists
        a. **Structuralists**
        b. **Gestalt psychologists**
        c. Evidence for rules: who won the debate?
    2. **Rules of organization**
        a. **Figure-ground rule**
        b. **Similarity rule**

c. **Closure rule**

d. **Proximity rule**

e. **Simplicity rule**

f. **Continuity rule**

D. *Perceptual Constancy*

1. Size, shape, brightness, and color constancy

2. **Perceptual constancy** in a potentially chaotic world

☐ How does perceptual constancy make our world understandable?

   a. **Size constancy**

   b. **Shape constancy**

   c. **Brightness constancy** and **color constancy**

E. *Depth Perception*

1. Binocular (two eyes) depth cues

   a. **Depth perception**

   b. **Binocular depth cues**

2. **Convergence**

3. **Retinal disparity**

4. **Monocular depth cues**: organizational rules

   a. **Linear perspective**

   b. **Relative size**

   c. **Interposition**

   d. **Light and shadow**

   e. **Texture gradient**

   f. **Atmospheric perspective**

   g. **Motion parallax**

F. *Illusions*

1. Strange perceptions

   a. **Illusion**

   b. **Impossible figure**

   c. Moon illusion

   d. **Ames room**

   e. Ponzo illusion

   f. Müller-Lyer illusion

2. Learning from illusions

☐ How can an illusion help us understand the process of perception?

G. *Research Focus: Subliminal Perception*

    1. Can "unsensed messages" change behavior (popcorn controversy)?

    2. Changing specific behaviors (experiment)

        a. **Subliminal messages**

        b. **Self-fulfilling prophecies**

    3. Changing perceptions (experiment)

H. *Cultural Diversity: Influence on Perceptions*

    1. What do **cultural influences** do?

    2. Perception of photos (color versus black-and-white)

    3. Perception of images (analytical versus holistic thinking)

    4. Perception of motion (Western cultural influences)

    5. Perception of 3 dimensions (formal education)

    6. Perception of beauty (cultural values)

    7. **Perceptual sets** (learned expectations)

I. *ESP: Extrasensory Perception*

    1. Definition and controversy

        a. **Extrasensory perception (ESP)**

            (1) Telepathy

            (2) Precognition

            (3) Clairvoyance

            (4) Psychokinesis

        b. **Psi**: believing in ESP

        c. Testimonials as evidence

    2. Trickery and magic (the Amazing Randi)

    3. ESP experiment: **Ganzfeld procedure**

    4. Status of ESP and TV psychics (importance of replication)

J. *Application: Creating Perceptions*

    1. Creating movement: **phi movement** (Max Wertheimer)

    2. Creating movies

        a. **Real motion**

        b. **Apparent motion**

    3. Creating **virtual reality**

        a. Remote and robotic surgery

        b. Psychotherapy

    4. Creating first impressions

Language Workout

What's That?

p. 122   **absolute** value = basic, unquestioned
white spots that usually **stand out** = look distinct

p. 124   we'll **take the liberty of** calling = risk, take a chance

p. 125   a series of **discrete** steps = completely separate

p. 126   a **heated** debate = full of strong emotions
a set of **innate** rules = contained within, inseparable

p. 133   a **fixed** peephole = unmoving

p. 135   take **legislative** action = creating new laws
a self-fulfilling prophecy = a prediction that makes itself happen

p. 136   Americans are much more likely to **zero in on** = immediately see
That's **where the money is** = the center of interest

p. 138   26% believe in **psychics** = people who claim psychic powers
seeing the **auras** of people = invisible atmosphere around a person
the **scrutiny** of scientific investigation = close examination

p. 139   an **acoustically isolated** room = closed to outside sounds
to **rule out** the potential for trickery = eliminate, prevent
questions from **perfect strangers** = complete strangers
self-proclaimed psychics = self-called (not approved by experts)

p. 140   **mind-blowing** three-dimensional world = amazing

p. 141   a **debilitating** fear of spiders = weakening

What's the Difference?

WHY A COMMA? (Part 2)

In the last module, you read about the use of commas to show where the introductory material ended and the important action, the main subject and verb, began. BUT WAIT! Did you notice three commas in that first sentence?

Of course, the first comma is used to let us know that "you read" is the important action in the sentence. But what are those the commas before and after "the main subject and verb" doing? These last two commas are working together to tell us that "the important action" means "main subject and verb." Look at this example from the text.

> Although it seemed like an ordinary week, Maria and her 7-year-old daughter, Gabrielle, would be involved in three relatively normal events that could change their lives forever. (p. 121)

Notice the commas before and after "Gabrielle." This extra information about the 7-year-old daughter's name is helpful, so the writer includes it in the sentence. The commas let us know that it is extra information. We can remove all the information between the two commas and sentence doesn't change its meaning. We call these pairs of commas "interrupters."

For higher-intensity stimuli, such as heavy weights, a much larger difference in intensity was required. (p. 123)

One group, called the structuralists, strongly believed that we added together thousands of sensations to form a perception. (p. 126)

Writers use interrupters to give examples or specific names that will help the reader understand the sentence.

Although we most often see interrupters in the middle of sentences, an interrupter can also appear at the end of a sentence. In this case, we don't need a comma at the end because we are using a period to identify the end of the sentence. From the textbook: Weber's law has many practical applications, such as how to detect a difference in the softness of towels. (p. 123)

TRY IT: Where would you put the commas in the follow sentences?

My friend Kazuhiro is an excellent soccer player for the school team.
Ali is taking several classes biology, chemistry, and computer programming that require lab time.
Veronica is from Quito the capitol of Ecuador.

Flex Your Word Power

Are you **clear** on the many meanings of the word **clear**? Glass can be **clear** or opaque.

The windshield of a car should always be _____.
However, a bathroom window should be _____.

An explanation can be **clear** or confusing.

This study guide is excellent because the examples are so _____.
Learning many different theories can be _____.

Air can be **clear** or hazy.

The view from the mountain top is especially _____.
The pollution from the factories makes everything look _____.

An action can look **clear** or blurry.

Keith's new digital camera takes pictures that are very _____.
Marci moved her head, so this photo looks _____.

Answers

My friend, Kazuhiro, is an excellent soccer player for the school team.
Ali is taking several classes, biology, chemistry, and computer programming, that require lab time.
Veronica is from Quito, the capitol of Ecuador.
The windshield of a car should always be **clear.**
However, a bathroom window should be **opaque.**
This study guide is excellent because the examples are so **clear.**
Learning many different theories can be **confusing.**
The view from the mountaintop is especially **clear.**
The pollution from the factories makes everything look **hazy.**
Keith's new digital camera takes pictures that are very **clear.**
Marci moved her head, so this photo looks **blurry.**

The Big Picture

Which statement below offers the best summary of the larger significance of this module?

A   Perception is the constant bombardment of sensory data on several specialized areas of the brain.

B   Both sensation and perception are inborn biological processes — once again demonstrating that psychology is basically just biology.

C   Through the several processes of perception, the mind creates the reality we take for granted. In a way, what is real is the picture of the world we create in our minds.

D   Considering how illusions and the various perceptual rules work, we can only conclude that there is no real world, and that psychology is little more than guesswork and shots taken in the dark.

E   The next time a teacher marks one of your answers "Wrong," just point out that, according to psychology, "it's all in how you look at it!"

True-False

_____   1. A threshold is a point above which we are aware of a stimulus.

_____   2. A biologist calls it "sensation" and a psychologist calls it "perception," but they are both talking about the same thing.

_____   3. The brain follows a number of perceptual rules in order to make sense out of the mass of visual stimuli it receives.

_____   4. If it were not for perceptual constancies, the world would seem ever-changing and chaotic.

_____   5. In the Müller-Lyer illusion, one boy looks like a giant and the other like a midget.

_____   6. Illusions are amusing, but can't teach us anything because they are unreal.

_____   7. Anthropologists have discovered that how you see things depends at least in part on the culture in which you were raised.

_____   8. A perceptual set is a kind of stubbornness that makes subjects stick to the first answer they give even if they realize they were wrong.

_____   9. There is a large body of accepted scientific evidence that supports the existence of ESP.

_____   10. Horses at the track, real motion; movie replay of the race, apparent motion.

Flashcards 1

_____ 1. closure rule

_____ 2. continuity rule

_____ 3. figure-ground rule

_____ 4. Gestalt psychologists

_____ 5. illusion

_____ 6. impossible figure

_____ 7. shape constancy

_____ 8. simplicity rule

_____ 9. size constancy

_____ 10. threshold

a. a point above which a stimulus is perceived and below which it is not perceived

b. our tendency to organize stimuli in the simplest way possible

c. found rules that specify how individual elements are organized into meaningful patterns or perceptions

d. tendency to perceive an object as remaining the same size even when its image on retina grows or shrinks

e. our tendency to favor smooth or continuous paths when interpreting a series of points or lines

f. a perceptual experience of perceiving a strange object as being so distorted that it could not really exist

g. tendency to see an object as keeping its same form in spite of viewing it from different angles

h. perceptual experience in which a drawing seems to defy basic geometric laws

i. our tendency to automatically identify an element of more detail, which then stands out from the rest

j. our tendency to fill in any missing parts of a figure in order to see the figure as complete

Flashcards 2

_____ 1. Ames room

_____ 2. apparent motion

_____ 3. convergence

_____ 4. extrasensory perception (ESP)

_____ 5. Ganzfeld procedure

_____ 6. perceptual sets

_____ 7. phi movement

_____ 8. self-fulfilling prophecies

_____ 9. subliminal messages

_____ 10. virtual reality

a. binocular cues for depth that depend on signals from muscles as they move both eyes inward to focus

b. a perceptual experience of being inside an object or environment or action that is simulated by computer

c. having strong beliefs about changing some behavior then acting, unknowingly, to change the behavior

d. a controlled method for eliminating trickery, error, and bias while testing telepathic communication

e. illusion that closely positioned stationary lights flashing at regular intervals seem to be moving

f. a group of presumed psychic experiences that lie outside the normal sensory processes or channels

g. learned expectations that are based on our personal, social, or cultural experiences and change perceptions

h. a demonstration that our perception of size can be distorted by changing depth cues

i. brief auditory or visual messages that are presented below the absolute threshold

j. illusion that a stimulus or object is moving in space when, in fact, the stimulus or object is stationary

Multiple-choice

_____ 1. An absolute threshold is the intensity level that you can
    a. detect every time it is presented
    b. guess is there, even if you can't quite detect it
    c. just barely detect
    d. detect 50 percent of the time

_____ 2. A subliminal stimulus has an intensity that gives a person _____ of detecting it
    a. less than a 50% chance
    b. more than a 50% chance
    c. no chance at all
    d. a 100% chance

_____ 3. Weber's law of the just noticeable difference explains why
    a. you study better if you have the radio on
    b. your parents don't believe you really turned your stereo down
    c. kids like heavy metal and their parents like Montovani
    d. the Destiny's Child singers all have different names

_____ 4. Sensation is to perception as _____ is to _____
    a. grownup / child
    b. complete / unfinished
    c. word / story
    d. movie / reality

_____ 5. Which *one* of the following is the correct sequence in perception?
    a. stimulus – sensation – perception – meaning
    b. meaning – stimulus – sensation – perception
    c. sensation – stimulus – perception – meaning
    d. perception – stimulus – meaning – sensation

_____ 6. Gestalt psychologists differed from structuralists in believing that
    a. you add together hundreds of basic elements to form complex perceptions
    b. perceptions result from our brain's ability to organize sensations according to a set of rules
    c. "the whole is equal to the sum of its parts"
    d. "the parts are more real than the whole"

_____ 7. The perceptual rule that makes important things stand out is called
    a. closure
    b. proximity
    c. figure dominance
    d. figure-ground

_____ 8. The perceptual rule that we tend to favor smooth or continuous paths when interpreting a series of points or lines is called
   a. shortest distance
   b. continuity
   c. closure
   d. simplicity

_____ 9. Which one of the following is *not* a perceptual constancy
   a. shape constancy
   b. size constancy
   c. motion constancy
   d. color constancy

_____ 10. Thank goodness for size constancy — without it you would
   a. never know for sure how big or small anything really was
   b. immediately get bigger after a single large meal
   c. see things change in size whenever the light changed in brightness
   d. think your Honey is getting smaller and smaller while walking away from you

_____ 11. The advantage to the human species of having two eyes is
   a. figure-ground discrimination
   b. monocular cues
   c. retinal disparity
   d. eyeglasses balance on the nose better

_____ 12. Which one of the following is *not* a monocular depth cue?
   a. retinal disparity
   b. linear perspective
   c. relative size
   d. motion parallax

_____ 13. The reason you couldn't figure out the two-pronged/three-pronged impossible figure in the textbook is that
   a. seeing it in a textbook aroused test anxiety and that threw you off
   b. you were attempting to see it as an object in the real world
   c. Westerners aren't as good at this kind of puzzle as Africans are
   d. it was just a joke

_____ 14. The reason people seem to change size as they change sides in the Ames room is that
   a. the room is not actually rectangular
   b. hidden mirrors distort the images you see as you look in
   c. a lens in the peephole forces you to view them upside down
   d. the subtle coloring of the walls creates a hypnotic trance in the viewer

_____ 15. One explanation why the Müller-Lyer illusion lines don't appear to be the same length is that
   a. our previous experience with arrows tells us they *aren't* all the same
   b. they really aren't quite the same — there is a tiny difference in length
   c. your experience with the corners of rooms makes you see the arrows differently
   d. this famous illusion remains unexplained (even Professors Müller and Lyer couldn't explain it)

_____ 16. Should you scrap this Study Guide and buy a subliminal message tape? Research suggests that any improvement you get with those tapes is probably due to
  a. the effects of extra practice
  b. turning the volume up too high
  c. the Ponzo illusion
  d. a self-fulfilling prophecy

_____ 17. The many brass coils worn by Burmese girls in the past are an example of how
  a. culture influences the concept of beauty
  b. Western cultural influences shape perception
  c. formal education affects perception
  d. analytical thinking affects perception

_____ 18. Because of a/n _____, you probably saw the body builder in the textbook as a big guy
  a. impossible figure
  b. perceptual set
  c. formal education
  d. holistic thinking approach

_____ 19. Which one of the following is *not* an ESP experience?
  a. replication
  b. telepathy
  c. clairvoyance
  d. psychokinesis

_____ 20. Tops on the list of people *not* to invite to an ESP demonstration:
  a. Gustav Fechner
  b. E. H. Weber
  c. Max Wertheimer
  d. Amazing Randi

_____ 21. Many people believe in it, but convincing evidence of ESP has been undercut by the
  a. hocus-pocus that surrounds ESP demonstrations
  b. refusal of psychologists to investigate it seriously
  c. inability to repeat positive results
  d. fact that some people have it and others don't

_____ 22. The purpose of the Ganzfeld procedure is to
  a. win the challenge posed by James Randi
  b. separate the effects of real motion from those of apparent motion
  c. eliminate trickery, error, and bias during experiments testing ESP
  d. investigate the powers of TV psychics like Miss Cleo

_____ 23. When John Wayne grabs the reins on the stagecoach, we see the horses as really flying because our brains
  a. apply the principle of closure and fill in the blanks between frames of the movie
  b. "suspend doubt" as we get more and more involved in the movie
  c. accept the data coming in from the retina and optic nerve
  d. know that the horses in the movie really were moving as they were being filmed

_____ 24. When "virtual reality" becomes an accomplished fact, you will be able to
  a. watch Star Trek reruns in 3-D
  b. dial up famous psychologists on your computer at home
  c. learn all the facts you need in psych while you sleep
  d. trade in your psych textbook for a headset and a DVD

_____ 25. The textbook showed Arnold Schwarzenegger with the skin color of an African American in order to illustrate the fact that
  a. we recognize Arnold as Arnold, regardless of skin color
  b. racial stereotypes affect first impressions
  c. younger people (students) are not affected by racial stereotypes
  d. attractive facial features can overcome a foreign accent

Short Essay

1. Describe the relationship between sensation and perception and explain its importance in psychology.

2. Why would we be helpless without the operation of the perceptual rules of organization, constancies, and depth perception?

3. Perceptual illusions are fun, but what do they have to teach us about psychology?

4. Describe the impact of culture on perception. Illustrate your answer with examples.

5. What is your opinion on the reality of ESP?

Do You Believe in ESP?

Tell the truth — do you believe that at least a few people possess the special power of perception we call ESP?

If you answered "yes," doesn't that create a problem with psychology as a science? Can a science of behavior be valid if some human abilities may sometimes fall outside its scope?

If you believe in ESP, how can you believe that psychology is a science? (That's okay, lots of people don't think psychology is completely scientific.)

If you believe that psychology can be, should be, must be a science, how can you believe in ESP?

Answers for Module 6

The Big Picture

A This is more like sensation, and not at all what perception is or how it works.
B Both sensation and perception are influenced by culture and learning.
C Correct! You see the "big picture" for this Module.
D This philosophical position is too large a leap from the wonders of perception. We have every reason to assume that there is a real world out there and that we can understand it.
E It's just a joke!

True-False (explanations provided for False choices; page numbers given for all choices)

1	T	122	
2	F	124	Perception creates meaningful experience out of sensory input.
3	T	126	
4	T	128	
5	F	133	That happens in the Ames room; the Müller-Lyer illusion compares two lines.
6	F	133	We learn from illusions that perception is an active process.
7	T	136	
8	F	137	A perceptual set is a learned tendency to see things only one way.
9	F	138	There is little scientific evidence (some would say "none") supporting ESP.
10	T	140	

Flashcards 1

1 j	2 e	3 i	4 c	5 f	6 h	7 g	8 b	9 d	10 a

Flashcards 2

1 h	2 j	3 a	4 f	5 d	6 g	7 e	8 c	9 i	10 b

Multiple-Choice (explanations provided for incorrect choices)

1 a Remember that "threshold" means where you cross over.
   b But how would you know it is there?
   c This is more like a subliminal stimulus.
   d Correct! See page 122.

2 *a Correct! See page 122.*
   b Then it would hardly be subliminal.
   c There is some chance, but how much?
   d Then what would "sub" mean?

3 a Distraction, not volume, probably explains why you like the radio on.
   b Correct! See page 123.
   c Kids don't really like louder noises (they just think they do).
   d It's just a joke!

4 a The relationship between raw material and finished product explains sensation and perception.
   b The relationship between raw material and finished product explains sensation and perception.
   c Correct! See page 124.
   d The relationship between raw material and finished product explains sensation and perception.

5 *a Correct! See page 124.*
   b How could meaning come first?
   c How could the sensation come before the stimulus?
   d Sensation creates the raw materials for the perception.

6 a That would be more true of the structuralists.
   b Correct! See page 126.
   c The famous quote is "more than" the sum of the parts.
   d This has the famous quote backwards.

7   a   Closure refers to the tendency to see figures as complete.
    b   Proximity refers to the tendency to group objects that are close together.
    c   Figure dominance is not the correct technical term for this perceptual principle.
    d   Correct! See page 127.

8   a   This is not a correct term in psychology.
    b   Correct! See page 127.
    c   Closure refers to the tendency to complete figures.
    d   Simplicity refers to the preference for simple figures.

9   a   Shape constancy is one of the perceptual constancies.
    b   Size constancy is one of the perceptual constancies.
    c   Correct! See page 128.
    d   Color constancy is one of the perceptual constancies.

10 a   Figure ground organization is not directly related to size constancy.
    b   Size constancy refers to perceived size, not real size.
    c   Light cues are not directly involved in size constancy.
    d   Correct! See page 128.

11 a   Figure-ground discrimination can be achieved with one eye.
    b   It has to do with binocular cues.
    c   Correct! See page 129.
    d   It's just a joke!

12 *a   Correct! See page 130.*
    b   Linear perspective is a monocular depth cue.
    c   Relative size is a monocular depth cue.
    d   Motion parallax is a monocular depth cue.

13 a   Test anxiety was not involved in your perception of the gadget.
    b   Correct! See page 132.
    c   This answer refers to an explanation of the Müller-Lyer illusion.
    d   It was not a joke, but this answer is!

14 *a   Correct! See page 133.*
    b   The Ames room is clever, but it's not done with mirrors.
    c   There is no lens in the peephole.
    d   The Ames room does not depend on a hypnotic trance.

15 a   This illusion does not depend on our experience with arrows.
    b   The lines are exactly the same length, all right.
    c   Correct! See page 133.
    d   The good professors couldn't explain it, but modern cognitive psychologists have an answer.

16 a   These tapes do not require practice (which is one reason why they don't work).
    b   High volume would only wake you up!
    c   The Ponzo illusion involves visual cues.
    d   Correct! See page 135.

17 *a   Correct! See page 137.*
    b   The Burmese are not Western.
    c   Traditional Burmese did not have widespread formal education.
    d   It is not analytical thinking but cultural influence.

18 a   He had an unusual figure, but why didn't we see that he was short?
    b   Correct! See page 137.
    c   Formal education is not involved.
    d   Holistic thinking is not involved.

19 *a   Correct! See page 138.*
    b   Telepathy is the supposed ability to transfer one's thoughts to another or read the thoughts of others.
    c   Clairvoyance is the supposed ability to see objects that are out of view.
    d   Psychokinesis is the supposed ability to move objects by thoughts.

20 a   Gustave Fechner defined the absolute threshold — he's O.K.
    b   E. H. Weber discovered "Weber's Law" — he's O.K.
    c   Max Wertheimer discovered phi movement — he's O.K.
    d   *Correct! See page 138.*

21 a   There has been considerable scientific research aimed at proving ESP.
    b   There has been considerable scientific research aimed at proving ESP.
    c   *Correct! See page 139.*
    d   If some people have it, then ESP must be a fact.

22 a   The Ganzfeld procedure is designed to dispute ESP, not support it.
    b   The Ganzfeld procedure is about ESP, not motion.
    c   *Correct! See page 139.*
    d   The Ganzfeld procedure is designed to dispute ESP results, not psychic predictions.

23 **a   *Correct! See page 140.***
    b   Since we see movies, the answer must involve a principle of perception.
    c   Since we see movies, the answer must involve a principle of perception.
    d   Since we see movies, the answer must involve a principle of perception.

24 a   Virtual reality is way better than 3-D.
    b   We already have computer simulation programs for psychology.
    c   Most research casts doubt on so-called "subliminal perception."
    d   *Correct! See page 141.*

25 a   Most readers did *not* recognize Arnold, at least not right away.
    b   *Correct! See page 141.*
    c   Sadly, not true.
    d   Maybe, but Arnold's speech patterns were not involved here.

Short Essay

1. The goal of psychology is to explain, predict, and control human behavior. One problem psychology must solve is how physical energy, like light waves, is transformed into thoughts and actions. Perception is the final step in that process. Through a series of perceptual rules, the brain almost instantly and almost automatically changes nerve impulses into recognizable and usable images. This completes the process of transduction and sets the stage for all human thought, feeling, and action.

2. If the perceptual rules of organization, constancies, and depth perception were suddenly abolished, our worlds would lose all stability, recognizability, and meaning. They would become like a cruel and terrifying form of insanity. Nothing would have meaning for us. Objects would continually change their size, shape, and color. People would seem larger or smaller as they came and went. In fact, we would not recognize them as people at all, but perhaps oozing blobs of changing material. Thank goodness for perception!

3. Perceptual illusions, such as the two-pronged/three-pronged impossible figure in the textbook, make us realize how hard we work to change electrical signals into meaningful messages. In this case, our brain is presented with an impossible problem. An artist has cleverly created a two dimensional drawing that we cannot turn into a three dimensional object in the real world. We keep trying, going back and forth from the two-pronged to the three-pronged end. Our struggle lets us actually experience the process.

4. One of the strengths of Rod Plotnik's textbook is that it takes full account of the impact of culture on psychological processes. The process of transduction is also affected by learning. There are numerous examples of the effect of culture on perception. Africans with no formal education did not see the two/three-pronged illusion. Traditional Burmese women were considered more beautiful with their necks stretched by brass coils. We see a small body builder as taller and heavier than he actually is. Culture is powerful!

5. You may believe in ESP or not (in surveys, most people say they do). In your answer, you should consider the opposing evidence of testimonials claiming ESP versus the scant scientific evidence for it. Your answer should include discussion of the rigorous Ganzfeld procedure (you might describe the experiment with Zener cards) and the scientific requirement of replication. By the way, for those who believe in ESP, James Randi still has $10,000 waiting for you!

Module 7

Sleep & Dreams

Do Dreams Have Meaning?

Freud is dead… Freud is dead… Freud is dead…. Keep repeating it long enough, and maybe Freud will go away. He has a way of coming back, though, no matter how often psychology pronounces him dead wrong.

One of Freud's most provocative ideas is the notion that all dreams have meaning. He thought it was his most important discovery, and wrote, "Insight such as this falls to one's lot but once in a lifetime." Dreams were important to Freud because they allowed the best look into the workings of the unconscious. When you learn more about Freud's theory of personality (in Module 19) and his technique of psychoanalysis (in Module 24), you will see that he thought of dreaming, with unconscious meanings hidden behind innocent sounding or bizarre surface stories, as a model for all human psychic life. (See "For Psych Students Only…" box for more on Freud's theory of dreams.)

The newer theories of dreaming discussed in Module 7 discount or reject Freud's theory, perhaps partly because — you knew this was coming — Freud says dreams represent sexual wishes. Building on laboratory research into sleep and brain biology, however, the new theories are filling in blanks Freud could only guess at.

Turn Your Bed into a Research Laboratory

The deciding evidence in the battle over the meaningfulness of dreams may be your own dreams. Why not use them as a research project? Many people find it useful to keep a dream journal, which helps them get down more details than we normally remember and also serves as a record that can be reviewed from time to time. The cares and worries of the day quickly chase dream details away, so try waking up slowly and peacefully. If you sense that you had a dream, keep your eyes closed and stay with it. Tell it to yourself a few times. Then get up (or grab your bedside pencil and pad if it is still night) and write down as much as you remember.

The hard part, of course, is trying to interpret the dream. Here's how. Review the story of the dream, then ask how it connects to your life. This is a process of indirection and confusion, and you have to go where the dream leads, no matter how apparently meaningless it seems. The *crucial clues* will be what Freudians call your *associations* to the dream, the things that come to mind as you think about each element of the dream. What feelings does it arouse? What thoughts (none sexual, of course) pop into your mind? How do the feelings and thoughts associated with the dream relate to issues in your psychological life? Is it possible that your dream does have meaning?

Effective Student Tip 7

Stay Focused

Everyone tells you how great it is that you are in college, but sometimes it seems like they don't really understand what you are up against. You may be away from home for the first time, trying to get along with your roommates, cheering on your college team, and worrying about how to get a date. Your parents and friends back home expect letters and phone calls. If you are a returning student, your children miss you, your spouse resents getting less attention, and your boss still asks you to stay late to finish that big project. In any case, you are discovering how easy it is to become distracted from your basic purpose for being in college.

No matter how important a party, your friend's need to talk all night, or extra work at the office may seem at the time, learning and succeeding are what college is really all about. The most important attributes of college are what happens in your classrooms and at your desk, when it's time to study.

Keep your emotional radar attuned to incoming distractions. When all you hear is the beep, beep, beep of threats to learning and succeeding, it's time to defend yourself. Remind yourself why you are in college. Then make the necessary adjustments to get back to the work you came to college to do.

Your response...

Think about a typical day in your college life. What distractions do you often face?

Learning Objectives

1. Understand consciousness as a *continuum* of awareness of one's thoughts and feelings, from full alertness to unconsciousness, in which sleep and dreaming are complex and fascinating components.

2. Learn the basic biology of sleeping and waking and the biological clocks and circadian rhythms that control them.

3. Explain the interplay of stages and types of sleep that together take up one-third of our lives.

4. Learn what research says about your personal style as a morning person or a night person.

5. Appreciate the winter depression called seasonal affective disorder (SAD) as an example of cultural differences in psychology.

6. Consider the competing theories of dreaming and dream interpretation and how they relate to larger theories of psychology.

7. Understand common sleep problems and their treatment and apply your new understanding to your own life, if necessary.

Key Terms

Everyone is fascinated by the topics in this module, especially sleep and dreaming. Learn these terms and you will be able to explain everything your friends want to know (well, enough to keep them listening).

activation-synthesis theory of dreams
adaptive theory
alpha stage
altered states of consciousness
automatic processes
benzodiazepines and non-benzodiazepines
biological clocks
circadian rhythm
consciousness
continuum of consciousness
controlled processes
daydreaming
dreaming
entering the spiritual world theory of dreams
evening persons

extensions of waking life theory of dreams
Freud's theory of dreams
implicit or nondeclarative memory
insomnia
interval timing clock
jet lag
light therapy
melatonin
morning persons
narcolepsy
night terrors
nightmares
non-REM sleep
questionnaire
REM behavior disorder
REM rebound

REM sleep
repair theory
reticular formation
seasonal affective disorder (SAD)
sleep
sleep apnea
sleepwalking
stage 1 sleep
stage 2 sleep
stage 4 sleep
stages of sleep
suprachiasmatic nucleus
unconscious (Freud)
unconsciousness (physical)
VPN (ventrolateral preoptic nucleus)

Outline

- *Introduction*
  1. Living in a cave (Stefania)
  - ☐ What was the purpose of placing a person in a cave for four months?
  2. Chance discovery (REM sleep)

A. *Continuum of Consciousness*
  1. Different states
     a. **Consciousness**
     b. **Continuum of consciousness**
        (1) **Controlled processes**
        (2) **Automatic processes**
        (3) **Daydreaming**
        (4) **Altered states of consciousness**
        (5) **Sleep** and **dreaming**
        (6) **Unconscious** (Sigmund Freud's theory) and **implicit or nondeclarative memory**
        (7) **Unconsciousness** [physical]
  2. Several kinds

B. *Rhythms of Sleeping & Waking*
  1. Biological clocks
     a. **Biological clocks**
     b. **Circadian rhythm**
     b. Length of day
  2. Location of biological clocks
     a. **Suprachiasmatic nucleus**
     b. **Interval timing clock**
  3. Circadian problems and treatments
     a. Accidents
     b. **Jet lag**
     c. Resetting clock: **light therapy**
     d. **Melatonin**

C. *World of Sleep*
  1. **Stages of sleep**
     a. **Alpha stage**
     b. **Non-REM sleep**
        (1) **Stage 1 sleep**

        (2) **Stage 2 sleep**

        (3) Stage 3 and **Stage 4 sleep**

   c. **REM sleep**

        (1) Characteristics of REM sleep (**REM behavior disorder**)

        (2) REM — dreaming (**REM rebound**) and remembering

2. Awake and alert

3. Sequence of stages

D. Research Focus: Circadian Preference

1. Research: are you a morning person or a night person?

   a. **Questionnaire**

   b. **Morning persons**

   c. **Evening persons**

☐ Are you a morning person or a night person?

2. Body temperature

3. Behavioral differences

E. Questions about Sleep

1. How much sleep do I need?

   a. Infancy and childhood

   b. Adolescence and adulthood

   c. Old age

☐ How much sleep do you personally seem to need?

2. Why do I sleep?

   a. **Repair theory**

   b. **Adaptive theory**

3. What if I miss sleep?

☐ What happens to you when you miss sleep?

   a. Effects on the body

   b. Effects on the brain

4. What causes sleep?

   a. Master sleep switch: **VPN (ventrolateral preoptic nucleus)**

   b. **Reticular formation**

   c. Going to sleep

F. Cultural Diversity: Incidence of SAD

1. Problem and treatment of **seasonal affective disorder (SAD)**

2. Occurrence of SAD

3. Cultural differences

G. *World of Dreams*

  1. Theories of dream interpretation

    a. **Freud's theory of dreams** (Sigmund Freud's *The Interpretation of Dreams*, 1900)

    b. **Extension of waking life theory of dreams** (Rosalind Cartwright)

    c. **Activation-synthesis theory of dreams** (J. Alan Hobson)

    d. **Entering the spiritual world theory of dreams** (Inuit beliefs)

  2. Typical dreams

H. *Application: Sleep Problems & Treatments*

  1. Occurrence

  ☐ Have you experienced a sleep problem? What was it like? What did you do about it?

  2. **Insomnia**

    a. Psychological causes

    b. Physiological causes

    c. Non-drug treatment for insomnia (cognitive-behavioral: establishing an optimal sleep pattern)

    d. Drug treatment for insomnia (**benzodiazepines** and **non-benzodiazepines**)

  3. **Sleep apnea**

  4. **Narcolepsy**

  5. **Night terrors** in children

  6. **Nightmares**

  7. **Sleepwalking**

Keep a Dream Journal

Many self-observing people have benefited from keeping dream journals. Have a notepad and pen on your nightstand. When you have a dream (see other material in this Study Guide module on catching and interpreting dreams), jot down the essential points. Later, write a fuller version in your Dream Journal. It is fascinating to re-read these dreams after you have accumulated a number of them. Patterns may emerge. Common themes will be revealed. You will learn more about yourself.

Language Workout

What's That?

p. 147   a **hardy** subject = strong, not easily tired
seemed to **come and go** = move from strong to weak
a publicity **stunt** = unusual act to get attention

p. 148   **evasive** action = avoiding
all external **restraints** = controls

p. 149   **implicit** memory = not directly expressed or seen

p. 151   in a **lousy** mood = irritable, bad mood
to win **patents** = legal protection for inventions
(problems) that **plague** shift workers = disturb again and again

p. 153   which **goes by** the initials REM = uses

p. 156   activities during the day **deplete** key factors = use until empty
that are **replenished** = refilled
theories are not really **at odds** = conflicting, at war

p. 157   they **lapse into** (coma) = fall into

p. 160   she says something about her **acne** = skin problem
swamis = religious person, especially in traditions of India
Insights such as this **fall to one's lot** = are experienced

p. 161   **sighted** people = people who can see

p. 166   the medical **establishment** = official leaders or authorities
I was operating **in a daze** = in a confused state
a **grueling** internship = very difficult, tiring

What's the Difference?

NOUN CLAUSES

Why do you sleep? is a question. **Why you sleep** (p. 147) is <u>not</u> a question. It's a clause that does the same job as a noun. We call this a noun clause.

Like a noun, you can use it as the <u>subject of a sentence</u>:
Why you sleep is an important topic.

Like a noun, you can use it as the <u>object of a sentence</u>:
Scientists are studying **why you sleep.**

Like a noun, you can use it as the <u>object of a preposition</u>:
Experts have different explanations of **why you sleep.**

How much sleep you need (p. 147): **How much sleep do you need?** is a question. **How much sleep you need** is a noun clause. **How _____** depends on your age.

Where we'll begin (p. 147): **Where will we begin?** is a question. **Where _____** is a noun clause. The first page of the first chapter is **where _____**.

How does a baby learn? is a question.

How _____ is a noun clause.

How _____ seems to be the same in all cultures.

When did Freud die? is a question.

When _____ is a noun clause.

The year 1939 is **when** _____.

Meet the Word Family: deprive, deprived, deprivation

Deprive (verb)

To **deprive** someone or something means to take away something important when people are **deprived of** REM sleep (p. 153)

The baby cried when the mother deprived him of _____.

Losing her job will deprive Lydia of _____.

The heavy clouds today are depriving everyone of _____.

Deprived (adjective)

people or animals who are sleep **deprived** (p. 157)

The house plants died because they were _____ deprived.

Poor people are _____ deprived.

The people who weren't allowed to vote were _____ deprived.

Deprivation (noun)

The record for sleep **deprivation** (p. 157)

Feelings of hunger are the result of _____ deprivation.

Depression can be caused by deprivation of _____.

Deprivation of _____ in childhood can lead to weakness in bones in adults.

Answers

How much sleep you need depends on your age.

Where we'll begin is a noun clause.

The first page of the first chapter is **where we'll begin**.

How a baby learns is a noun clause.

How a baby learns seems to be the same in all cultures.

When Freud died is a noun clause.

The year 1939 is **when Freud died**.

The baby cried when the mother deprived him of **(his bottle) (his toy)**.

Losing her job will deprive Lydia of **(her income) (money)**.

The heavy clouds today are depriving everyone of **(sunlight)**.

The house plants died because they were **(light)(water)** deprived.

Poor people are **(economically)** deprived.

The people who weren't allowed to vote were **(politically)** deprived.

Feelings of hunger are the result of **(food)** deprivation.

Depression can be caused by deprivation of **(love) (light)**.

Deprivation of **(milk) (vitamins)** in childhood can lead to weakness in bones in adults.

The Big Picture

Which statement below offers the best summary of the larger significance of this module?

A   In everyday life, we seem to live in two states: awake and asleep. In actuality, there are many subtle degrees of consciousness that psychology is only beginning to explore and understand.

B   A new spirit of common sense is coming into the psychological study of consciousness. We are either conscious or unconscious, dreams mean very little, and sleep disturbances are minor problems.

C   This module raises disturbing questions about just how scientific the study of psychology really is. Most of what is presented comes from personal experience and insight, and very little from empirical research.

D   The puzzling experience of living in a cave and the existence of morning persons and evening persons cast doubt on the existence of biological clocks and biological regulation. Humans are controlled by culture and learning.

E   If we were all meant to be 'A' students, the Almighty would not have given us a need for sleep.

True-False

_____   1. Human beings are always in one of two distinct states: awake and conscious or asleep and unconscious.

_____   2. One adjustment problem faced by humans is that the circadian rhythm of our biological clocks is set not for 24 hours but for about 24 hours and 18 minutes.

_____   3. Getting extra hours of sleep in a dark room is a fast way to reset our biological clocks.

_____   4. Researchers study sleep by measuring brain waves.

_____   5. Once you sink into true sleep, your bodily activity remains constant until you awake in the morning.

_____   6. The existence of the REM rebound effect suggests that dreaming must have some special importance to humans.

_____   7. Research on sleep deprivation and performance proves that the "repair theory" of sleep is correct.

_____   8. Everyone dreams.

_____   9. As with everything else in his theories, Freud's explanation of dreams has a sexual twist.

_____   10. The activation-synthesis theory of dreams places great importance on getting to the underlying meaning of each dream.

Flashcards 1

_____ 1. activation-synthesis theory of dreams

_____ 2. adaptive theory

_____ 3. circadian rhythm

_____ 4. continuum of consciousness

_____ 5. entering spiritual world theory of dreams

_____ 6. extensions of waking life theory of dreams

_____ 7. Freud's theory of dreams

_____ 8. REM rebound

_____ 9. REM sleep

_____ 10. repair theory

a. says dreaming represents the random and meaningless activity of nerve cells in the brain

b. says sleep replenishes key factors in brain and body depleted by activities during day; sleep as restorative

c. says dreams are ways of contacting souls of animals, supernaturals, departed relatives in search of help

d. wide range of experiences from being aware and alert to being unaware and unresponsive

e. an increased percentage of time spent in REM sleep when we are deprived of REM sleep on previous night

f. sleep during which eyes move rapidly back and forth behind closed eyelids; associated with dreaming

g. says sleep evolved to prevent energy waste and exposure to dangers of nocturnal predators

h. a biological clock that is genetically programmed to regulate physiological responses in a 24-25 hour day

i. says dreams are wish fulfillments, satisfaction of unconscious sexual or aggressive desires

j. says our dreams reflect the same thoughts, fears, concerns, and problems as are present when awake

Flashcards 2

_____ 1. altered states of consciousness

_____ 2. automatic processes

_____ 3. controlled processes

_____ 4. jet lag

_____ 5. light therapy

_____ 6. narcolepsy

_____ 7. night terrors

_____ 8. seasonal affective disorder (SAD)

_____ 9. sleep apnea

_____ 10. unconscious (Freud)

a. using meditation, drugs, or hypnosis to produce an awareness that differs from normal state

b. repeated periods during sleep when a person stops breathing for 10 seconds or longer; tiredness results

c. a mental place sealed off from voluntary recall where we place threatening wishes or desires

d. when one's internal circadian rhythm is out of step with external clock time; fatigue, disorientation.

e. frightening child sleep experiences starting with a scream, followed by sudden waking in a fearful state

f. a chronic disorder marked by sleep attacks or short lapses of sleep throughout the day; muscle paralysis

g. a pattern of depressive symptoms beginning in fall and winter and going away in spring

h. use of bright artificial light to reset circadian rhythms and to combat insomnia and drowsiness from jet lag

i. activities that require full awareness, alertness, and concentration to reach some goal; focused attention

j. activities that require little awareness, take minimal attention, and do not interfere with other activities

Multiple-Choice

_____ 1. Rod Plotnik opens the module on consciousness with the story of Stefania's four-month stay in a cave to illustrate the fact that
   a. body time runs slower than celestial time
   b. without sunlight, humans begin to lose their grip on reality
   c. without sunlight, Stefania's night vision became very acute
   d. we would all be much more cheerful if there were no clocks around

_____ 2. We naturally think in terms of the two states called "conscious" and "unconscious," but actually there is/are
   a. three states, including the "high" from drugs
   b. four states: conscious, drowsy, dreaming, and unconscious
   c. a continuum of consciousness
   d. no measurable difference between consciousness and unconsciousness

_____ 3. Psychologists call activities that require full awareness, alertness, and concentration
   a. automatic processes
   b. altered states
   c. comas
   d. controlled processes

_____ 4. Activities that require little awareness, take minimal attention, and do not interfere with other ongoing activities are called
   a. implicit activities
   b. altered states of consciousness
   c. automatic processes
   d. unconsciousness

_____ 5. Have you noticed that you often wake up just before the alarm clock goes off? Credit it to the fact that we humans have a built-in
   a. aversion to jangling noise, which we try to avoid
   b. biological clock
   c. sense of responsibility
   d. brain mechanism that is always monitoring the external environment, even during sleep

_____ 6. If human beings were deprived of all mechanical means of telling time (like clocks), they would
   a. still follow schedules and be punctual, thanks to their biological clocks
   b. follow a natural clock with a day about 30 hours long
   c. not stick to strict schedules the way we do now
   d. lose all sense of when things should be done

_____ 7. The brain structure that regulates many circadian rhythms is called the
   a. internal timing clock
   b. suprachiasmatic nucleus
   c. resetting clock center
   d. biological stopwatch

_____ 8. Once you begin to understand the biology of sleeping and waking, you realize that
   a. we should allow people to sleep whenever and as long as they want to
   b. most people waste hours in non-productive sleep they could do without
   c. humans are evolving into a species that only needs a couple of hours of sleep a day
   d. there is a disconnect between human biology and modern culture

_____ 9. The most promising new treatment for jet lag appears to be
   a. periods of bright light
   b. avoidance of food for 24 hours before a long flight
   c. surgical resetting of the biological clock
   d. drugs that induce sleep in the new time zone

_____ 10. Sleep can be divided into _____ sleep and _____ sleep
   a. alpha / beta
   b. REM / non-REM
   c. REM / pre-REM
   d. stage 1 / stage 2

_____ 11. Dreams are most likely to occur during
   a. stage 1 (theta waves)
   b. EEG sleep
   c. non-REM sleep
   d. REM sleep

_____ 12. REM behavior disorder is a condition in which
   a. you appear to be looking around even though obviously you can't see anything
   b. you have dreams, but they don't make any sense
   c. voluntary muscles are not paralyzed and sleepers can and do act out their dreams
   d. voluntary muscles are paralyzed and you can't move no matter how hard you try

_____ 13. Evidence that dreaming is a necessary biological process is provided by
   a. REM behavior disorder
   b. REM rebound
   c. stage 4 sleep
   d. alpha stage sleep

_____ 14. Rod Plotnik (author of your textbook) compares sleeping all night to
   a. riding a roller-coaster
   b. boating on a calm lake
   c. wading in deep water
   d. driving a luxury automobile

_____ 15. Why do you sleep? The answer is best explained by
   a. the adaptive theory
   b. the repair theory
   c. the exhaustion theory
   d. combining the repair theory and the adaptive theory

_____ 16. Research shows that sleep deprivation
   a. is a serious medical problem
   b. only occurs after 11 days without sleep
   c. is a minor problem, mostly affecting high school and college students
   d. is not a problem, because the body will go to sleep when necessary

_____ 17. The VPN (ventrolateral preoptic nucleus) acts as a
   a. clue that makes it possible to tell if a sleeper is dreaming
   b. master on-off switch for sleep
   c. censor that disguises sexual and aggressive wishes in dreams
   d. light enhancer that combats feelings of depression during the winter months

_____ 18. Research in both Iceland and New Hampshire showed that seasonal affective disorder (SAD) is caused by
   a. an above average number of days of bright light
   b. a combination of diminished light and low temperature
   c. personal tragedy and family problems
   d. cultural factors as well as the amount of sunlight

_____ 19. According to Freud's famous theory, at the heart of every dream is a
   a. clue to the future
   b. disguised wish
   c. hate-filled thought
   d. shameful sexual memory

_____ 20. Rosalind Cartwright points out that dreams are difficult to understand because
   a. people don't remember their dreams very well
   b. most people don't remember their dreams at all
   c. dreams have very little to do with everyday life
   d. most dreams are dull, like typical everyday life

_____ 21. The activation-synthesis theory says that dreams result from
   a. a biological need to pull together and make sense of the day's activities
   b. "batch processing" of all the information gathered during the day
   c. random and meaningless chemical and neural activity in the brain
   d. the need to express hidden sexual and aggressive impulses

_____ 22. For thousands of years, the Inuit (Eskimo) people have believed that dreams are
   a. ways to enter the spiritual world, where the souls of animals, supernaturals, and departed relatives are made known
   b. solutions to practical, everyday problems that come to us during dreaming
   c. representations of evil forces that must never be spoken about
   d. tricks played on humans by mischievous gods, and therefore are meaningless

_____ 23. The best advice for combating insomnia is to
   a. get in bed at the same time every night and stay there no matter what happens
   b. get out of bed, go to another room, and do something relaxing if you can't fall asleep
   c. review the problems of the day as you lie in bed trying to go to sleep
   d. try sleeping in another room, or on the couch, if you can't fall asleep in your bed

_____ 24. Which one of the following is *not* a sleep problem?
   a. narcolepsy
   b. night terrors
   c. oversleeping
   d. sleepwalking

_____ 25. The sleep problem that involves repeated stopping of breathing is called
   a. benzodiazepine deficiency
   b. narcolepsy
   c. night terror
   d. sleep apnea

Short Essay

1. Describe the idea and components of the continuum of consciousness.

2. What are biological clocks and why do we have them?

3. Describe the stages of sleep and what occurs in them.

4. Explain which theory of dreaming seems most persuasive to you and how your personal experience supports that theory.

5. Describe a sleep problem or disturbance you have experienced (whether mild or serious) and relate how you tried to deal with it.

For Psych Majors Only...

How to Construct a Dream (Sigmund Freud): If every dream represents a secret wish disguised as a jumbled, apparently meaningless story, how is the disguise constructed? Freud describes the "dream work" as four processes:

   1. **Condensation** is the compression of several thoughts into a single element, which has the effect of making the dream seem *incoherent*.

   2. **Displacement** is the transfer of psychical intensity from the actual dream thoughts to other ideas, which has the effect of making the dream seem *meaningless*.

   3. **Symbolism** is the transformation of the dream thoughts into apparently unconnected pictorial arrangements or scenes, which have the effect of making the dream seem *illogical*.

   4. **Secondary elaboration** is the interpretative revision of the dream content or scenes into stories, however absurd, which has the effect of making the dream seem *strange*, perhaps ridiculous or frightening, but *not connected to the dreamer*.

   The next time you remember a dream fairly clearly, try using these ideas to take it apart. It's not easy, but you may gain insight into the meaning of your dreams, and also into the provocative genius of Sigmund Freud.

Answers for Module 7

The Big Picture

A *Correct! You see the "big picture" for this Module.*
B Each part of this statement is false, as is the statement as a whole.
C The psychology of consciousness, sleep, and dreams rests on highly scientific research findings.
D Just the opposite is true; the examples support the idea of biological regulation.
E It's just a joke!

True-False (explanations provided for False choices; page numbers given for all choices)

1	F	148	There is a continuum of consciousness.
2	T	150	
3	F	151	Exposure to bright light is a fast way to reset our biological clocks.
4	T	152	
5	F	152	There are four stages of sleep that alternate during the night.
6	T	153	
7	F	156	However logical it sounds, the repair theory of sleep is not supported by research.
8	T	160	
9	T	160	
10	F	161	Finding the underlying meaning of dreams is emphasized by the Freudian theory.

Flashcards 1

1 a	2 g	3 h	4 d	5 c	6 j	7 i	8 e	9 f	10 b

Flashcards 2

1 a	2 j	3 i	4 d	5 h	6 f	7 e	8 g	9 b	10 c

Multiple-Choice (explanations provided for incorrect choices)

1   *a*   *Correct! See page 147.*
    b   Stefania's mental health remained good.
    c   Night vision was not a factor in this experiment.
    d   Maybe true, but cheerfulness was not a factor in this experiment.

2   a   There are more than three states of consciousness.
    b   There are more than four states of consciousness.
    c   *Correct! See page 148.*
    d   Consciousness and unconsciousness are distinct and different states.

3   a   Automatic processes require little awareness.
    b   In altered states of consciousness, awareness and alertness are diminished.
    c   A coma is just the opposite.
    d   *Correct! See page 148.*

4   a   This is not a correct term in psychology.
    b   Altered states of consciousness, such as meditation or psychoactive drugs, do interfere.
    c   *Correct! See page 148.*
    d   Unconsciousness absolutely prohibits other activities.

5   a   Perhaps, but how would we know when to wake up and turn it off?
    b   *Correct! See page 150.*
    c   Ha! ha! ha! ha!
    d   There is no such brain mechanism.

6   a   Belief in the value of schedules and punctuality is a cultural phenomenon.
    b   A day, according to our natural circadian rhythm, is about 24-25 hours long.
    c   *Correct! See page 150.*
    d   In preindustrial societies, humans followed many environmental and bodily cues in coordinating their activities.

7 a This is not a correct term in psychology.
   b *Correct! See page 150.*
   c This is not a correct term in psychology.
   d This is not a correct term in psychology.

8 a How could modern society function under such circumstances?
   b Most people get less sleep than is good for them.
   c There is nothing to suggest that humans need less sleep than they did earlier in their evolution.
   d *Correct! See page 150.*

9 **a** *Correct! See page 151.*
   b Food is not the issue in jet lag.
   c Surgery after every trip? [Test-taking tip: be wary of statements that defy all common sense.]
   d What if the problem is to stay awake?

10 a The alpha stage is just as you are going to sleep; there is no beta stage.
    b *Correct! See page 152.*
    c Half correct; there is no "pre-REM" sleep.
    d There are 4 stages of sleep but 2 categories.

11 a Dreams begin to occur after stage 2 sleep.
    b This is not a correct technical term in sleep research.
    c Read page 165 on the difference between REM and non-REM sleep.
    d *Correct! See page 153.*

12 a This is a description of REM sleep.
    b Dreams typically do not make much sense.
    c *Correct! See page 153.*
    d During dreaming, the normal condition is for your body to lose muscle tension.

13 a This hints at it, but REM rebound suggests that our body demands dreaming.
    b *Correct! See page 153.*
    c Dreaming does not occur in stage 4 sleep.
    d Dreaming does not occur in the alpha stage.

14 **a** *Correct! See page 154.*
    b It is far from a calm, steady process.
    c This analogy would make sleeping too difficult and troubling.
    d If only!

15 a This is half the story.
    b This is half the story.
    c This is not a correct term in psychology.
    d *Correct! See page 156.*

16 **a** *Correct! See page 157.*
    b As far as we know, only one person ever went 11 days without sleep.
    c Sleep deprivation is a serious and widespread problem in modern society.
    d As shown by the record of 11 days, with exertion sleep can be postponed for a long time.

17 a That would be REM sleep.
    b *Correct! See page 157.*
    c The VNP is not a psychological mechanism.
    d That would be melatonin.

18 a Just the opposite is true.
    b Temperature is not a factor in SAD.
    c Personal tragedy and family problems are not primary factors in SAD.
    d *Correct! See page 159.*

19 a Freud did not believe that dreams foretell the future.
    b *Correct! See page 160.*
    c Freud did not believe that dreams are primarily sadistic.
    d Freud linked dreaming to sex, but not necessarily to shame.

20 **a** *Correct! See page 160.*
    b A few people can't remember their dreams, but most remember some of them.
    c Her theory of extensions of waking life says just the opposite.
    d Dreams reflect everyday life, but they can be dramatic, exciting, scary, etc.

21 a No such biological need has been discovered.
    b This would be true of an information processing theory of dreams.
    c *Correct! See page 161.*
    d This is true of Freud's theory of dreams.

22 **a** *Correct! See page 161.*
    b This is closer to the extension of waking life theory of dreaming.
    c Dreams are often discussed and interpreted in this culture.
    d They believe that dreams are meaningful and useful.

23 a This advice only makes insomnia worse.
    b *Correct! See page 162.*
    c This advice will only make it harder to fall asleep.
    d This advice will make it difficult to form good sleep habits.

24 a Narcolepsy is a relatively rare sleep problem.
    b Night terrors are a common childhood sleep problem.
    c *Correct! See page 163.*
    d Sleepwalking is a relatively rare sleep problem.

25 a This is not a correct term in psychology.
    b Narcolepsy is falling asleep many times during the day.
    c Night terrors are frightening experiences in which children wake up screaming with fear.
    d *Correct! See page 163.*

Short Essay

1. Most people assume that we are either conscious (awake) or unconscious (asleep). Modern psychology knows that there is actually a continuum of consciousness consisting of at least seven different experiences. From most to least conscious, these experiences are: controlled processes, automatic processes, daydreaming, altered states, sleep and dreaming, the unconscious mind (Freud) or implicit (declarative) memory, and physical unconsciousness. Understanding the range helps us understand each part better.

2. Biological clocks are internal timing devices that are genetically set to regulate various physiological responses for different periods of time. These clocks are governed by the suprachiasmatic nucleus in the brain. Earlier in evolution, biological clocks and circadian rhythms helped humans stay in tune with nature. Even now, biological clocks keep us from straying too far from the tasks like eating, sleeping, and reproducing that keep the species going.

3. Sleep is far from an unbroken, steady state. Based on studies of changes in brain waves, physiological arousal, and dreaming, sleep is more like a roller-coaster ride. In the alpha stage, you become drowsy and drift into stage 1, which lasts 1-7 minutes. Stage 2 is the first stage of real sleep. About 30-45 minutes after falling asleep, you go through stages 3 and 4, the latter being deep sleep. REM sleep, during which dreams occur, can happen 5-6 times over stages 2-4. These stages are depths, rather than sequences, of sleep.

4. You may be persuaded either by Freud's theory of dreams, the extensions of waking life theory, the activation-synthesis theory, or even, in some modern form, the theory that dreams help you enter the spiritual world. You might favor some combination of these theories. However you argue, you should take account of a theory's strengths, weaknesses, and main competitors. Try to capture the essence of the theory you favor and why it best fits your own ideas about psychology.

5. I hope you have not experienced any of the serious sleep problems described in the textbook. If you have, you know all too well what to write about (be sure to tell what seems to help you). But it would be a rare student who has not at least struggled with periods of insomnia. If that fits you, describe the circumstances and what you tried to do about it. Comment on the program Rod Plotnik (textbook author) offers for establishing an optimal sleep pattern. Would the program, or parts of it, work for you?

Module 8

Hypnosis & Drugs

We'll Have Ours Straight

Nature lovers have a kind of warped view of life. In general, we prefer it undiluted. When we're outdoors, we don't wear headsets because we would rather hear the birds, waves, and wind. When we're having fun, we would rather have all our senses set on normal, neither excited nor dulled by psychoactive agents, legal or otherwise.

For most humans, however, and apparently for most of human history, normal consciousness isn't quite satisfying. Sometimes we want it heightened, sometimes we need it muted. Hence the long history of human attempts to alter consciousness and mood through self-medication. Almost all of us have found some technique, or some substance, that adjusts our consciousness and mood to the point where it feels just right.

This module discusses two methods of altering consciousness. Hypnosis is either a state of great suggestibility or an alternate route to deeper truths about ourselves. Rod Plotnik discusses the debate over what hypnosis is, how it works, and what it can do. But regardless of your position in this debate, hypnosis is different from ordinary consciousness. Psychoactive drugs are a mind-altering power of a different sort.

Why Do We Use Drugs?

In textbook after textbook I've seen, the section on drugs reads like something you would get in pharmacy school. Good, solid technical information on psychoactive drugs, including the most recent illegal drugs to hit the streets, but nothing on the really important issue — why we use psychoactive drugs at all, let alone to such excess.

Rod Plotnik raises that question, and suggests provocative answers. Rod offers a balanced, dispassionate survey of contemporary drug use and abuse. Rather than succumbing to hysteria or personal beliefs, the common failing of so many politicians and public spokespersons, Rod carefully reviews the biological facts, the cultural connections, and the historical record of drug use and society's attempts to curtail it. If you read Rod's discussion carefully, you may discover that some of the things you always knew were "true" about drugs may not be true after all.

Personally, I'm dead set against any use of psychoactive drugs [...says he, after gulping down a can of caffeine-laced cola!], but I don't think it does any good to tell you that. Rod has it right. Instead of moralizing (as I did earlier), let's investigate the psychological processes by which almost all of us "self-medicate," in our continual attempt to control and manage our thoughts, feelings, and behavior. This is exciting stuff.

Effective Student Tip 8

People Power

One of my arguments for setting a goal of perfect attendance is that when you go to class every day the group takes over. It's not that you feel like a captive, but more like a member of a family that is determined not to let you fail. In a good class, I often notice that the regulars kind of take an informal attendance, not satisfied until all the other regulars have arrived, or pointedly worrying about the one who hasn't.

These friendships become the basis for study groups, invaluable for struggling students and even more valuable for the students helping them. (Here is a paradox of instruction: the teacher always learns more than the student, because in order to teach something to someone else you first have to really understand it yourself). Study groups give their members ten times more opportunities to ask questions and talk than class time allows. That adds up to lots more practice.

Another reason to get acquainted with your classmates is the opportunity to make new friends and expand your cultural horizons. Most colleges attract students from every part of the city and from all over the world. Finally, there is the fact that we humans may be the most social species on earth. Biologically speaking, other people replace our missing instincts. Practically speaking, friends make life fun.

Your response...

Do you talk to your classmates? How easily do you make new friends? Do you ever feel lonely?

Learning Objectives

1. Understand hypnosis and drug use as altered states of consciousness — a prelude to the study of normal conscious processes that is coming in the next several modules.

2. Learn the basic facts about hypnosis and the essence of the controversy about what hypnosis is and how it works.

3. Appreciate the underlying reasons for drug use, the similarities of drug use in brain chemistry, and the social lessons in the history of drug abuse and control.

4. Learn the relationship of stimulants, opiates, and hallucinogens and the properties of the major drugs in each category.

5. Consider the significance of cultural risk factors as determinants of national differences in alcoholism rates.

6. Consider the implications of research on a popular drug prevention program (DARE).

7. Learn the essential ingredients of good treatment programs for drug abuse.

Key Terms

Most of these key terms are as timely as today's news, where you are likely to find them. All you need to do is sharpen up your definitions.

addiction

age regression

alcohol

alcoholism

altered state theory of
   hypnosis

caffeine

cocaine

DARE (Drug Abuse Resistance
   Program)

dependency

designer drugs

hallucinogens

hypnosis

hypnotic analgesia

hypnotic induction

imagined perception

LSD

marijuana

MDMA or ecstasy

mescaline

methamphetamine

nicotine

opiates

posthypnotic amnesia

posthypnotic suggestion

psilocybin

psychoactive drugs

sociocognitive theory of
   hypnosis

stimulants

substance abuse

tolerance

withdrawal symptoms

Outline

- *Introduction*
    - ☐ How are hypnosis and drug use somewhat alike?
    1. Hypnosis (Rod and Paul at the nightclub)
    2. Drugs (Albert Hoffman's bad trip)

A. *Hypnosis*

    1. Definition of **hypnosis**

    2. Three often asked questions about hypnosis

        a. Who can be hypnotized?

        b. Who is susceptible?

        c. How is someone hypnotized?

           (1) **Hypnotic induction**

           (2) Method to induce hypnosis

    3. Theories of hypnosis

        a. **Altered state theory of hypnosis**

        b. **Sociocognitive theory of hypnosis**

    4. Behaviors

        a. **Hypnotic analgesia**

        b. **Posthypnotic suggestion**

        c. **Posthypnotic amnesia**

        d. **Age regression**

        e. **Imagined perception**

    5. Medical and therapeutic applications

        a. Medical and dental uses

           (1) Brain scans

           (2) Thoughts or expectations

        b. Therapeutic and behavioral uses

B. *Drugs: Overview*

    1. Reasons for use (**psychoactive drugs**)

    2. Definition of terms

    ☐ Why is it significant that Freud had a problem? What does it say about drugs? About psychology?

        a. **Addiction**

        b. **Tolerance**

        c. **Dependency**

        d. **Withdrawal symptoms**

    3. Use of drugs

    4. Effects on nervous system

        a. Drugs affect neurotransmitters

           (1) Mimicking neurotransmitters

           (2) Blocking reuptake

        b. Drugs affect the brain's reward/pleasure center

        (1) Activating the brain's reward/pleasure center

        (2) Addiction/dependency

C. Stimulants

  1. **Stimulants**

☐ Rod Plotnik quotes a great marketing slogan used to sell amphetamines in Sweden in the 1940s. When we look back on our own times, what ad campaigns may seem equally irresponsible?

  2. Amphetamines

     a. Drug: **methamphetamine**

     b. Nervous system

     c. Dangers

  3. Cocaine

     a. Drug: **cocaine**

     b. Nervous system

     c. Dangers

  4. Caffeine

     a. Drug: **caffeine**

     b. Nervous system

     c. Dangers

  5. Nicotine

     a. Drug: **nicotine**

     b. Nervous system

     c. Dangers

D. Opiates

  1. Opium, morphine, heroin

     a. Drug: **opiates**

     b. Nervous system

     c. Dangers

  2. Treatment

E. Hallucinogens

  1. Definition: **hallucinogens**

  2. LSD

     a. Drug: **LSD**

     b. Nervous system

     c. Dangers

        3. Psilocybin ("magic mushrooms")

          a. Drug: **psilocybin**

          b. Nervous system

          c. Dangers

        3. Mescaline (peyote cactus)

          a. Drug: **mescaline**

          b. Nervous system

          c. Dangers

        4. **Designer drugs**

          a. Drug: **MDMA** or **ecstasy**

          b. Nervous system

          c. Dangers

F. *Alcohol*

    1. History and use

    2. Definition and effects

      a. Drug: **alcohol**

      b. Nervous system

      c. Dangers (review Module 3, page 55)

    3. Risk factors

      a. Psychological risk factors

      b. Genetic risk factors

    4. Problems with alcohol

G. *Cultural Diversity: Alcoholism Rates*

    1. **Alcoholism**

    2. Cultural influences

      a. Genetic risk factors (facial flushing)

      b. Cultural risk factors

      c. Across cultures

H. *Marijuana*

    1. Use and effects

      a. Medical marijuana

      b. Gateway effect

    2. Marijuana

      a. Drug: **marijuana**

      b. Nervous system

      c. Dangers

I. Research Focus: Drug Prevention

1. Effectiveness of **DARE (Drug Abuse Resistance Program)**

2. Research on effectiveness of DARE Program

   a. Method and procedure

   b. Results and discussion

   b. Conclusion

J. Application: Treatment for Drug Abuse

1. Case history

2. **Substance abuse** and treatment

3. Treatment

   a. Step 1: admit the problem

   b. Step 2: enter a program (four goals)

   c. Step 3: get therapy (three therapies)

   d. Step 4: stay sober (relapse prevention)

For hip students only...

A Special Quiz on Psychoactive Drugs: Sorry, but suspicious results may be sent home to your parents!

_____ 1. alcohol   a. America's number one cash crop

_____ 2. caffeine   b. creates a vicious circle of highs, depression, and intense craving for more

_____ 3. cocaine   c. most widely used drug in the world, relatively harmless

_____ 4. ecstasy   d. very clear and vivid visual hallucinations

_____ 5. heroin   e. responsible for the most drug deaths

_____ 6. LSD   f. designer drug

_____ 7. marijuana   g. oldest drug made by humans; still society's biggest drug problem

_____ 8. mescaline   h. speed, crank, crystal, ice

_____ 9. nicotine   i. opium poppy

_____ 10. methamphetamine   j. severe bad trips could lead to psychotic reactions

Scoring:

1 to 3 correct	*You've been in a monastery, right?*
4 to 6 correct	*I'm new on campus myself!*
7 to 9 correct	*This seems very suspicious.*
all 10 correct	*Report to Student Health immediately — you know too much!*

Answers to "A Special Quiz on Psychoactive Drugs"

1 g   2 c   3 b   4 f   5 i   6 j   7 a   8 d   9 e   10 h

Language Workout

What's That?

p. 169   we all **filed out** = walked out
          pieces of furniture assumed **grotesque** [forms] = strange, ugly

p. 170   **compliance** = agreeing to follow other people's decisions

p. 172   [Clients] had **undergone** hypnosis = experienced
          After an **exhaustive** review = complete, with every detail
          Try to **swat** that fly = hit
          not merely **faking** their responses = pretending false action

p. 173   the world's leading **practitioner** = user, person who practices method
          a **terminal** disease = leading to death

p. 174   [Freud] tried to **cut down** = reduce his usage
          it was beyond his human power to **bear** = tolerate

p. 176   **stiffer** penalties = stronger
          available on **the black market** = illegal, hidden economy
          authorities **raided** [laboratories] = attacked
          its chemical **makeup** = composition, organization
          Tara, who was a **heavy** amphetamine user = very frequent
          a **crackdown** on amphetamines = strong action by police

p. 177   go through **a vicious circle** = series of actions where each solution makes a new problem

p. 178   a **nicotine patch** = treatment applied to skin, like a band-aid

p. 180   the **net** effect is increased stimulation = final
          frightening **flashbacks** = surprise return of drug effects

p. 181   use peyote as a **sacrament** = an important religious practice

p. 182   a **fraternity pledge** died = college student trying to enter a social organization

p. 183   **manslaughter** convictions = killing
          husbands **batter** their wives = beat, hit
          college women said they had **binged** = uncontrolled eating or drinking
          college freshmen who **drop out** = leave school

p. 186   researchers identified and **synthesized** THC = artificially produced
          joints of marijuana = cigarette-like shape

p. 187   politicians gave **glowing** testimonials = full of praise

p. 188   Martin's **knack** for learning helped him = ability
          alcohol reduced his feelings of **self-loathing** = self-hating
          his wife **could stand** his drinking no longer = tolerate, live with
          Martin sat home with his **booze** = liquor
          treatment to **get straightened out** = stop harmful behavior
          it represents a **hurdle** = obstacle, problem

p. 192   evidence used by Kishline to **back up** the claims = prove

What's the Difference?

Are you an **intro**vert or an **extro**vert?

The prefix **intro** means inward while **extro** means outward.

So **intro**version (p. 170) is a tendency to think and act inward, unsocial, and **extro**version (p. 170) is a tendency to think and act outward, social.

Do you know any **intro**verts? They are less likely to talk to you than **extro**verts.

Now, which one do you think you are more like?

Meet the Word Family: abstain, abstinent, abstinence

Abstain (verb).

To **abstain** is to decide to not do something.

to take personal responsibility to **abstain from** drinking (p. 189)
Librarians always ask people to **abstain from** talking in the library.
The doctor advised Halina to **abstain from** food for 24 hours before her operation.

Abstinent (adjective)

how many clients remain **abstinent** (p. 189)

Abstinent guests are popular at parties because they can safely drive other people home.
It's hard to stay **abstinent** when everyone around is eating and drinking.

Abstinence (noun)

that total **abstinence** is the only solution (p. 189)

The war was a time of **abstinence** for everyone.

In the month of Ramadan, Muslims practice **abstinence from** eating and drinking during daylight hours.

Test Yourself

Read the following passage and choose the best word to fill the blank. You will need to use one word more than once.

  abstain / abstinent / abstinence

Darryl is very lazy; he _____ from exercise as much as possible. But he is not at all _____ when it's time for dinner. He prefers _____ from exercise, not from hamburgers. However, his friends _____ from criticizing him.

_____

Answers

Darryl is very lazy; he **abstains** from exercise as much as possible. But he is not at all **abstinent** when it's time for dinner. He prefers **abstinence** from exercise, not from hamburgers. However, his friends **abstain** from criticizing him.

The Big Picture

Which statement below offers the best summary of the larger significance of this module?

A This module comes right out and says it: the War on Drugs not only is a waste of time, but it may be contrary to human health. We need the pleasures that drugs provide and we can tolerate a few victimless crimes.

B The material on hypnosis is a stage-setter for the message of this module. If we have so little control over our behavior, we cannot allow even the smallest existence of a drug culture. Zero tolerance is our only hope.

C When we crack down on one psychoactive drug, people who are weak just find some other mood-altering substance. That's why the module concludes that government regulation of the drug trade is the only sensible answer.

D As much as we might not like to admit it, drug use may be almost "natural." We seem driven to alter our consciousness, perhaps to make life more bearable, and history suggests that almost nothing will stop us.

E Say something about this module? Well, its like totally awesome... you know what I mean?... like, you know?... whatever... oh man, I'm really wasted!

True-False

_____ 1. Stage hypnotism really isn't so remarkable, since everyone can be hypnotized.

_____ 2. According to the altered state theory, during hypnosis a person enters a special state of consciousness that is different from the normal waking state.

_____ 3. The debate in psychology about hypnosis concerns whether entertainers should be allowed to exploit hypnosis for profit.

_____ 4. One good use for hypnosis is to reduce pain during medical or dental procedures.

_____ 5. Hypnosis is more effective than any other technique in helping people quit smoking.

_____ 6. History shows that if our government would follow a consistent policy, one by one all illegal drugs could be eradicated.

_____ 7. Psychoactive drugs create effects on behavior by interfering with the normal activity of neurotransmitters.

_____ 8. Illegal drugs are scary, but legal drugs like alcohol and nicotine do by far the greatest harm.

_____ 9. Your risk for becoming an alcoholic rises significantly if members of your family were alcoholics.

_____ 10. Research proves that in DARE (Drug Abuse Resistance Program) we finally have a program that works — if only we had the resolve to use it in every school in the nation.

Flashcards 1

_____ 1. age regression

_____ 2. altered state theory of hypnosis

_____ 3. hypnosis

_____ 4. hypnotic analgesia

_____ 5. hypnotic induction

_____ 6. imagined perception

_____ 7. posthypnotic amnesia

_____ 8. posthypnotic suggestion

_____ 9. psychoactive drugs

_____ 10. sociocognitive theory of hypnosis

a. says hypnosis is a state during which a person experiences different sensations and feelings

b. experiencing sensations, perceiving stimuli, or performing behaviors from one's imagination

c. giving hypnotized subject an idea about performing a particular behavior upon coming out of hypnosis

d. not remembering what happened during hypnosis if hypnotist told you that you wouldn't

e. various methods to induce hypnosis, including asking subjects to close their eyes, go to sleep

f. reduction in pain after hypnosis, suggestions that reduce anxiety and promote relaxation

g. procedure for experiencing changes in sensations, perceptions, thoughts, feelings, or behaviors

h. says hypnosis is state of powerful social or personal influences and pressures to conform to suggestions

i. drugs that increase the activity of the nervous system and result in heightened alertness and arousal

j. subjects under hypnosis being asked to return or regress to an earlier period, such as early childhood

Flashcards 2

_____ 1. addiction

_____ 2. caffeine

_____ 3. dependency

_____ 4. designer drugs

_____ 5. hallucinogens

_____ 6. nicotine

_____ 7. opiates

_____ 8. stimulants

_____ 9. tolerance

_____ 10. withdrawal symptoms

a. change in nervous system so a person needs to take the drug to prevent painful withdrawal symptoms

b. a behavioral pattern marked by overwhelming and compulsive desire to use a drug; tendency to relapse

c. manufactured or synthetic illegal drugs designed to produce psychoactive effects

d. a mild stimulant that produces moderate physiological arousal; alertness, decreased fatigue

e. drugs that increase activity of nervous system and result in heightened alertness, arousal, and euphoria

f. drugs that produce strange and unreal perceptual, sensory, and cognitive experiences

g. addictive drugs that come from the opium poppy, such as opium, morphine, heroin; highly addictive

h. dangerous drug that first produces arousal but then has calming effect [hint: it's legal!]

i. original dose of drug no longer produces the desired effect, so person must take increasingly larger doses

j. painful physical and psychological symptoms that occur after drug-dependent person stops using drug

Multiple-Choice

_____ 1. Rod Plotnik tells the story about attending a stage hypnotist's act to illustrate the point that
- a. a trained psychologist cannot be hypnotized
- b. hypnotism produces remarkable effects, but there is debate about what it really is
- c. hypnotism is an art that many have attempted to learn, but only a rare few have mastered
- d. entertainment pays better than psychology

_____ 2. Which one of the following is _not_ a necessary part of hypnotic induction?
- a. swing a watch (and it must be a pocket watch) slowly back and forth until the subject's eyes glaze over
- b. create a sense of trust
- c. suggest that the subject concentrate on something
- d. suggest what the subject will experience during hypnosis

_____ 3. The main issue in the psychological debate over hypnosis is
- a. not whether it exists, but how it is induced
- b. why subjects tend to play along with the hypnotist
- c. whether hidden observers really can spot stage hypnotist's tricks
- d. whether it is a special state of consciousness

_____ 4. The sociocognitive theory of hypnosis says that hypnosis is based on a/n
- a. special ability of responding to imaginative suggestions and social pressures
- b. altered state of consciousness
- c. good natured desire to go along with what people want
- d. extreme tendency to give in to authority

_____ 5. Which one of the following is _not_ an effect claimed for hypnosis?
- a. age regression
- b. imagined perception
- c. hypnotic analgesia
- d. superhuman acts of strength

_____ 6. The hypnotist tells Janet, "When you wake up, you will not remember what you did on stage tonight." This instruction produces
- a. posthypnotic amnesia
- b. hypnotic suggestion
- c. posthypnotic ordering
- d. hypnotic analgesia

_____ 7. Research into the use of hypnosis to change problem behaviors suggests that hypnosis
- a. is a miracle treatment in changing behavior
- b. does not help in attempts to change behavior
- c. can be useful in combination with other treatments
- d. is useful in helping people quit smoking, but not in weight loss

_____ 8. Why do people use drugs? The answer involves
   a. personality factors — there are as many reasons as there are drug users
   b. pharmacological, psychological, and cultural factors
   c. the power of chemistry, which creates a "one try and you're hooked" result
   d. the pressures of modern society (ancient peoples didn't have drugs)

_____ 9. Many students are shocked to learn that the great psychologist Sigmund Freud had a serious drug problem:
   a. cocaine
   b. nicotine
   c. alcohol
   d. marijuana

_____ 10. "Tolerance" for a drug means that the brain and the body
   a. adjust to the drug and use it with no ill effects
   b. no longer get any effect from using the drug
   c. shut out the drug, which passes harmlessly through the system
   d. require increasingly larger doses of the drug to achieve the same effect

_____ 11. Basically, all drugs work by interfering with the normal operation of
   a. neurotransmitters in the brain
   b. glucose in the blood
   c. DNA in the genes
   d. sensory receptors in the eyes, ears, nose, tongue, and skin

_____ 12. Only 60 years ago, a now-illegal drug was marketed in Sweden under the slogan
   a. "Things go better with caffeine!"
   b. "Two pills beat a month's vacation."
   c. "I'd walk a mile for a Camel."
   d. "Hey Dude, where's my joint?"

_____ 13. Specifically, drugs cause addiction and dependency by
   a. destroying brain centers that control will power
   b. activating the brain's pain center
   c. interfering with the normal levels of dopamine in the brain
   d. making sexual behavior impossible without drugs

_____ 14. All of the following are stimulants *except*
   a. cocaine
   b. caffeine
   c. alcohol
   d. nicotine

_____ 15. One sad lesson from the history of amphetamine, cocaine, and methamphetamine use is that
   a. cracking down on one illegal drug leads to an increase in use of another illegal drug
   b. the more dangerous the illegal drug, the harder it is to suppress it
   c. the most dangerous drugs are the depressants
   d. there is a certain class of people who must — and will — have drugs

_____ 16. The main reason it is so tough to quit smoking is that
   a. tolerance for nicotine takes a long time to develop
   b. physical addiction can continue for years after quitting
   c. withdrawal symptoms are so painful
   d. psychological dependency is deepened by the fact that smoking solves problems

_____ 17. The three main effects of _____ are pain reduction, euphoria, and constipation
   a. opiates
   b. stimulants
   c. hallucinogens
   d. designer drugs

_____ 18. Which one of the following does _not_ belong with the others?
   a. peyote
   b. LSD
   c. psilocybin
   d. heroin

_____ 19. The clear lesson of the history of prohibition (1920 to 1933) is that
   a. it may be impossible to ban a drug that is so popular and widely used
   b. we must abandon our on-again/off-again enforcement strategies and declare an all-out war on drugs
   c. eventually people get tired of any drug
   d. legalization would reduce the problem to manageable dimensions

_____ 20. Despite all the drug abuse horror stories we hear, the truth is that the two most costly and deadly drugs in our society are
   a. heroin and cocaine
   b. marijuana and ecstasy
   c. psilocybin and mescaline
   d. alcohol and tobacco

_____ 21. Studies of national rates of alcoholism around the world suggest that alcoholism is a/n
   a. individual problem, relatively unaffected by where the individual lives
   b. partly genetic and partly cultural problem
   c. genetic problem, independent of national origins
   d. family problem, passed down through the generations

_____ 22. One reason offered for enforcing tough penalties against marijuana use is the
   a. lack of evidence that marijuana has any medical value
   b. medical abuse of marijuana caused by liberal doctors
   c. theory of the gateway effect
   d. success of the DARE program

_____ 23. After years of studying the harmfulness of marijuana, scientists have concluded that it
   a. eventually causes brain damage
   b. often leads to mental illness
   c. typically leads to the use of hard drugs
   d. may or may not be dangerous in the long run — the research is not yet definitive

_____ 24. The story of "Martin," the high school drinker who became a drug-abusing doctor, suggests that
    a. environmental causes like poverty don't help explain substance abuse
    b. instead of blaming addicts, we should offer them treatment
    c. if alcohol had been illegal, Martin never would have gotten into hard drugs
    d. Martin should have been left alone, unless he actually harmed a patient

_____ 25. Good news/bad news — an eight-year study of three therapies for alcoholism showed that
    a. psychoanalytic therapy is the most effective, but the costs are prohibitively high
    b. the programs had initial success, but in four months all the subjects were drinking again
    c. the programs were equally effective, but the overall success rate was only 30-45 percent
    d. all three therapies have some strengths, but nothing beats individual will power

Short Essay

1. What are the arguments that hypnosis is or is not a special state of consciousness?

2. Explain the brain chemistry of drug use, addiction, and dependency (non-technical terms are okay).

3. How do stimulants, opiates, and hallucinogens differ? Illustrate your explanation with examples of each.

4. Consider the fact that humans have used drugs for thousands of years. What does that say about how we should approach the social and personal problems of drug use?

5. DON'T WRITE THIS DOWN! But consider your own involvement in drug use, or your rejection of it. What have you tried, what were the effects, and what do you think about it now? If you don't use drugs, what keeps you from it? Suppose the President called and asked you what to do about drug use. What advice would you give?

Multiple-Choice Questions

Most multiple-choice questions have a stem and four alternatives. The first trick in handling multiple-choice questions is to know what the question is asking. One way to think about this is to ask yourself, "Which alternative turns the stem into a true statement?"

Answers for Module 8

The Big Picture

A Plotnik raises questions, but he does not make any of these extreme statements.
B Hypnosis does not destroy self-control, nor does zero tolerance seem to work very well.
C The module offers no such conclusion.
D *Correct! You see the "big picture" for this Module.*
E It's just a joke!

True-False (explanations provided for False choices; page numbers given for all choices)

1	F	170	Not everyone can be hypnotized.
2	T	171	
3	F	171	The debate concerns whether hypnosis is a special state of consciousness.
4	T	172	
5	F	173	Research suggests that hypnosis is no more effective than other treatments.
6	F	175	History suggests swings in drug popularity that are not the result of legal action.
7	T	175	
8	T	175	
9	T	185	
10	F	187	DARE is an admirable program, but research has not proven its effectiveness.

Flashcards 1

1 j   2 a   3 g   4 f   5 e   6 b   7 d   8 c   9 i   10 h

Flashcards 2

1 b   2 d   3 a   4 c   5 f   6 h   7 g   8 e   9 i   10 j

Multiple-Choice (explanations provided for incorrect choices)

1 a Of course they can. That's what Rod Plotnik was worried about!
   b *Correct! See page 169.*
   c With adequate training, almost anyone can learn hypnotism.
   d Why would Plotnik want to make this point, even if it were true?

2 *a* *Correct! See page 170.*
   b Trust is essential to hypnotism.
   c Suggestion is the key feature of hypnotism.
   d Suggestion is the key feature of hypnotism. In this case, the subject believes the behavior is caused by hypnosis.

3 a There is considerable debate over how real hypnosis is.
   b It is well established that hypnotized subjects are highly suggestible.
   c This is a misstatement of the "hidden observer" phenomenon. See page 171.
   d *Correct! See page 171.*

4 *a* *Correct! See page 171.*
   b Just the opposite is true.
   c It is based on responsiveness and social pressure, but not on being good-natured.
   d It is based on responsiveness and social pressure, but on giving in to authority.

5 a Age regression refers to asking hypnotized subjects to re-experience an earlier age.
   b Imagined perception refers to asking hypnotized subjects to experience something that does not exist.
   c Hypnotic analgesia refers to suggesting that a hypnotized subject will not experience pain.
   d *Correct! See page 172.*

6 *a* *Correct! See page 172.*
   b This is not a correct technical term in hypnosis.
   c This is not a correct technical term in hypnosis.
   d Hypnotic analgesia refers to suggesting that a hypnotized subject will not experience pain.

7   a   Then we assume you are going to a psychology tutor who uses hypnosis?
    b   Some people have reported success in changing behaviors with hypnosis.
    c   *Correct! See page 173.*
    d   If it were good for one problem, it would be good for related problems.

8   a   If this were true there would be no way to understand and treat drug abuse.
    b   *Correct! See page 174.*
    c   Most drugs are not nearly this powerful.
    d   Drugs have been used for at least 6,000 years.

9   a   Freud experimented with cocaine, but that isn't the drug that eventually killed him.
    b   *Correct! See page 174.*
    c   This was not a problem for Freud.
    d   This was not a problem for Freud.

10 a   This is only partly true — the drug isn't giving the same high, but it still hurts the body.
    b   This is partly true — there is less of the desired effect.
    c   Harm continues to be done.
    d   *Correct! See page 174.*

11 *a*   *Correct! See page 175.*
    b   Possible side effects of illegal drugs on blood glucose do not explain how these drugs work.
    c   Illegal drugs have no significant effect on DNA in the genes.
    d   Illegal drugs affect the brain, not sensory receptors.

12 a   An American slogan for soda implies this.
    b   *Correct! See page 176.*
    c   This was a famous slogan for cigarettes.
    d   It's just a joke!

13 a   We do not know of brain centers that control "will power."
    b   There is no pain center in the brain.
    c   *Correct! See page 175.*
    d   Other than relaxing inhibitions, drug use tends to interfere with normal sexual response.

14 a   Cocaine is a stimulant.
    b   Caffeine is a stimulant (the student's friend!).
    c   *Correct! See page 176.*
    d   Nicotine is a stimulant.

15 *a*   *Correct! See page 177.*
    b   As shown by efforts to ban alcohol and marijuana, it is harder to suppress less dangerous drugs.
    c   Stimulants like amphetamines and cocaine are more dangerous.
    d   This prejudice is a stereotype that is contradicted by every survey of drug use.

16 a   This would not explain why it is so tough to quit smoking.
    b   Fortunately, this is untrue. The physical addiction ends quickly.
    c   *Correct! See page 178.*
    d   Other than providing a brief, calming break from stressful activities, smoking does not solve problems.

17 *a*   *Correct! See page 179.*
    b   Stimulants cause heightened alertness, arousal, euphoria, and decreased appetite and fatigue.
    c   Hallucinogens produce strange and unusual perceptual, sensory, and cognitive experiences.
    d   Designer drugs mimic the psychoactive effects of already existing illegal drugs.

18 a   Peyote is a hallucinogen; heroin is an opiate.
    b   LSD is a hallucinogen; heroin is an opiate.
    c   Psilocybin is a hallucinogen; heroin is an opiate.
    d   *Correct! See page 180.*

19 *a*   *Correct! See page 182.*
    b   Like Prohibition? History says it won't work.
    c   Rather than disinterest, people continually shift their drug usage seeking the optimal ratio of costs to benefits.
    d   There is no clear evidence that legalization would work any better than prohibition.

20 a   Bad as these are, two others do far more damage in our society.
    b   Bad as these are, two others do far more damage in our society.
    c   Bad as these are, two others do far more damage in our society.
    d   *Correct! See page 183.*

21 a   Just the opposite is true.
    b   *Correct! See page 185.*
    c   This is not suggested by rates of alcoholism around the world.
    d   This is not suggested by rates of alcoholism around the world.

22 a   There is evidence that marijuana has some medical value.
    b   There may be some unethical doctors, but this is a small part of the problem.
    c   *Correct! See page 186.*
    d   Research throws the effectiveness of the DARE program into serious doubt.

23 a   There is no firm evidence for this claim.
    b   There is no firm evidence for this claim.
    c   Sometimes, but not inevitably.
    d   *Correct! See page 186.*

24 a   Martin may not fit, but abundant evidence connects drug abuse and environmental conditions.
    b   *Correct! See page 188.*
    c   Prohibition didn't work before, and Martin's psychological problems still would have been there.
    d   Society could not allow Martin to write illegal prescriptions, which could eventually have harmed others.

25 a   Psychoanalysis was not one of the three therapies evaluated.
    b   Some subjects, from 30-45%, stayed sober for a year.
    c   *Correct! See page 189.*
    d   Individual will power, which would be difficult to define and measure, was not a variable in this study.

Short Essay (sample answers)

1. "Hypnotized" subjects show remarkable degrees of compliance with requests, no matter how outlandish, and many people believe they have received medical or therapeutic help through hypnosis. The question is why? The altered state theory says hypnosis is a special state of consciousness that disconnects subjects from reality. The sociocultural theory says that hypnosis results from having the special ability of responding to imaginative suggestions and social pressures. Research continues.

2. All drugs work by mimicking, or even changing, the chemistry of the brain's information system. Neurotransmitters carry information back and forth. Some drugs mimic how neurotransmitters work, removing neurotransmitters by blocking their normal reuptake. Some drugs directly activate the brain's reward/pleasure center by increasing dopamine levels. Other drugs become substitutes for dopamine. When the user's reward/pleasure center becomes dependent on outside drugs, addiction occurs.

3. Stimulants, opiates, and hallucinogens all change brain chemistry and alter consciousness, but do it in different ways. Stimulants (methamphetamine, cocaine, caffeine, and nicotine) increase the activity of the CNS and heighten arousal and alertness. Opiates (opium, morphine, and heroin) reduce pain and produce a pleasurable state between waking and sleeping. Hallucinogens (LSD, psilocybin, and mescaline) produce strange and unusual perceptual, sensory, and cognitive experiences. But all these effects have a high cost.

4. The 6,000-year history of drug use provides ample, if worrisome, evidence that using drugs to alter consciousness may be a permanent feature of the human experience. Attempts to outlaw drugs have been unsuccessful (alcohol) or uneven (caffeine and nicotine remain legal). Like most psychologists, Rod Plotnik seems to favor treatment over punishment. But even when treatment is available — and many drug users and abusers resist treatment — the success rate are meager, perhaps 35%. Just say No!

5. I may have been kidding when I said "DON'T WRITE THIS DOWN!", but this question has a serious purpose. A course in psychology is an obvious opportunity to examine an aspect of your life that may be disturbing to you, or which may be under attack from classmates, the media, and other social pressures. Better self-understanding can only help you change, if you use, or strengthen your resolve, if you don't. Think about it, privately or with a trusted friend or teacher or counselor, but think about it honestly.

Classical Conditioning

The Paradox of Behaviorist Psychology

Most students begin reading about the psychology of learning with good intentions, but soon give up. It's just too darn complicated. They have run smack into The Paradox.

In truth, the basic principles of learning discovered by Pavlov, Skinner, and others (described in Modules 9 and 10) are elegantly simple, wonderfully powerful, and among the most useful products of psychology. Once you do understand them you'll say, "I sort of knew that already." The problem is the language they come wrapped in.

Ivan Pavlov was a pure scientist, a Nobel prize winner. Naturally, he used the precise, mathematical language of the laboratory. The psychologists who followed Pavlov, the ones we call behaviorists, also prided themselves on being laboratory scientists. One of the strongest points in favor of the behaviorist approach is its insistence that psychology stick to observable, measurable phenomena (no murky, mentalistic concepts like Freud's unconscious). We teachers can appreciate this approach, because we studied it thoroughly in graduate school. But when undergraduate students encounter behaviorism, they don't have much time to learn the technical language. Yet we expect them to gulp it all down in a couple of weeks. Most gag instead.

These poor beleaguered psychology students have a point. Reform in our terminology is long overdue. The first term we could do without is "conditioning." We're really talking about *learning*. Classical conditioning and operant conditioning are also learning, each by a different route, but learning all the same. Even the terms "stimulus" and "response" say more about Pavlov's fame than about how human life really works.

We're Mad As Hell and We're Not Going to Take It Anymore!

Your instructor will tell you which terms to learn, but as you study you can make some mental translations. Keep in mind that we're always talking about *learning*. When you read "classical conditioning," remind yourself that you are reading about Pavlov's kind of learning, where a dog's natural reflex to drool at meat got connected to something else (a bell). When you bump into a technical term like Skinner's "positive reinforcement," make up an everyday-life story that illustrates the term: "If my little brother cleans up his room and my parents reward him with extra allowance money, he will be more likely to clean up his room again next week."

Don't let yourself be cheated out of what may be the most useful ideas in psychology, just because the language is difficult. Fight back!

> Check it out! PowerStudy 2.0 includes a 40-50 minute presentation that uses animations, visuals, and interactive activities as well as quizzing to help you understand concepts in this module.

Effective Student Tip 9

Adopt a Strategy of Effectiveness

You're probably getting more advice about how to be successful in college than you know what to do with. By itself, any specific piece of advice tends to get lost in the crowd. You need a way to pull the really good advice together and put it to regular use. You need a *strategy* of success.

An overall strategy is important because it gives you a way of evaluating any particular suggestion and of adjusting to whatever conditions arise. It is more than a single game plan, because it is both more comprehensive and more flexible. If your game plan for the next test is to work like the devil, what do you do if hard work doesn't seem to be enough?

Any plan is better than no plan, but I suggest a special kind of strategy, a strategy of effectiveness. The strategy of effectiveness is simply this: (1) You recognize that you have a basic need to be effective in everything you do, especially your college work, since that's your most important task right now. (2) You measure everything you do in college by asking, "Is this procedure getting the job done?" (In other words, is it effective?) (3) Whenever a method isn't working, instead of continuing to do the same ineffective things you make a specific procedural change.

Your response...

Do you have an overall strategy for getting through college? [Most students don't.]

Learning Objectives

1. Understand classical conditioning, first described by Ivan Pavlov, as one of the three powerful theories of learning that behaviorists believe govern all human action.

2. Learn the basic mechanisms of classical conditioning as illustrated by Pavlov's famous salivating dog experiment.

3. Explain the classical conditioning concepts of generalization, discrimination, extinction, and spontaneous recovery.

4. Explain the role adaptive value plays in taste aversion learning and conditioned emotional responses

5. Consider the differences in the three basic explanations of how and why conditioning occurs.

6. Appreciate how conditioning can affect emotional responses, as illustrated by John B. Watson's famous experiment with "Little Albert."

7. Describe how the behavioral therapy called systematic desensitization works to eliminate a conditioned fear.

Key Terms

Fight back! Translate these technical terms into everyday language about learning.

adaptive value	conditioned stimulus (CS)	operant conditioning
anticipatory nausea	contiguity theory	preparedness
classical conditioning	discrimination	spontaneous recovery
cognitive learning	extinction	stimulus substitution
cognitive perspective	generalization	systematic desensitization
conditioned emotional response	law of effect	taste-aversion learning
conditioned response (CR)	learning	unconditioned response (UCR)
	neutral stimulus	unconditioned stimulus (UCS)

Outline

* *Introduction*

  □ "Learning" is one of those everyday terms about which we say, "I know what it means..." until we attempt a formal definition. How would you define learning? Seriously... give it a try.

  1. It's only aftershave (Carla's phobia)

  2. It's only a needle (Rod's needle fear)

  3. It's only dish soap (Michelle's conditioned nausea)

     a. Conditioning

     b. **Learning**

A. Three Kinds Of Learning

1. **Classical conditioning**

   a. Ivan Pavlov's famous experiment

   b. Conditioned reflex

   c. Learning through pairing stimuli

2. **Operant conditioning**

   a. **Law of effect** (E. L. Thorndike)

   b. Consequences and learning (B. F. Skinner)

   c. Learning through effects or consequences of actions

3. **Cognitive learning**

   a. Mental processes

   b. Observation and imitation (Albert Bandura)

   c. Learning through observing and thinking

B. Procedure: Classical Conditioning

1. Pavlov's experiment

   ☐ There is a beautiful logic to the way Pavlov worked out conditioning in his famous experiment with the drooling dog. Can you tell the story?

   a. Step 1: Selecting stimulus and response

       (1) **Neutral stimulus**

       (2) **Unconditioned stimulus (UCS)**

       (3) **Unconditioned response (UCR)**

   b. Step 2: Establishing classical conditioning

       (1) Neutral stimulus

       (2) Unconditioned stimulus (UCS)

       (3) Unconditioned response (UCR)

   c. Step 3: Testing for conditioning

       (1) **Conditioned stimulus (CS)**

       (2) **Conditioned response (CR)**

2. Terms in classical conditioning

   ☐ See if you can apply Pavlov's logic to the example of poor Carla. Use the three steps below.

   a. Step 1: Selecting stimulus and response

   b. Step 2: Establishing classical conditioning

   c. Step 3: Testing for conditioning

C. *Other Conditioning Concepts*

   1. **Generalization**

   2. **Discrimination**

   3. **Extinction**

   4. **Spontaneous recovery**

D. *Adaptive Value and Uses*

   1. **Adaptive value**

   2. **Taste aversion learning**

   3. Explanation: **preparedness**

   4. Classical conditioning and adaptive value

      a. Bluejays and butterflies

      b. Hot fudge sundaes

   5. Classical conditioning and emotions: **conditioned emotional response**

   6. Classical conditioning in the brain

E. *Three Explanations*

   1. What is learned?

   2. Stimulus substitution and contiguity theory

      a. **Stimulus substitution** (Pavlov)

      b. **Contiguity theory**

   3. **Cognitive perspective** (Robert Rescorla)

      a. Predictable relationship

      b. Backward conditioning

F. *Research Focus: Conditioning Little Albert*

   1. Can emotional responses be conditioned?

      a. John Watson and Rosalie Rayner (1920)

      b. "Little Albert"

   2. Method: identifying terms

   3. Procedure: establish and test for classical conditioning

   4. Results and conclusions

G. *Cultural Diversity: Conditioning Dental Fears*

   1. In the dentist's chair

   2. Cultural practices

   3. Origins

   4. Effects of fear

H. *Application: Conditioned Fear & Nausea*

1. Examples of classical conditioning

   a. Conditioned emotional response

   b. **Anticipatory nausea**

   c. Conditioning anticipatory nausea

2. **Systematic desensitization**

   a. Systematic desensitization procedure: three steps

      (1) Step 1: learning to relax

      (2) Step 2: making an anxiety hierarchy

      (3) Step 3: imagining and relaxing

   b. Effectiveness of systematic desensitization

For Psych Majors Only...

How Behaviorism Revolutionized Psychology: Living in an age of scientific psychology, it is hard for us to comprehend how profoundly behaviorism revolutionized psychology. William James, the 'father' of American psychology, was more a philosopher than psychologist. He and others in the new field relied on the method of introspection, rather than on laboratory research, to figure out how the mind worked.

Watson, extending Pavlov's scientific method to the study of human behavior, urged the following rule: Given the stimulus, predict the response; given the response, find the stimulus; given a change in response, find a change in the stimulus.

My mother took a psychology course when she attended the University of Wisconsin in the early 1920s. Psychology was only a small part of the philosophy department, but the air was charged with Watson's crusade. She still remembers her young professor's challenge to his students: *"Stimulus and response, stimulus and response — learn to think in terms of stimulus and response!"*

Language Workout

What's That?

p. 195   I **assured** Carla = said it was true or possible
One [side effect] is severe **nausea** = sick feeling in stomach
its odor made her **salivate** = produce liquid in mouth (saliva)

p. 200   Rat **exterminators** = workers who destroy [rats]
bait poison = material used to catch or trap
They baited **grazing** areas = open areas of grass where animals eat
sheep flesh **laced** with a chemical = combined with

p. 201   For example, blue jays **feast on** butterflies = eat with pleasure
One purpose of salivation is to **lubricate** your mouth = make slippery

p. 202   a pizza [becomes] **bonded** = connected

p. 204   was described as healthy, **stolid** = without emotion
which made a loud noise and elicited **startle** = surprise
Watson's demonstration **laid the groundwork** = formed the basis

p. 210   stomach **cramps** = pains
demanded that olestra be **taken off the market** = removed from stores
The olestra warning **was lifted** = removed

Build Your Word Power

The endings of words, called suffixes, can tell us just how the word is used. By knowing these wording endings, you'll be able to identify the word families that you meet. Let's look at some common suffixes from your text:

which a person imagines or visual**izes** fearful or anxiety-evoking stimuli (p. 207)

> The **-ize** ending makes the adjective **visual** into a verb.
>
> **Visual** = able to see. **Visualize** = to be able to see.
>
> So if **General** means not specific, **generalize** would mean _____.

By adding **-ation**, the verb becomes a noun.

> **Visualize** = to be able to see. **Visualization** = the action of being able to see.
>
> **Generalize** = _____. **Generalization** = the action of being not specific.
>
> **Sensitize** = to make full of feeling. **Sensitization** = _____.

Flex Your Word Power

anticipate = expect, plan ahead

> Pavlov's dog **anticipated** food when it heard the bell.
>
> No one can **anticipate** all the surprises that life might bring.

in anticipation of = expecting, before

The dog's mouth began to salivate **in anticipation of** the food.

Marta cleaned her house completely **in anticipation of** her mother's visit.

anticipatory = planned, before something happens

Pavlov considered this sort of **anticipatory** salivation to be a bothersome problem. (p. 196)

Dinner wasn't ready yet, but Toshio enjoyed the smells in the kitchen with **anticipatory** pleasure.

What's the Difference?

Extinguish (verb) means to bring to a complete end

Marco blew hard **to extinguish** the candle.

the smell of the aftershave had been **extinguished** (p. 199)

Extinction (noun) means the process of ending, erasing a conditioned response

Carla worked with a therapist on **the extinction of** her reaction to the aftershave.

The extinction of this conditioned response was a goal of her therapy.

Test Yourself

Read the following passage and choose the best word to fill the blank:

anticipate / in anticipation of / anticipatory

Mrs. Billings knew that she was pregnant, but she was surprised when the doctor told her to _____ the birth of twins. In the months before she had the babies, her husband made some _____ changes to their house; in fact, he built a new bedroom for the newcomers. Mrs. Billings kept a suitcase ready, with a nightgown and personal items, _____ of a sudden trip to the hospital.

Answers

So if General means not specific, generalize would mean **to be not specific**.
Generalize: to **be not specific**
  Generalization: the action of being not specific
Sensitize: to make full of feeling
  Sensitization: **the action to make full of feeling**
Mrs. Billings knew that she was pregnant, but she was surprised when the doctor told her to **anticipate** the birth of twins. In the months before she had the babies, her husband made some **anticipatory** changes to their house; in fact, he built a new bedroom for the newcomers. Mrs. Billings kept a suitcase ready, with a nightgown and personal items, **in anticipation of** a sudden trip to the hospital.

The Big Picture

Which statement below offers the best summary of the larger significance of this module?

A   Begining with Ivan Pavlov's famous experiment with the salivating dog, behaviorists have performed remarkable feats of animal training. Almost all of their attempts to create such learning in humans, however, have failed.

B   Conditioning offers a powerful explanation of learning to fear things like rats, poisons, chemotherapy, etc. All that is lacking for a complete psychology of learning is a way to condition people to *like* things.

C   By demonstrating learning through "classical conditioning," Pavlov pioneered an objective, laboratory psychology. When Watson showed conditioning in humans, the stage was set for a scientific psychology of human behavior.

D   Although the behaviorists did demonstrate how simple behaviors can be taught and learned, behaviorist concepts cannot begin to explain the rich complexity of human behavior. Behaviorism is a very limited theory.

E   You think drooling to a bell was amazing? Wait 'til you hear what *my* dog did to my homework!

True-False

_____   1. Learning is a relatively permanent change in behavior as a result of experience.

_____   2. Ivan Pavlov's famous explanation of learning was so persuasive that no other theory has challenged it since.

_____   3. The key to Pavlov's experiment was finding a reward that would make the dog salivate.

_____   4. At first, UCS → UCR, but after the conditioning procedure, CS → CR.

_____   5. Once conditioning has taken place, *generalization* may cause similar stimuli to elicit the response, but *discrimination* should work to establish control by the specified stimuli.

_____   6. Bluejays avoid eating monarch butterflies because of taste-aversion learning.

_____   7. The cognitive perspective says classical conditioning happens when a new stimulus replaces an old one through association.

_____   8. In John Watson's classic experiment, Little Albert gradually learned to like a previously feared white rat when he was given candy for petting it.

_____   9. If you are like most people, the sound of the dentist's drill has become an unconditioned stimulus.

_____   10. The goal of systematic desensitization is to *uncondition* conditioned stimuli and make them neutral again.

Flashcards 1

_____ 1. conditioned response (CR)

_____ 2. conditioned stimulus (CS)

_____ 3. discrimination

_____ 4. extinction

_____ 5. generalization

_____ 6. neutral stimulus

_____ 7. spontaneous recovery

_____ 8. stimulus substitution

_____ 9. unconditioned response (UCR)

_____ 10. unconditioned stimulus (UCS)

a. tendency for the conditioned response to reappear after being extinguished

b. a formerly neutral stimulus that has acquired the ability to elicit the same response as UCS does

c. learning to make a particular response to some stimuli but not to others

d. explains classical conditioning as a neural bonding of a neutral and an unconditioned stimulus

e. an unlearned, innate, involuntary physiological reflex that is elicited by the unconditioned stimulus

f. failure of a conditioned stimulus to elicit a response when repeatedly presented without the UCS

g. new response elicited by a conditioned stimulus; similar to the unconditioned response

h. some stimulus that triggers or elicits a physiological reflex, such as salivation or eye blink

i. tendency for a stimulus that is similar to the original conditioned stimulus to elicit the same response

j. some stimulus that produces a response, but does not produce the reflex being tested

Flashcards 2

_____ 1. anticipatory nausea

_____ 2. classical conditioning

_____ 3. cognitive learning

_____ 4. conditioned emotional response

_____ 5. contiguity theory

_____ 6. law of effect

_____ 7. learning

_____ 8. preparedness

_____ 9. systematic desensitization

_____ 10. taste-aversion learning

a. procedure in which a person eliminates anxiety-evoking stimuli by relaxation; counterconditioning

b. a relatively enduring or permanent change in behavior that results from experience with stimuli

c. feeling fear or pleasure when experiencing a stimulus that initially accompanied a painful or pleasant event

d. learning in which a neutral stimulus acquires the ability to produce a response (Ivan Pavlov)

e. feelings of sickness elicited by stimuli that are associated with receiving chemotherapy treatments

f. if actions are followed by a pleasurable consequence or reward, they tend to be repeated (E. L. Thorndike)

g. explains classical conditioning as occurring because two stimuli are paired closely together in time

h. associating sensory cues (smells, tastes, sound, or sights) with getting sick, then avoiding those cues

i. a kind of learning that involves mental processes alone; may not require rewards or overt behavior

j. biological readiness to associate some combinations of conditioned and unconditioned stimuli

Multiple-Choice

_____ 1. Rod Plotnik begins this module with the story of Carla and the dentist's aftershave to show how
   a. learning often occurs when we least expect it
   b. learning is more likely to occur in some environments than in others
   c. we can learn a response simply because it occurs along with some other response
   d. we can like something very much, then turn against it for no clear reason

_____ 2. Plotnik also tells about a bad medical experience of his own, in order to show how
   a. thoughtless doctors can poison your mind toward medicine in general
   b. strong fear can become attached to simple events
   c. not long ago, a simple medical procedure like getting a shot was extremely painful
   d. when going to the dentist also means getting a shot, it can be more than a child can bear

_____ 3. All of the following are approaches to understanding how learning occurs _except_
   a. classical conditioning
   b. operant conditioning
   c. physical learning
   d. cognitive learning

_____ 4. A theory of learning that became part of operant conditioning was
   a. Bandura's cognitive learning
   b. Pavlov's classical conditioning
   c. Plotnik's fear conditioning
   d. Thorndike's law of effect

_____ 5. Operant conditioning differs from classical conditioning in placing the emphasis on
   a. consequences that follow some behavior
   b. pairing a neutral stimulus with an unconditioned response
   c. waiting until the subject accidentally performs the right behavior
   d. allowing subjects to watch others perform some behavior

_____ 6. Albert Bandura found that he could get children to play aggressively (punching a doll) by
   a. offering them a reward (candy) for hitting the doll
   b. showing them a film of adults happily punching the doll
   c. giving them a learning session in which they practiced punching the doll
   d. sternly forbidding them to punch the doll

_____ 7. Since S → R, then obviously UCS → UCR, so naturally CS →
   a. UCS
   b. UCR
   c. CR
   d. neutral stimulus

_____ 8. In Pavlov's experiment, the actual learning took place when the
   a. neutral stimulus was paired with the unconditioned stimulus
   b. conditioned reflex was presented again and again
   c. unconditioned stimulus was paired with the conditioned stimulus
   d. paired unconditioned and neutral stimuli were presented together in several trials

_____ 9. Now even the smell of her own shampoo can make Carla anxious: this is an example of
    a. generalization
    b. extinction
    c. discrimination
    d. spontaneous recovery

_____ 10. But the smell of her nail polish does _not_ make Carla feel anxious; this is an example of
    a. generalization
    b. extinction
    c. spontaneous recovery
    d. discrimination

_____ 11. When a conditioned stimulus (tone) is repeatedly presented _without_ the unconditioned stimulus (meat), _____ eventually will occur
    a. generalization
    b. discrimination
    c. extinction
    d. spontaneous recovery

_____ 12. We seem to be biologically ready to associate some combinations of conditioned and unconditioned stimuli in as little as a single trial, a phenomenon called
    a. conditioned nausea
    b. phobia
    c. taste-aversion learning
    d. preparedness

_____ 13. Bluejays love butterflies, but they won't eat monarch butterflies, because
    a. taste aversion learning teaches them to avoid the distinctive coloring pattern
    b. an inborn hatred of black and orange makes them avoid monarchs
    c. one bite of a monarch brings instant death to a bluejay
    d. monarchs have an evasive flight pattern that makes them almost impossible to catch

_____ 14. From the point of view of a behavioral psychologist, Rod Plotnik's fear of needles is a/n
    a. expression of an unconscious conflict
    b. representation of a hidden wish
    c. conditioned emotional response
    d. unconditioned response

_____ 15. At the physical level, conditioning depends on the operation of
    a. taste buds
    b. muscle fibers
    c. nerves radiating out from the spinal cord
    d. structures in the brain

_____ 16. Which one of the following is _not_ a theory about why conditioning occurs?
    a. all stimuli (neutral, unconditioned, and conditioned) occur randomly
    b. after repeated pairing, the neutral stimulus substitutes for the unconditioned stimulus
    c. two stimuli are contiguous (paired close together in time)
    d. we learn that the neutral stimulus predicts the occurrence of the unconditioned stimulus

_____ 17. The contiguity theory says that classical conditioning occurs because
   a. whichever stimulus is remembered better comes to predominate
   b. a new stimulus comes to substitute for an earlier one
   c. one stimulus predicts the occurrence of another
   d. two stimuli are paired close together in time

_____ 18. According to Robert Rescorla's cognitive explanation of Pavlov's experiment, the conditioned reflex gets established because
   a. the dog wants to do what Pavlov seems to want it to do
   b. the dog learns that the tone predicts the presentation of the food
   c. Pavlov unwittingly tips off the dog by looking at the food tray
   d. Pavlov simply waits until the dog makes the right response

_____ 19. John Watson was excited by Pavlov's discovery of the conditioned reflex because it
   a. provided the first look inside the thinking mind
   b. explained the operation of cognitive factors in learning
   c. explained learning in terms of observable, not mental or cognitive, behaviors
   d. showed that canine and human brains work in much the same way

_____ 20. To the early behaviorists, Watson's Little Albert experiment showed that
   a. human learning is very different from animal learning
   b. humans have an inborn fear of rats
   c. even infants can learn
   d. observable behaviors explain human psychology better than inner conflicts or thoughts

_____ 21. The reason for Little Albert's fame in psychology is the fact that
   a. Watson showed that emotional responses could be classically conditioned in humans
   b. Pavlov was unable to replicate his salivation procedure with Little Albert
   c. Rescorla used the Little Albert experiment to disprove Pavlov
   d. Carla learned not to fear the dentist through the example of this brave little boy

_____ 22. Cultural differences affecting conditioning are revealed by
   a. American children's fear of getting shots
   b. varying national rates of dental fears in children
   c. the fact that dental procedures in every country are painful
   d. the common tendency around the world to avoid dental treatment if at all possible

_____ 23. American children show more dental fear than Scandinavian children because
   a. American dentists are not as well trained
   b. American children have seen many scary movies about cruel dentists
   c. health care systems in the two societies are different
   d. Scandinavian dentists give their patients lots of candy for not crying

_____ 24. A classically conditioned response often observed in patients receiving chemotherapy is
   a. anticipatory nausea
   b. pleasure
   c. taste-aversion learning
   d. preparedness

_____   25. Which one of the following is *not* necessary to the systematic desensitization procedure
        a. learning to relax
        b. identifying unconscious conflicts
        c. making an anxiety hierarchy
        d. imagining and relaxing while moving up and down the anxiety hierarchy

Short Essay

1. Recount Pavlov's famous salivating dog experiment and explain why it was such a bombshell in psychology.

2. How does classical conditioning occur in the brain and why does it have adaptive value?

3. How has psychology tried to explain why conditioning occurs? Explain stimulus substitution, contiguity theory, and the cognitive perspective.

4. Describe John B. Watson's famous conditioning experiment with "Little Albert" and explain why Watson thought it would revolutionize psychology.

5. Remember what happened to little Rod Plotnik in the doctor's office? Describe an exaggerated emotional response of your own, and speculate on how it was conditioned and how it might be unconditioned by a behavioral therapy like systematic desensitization.

Test-Taking Tips 1

You don't have to remember *everything* in order to get the question right. Often, carefully reading the question, plus relying on your own knowledge and intelligence, will reveal the correct answer.

- Be wary of answers stated in extreme terms like "always," "never," or "100 percent."

- Be wary of answers that defy all common sense.

Answers for Module 9

The Big Picture (explanations provided for incorrect choices)

A There is a wealth of research showing conditioning in humans.
B We are conditioned to like things all the time; it's called advertising!
C *Correct! You see the "big picture" for this Module.*
D Anti-behaviorists make this argument, but behaviorists have explanations for almost all human behavior.
E It's just a joke!

True-False (explanations provided for False choices; page numbers given for all choices)

1	T	195	
2	F	196	Many different theories of learning have been advanced since Pavlov.
3	F	197	Reward relates to Skinner; Pavlov used pairing.
4	T	197	
5	T	199	
6	T	201	
7	F	202	According to the cognitive perspective, a stimulus predicts a reinforcement.
8	F	204	"Little Albert" left the hospital before Watson could "uncondition" the fear.
9	F	205	The sound of the drill is a conditioned (not natural) stimulus.
10	T	207	

Flashcards 1

1 g	2 b	3 c	4 f	5 i	6 j	7 a	8 d	9 e	10 h

Flashcards 2

1 e	2 d	3 i	4 c	5 g	6 f	7 b	8 j	9 a	10 h

Multiple-Choice (explanations provided for incorrect choices)

1 a Sometimes true, but why would Plotnik want to emphasize that?
   b Learning can occur in any environment.
   c Correct! See page 195
   d Scientific psychology assumes that for every effect there must be a cause.

2 a There was nothing wrong with Rod's doctor.
   b Correct! See page 195.
   c Not true.
   d It did not happen at the dentist's office.

3 a Classical conditioning is a recognized approach to learning.
   b Operant conditioning is a recognized approach to learning.
   c Correct! See page 196.
   d Cognitive learning is a recognized approach to learning.

4 a Cognitive learning is a challenge to operant conditioning.
   b Operant conditioning is a new and different theory of conditioning.
   c Plotnik described his fear, but did not offer a new theory.
   d Correct! See page 196.

5 *a Correct! See page 196.*
   b This is classical conditioning.
   c This is Thorndike's experimental procedure.
   d This is Bandura's cognitive learning.

6 a That's the point — no external reward was necessary.
   b Correct! See page 196.
   c That's the point — no teaching was necessary.
   d Because children are contrary? But they were not forbidden to punch the doll.

7   a   Substitute words for letters, "causes" for the arrow, and you get the answer in Pavlov's laboratory language.
      b   Substitute words for letters, "causes" for the arrow, and you get the answer in Pavlov's laboratory language.
      c   *Correct! See page 197.*
      d   Substitute words for letters, "causes" for the arrow, and you get the answer in Pavlov's laboratory language.

8   a   Partly true, but one pairing was not enough for a dog.
      b   The conditioned reflex is the end result (what was learned).
      c   The conditioned stimulus does not exist until the learning has taken place.
      d   *Correct! See page 197.*

9   *a*   *Correct! See page 199.*
      b   Extinction occurs when there is no stimulus over a period of time.
      c   In discrimination, learning is narrowed to a specific appropriate response.
      d   Spontaneous recovery occurs after extinction.

10   a   In generalization, learning spreads to similar objects and situations.
      b   Extinction occurs when there is no stimulus over a period of time.
      c   Spontaneous recovery occurs after extinction.
      d   *Correct! See page 199.*

11   a   In generalization, learning spreads to similar objects and situations.
      b   In discrimination, learning is narrowed to a specific appropriate response.
      c   *Correct! See page 199.*
      d   Spontaneous recovery occurs after extinction.

12   a   This is an effect of learning, not a cause of learning.
      b   This is an effect of learning, not a cause of learning.
      c   This is an effect of learning, not a cause of learning.
      d   *Correct! See page 200.*

13   *a*   *Correct! See page 201.*
      b   That's the point — it's not inborn.
      c   Not true.
      d   Not true (just ask any lepidopterist).

14   a   This would be true of a psychoanalytic psychologist.
      b   This would be true of a psychoanalytic psychologist.
      c   *Correct! See page 201.*
      d   That would mean fears are inborn, not learned.

15   a   The new connections are not made in the taste buds.
      b   The new connections are not made in the muscles.
      c   The new connections are not made in the nerves.
      d   *Correct! See page 201.*

16   *a*   *Correct! See page 202.*
      b   This is the stimulus substitution theory of conditioning.
      c   This is the contiguity theory of conditioning.
      d   This is the cognitive theory of conditioning.

17   a   Although it sounds cognitive, this is not a theory of conditioning.
      b   This is the stimulus substitution theory of conditioning.
      c   This is the cognitive theory of conditioning.
      d   *Correct! See page 202.*

18   a   This statement does not fit the facts in Pavlov's experiment.
      b   *Correct! See page 202.*
      c   This statement does not fit the facts in Pavlov's experiment.
      d   This statement does not fit the facts in Pavlov's experiment.

19   a   Pavlov studied outside behavior, not inside thinking.
      b   Watson and the behaviorists were interested in learned behavior, not cognition.
      c   *Correct! See page 204.*
      d   Pavlov was not studying the brain.

20 a Behaviorists believe just the opposite.
    b Little Albert was not afraid of the white rat.
    c That fact was generally accepted.
    d Correct! See page 204.

21 ***a Correct! See page 204.***
    b Pavlov was not involved with Little Albert.
    c Rescorla was not involved with Little Albert.
    d Carla was not involved with Little Albert.

22 a Perhaps true, but this would not explain varying national rates.
    b Correct! See page 205.
    c Not true of modern dentistry.
    d That wouldn't explain dental fears.

23 a This is not true.
    b This is not true.
    c Correct! See page 205.
    d This is not true.

24 ***a Correct! See page 206.***
    b Have you known a person undergoing chemotherapy?
    c Taste is not the crucial element.
    d Preparedness is a tendency to learn, not a response.

25 a Relaxation is of key importance to the systematic desensitization procedure.
    b Correct! See page 207.
    c A hierarchy of feared situations is essential to the systematic desensitization procedure.
    d Moving through the hierarchy is part of the systematic desensitization procedure.

Short Essay (sample answers)

1. Pavlov showed that dogs naturally salivate when food is presented (easier to swallow). Next, he presented a sound. Naturally, the dog did not salivate. Now, just before presenting the food, Pavlov presented the sound. The dog salivated because of the food. But here was the surprise. After a few such trials, the dog salivated to the sound alone. A neutral stimulus had acquired the power of an unconditioned stimulus. Pavlov called this learned behavior a conditioned response. No reference to the mind or thinking was necessary.

2. Both motor responses, such as the eye blink reflex, and emotional responses, such as fear of needles and injections, are susceptible to classical conditioning. Motor response conditioning is dependent on the cerebellum and emotional response conditioning is dependent on the amygdala. Such conditioning occurs rapidly and automatically. This smooth learning process, while sometimes causing problems (like phobias) in modern society, helps us adapt and survive. We don't have time to think about everything!

3. Psychologists knew Pavlov was not a magician. Something had to explain why conditioning occurred. At first, it was thought that the new stimulus took the place of the natural stimulus. Problem was, the substitution was not perfect. Next it was proposed that the learning took place because the old and new stimuli were associated in time (contiguous). The newest explanation, a cognitive one, suggests that the subject learns that the new stimulus predicts the occurrence of the old, unconditioned stimulus.

4. Watson first showed that little Albert showed no fear of a white lab rat and other animals. Then Watson made a loud noise in the presence of the rat and Albert cried and showed fear. Two months later, Albert was shown the rat again and again cried and showed fear. Watson announced that the child had acquired a new emotional response from a simple experience. Now psychology would not need to consider thinking and inner conflicts, only observable behavior. At last, said Watson, psychology could become a real science.

5. Is there something you are "phobic" about? (One of my students was afraid of statues in the park!) Can you trace the fear back to its first occurrence? Can you explain why the experience may have been especially powerful, beyond what it normally would have been? Finally, can you imagine a way by which you might "unlearn" the fear? What would you have to do? You might explore how a behavioral therapy like systematic desensitization could help you.

Module 10

Operant & Cognitive Approaches

B. F. Skinner and the Behavioral Approach

Which psychologist has had the greatest impact? The only obvious alternative to B. F. Skinner is Sigmund Freud himself. Even then, many would give Skinner the award for discovering actual laws of behavior and their practical applications. Skinner made psychology a science and discovered a series of principles that have become a permanent part of psychology.

As a scientist, Skinner spent his career pursuing principles of behavior that could be demonstrated in the laboratory. But he was equally concerned with what psychology is *not*. Often criticized for a mechanistic approach to psychology, Skinner once protested, "I have feelings!" The point he was trying to make was that no matter how real and important feelings are, they are difficult to study objectively. Skinner refused to speculate about any psychological phenomena that could not be subjected to rigorous laboratory investigation. Rod Plotnik tells a fascinating story about how Skinner stuck to his scientific guns to the end of his life, even at the cost of offending those who had come to admire him.

Is "Cognitive Learning" a Contradiction in Terms?

For Skinner and the "radical" behaviorists, as they came to be called, learning meant the principles of acquiring and modifying behavior as explained *without* reference to any nonobservable phenomena like cognition or mind. "Cognitive" learning, which Plotnik covers in this module, brings in what Skinner called nonobservable, and hence nonscientific, mental activity.

For most psychologists, even many of Skinner's young disciples like Albert Bandura, this uncompromising stand seemed to require a deliberate turning away from factors that were obvious and suggestive of further insights about learning. They were unwilling to leave so much out. So, without rejecting Skinner's classic discoveries, they entered the forbidden territory of the mind anyway. The result has been a very fruitful combining of behavioral principles and cognitive processes. Because the combined cognitive-behavioral approach has been willing to speculate about mental processes, it has developed many innovative and effective therapeutic applications. When the Skinnerians were at the peak of their influence, they assumed that since they understood the laws of behavior, it would be a simple matter to apply those laws to curing human psychological suffering. It didn't work out that way, since real life is so much more complicated than the laboratory, and many of Skinner's frustrated followers drifted into the cognitive camp.

> Check it out! PowerStudy 2.0 includes a 40-50 minute presentation that uses animations, visuals, and interactive activities as well as quizzing to help you understand concepts in this module.

Effective Student Tip 10

Build Effective Routines

Anyone who loves computers also values orderly procedures. To get the most out of your computer, you must learn procedures and follow them.

Why not apply the same tactic to your college studies? When it comes to advice about how to do better in college, there are tons of useful techniques, hints, tips, tricks, and shortcuts out there. Become a consumer of useful procedures. Adapt them to your needs. Invent your own. Gather advice about how to be successful in school, but do it with a difference.

First, take a *procedural* point of view. Pay less attention to advice that is mainly sloganeering ("You *must* work harder!") and more to specific procedures (see Tip 19, "Three Secrets of Effective Writing," for example).

Second, gather all these useful procedures under the umbrella of *effectiveness*. Judge every procedure by whether it makes you a better student. If it works, keep it in your arsenal of useful procedures. If it doesn't, drop it. I once had a friend who decided to make himself lean and strong by eating *nothing but apples*. Excited about his new plan, for several days he was never without his bag of apples. It didn't work.

Your response...

What advice have you gotten that wasn't really very helpful? What was wrong with the advice?

Learning Objectives

1. Understand operant conditioning, B. F. Skinner's theory of learning, as the linchpin of the behavioral approach to learning, itself one of the six major theories of psychology.

2. Learn the basic principles and procedures of operant conditioning, and how these and other conditioning concepts differ from those of classical conditioning (discussed in the previous module).

3. Explain how the idea of consequences lies at the heart of reinforcement and punishment.

4. Understand the four basic schedules of reinforcement, how they are measured, and how they explain much (most?) behavior in humans and other animals.

5. Explain how the power of operant conditioning is modified by both the cognitive learning principles of observational learning and insight learning as well as the biological principles of imprinting and prepared learning.

6. Learn how the very effective Suzuki method of learning to play a musical instrument matches Bandura's social learning principles.

7. Consider your position on using punishment in therapy (autism) in particular and child rearing (spanking) in general.

Key Terms

Keep on fighting back! (See Module 9 of the Study Guide.) Here is more technical laboratory language, but each key term is still about how we learn stuff. Try to make up a little story for each one. Two hints to make it easier: (1) Many of these terms are already in the vocabulary of educated people, so you may already understand them; (2) If you read Module 9, on classical conditioning, note that several of the key terms below have already been covered.

---

autism
behavior modification
biofeedback
biological factors
cognitive learning
cognitive map
continuous reinforcement
critical or sensitive period
cumulative record
discrimination
discriminative stimulus
ethologists
extinction
fixed-interval schedule
fixed-ratio schedule

generalization
imprinting
insight
law of effect
learning-performance
   distinction
negative punishment
negative reinforcement
noncompliance
operant conditioning
operant response
partial reinforcement
pica
positive punishment
positive reinforcement
positive reinforcer

preparedness or prepared
   learning
primary reinforcer
punishment
reinforcement
schedule of reinforcement
secondary reinforcer
self-injurious behavior
shaping
social cognitive learning
social cognitive theory
spontaneous recovery
superstitious behavior
time-out
variable-interval schedule
variable-ratio schedule

Outline

- *Introduction*
    1. Learning 45 commands: **operant conditioning**
    2. Learning to golf: cognitive learning (observation and imitation)

A. *Operant Conditioning*

    1. Background: Thorndike and Skinner

        a. Thorndike's law of effect

            (1) **Law of effect**

            (2) Effects strengthen or weaken behavior

        b. Skinner's operant conditioning

            (1) **Operant response**

            (2) Voluntary behavior and consequences

    2. Principles and procedures

    ☐ You could almost say that the process of shaping is at the heart of operant conditioning. Why?

        a. **Shaping**

            (1) Shaping: facing the bar

            (2) Shaping: touching the bar

            (3) Shaping: pressing the bar

        b. Immediate reinforcement: **superstitious behavior**

    3. Examples of operant conditioning

        a. Toilet training

            (1) Target behavior

            (2) Preparation

            (3) Reinforcers

            (4) Shaping

        b. Food refusal

            (1) Target behavior

            (2) Preparation

            (3) Reinforcers

            (4) Shaping

    4. Operant versus classical conditioning

    ☐ How do classical conditioning and operant conditioning differ? What do they have in common?

        a. Operant conditioning

            (1) Goal

            (2) Voluntary response

        (3) Emitted response

        (4) Contingent on behavior

        (5) Consequences

   b. Classical conditioning

        (1) Goal

        (2) Involuntary response

        (3) Elicited response

        (4) Conditioned response

        (5) Expectancy

B. *Reinforcers*

   1. Consequences

      a. **Reinforcement**

      b. **Punishment**

      c. **Pica**

      d. Changing the consequences

   2. Reinforcement

      a. **Positive reinforcement: positive reinforcer**

      b. **Negative reinforcement**

   3. Reinforcers

      a. **Primary reinforcer**

      b. **Secondary reinforcer**

   4. Punishment

      a. **Positive punishment**

      b. **Negative punishment**

      c. **Self-injurious behavior**

      d. Positive punishment (example)

C. *Schedules of Reinforcement*

   1. Skinner's contributions: **schedule of reinforcement**

   2. Measuring ongoing behavior: **cumulative record**

   3. Schedules of reinforcement

      a. **Continuous reinforcement**

      b. **Partial reinforcement**

   4. Partial reinforcement schedules

   ☐ Can you think of an example from everyday life for each of the four schedules of reinforcement?

      a. **Fixed-ratio schedule**

      b. **Fixed-interval schedule**

      c. **Variable-ratio schedule**

      d. **Variable-interval schedule**

   5. Applying Skinner's principles

D. *Other Conditioning Concepts*

   1. **Generalization**

   2. **Discrimination** and **discriminative stimulus**

   3. **Extinction** and **spontaneous recovery**

E. *Cognitive Learning*

   1. Three viewpoints of **cognitive learning**

      a. Against: B. F. Skinner

      b. In favor: Edward Tolman (**cognitive map**)

      c. In favor: Albert Bandura (**social cognitive learning**)

   2. Observational learning

    ☐ Some psychologists say Bandura's classic Bobo doll experiment disproves Skinner. How so?

      a. Bobo doll experiment

         (1) Procedure

         (2) Results

         (3) Conclusion

      b. Learning versus performance (**learning-performance distinction**)

   3. Bandura's **social cognitive theory**

      a. Social cognitive learning: four processes

         (1) Attention

         (2) Memory

         (3) Imitation

         (4) Motivation

      b. Social cognitive learning applied to fear of snakes

         (1) Background

         (2) Treatment

         (3) Results and conclusion

   4. Insight learning

      a. **Insight** (Wolfgang Köhler)

      b. Insight in animals (how Sultan got the banana)

      c. Insight in humans (the "ah ha" experience)

F. *Biological Factors*

   1. Definition: **biological factors**

   2. Imprinting

      a. **Ethologists**

      b. **Imprinting** (Konrad Lorenz)

         (1) **Critical or sensitive period**

         (2) Irreversible

   3. Prepared learning

      a. Incredible memory (birds): **preparedness or prepared learning**

      b. Incredible sounds (human infants)

G. *Research Focus: Noncompliance*

   1. How can parents deal with "No!"

      a. **Noncompliance**

      b. **Time-out**

   2. Study: using time-out to reduce noncompliance

H. *Cultural Diversity: East Meets West*

   1. Suzuki method (teaching violin) and Bandura's social cognitive learning

   2. Different cultures but similar learning principles: teacher Suzuki and researcher Bandura

      a. Attention

      b. Memory

      c. Imitation

      d. Motivation

I. *Application: Behavior Modification*

   1. Definitions

      a. **Behavior modification**

      b. **Autism**

   2. Behavior modification and autism

      a. Program (Ivar Lovaas)

      b. Results

      c. Follow-up

   3. **Biofeedback**

   4. Pros and cons of punishment

   ☐ Do you believe in spanking? Were you spanked as a child? Do you spank your own children?

      a. Spanking: positive punishment

      b. Time-out: negative punishment

For Psych Majors Only. . .

How to Trade Bad Habits for Good: The central idea of behaviorism is that all human behavior is learned, the result of reinforcement through consequences. Your bad habits are not intrinsic parts of you, they are the result of learning. If that is true, then you can unlearn them, too, or crowd them out by learning new and better habits.

How can you accomplish this? By keeping the focus on behavior, understanding behavior as a transaction with the environment, and constructing better environments that support better habits. Of course this is easier said than done, because you have a long and largely forgotten learning history and also because social environments are complicated structures.

Have you noticed that nothing has been said about faults and weaknesses, blame or guilt? They have no place in behavior analysis. That's why the title of this box is not strictly accurate — habits are neither 'good' nor 'bad' in and of themselves. Behavior is simply behavior. How well any given behavior serves our purposes, however, leads to value judgments that can become guides to action.

Test-Taking Tips 2

Carefully reading the question, plus your own general knowledge and intelligence, often reveals the correct answer. Some hints:

- Be wary of answers that appear to be way off the point.
- Be wary of answers that contain nonsense statements or that do not make sense.

Language Workout

What's That?

p. 213   the learning process is **out in the open** = clear, not hidden
as a **toddler** = baby learning to walk
. **beaning** his dad on the head = hitting

p. 215   a naïve rat does not usually **waltz over** = go directly

p. 216   give flowers to your **honey** = boyfriend or girlfriend
Baseline = basic behavior, before attempts to change it

p. 218   **playing hookey** from school = being absent

p. 219   **coupon** [COO-pahn] = a ticket that promises payment
the driver could **get rolling** = start driving
spanking = hitting child on backside as punishment
a child's **allowance** = weekly money given by parents to child

p. 220   **slot machine** = gambling machine
the pen moves up a **notch** = step, unit of measurement

p. 223   caused many in the audience to **gasp** = make sound of surprise

p. 226   **vainly** grasp at the out-of-reach banana = unsuccessfully
he seemed to **hit on** the solution = find

p. .229   **phenomenal** memories = extraordinary
humans' vocal **apparatus** = equipment

p. 230   **carry out** a request = perform
temper tantrums = child's outburst marked by losing control

p. 232   stop constant **rocking** = moving back and forth

p. 236   Dr. Den Trumbull, a **pediatrician** = doctor for babies and children
lead to problems **down the line** = later

What's the Difference?

a simple but clever way to measure reasoning in a more **objective** way (p. 214)

A **subjective** statement focuses on the **subject**: the person making the statement.
It is **subjective** because it expresses personal opinions, feelings, and biases.
Subjective = This hamburger tastes good.

An **objective** statement focuses on the **object**: the thing or action that is observed.
It is **objective** because it reports only facts that can be measured or proved.
Objective = This hamburger weighs 10.6 ounces.

Subjective statements often contain words of judgment, like should" or "better."
Objective statements often contain words of description or measurement.

Now try it: think about each of the statements below. If you think the statement is **Subjective**, write **S** in the blank. If you think the statement is **Objective**, write **O** in the blank.

____ "Textbooks cost too much."

____ "Apples have more vitamins than potatoes."

____ "Everyone should eat an apple every day."

____ "Most children like chocolate."

____ "It is better to be clean than dirty."

____ "American football is a more violent game than soccer."

Making Connections

When you are reading, it's vitally important to understand all the logical help that writers give you. Certain words will help you by showing you the connection between one sentence and the next one.

Is the next sentence about *more* of the same? The writer should tell you with words like:

moreover / furthermore / in addition

Jack liked to watch golf on television. **Moreover,** he loved to pretend to play golf.

After watching the model, children kicked and hit the Bobo doll. **Furthermore,** they yelled, "Hit him! Kick him!"

Tolman showed that rats learned the layout of a maze. **In addition,** the rats formed a cognitive map.

Practicing this kind of thinking will help you understand what you read more quickly and more deeply. Let's try more, but remember that there is no one right answer:

Faysal never eats meat. **Moreover,** _____.

It rained all night. **Furthermore,** _____.

Bogdana works hard during the week. **In addition,** _____.

Answers

Subjective: "Textbooks cost too much." = "too much" is an opinion
Objective: "Apples have more vitamins than potatoes." = this can be proven
Subjective: "Everyone should eat an apple every day." = "should" is an opinion
Objective: "Most children like chocolate." = this can be proven with statistics
Subjective: "It is better to be clean than dirty." = most people share this opinion, but it is still an opinion.
Subjective: "American football is a more violent game than soccer." = what is or is not "violent" is an opinion, although it is possible to count the number of violent acts and compare them.
Faysal never eats meat. **Moreover,** he (never eats eggs)(wears a cloth belt) (does not wear leather).
It rained all night. **Furthermore,** (it is still raining now) (it might rain later).
Bogdana works hard during the week. **In addition,** she (has a weekend job) (goes to school on Saturdays).

The Big Picture

Which statement below offers the best summary of the larger significance of this module?

A   If B. F. Skinner is correct, most human behaviors are learned through the reinforcing powers of consequences. Because learning can be studied objectively and experimentally, psychology can become a real science of behavior.

B   Skinner and the behaviorists reduced psychology to a study of rats and pigeons. They lost sight of the fact that humans are unique, individual, and not reducible to a set of laws organized around reinforcement.

C   Skinner thought his "operant conditioning" would replace Pavlov's "classical conditioning" as the fullest description of human behavior. Today we know that most human behavior is based on reflexes, and so Pavlov wins.

D   The behaviorists launched a revolution that led to a wealth of research in psychology. By the time he died, however, Skinner had turned to a belief in the importance of biological and cognitive factors to explain behavior.

E   Most research subjects are rats, pigeons, and psych students. A cynic once observed that the first two are not human, and the third may not be.

True-False

_____   1. Classical conditioning concerns involuntary (reflex) behavior while operant conditioning concerns voluntary behavior.

_____   2. The secret of successful shaping is waiting until the animal emits the desired final target behavior, then immediately applying reinforcement.

_____   3. The key to operant conditioning is making consequences contingent on behavior.

_____   4. Positive reinforcement makes behavior more likely to occur again; negative reinforcement makes it less likely to occur again.

_____   5. If you want effective learning, you must use primary reinforcers instead of secondary reinforcers.

_____   6. Schedules of reinforcement are the specific times of the day when animals in learning experiments must receive their reinforcement.

_____   7. Social cognitive learning shows how there is a difference between learning a behavior and performing that behavior.

_____   8. The difference between social cognitive learning and operant conditioning is that the former does not depend on external reinforcement.

_____   9. A good example of social cognitive learning was when Sultan piled up several boxes so he could reach the banana.

_____ 10. The great power of reinforcement extends only so far — until it bumps into a biological restraint.

Flashcards 1

_____ 1. continuous reinforcement

_____ 2. negative punishment

_____ 3. negative reinforcement

_____ 4. partial reinforcement

_____ 5. positive punishment

_____ 6. positive reinforcement

_____ 7. punishment

_____ 8. reinforcement

_____ 9. schedule of reinforcement

_____ 10. shaping

a. the presentation of a stimulus that increases the probability of a behavior occurring again

b. a rule that determines how and when the occurrence of a response will be followed by a reinforcer

c. a consequence that occurs after behavior and decreases chance of that behavior occurring again

d. a situation in which responding is reinforced only some of the time

e. a procedure of successive reinforcement of behaviors that lead up to or approximate the desired behavior

f. a consequence that occurs after behavior and increases the chance of that behavior occurring again

g. removing a reinforcing stimulus (allowance) after response; decreases chances of response recurring

h. presenting an aversive stimulus (spanking) after a response; decreases chances of response recurring

i. every occurrence of the operant response results in delivery of the reinforcer

j. an aversive stimulus whose removal increases the likelihood of the preceding response occurring again

Flashcards 2

_____ 1. behavior modification

_____ 2. cognitive map

_____ 3. fixed-interval schedule

_____ 4. fixed-ratio schedule

_____ 5. imprinting

_____ 6. insight

_____ 7. preparedness or prepared learning

_____ 8. superstitious behavior

_____ 9. variable-interval schedule

_____ 10. variable-ratio schedule

a. inherited tendencies or responses that are displayed by newborn animals encountering certain stimuli

b. a treatment or therapy that modifies problems by using principles of learning and conditioning

c. a reinforcer occurs only after a fixed number of responses made by the subject

d. an innate or biological tendency of animals to recognize and attend to certain cues and stimuli

e. a mental representation in the brain of the layout of an environment and its features

f. a reinforcer occurs following the first response that occurs after a fixed interval of time

g. a reinforcer occurs following the first response after a variable amount of time has gone by

h. a mental process marked by the sudden solution to a problem; the "ah ha" phenomenon

i. a subject must make a variable or different number of responses for delivery of each reinforcer

j. any behavior that increases in frequency because of accidental pairing with the delivery of a reinforcer

Multiple-Choice

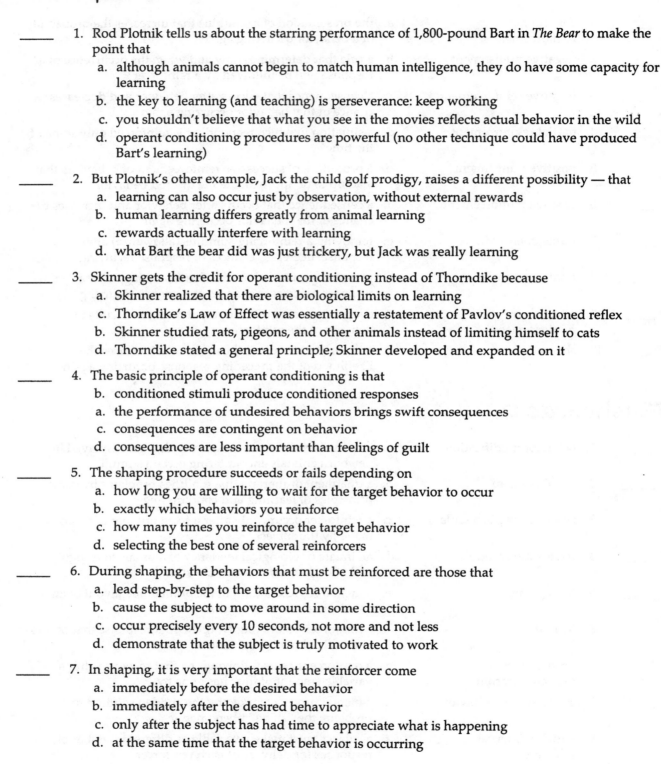

_____ 1. Rod Plotnik tells us about the starring performance of 1,800-pound Bart in *The Bear* to make the point that
   a. although animals cannot begin to match human intelligence, they do have some capacity for learning
   b. the key to learning (and teaching) is perseverance: keep working
   c. you shouldn't believe that what you see in the movies reflects actual behavior in the wild
   d. operant conditioning procedures are powerful (no other technique could have produced Bart's learning)

_____ 2. But Plotnik's other example, Jack the child golf prodigy, raises a different possibility — that
   a. learning can also occur just by observation, without external rewards
   b. human learning differs greatly from animal learning
   c. rewards actually interfere with learning
   d. what Bart the bear did was just trickery, but Jack was really learning

_____ 3. Skinner gets the credit for operant conditioning instead of Thorndike because
   a. Skinner realized that there are biological limits on learning
   c. Thorndike's Law of Effect was essentially a restatement of Pavlov's conditioned reflex
   b. Skinner studied rats, pigeons, and other animals instead of limiting himself to cats
   d. Thorndike stated a general principle; Skinner developed and expanded on it

_____ 4. The basic principle of operant conditioning is that
   b. conditioned stimuli produce conditioned responses
   a. the performance of undesired behaviors brings swift consequences
   c. consequences are contingent on behavior
   d. consequences are less important than feelings of guilt

_____ 5. The shaping procedure succeeds or fails depending on
   a. how long you are willing to wait for the target behavior to occur
   b. exactly which behaviors you reinforce
   c. how many times you reinforce the target behavior
   d. selecting the best one of several reinforcers

_____ 6. During shaping, the behaviors that must be reinforced are those that
   a. lead step-by-step to the target behavior
   b. cause the subject to move around in some direction
   c. occur precisely every 10 seconds, not more and not less
   d. demonstrate that the subject is truly motivated to work

_____ 7. In shaping, it is very important that the reinforcer come
   a. immediately before the desired behavior
   b. immediately after the desired behavior
   c. only after the subject has had time to appreciate what is happening
   d. at the same time that the target behavior is occurring

_____   8. Superstitious behavior is any behavior that increases in frequency because
  a. somehow you just know that it will happen again
  b. the belief system of the subject contains elements of superstition
  c. it appears to happen by accident, with no understandable cause
  d. its occurrence is accidentally paired with the delivery of a reinforcer

_____   9. You could argue that Skinner's discoveries are more important than Pavlov's in that
  a. beginning a quarter of a century later, Skinner could build on Pavlov's discoveries
  b. American science offers more freedom than Russian science
  c. almost all important human behavior is voluntary (not reflex) behavior
  d. the conditioned reflex isn't fully explained until you bring in the concepts of both positive and negative reinforcement

_____ 10. Which one of the following pairs is *not* a difference between *operant* and *classical* conditioning?
  a. consequences of behavior / conditioned reflex
  b. voluntary behavior / physiological reflex
  c. emitted response / elicited response
  d. decreases rate of behavior / increases rate of behavior

_____ 11. The main difference between reinforcement and punishment is that
  a. reinforcement increases rates of behavior, but punishment decreases them
  b. reinforcement is very effective, but punishment rarely is
  c. reinforcement leads to good behavior, but punishment often creates pica
  d. people obviously dislike punishment, but they don't really like reinforcement much more

_____ 12. The student on probation who finally buckles down and begins studying in earnest is under the control of an operant conditioning procedure called
  a. positive reinforcement
  b. negative reinforcement
  c. punishment
  d. extinction

_____ 13. The little child who gets a good hard spanking for running out into the street is experiencing an operant conditioning procedure called
  a. positive reinforcement
  b. negative reinforcement
  c. positive punishment
  d. extinction

_____ 14. When your date shakes your hand and says, "Thanks for a wonderful evening," you reply, "Gee, I was kind of hoping for a _____
  a. token of your affection
  b. partial reinforcement
  c. secondary reinforcer
  d. primary reinforcer

_____ 15. "Positive punishment" is an awkward term (psychology be cursed!) to express the idea of
   a. punishment strong enough to really work
   b. punishment based on taking something pleasant away from you
   c. punishment based on "giving" you something unpleasant
   d. a positive rather than a negative approach to discipline

_____ 16. "Poor fool," you think to yourself when your friend tells you she lost on the lottery again, "another helpless victim of the _____ schedule of reinforcement"
   a. fixed-ratio
   b. variable-ratio
   c. fixed-interval
   d. variable-interval

_____ 17. Skinner opposed cognitive theories of learning to the end of his life because
   a. it is difficult to admit that the work of a lifetime was misguided
   b. they are based on philosophical speculation rather than on laboratory research
   c. they bring in the "mind," which he said couldn't be observed or measured directly
   d. you can't teach an old dog new tricks

_____ 18. Although you haven't made a conscious effort to memorize the campus area, you probably can get to any point on it relatively easily; Edward Tolman would say you
   a. exhibited attention, memory, imitation, and motivation
   b. learned through observation as you moved around campus
   c. can call on the power of insight when necessary
   d. automatically developed a cognitive map

_____ 19. Which one of the following was _not_ an important outcome in Albert Bandura's famous Bobo doll experiment?
   a. the children did not imitate the adult model until they were given a reward
   b. the children learned even though they did not receive tangible rewards
   c. the children learned even though they were not engaging in any overt behavior
   d. some subjects did not imitate the model (proving learning had occurred) until they were reinforced for doing so

_____ 20. Which one of the following is _not_ a factor in Bandura's theory of social cognitive learning?
   a. attention
   b. memory
   c. rehearsal
   d. motivation

_____ 21. According to the learning-performance distinction,
   a. learning may occur but not be immediately evident in behavior
   b. learning may not occur in situations calling for immediate performance
   c. girls probably learn better than boys but may not perform as well on tests
   d. girls are naturally aggressive but hide aggressive performance better

_____ 22. The important thing about the solution Sultan came up with for the out-of-reach banana problem was
   a. how an old conditioned reflex spontaneously recovered
   b. how he used trial and error
   c. how he built on previously reinforced behavior
   d. what was *missing* in his solution — namely, all the factors above

_____ 23. Limitations on the power of operant conditioning to explain behavior were discovered by
   a. ethnologists studying pica in baby ducks during the insensitive period
   b. ethologists studying imprinting during the critical period for learning
   c. ethicists studying the virtue of punishing self-injurious behaviors of autistic children
   d. ethanologists studying the power of biological products to get us around

_____ 24. A _____ is a negative punishment often used for the childhood problem of noncompliance
   a. time-out
   b. spanking
   c. parent yelling "No!"
   d. gentle frown

_____ 25. The Suzuki method of teaching violin to children closely resembles the processes of
   a. Pavlov's classical conditioning
   b. Bandura's social cognitive learning
   c. Skinner's operant conditioning
   d. Kohler's insight learning

Short Essay

1. Sketch the history of behaviorism, using the names Ivan Pavlov, John Watson, B. F. Skinner, and Albert Bandura.

2. How does operant conditioning differ from classical conditioning?

3. It could be argued that Skinner's crowning achievement is his exploration and definition of schedules of reinforcement. How so?

4. How does biology affect learning? Describe the biological limitations on conditioning.

5. Do you believe that research on rats and pigeons in the laboratory can help us understand how human beings operate in the real world?

Answers for Module 10

The Big Picture (explanations provided for incorrect choices)

A *Correct! You see the "big picture" for this Module.*
B Skinner believed that behavior was consistent across species (but animals make more willing subjects!). Schedules of reinforcement, for example, work the same for pigeons and people.
C Most human behavior is voluntary, not reflexive, so this conclusion is wrong.
D Skinner stuck to his guns on behavioral psychology versus cognitive explanations to the end.
E It's just a joke!

True-False (explanations provided for False choices; page numbers given for all choices)

1	T	213	
2	F	215	The secret is to reinforce a behavior that is a little closer to the target behavior.
3	T	217	
4	F	218	Negative reinforcement also makes behavior more likely to occur again.
5	F	219	Both primary and secondary reinforcers motivate behavior.
6	F	220	Schedules of reinforcement are payoff rules (not specific times) for different patterns of performance.
7	T	223	
8	T	223	
9	F	226	Sultan's behavior demonstrated insight learning.
10	T	228	

Flashcards 1

1 i	2 g	3 j	4 d	5 h	6 a	7 c	8 f	9 b	10 e

Flashcards 2

1 b	2 e	3 f	4 c	5 a	6 h	7 d	8 j	9 g	10 i

Multiple-Choice (explanations provided for incorrect choices)

1 a Perhaps true, but why would Plotnik emphasize this point?
   b Perseverance is involved, but it is by no means the main story.
   c This movie, although not a documentary, did attempt to present natural animal behavior.
   d Correct! See page 213.

2 *a Correct! See page 213.*
   b Skinner and the behaviorists believed just the opposite.
   c Some cognitive learning proponents say this, but most behaviorists disagree.
   d It was sort of a trick, but Bart *learned* how to do it.

3 a This is far from Skinner's main idea.
   b Skinner believed that the laws of learning applied to all animals, including humans.
   c Thorndike's explanation of learning was very different from Pavlov's.
   d Correct! See page 214.

4 a Not unless the situation has been set up that way.
   b This is true in classical conditioning.
   c Correct! See page 214.
   d The concept of guilt feelings belongs to psychoanalysis.

5 a In shaping, you don't wait for the target behavior to occur.
   b Correct! See page 215.
   c By the time you have the target behavior, shaping is complete.
   d Any reinforcer that works can be used in shaping.

6 *a Correct! See page 215.*
   b Then the subject would end up spinning around and getting nowhere!
   c Then the subject would learn to do something different every 10 seconds!
   d How would you know which behaviors show motivation and which don't?

7 a How would this reinforce the desired behavior? More likely, the previous behavior.
   b *Correct! See page 215.*
   c How would we know when (or whether) the subject appreciated what was happening?
   d The target behavior is the desired final behavior; first we have to reinforce the behaviors that lead up to it.

8 a Too mystical. Behaviorism explains you not by your ideas, but by your behavior.
   b It's not what the subject believes, but what happens just before a rewarding event occurs.
   c There is an understandable cause, if you analyze what the subject was doing before the rewarding event.
   d *Correct! See page 215.*

9 a Somewhat true, but Skinner's work is very different from Pavlov's.
   b Skinner believed that the laws of learning applied to all animals, including humans.
   c *Correct! See page 214.*
   d The conditioned reflex and positive and negative reinforcement are essentially different concepts.

10 a Consequences operant, conditioned reflex classical. This is a valid difference.
    b Voluntary operant, reflex classical. This is a valid difference.
    c Emitted operant, elicited classical. This is a valid difference.
    d *Correct! See page 217.*

11 **a** *Correct! See page 218.*
    b Punishment can be very effective, maybe even more effective than reinforcement.
    c Not true. Pica is a disorder involving eating inedible objects or unhealthy substances.
    d Only half true (they may not like *negative* reinforcement).

12 a Positive reinforcement is the strengthening of behavior by applying a desired consequence.
    b *Correct! See page 218.*
    c Punishment is the suppression of behavior through unpleasant consequences.
    d Extinction is the gradual elimination of behavior through the removal of a consequence.

13 a Positive reinforcement is the strengthening of behavior by applying a desired consequence.
    b Negative reinforcement is the strengthening of behavior through threats.
    c *Correct! See page 218.*
    d Extinction is the gradual elimination of behavior through the removal of a consequence.

14 a That would be your date giving you a poker chip you could trade in later.
    b That would be your date reinforcing you some times and not others.
    c What you got *was* a secondary reinforcer!
    d *Correct! See page 219.*

15 a It's not the strength of the punishment, but how it operates.
    b That would be "negative punishment" (another awkward term).
    c *Correct! See page 219.*
    d Sadly, any punishment is a negative approach to discipline.

16 a Fixed-ratio would be winning every X number of times she bought a ticket.
    b *Correct! See page 221.*
    c Fixed-interval would be winning every week regardless of how many tickets she bought.
    d Variable-interval would be winning every now and then regardless of how many tickets she bought.

17 a There was no reason for Skinner to doubt the value of his life's work.
    b Skinner knew cognitive theories of learning were based on laboratory research (but he was critical of it).
    c *Correct! See page 223.*
    d It's just a joke!

18 a These variables apply to Albert Bandura's theory of observational learning.
    b This idea applies to Albert Bandura's theory of observational learning.
    c This idea applies to Wolfgang Köhler's theory of insight learning.
    d *Correct! See page 223.*

19 **a** *Correct! See page 224.*
    b The absence of tangible reinforcement is of key importance to this experiment.
    c The absence of overt behavior is important in this experiment.
    d The later exhibition of the learning is important in this experiment.

20   a   Attention is one of the four processes necessary for observational learning.
      b   Memory is one of the four processes necessary for observational learning.
      c   *Correct! See page 225.*
      d   Motivation is one of the four processes necessary for observational learning.

21   *a*   *Correct! See page 224.*
      b   Bandura's experiment did not suggest this conclusion.
      c   Bandura's experiment did not suggest this conclusion.
      d   Bandura's experiment did not suggest this conclusion.

22   a   No, because this was a completely new problem for Sultan.
      b   No, because Sultan solved the problem suddenly.
      c   No, because no deliberate previous learning led up to Sultan's solution.
      d   *Correct! See page 226.*

23   a   Ethnologists study cultural differences. Review the meaning of pica. There is no insensitive period.
      b   *Correct! See page 228.*
      c   Behavior modification may raise ethical questions, but it does work.
      d   It's just a joke! (Ethanol in gas — get it?)

24   *a*   *Correct! See page 230.*
      b   That's the point — time-out avoids hitting the child.
      c   "No" is still aggressive and may not modify the child's behavior.
      d   Sure, that works!

25   a   Classical conditioning is reflex learning.
      b   *Correct! See page 231.*
      c   Operant conditioning does not emphasize cognitive learning.
      d   Insight learning is sudden rather than the result of practice.

Short Essay (sample answers)

1. Ivan Pavlov's discovery of the conditioned reflex changed the course of modern psychology and led to the behaviorist movement. John B. Watson showed that emotional responses could be classically conditioned in humans. B. F. Skinner shifted the emphasis from reflexes to consequences, and developed the laws of operant conditioning. Skinner described the schedules of reinforcement that govern behavior. Albert Bandura explored learning by observation and imitation, adding a cognitive element to behaviorism.

2. Skinner's operant conditioning of voluntary behavior greatly expanded the scope of Pavlov's classical conditioning of reflexes. Classical conditioning limits learning to pairing a new behavior with an existing reflex. Operant conditioning says all organisms constantly emit behavior, which in turn is reinforced or punished by the consequences it causes. Since almost all human behavior is voluntary, Skinner was able to explore learning fully, establishing the laws of reinforcement and describing schedules of reinforcement.

3. Skinner realized that continuous reinforcement is not necessary to maintain behavior. Partial reinforcement works as well or better. In humans, few activities are continuously reinforced. So Skinner set out to describe the various relationships between behavior and reinforcement. Through research, he established the very precise rules that govern these relationships and went on to apply them to the great majority of behaviors engaged in by humans and other animals. Few "laws" of behavior have such precision and applicability.

4. At first, behaviorists thought they could explain any behavior through the laws of reinforcement. But there are biological factors in behavior and learning. Ethologists like Konrad Lorenz, who observed that ducklings automatically follow anything near them, explored critical or sensitive periods in learning. Preparedness or prepared learning explains why animals may pay special attention to certain cues. Human infants' brains are wired to be prepared to learn, at first, all the sounds that make up human languages.

5. One of the strongest and most persistent criticisms of behaviorism is that laboratory research on animals cannot explain the most important features of human behavior in the real world. But behaviorists like Skinner seemed to show in their laboratories that human behavior, although perhaps more complicated, is governed by the same laws of behavior as other creatures. Where do you come down on this essential dispute? What do you think of modern behaviorism? What evidence supports your conclusion?

Module 11

Types of Memory

Nothing in This Module Is True

The biological and cognitive approaches to psychology have made great strides in the last two decades. One of the results is a much clearer picture of how memory works. Even so, there is a sense in which none of it is true.

The answers we want are buried at least two layers down. First, how does the physical brain work? We are learning more about the brain every day, yet for all their discoveries neuroscientists have barely scratched the surface. The need to understand elusive electrical activity, not just gray matter, complicates the task. Second, how does the mind work? If the mind is an abstraction, a concept (unless you say mind and brain are the same thing), we cannot apprehend it directly, making it even more difficult to understand.

Today we are fond of comparing the mind to a computer, simply because the computer is the most powerful mechanical thinking device we know, and therefore makes a good comparison. Yet when we develop a *new* generation of thinking machines, perhaps based on liquid instead of silicone chips, we will stop comparing the mind to a computer and compare it to the new device instead, since the new device will seem much more like the human mind. The mind is not really a computer; the computer merely makes a good model for understanding the mind, at least today.

The Beauty of a Good Model

No wonder that dress looks so beautiful on the model sashaying down the runway in the fashion show. The model isn't an actual human being — obviously, no one could be that tall, that thin, that perfect! Consequently, when draped around this abstraction of a human, we can see much more clearly how the clothing itself really looks.

A model helps us understand the real world because it is an ideal against which we can compare specific phenomena. When we try to understand the workings of the mind, all we see are awkward elbows and knees. We need a model to help us visualize what it must really be like.

What we are struggling to understand is how the process of grasping the world and putting parts of it in our heads must work. Many of the formulations Rod Plotnik presents in Module 11 are models of what this process may be like. Because this is not yet certain knowledge, several theories, or models, compete for our acceptance. I think you can learn these theories better if you keep in mind the idea that they are models, not reality.

> Check it out! PowerStudy 2.0 includes a 40-50 minute presentation that uses animations, visuals, and interactive activities as well as quizzing to help you understand concepts in this module.

Effective Student Tip 11

High Grades Count Most

Here is a hard truth. Unfair, maybe, but true. Anyone who looks at your transcript, whether for admission to another school or for employment, is going to be looking for the *high* grades. It's difficult for them to tell exactly what 'C' means. In some schools, 'C' may mean little more than that you attended class. The grade 'B' begins to say more about your abilities and character, but it is an 'A' that is really convincing. No matter in what course or at what school, an 'A' says you did everything asked of you and did it well. That's a quality admissions people and personnel officers look for.

High grades have other rewards, too. You get on the school's honors list. You can join honors societies. You qualify for scholarships. With every 'A', your sense of effectiveness goes up a notch. You are more confident and enjoy greater self-esteem. (Keeps Mom and Dad happy, too!)

Tailor your work toward earning high grades. Take fewer courses, stay up later studying, write papers over, ruthlessly cut fun out of your life [just kidding].

Earning high grades in a few courses beats getting average grades in many courses. The fastest route toward your goal is a conservative selection of courses in which you do well, resulting in a good record and confidence in your effectiveness as a student.

Your response...

Can you remember a time when you thought you had an 'A', then didn't get it? What went wrong?

Learning Objectives

1. Understand memory and memory processes as models — inferred explanations of brain functions for which we do not as yet have the tools to investigate directly at the physiological level.

2. Learn the three basic types of memory and how they work together as an integrated process to help us retain and use the information we need as thinking (not just reacting) animals.

3. Know the component parts, functions, and steps in the three types of memory.

4. Understand the processes of encoding and the implications of different memory strategies for students attempting to master complex materials.

5. Consider your position on the repressed memory controversy and how accusations of child abuse should be handled.

6. Appreciate cultural differences in memory processes through cross-cultural research in memory.

7. Learn how the unusual abilities of photographic memory, eidetic imagery, and flashbulb memory suggest the great potential power of human memory.

Key Terms

Many of these terms are based on a model of the mind. Get the model and it's easier to learn the terms.

automatic encoding
chunking
declarative memory
echoic memory
effortful encoding
eidetic imagery
elaborative rehearsal
encoding
episodic memory
flashbulb memories

iconic memory
interference
levels-of-processing theory
long-term memory
maintenance rehearsal
memory
photographic memory
primacy effect
primacy-recency effect

procedural or nondeclarative
  memory
recency effect
repression
retrieving
semantic memory
sensory memory
short-term or working
  memory
storing

Outline

- *Introduction*
    1. Incredible memory (Rajan Mahadevan)
    2. Repressed memory (Holly and her father)

3. Definitions

   a. **Memory**

   b. Three memory processes

      (1) **Encoding**

      (2) **Storing**

      (3) **Retrieving**

A. *Three Types of Memory*

  1. Three types of memory

   a. **Sensory memory**

   b. **Short-term (working) memory**

   c. **Long-term memory**

  2. Memory processes

B. *Sensory Memory: Recording*

  1. **Iconic memory** (visual)

  2. **Echoic memory** (auditory)

  ☐ How do iconic and echoic memory work? What is their purpose?

  3. Functions of sensory memory

   a. Prevents being overwhelmed

   b. Gives decision time

   c. Provides stability, playback, and recognition

C. *Short-Term Memory: Working*

  1. Definition: **short-term or working memory**

  2. Two features

   a. Limited duration

      (1) From two to 30 seconds

      (2) **Maintenance rehearsal**

   b. Limited capacity

      (1) About seven items or bits (George Miller)

      (2) Memory span test

      (3) **Interference**

  3. **Chunking**

  4. Functions of short-term memory

   a. Attending

   b. Rehearsing

   c. Storing

D. *Long-Term Memory: Storing*

   1. Putting information into long-term memory

      a. Sensory memory

      b. Attention

      c. Short-term memory

      d. **Encoding**

      e. **Long-term memory**

      f. **Retrieving**

   2. Features of long-term memory

      a. Capacity and permanence

      b. Retrieval and accuracy

      c. Accuracy of long-term memory

   3. Separate memory systems

   4. Primacy versus recency

      a. **Primacy effect** (first 4-5 items)

      b. **Recency effect** (last 4-5 items)

      c. **Primacy-recency effect** (beginning and end of list)

   ☐ Can you work out the logic of the memory processes involved in these concepts?

   5. Short-term versus long-term memory

   6. Declarative versus procedural or nondeclarative

      a. **Declarative memory**

         (1) **Semantic memory**

         (2) **Episodic memory**

      b. **Procedural or nondeclarative memory**

E. *Research Focus: Do Emotions Affect Memories?*

   1. Hormones and memories (James McGaugh)

   2. Memories of emotional events

      a. Procedure

      b. Results and conclusion

F. *Encoding: Transferring*

   1. Two kinds of **encoding**

      a. **Automatic encoding**

      b. **Effortful encoding**

   2. Rehearsing and encoding

      a. **Maintenance rehearsal**

      b. **Elaborative rehearsal**

3. **Levels-of-processing theory**

G. *Repressed Memories*

   1. Recovered memories

   2. Definition of repressed memories: **repression** (Sigmund Freud)

   3. Therapist's role in recovered memories (Elizabeth Loftus)

   4. Implanting false memories

   5. Accuracy of recovered memories

H. *Cultural Diversity: Oral versus Written*

   1. United States versus Africa

   2. Remembering spoken information

I. *Application: Unusual Memories*

   1. **Photographic memory**

   2. **Eidetic imagery**

   3. **Flashbulb memories**

     a. Impact and accuracy

     b. Most remembered events

     c. Multinational study

     d. Flashbulb memories: brains and hormones

     e. Memory: pictures versus impressions

For Psych Majors Only. . .

Gloomy Psychology: Here is a gloomy, possibly discouraging thought (considering how much you paid for your books): perhaps *nothing* in psychology is really true. Perhaps everything you are slaving so hard to learn is simply the best understanding we have now, soon to be replaced by better ways of understanding how psychology works.

I suggested that the computer is merely a temporary model for understanding the mind. Let's go further and suggest that *all* the wonderful theories you study in psychology are models, none ultimately "true." There is no "unconscious" region of the mind, no pure "schedule of reinforcement," and no ethereal "self." They are all fictions — fictions we need in order to make sense of the facts.

There is one happy possibility in this dismal thought. Think how eagerly psychology is waiting for the better model *you* may construct one day. Keep working on your favorite theories.

Language Workout

What's That?

p. 239   before the **packed** house = crowded with people
He did not **err** = make a mistake
such **gargantuan** memory powers = huge, great
for **allegedly** molesting her as a child = reportedly but not proven
subject to error and bias = have tendency to

p. 240   you are **bombarded** = attacked
a lone guitarist playing for **spare change** = extra money

p. 241   you are **absorbed in** reading a novel = completely interested

p. 245   brain damage can **wipe out** long-term memory = destroy
while completely **sparing** short-term memory = not affecting, protecting

p. 247   highly **charged** emotional situations = full of feeling
Because of safety **concerns** = worries
seeing a series of **slides** = a type of photograph
his feet were **severed** = cut off
McGaugh and his **colleagues** = co-workers, fellow researchers
lay the basis for similar studies = prepare, form

p. 248   **avid** sports fans = very enthusiastic

p. 250   Holly's memories first **surfaced** = came to conscious level
it has been **barred** in California's courts = forbidden
survivors of **incest** = sexual relations with family members

p. 254   able to recall (notes) **verbatim** = perfectly, every word

p. 258   absolutely no **shred** of doubt = a tiny piece

Making Connections

As was mentioned in the Language Workout for Module 10, it's vitally important to understand all the logical help that writers give you. Certain words will help you by showing you the connection between one sentence and the next one.

If the second sentence shows a <u>result</u> of the first sentence, certain words will tell you this: **consequently, as a result, thus, for this reason**

The first sentence provides the reason, while the second sentence gives the <u>result</u>.

Reason = Eric had an important job interview on Tuesday morning.
Result = **For this reason**, he ironed his shirt on Monday night.

Reason = It was snowing heavily in Ohio that evening.
Result = **As a result**, airplanes could not land at the Cleveland airport.

Reason = Nina had to watch the children.
Result = **Consequently**, she was not able to come to class.

Let's look at an example from the text:

There are also many examples of therapists who have helped clients recover and deal with terrible repressed memories. **Thus,** therapists are in the difficult position of trying to distinguish accurate accounts of repressed memories from those that may have been shaped or reinforced by suggestions or expectations of the therapist." (p. 250)

The reason = therapists help their clients recover and deal with the repressed memories
The result = therapists have to distinguish between the accurate accounts and their own expectations.

NOW YOU TRY IT. In the sentence below, how do you think the story will continue?

Esmeralda just signed a contract to play in a movie.
As a result, _____.

There is no <u>one</u> right answer. You could have written any of the following:
As a result, she is excited.
As a result, she is planning to move to Hollywood.
As a result, she might become rich and famous.

Practicing this kind of thinking will help you understand what you read more quickly and more deeply. Let's try more:

Faysal never eats meat. **Consequently,** _____.

It rained all night. **Thus,** _____.

The movie is almost four hours long. **For this reason,** _____.

Bogdana works hard during the week. **As a result,** _____.

Now, let's see what difference it makes if we reverse the order. In many cases, you'll have a completely different story:

_____. **Consequently,** Faysal never eats meat.

_____. **Thus,** it rained all night.

_____. **For this reason,** the movie is four hours long.

_____. **As a result,** Bogdana works hard during the week.

___

Answers

Faysal never eats meat. **Consequently,** he (is thin) (eats a lot of rice) (saves money).
It rained all night. **Thus,** (the streets are wet) (the roads are flooded).
The movie is almost four hours long. **For this reason,** (no one wants to see it) (you should buy lots of popcorn) (go to the bathroom before).
Bogdana works hard during the week. **As a result,** she (is tired by Friday) (has a lot of money) (has no extra time).
(He loves animals) (He thinks vegetarianism is healthy). **Consequently,** Faysal never eats meat.
(A storm began) (It's the rainy season). **Thus,** it rained all night.
(It's a long story) (The film covers 100 years). **For this reason,** the movie is four hours long.
(She needs money for her education) (She's saving to buy a car) (She has bills to pay). **As a result,** Bogdana works hard during the week.

The Big Picture

Which statement below offers the best summary of the larger significance of this module?

A   The study of memory shows that humans are destined to disappointment in their endeavors to learn. The best we can achieve is a fragmentary and temporary grasp of facts and ideas that are of importance to us.

B   The human brain is like a vast container, which we fill with facts and ideas from birth to death. Every time we attend to something in our environment, it goes into the box to be saved for later use.

C   In the future, psychology will use electrical and chemical examination to locate and identify every specific memory in the brain. Until then, we really can't say anything definitive about what memory is or how it works.

D   Although we are just beginning to find the precise mechanisms of memory in the brain, several theories, or models, of memory illustrate the processes that seem to be occurring as we perceive, learn, and remember.

E   Types of memory: long-term, short-term, and examination (real-short-term).

True-False

_____   1. Memory involves three basic processes: encoding, storing, and retrieving.

_____   2. There are four basic kinds of memory: flashbulb snapshots, temporary, impermanent, and permanent.

_____   3. Without the stage called sensory memory, we would drown in a sea of visual and auditory sensations.

_____   4. Short-term memory is capable of holding several dozen bits of information for several minutes.

_____   5. When you attempt to remember a list of animals, the recency effect takes precedence over the primacy effect.

_____   6. Encoding is transferring information from short-term to long-term memory.

_____   7. If you are studying for the next psych exam, elaborative rehearsal will be a more effective strategy than maintenance rehearsal.

_____   8. The best way to get information into long-term memory is to repeat it over and over again.

_____   9. A good strategy for remembering something is to associate it with some distinctive visual image.

_____   10. When you find someone who has unusual powers of memory, you can be fairly certain that the person possesses a photographic memory.

Flashcards 1

_____ 1. declarative memory

a. a form of sensory memory that holds auditory information for one or two seconds

_____ 2. echoic memory

b. another process that can hold only a limited amount of information (7 items) for short period (2-30 sec)

_____ 3. encoding

c. memories for performing motor tasks, habits, conditioning; not conscious or retrievable

_____ 4. iconic memory

d. an initial process that holds information in raw form for a brief period of time (instant to several seconds)

_____ 5. long-term memory

e. a form of sensory memory that holds visual information for about a quarter of a second

_____ 6. procedural memory

f. the process of getting or recalling information that has been placed into short-term or long-term storage

_____ 7. retrieving

g. the process of placing encoded information into relatively permanent mental storage for later recall

_____ 8. sensory memory

h. memories for facts or events (scenes, stories, faces, etc.); conscious and retrievable

_____ 9. short-term or working memory

i. the process of storing almost unlimited amounts of information over long periods of time

_____ 10. storing

j. making mental representations of information so that it can be placed or put into our memories

Flashcards 2

_____ 1. chunking

a. the ability to form sharp, detailed visual images of a page, then to recall the entire image at a later date

_____ 2. effortful encoding

b. better recall of information presented at the beginning and at the end of a task

_____ 3. eidetic imagery

c. vivid recollections, usually in great detail, of dramatic or emotionally charged incidents of great interest

_____ 4. elaborative rehearsal

d. process of pushing memories of threat or trauma into the unconscious, from which it cannot be retrieved

_____ 5. flashbulb memories

e. transfer of information from short-term into long-term memory by working hard to do so

_____ 6. interference

f. results when new information enters short-term memory and overwrites information already there

_____ 7. maintenance rehearsal

g. making meaningful associations between information to be learned and information already stored

_____ 8. photographic memory

h. simply repeating or rehearsing the information rather than forming any new associations

_____ 9. primacy-recency effect

i. the ability to examine material for 10-30 seconds and retain a detailed visual image for several minutes

_____ 10. repression

j. combining separate items of information into a larger unit, then remembering the unit as a whole

Multiple-Choice

_____   1. Rod Plotnik discusses Rajan Mahadevan, who memorized more than 30,000 digits of pi, because Rajan's rare abilities
      a. show that extreme concentration of mental ability in one area is usually accompanied by significant mental deficiencies in other areas
      b. are possessed only by people who are otherwise retarded or autistic
      c. could be duplicated by any of us… if we put our minds to it
      d. offer an extreme example of the memory processes we all use

_____   2. Plotnik also tells the story of Holly, who accused her father of molesting her when she was a child, to illustrate the controversial idea of
      a. repressed memories
      b. revenge accusations
      c. stored anger
      d. retrieving information

_____   3. Which one of the following is _not_ one of the three processes of memory?
      a. encoding
      b. storing
      c. deciphering
      d. retrieving

_____   4. The function of sensory memory is to
      a. hold information in its raw form for a brief period of time
      b. make quick associations between new data and things you already know
      c. weed out what is irrelevant in incoming information
      d. burn sensations into long-term memory for later retrieval and inspection

_____   5. Short-term memory can hold information for about
      a. 1 to 2 minutes
      b. one-tenth of a second
      c. 2 to 30 seconds
      d. 10 minutes

_____   6. _____ memory holds visual information for about a quarter of a second
      a. chunk
      b. iconic
      c. pictorial
      d. echoic

_____   7. Thanks to _____ memory, incoming speech sounds linger just long enough so we can recognize the sounds as words
      a. chunking
      b. iconic
      c. verbal
      d. echoic

_____ 8. Which statement below best describes what short-term or working memory is?
   a. your perceptual processes react to it
   b. you freeze it briefly in order to pay attention to it
   c. you work with it to accomplish some immediate task
   d. you retrieve it later when you need it again

_____ 9. Out of change at the pay phone, you frantically repeat the 11-digit number you just got from Information over and over again; that's called
   a. chunking
   b. maintenance rehearsal
   c. memory span stretching
   d. duration enhancement

_____ 10. A classic study by George Miller showed that short-term memory can hold
   a. one item or bit of information at a time
   b. an unlimited amount of information
   c. about a dozen items or bits
   d. about seven items or bits

_____ 11. Why doesn't information in short-term memory simply become permanent? Probably because of
   a. limited storage space in the brain
   b. fascination with the new and different
   c. incompatibility with previously processed information
   d. interference caused by newly arriving information

_____ 12. Using the process of _____, Rajan Mahadevan memorized more than 30,000 digits of pi
   a. chunking
   b. maintenance rehearsal
   c. memory span stretching
   d. duration enhancement

_____ 13. Short-term memory is also called _working_ memory, in order to emphasize that it is
   a. hard work, which most of us like to avoid
   b. an active process involving attending, rehearsing, and storing
   c. a fragile process that often breaks down (explaining why we forget things)
   d. something you can't do indefinitely without a period of rest

_____ 14. Plotnik advises you to think of long-term memory as a
   a. process of storing almost unlimited amounts of information
   b. process of storing much information, but only a fraction of what we learn
   c. place where information is deposited for possible future use
   d. place where important information is kept and unimportant information is discarded

_____ 15. If you attempt to remember a list of animal names, you will be more likely to remember
   a. the first few names
   b. the last few names
   c. both the first and last few names
   d. neither the first or last few names, but the ones occurring in the middle of the list

16. The memory function described in the previous question is called the
    a. paradoxical memory effect
    b. primacy effect
    c. recency effect
    d. primacy-recency effect

17. Remembering how you did on your last psych test involves _____ memory
    a. episodic
    b. semantic
    c. consequential
    d. procedural

18. The actual knowledge required for that test involves _____ memory
    a. episodic
    b. semantic
    c. consequential
    d. procedural

19. Your manual ability to write out the answers on the test involves _____ memory
    a. episodic
    b. semantic
    c. consequential
    d. procedural

20. Of the four memory concepts below, the one most important to you as a student is
    a. automatic encoding
    b. elaborative rehearsal
    c. maintenance rehearsal
    d. power-of-will encoding (willpower)

21. Rod Plotnik puts psychology to good use in his textbook by providing _____ to help you encode the material you must learn
    a. distinctive visual associations
    b. flashbulb memories
    c. maintenance rehearsal drills
    d. chunking strategies

22. The main problem with repressed memories of childhood abuse is that
    a. very few people can remember that far back
    b. we now know that the "unconscious" does not exist
    c. therapists may unwittingly help patients form memories that seem to explain their key problems
    d. so far, all the claimed cases of abuse in childhood have been proven to be lies

23. Students from rural Ghana remembered a story better than New York students because of the
    a. lower intelligence of Ghanaian students due to poverty and a poor diet
    b. oral tradition of their culture versus the written tradition of New Yorkers
    c. fact that the story was from their culture, which was foreign to New Yorkers
    d. cultural tradition of cynical New Yorkers not to believe *any* story

_____ 24. Unusual memory abilities in adults are called _____; in children they are called _____

    a. flashbulb memory / storybook memory

    b. iconic memory / echoic memory

    c. photographic memory / eidetic memory

    d. eidetic memory / photographic memory

_____ 25. Research shows that flashbulb memories are

    a. impressive and vivid, but not necessarily accurate

    b. blinding images that are impossible to forget

    c. always associated with tragedies, like where you were when September 11 happened

    d. frightening memories that you can't quite bring into clear detail

Short Essay

1. Summarize how three types of memory processes transform potentially useful information into available memories.

2. Contrast the two types of long-term memory by describing how they work.

3. What did you learn from this module that could help you become a more effective student?

4. What are the basic arguments for and against the existence of repressed memories of sexual abuse?

5. Describe the research Rod Plotnik offered in support of the idea that cultural influences affect memory processes.

Test-Taking Tips 3

More hints:

- Be wary of answers that seem way out of keeping for the subject involved.

- Be wary of answers that don't fit in with everything else you know about the subject.

Answers for Module 11

The Big Picture (explanations provided for incorrect choices)

A Far too pessimistic! Human memory is powerful and effective in guiding our lives.
B Far too simplistic! Both the selection of what to remember and the method of organizing it in the mind are complex processes.
C This may be true in the future, but until then we still have useful theories about how memory works.
D Correct! You see the "big picture" for this Module.
E It's just a joke!

True-False (explanations provided for False choices; page numbers given for all choices)

1	T	239	
2	F	240	The three basic kinds of memory are sensory, short-term, and long-term.
3	T	241	
4	F	242	Short-term memory is limited to about seven bits of information.
5	F	245	Both the recency effect and the primacy effect are in operation.
6	T	248	
7	T	249	
8	F	249	Associating information with other information is the best way.
9	T	249	
10	F	254	Unusual memory powers are explained by association rather than the rare photographic memory.

Flashcards 1

1 h	2 a	3 j	4 e	5 i	6 c	7 f	8 d	9 b	10 g

Flashcards 2

1 j	2 e	3 i	4 g	5 c	6 f	7 h	8 a	9 b	10 d

Multiple-Choice (explanations provided for incorrect choices)

1 a Rajan Mahadevan is normal in all other respects.
   b This statement is untrue.
   c There is no evidence that anyone could accomplish this feat.
   d Correct! See page 239.

2 *a Correct! See page 239.*
   b This is not a correct term in psychology.
   c This is not a correct term in psychology.
   d Retrieving is the everyday process of recalling information from storage.

3 a Encoding is one of the three memory processes.
   b Storing is one of the three memory processes.
   c Correct! See page 239.
   d Retrieving is one of the three memory processes.

4 *a Correct! See page 240.*
   b This is a function of long-term memory.
   c This is a function of short-term memory.
   d This is not how information is stored in long-term memory.

5 a At this length of time, we would be overwhelmed by new information.
   b This would hardly be enough time to consider the information.
   c Correct! See page 240.
   d Could you think of only one thing and nothing else going on around you for 10 minutes?

6 a Chunking refers to grouping bits of information into larger units.
   b Correct! See page 241.
   c This is not a correct technical term in the psychology of memory.
   d Echoic memory refers to holding auditory information for one or two seconds.

7   a   Chunking refers to grouping bits of information into larger units.
    b   Iconic memory refers to holding visual information for about a quarter of a second.
    c   This is not a correct technical term in the psychology of memory.
    d   *Correct! See page 241.*

8   a   Perceptual processes come before memory.
    b   Short-term memory is an active process.
    c   *Correct! See page 242.*
    d   This statement refers to long-term memory.

9   a   Chunking refers to grouping bits of information into larger units.
    b   *Correct! See page 242.*
    c   This is not a correct technical term in the psychology of memory.
    d   This is not a correct technical term in the psychology of memory.

10 a   If true, how could we follow directions or remember a phone number?
    b   This may be true of long-term memory.
    c   Close, but no cigar.
    d   *Correct! See page 242.*

11 a   No limits on storage space in the brain have been established.
    b   If this were the explanation, how would anything enter long-term memory?
    c   If this were the explanation, how would we learn anything truly new?
    d   *Correct! See page 242.*

12 *a*   *Correct! See page 243.*
    b   Maintenance rehearsal refers to intentionally repeating information so it remains longer in short-term memory.
    c   This is not a correct technical term in the psychology of memory.
    d   This is not a correct technical term in the psychology of memory.

13 a   Working is used in the sense of a process.
    b   *Correct! See page 243.*
    c   It operates as long as we are conscious.
    d   You couldn't take a break from it if you wanted to.

14 *a*   *Correct! See page 244.*
    b   It can store almost unlimited amounts of information.
    c   That's the point — it's a process, not a place.
    d   That's the point — it's a process, not a place.

15 a   This answer is only partly true.
    b   This answer is only partly true.
    c   *Correct! See page 245.*
    d   The names in the middle of the list are the most poorly remembered.

16 a   This is not a correct term in psychology.
    b   Half correct; see definitions.
    c   Half correct; see definitions.
    d   *Correct! See page 245.*

17 *a*   *Correct! See page 246.*
    b   Semantic information refers to general knowledge, book learning, facts, and definitions of words.
    c   This is not a correct technical term in the psychology of memory.
    d   Procedural information refers to knowledge about motor skills and conditioned reflexes.

18 a   Episodic information refers to knowledge about one's personal experiences.
    b   *Correct! See page 246.*
    c   This is not a correct technical term in the psychology of memory.
    d   Procedural information refers to knowledge about motor skills and conditioned reflexes.

19 a   Episodic information refers to knowledge about one's personal experiences.
    b   Semantic information refers to general knowledge, book learning, facts, and definitions of words.
    c   This is not a correct technical term in the psychology of memory.
    d   *Correct! See page 246.*

20   a   Automatic encoding refers to easily remembering interesting, personal, but not academic information.
      b   *Correct! See page 249.*
      c   Maintenance rehearsal refers to keeping information in short-term memory.
      d   This is not a correct term in psychology.

21   ***a***   *Correct! See page 249.*
      b   Think about why the marvelous pictures in the text are repeated in Concept Reviews and Summary Tests.
      c   Think about why the marvelous pictures in the text are repeated in Concept Reviews and Summary Tests.
      d   Think about why the marvelous pictures in the text are repeated in Concept Reviews and Summary Tests.

22   a   Most people remember many events from age 4 or 5 onward.
      b   Many psychologists continue to use the concept of the unconscious.
      c   *Correct! See page 250.*
      d   Sadly, most claims of child abuse may be true.

23   a   Intelligence was not a variable in this research.
      b   *Correct! See page 253.*
      c   The story was not from either culture.
      d   They may be worldly wise, and maybe cynical, but they love stories as much as anyone.

24   a   Flashbulb memories are occurrences, not abilities; there is no storybook memory.
      b   These term refer to visual and auditory memory.
      c   *Correct! See page 254.*
      d   This has the correct terms, but in the wrong order.

25   ***a***   *Correct! See page 255.*
      b   Flashbulb memories may last, but also may be forgotten.
      c   Not always, because some concern happy events like graduations or senior proms.
      d   Not all are frightening, but all flashbulb memories are clear and vivid.

Short Essay (sample answers)

1. Sensory memory receives and holds incoming environmental information in its raw form for an instant to several seconds while you consider what to do with it. Short-term or working memory holds information you are paying attention to for a brief time, from 2 to 30 seconds, while you rehearse the information you want to keep. Finally, that information is encoded for storage in long-term memory on a relatively permanent basis. The best way to encode and recall new information is to associate it with old information.

2. The two types of long-term memory are declarative and procedural — facts versus actions. Declarative memory involves memory for fact or events, such as scenes, stories, words, conversations, faces, or daily events. These memories can be semantic, basically factual, or episodic, more personal. Procedural or nondeclarative memory involves memories for motor skills, cognitive skills, and emotional behavior like fears learned through classical conditioning. Name of your old bike (declarative); how to ride it (procedural).

3. Your professor probably assigns a module of the textbook a week. How can you master the many terms and concepts? In your answer, you should talk about effortful encoding and elaborative rehearsal. Both involve working hard to repeat or rehearse information and actively making meaningful associations between new information you wish to remember and old or familiar information you already have stored in long-term memory.

4. Sigmund Freud brought the concept of repression into psychology. According to that idea, memories of painful traumatic events can be buried in the unconscious. Therapy, which is a kind of exploration of the unconscious mind, might bring such memories into consciousness. But Elizabeth Loftus and other researchers have demonstrated not only that some "recovered" memories are false, but also that false "memories" can be implanted in suggestible minds. The law correctly demands irrefutable evidence.

5. Does culture influence memory? Researchers read a dramatic (but neutral) story twice to both English-speaking college students in Ghana and college students in New York. Sixteen days later, and without having been forewarned, both groups of students were asked to write down as much as they could remember of the story. The Ghanaians, who grew up in a culture with a strong oral tradition, remembered significantly more than the New Yorkers, whose education emphasized a written tradition.

Remembering & Forgetting

What If You Could Remember Nothing?

Can you imagine how terrifying it must be to suffer from amnesia? In one form of amnesia, you can't remember back before a certain point. In a less common form, you can't construct new memories. In either case, you are rootless, adrift in a world with no clear sense of past, present, and future. You wouldn't really know who you are, why you exist, or what will happen to you.

What if you could *forget* nothing? Happily, there is no such psychiatric condition (although you could use such powers, along about now, with mid-term exams coming up). If you were incapable of ever forgetting anything you would be immobilized in a sea of indistinguishable bits and pieces of information, incapable of ever making a decision or taking action because the necessary review of past information and action would be never-ending.

The processes of remembering and forgetting are so immediate and so crucial that we take them for granted. But science, of course, takes nothing for granted. Rod Plotnik shows us what the science of psychology has learned about these vital memory processes.

Forget About It

When something is too painful to endure, a common psychiatric reaction is to forget it, in part or completely. Often victims of auto accidents experience temporary amnesia for the immediate events of the crash. All of us "forget" bad grades and other humiliating defeats.

As we have learned more about child abuse, we have come to realize how its victims often repress their trauma, in order to go on living. Uncovering these repressed memories has become an important part of psychotherapy. Many therapists are convinced that the suffering child cannot become well again unless the painful memories are dug out and worked through.

But memory is ever so much more complicated. Now we are also learning that it is quite possible to "remember" things that never happened. Rod Plotnik reveals the interesting and disturbing dangers of false memories, both those of eyewitness testimony in court cases and childhood memories in psychotherapy. Is it really possible that an eyewitness to a crime could make the wrong identification, or that a child could be wrong about having been sexually abused? Must we not believe what children and good people say when they testify in court? Forget about it!

> Check it out! PowerStudy 2.0 includes a 40-50 minute presentation that uses animations, visuals, and interactive activities as well as quizzing to help you understand concepts in this module.

Effective Student Tip 12

Manage Your Grade

True, we professors set the course standards and assign the final grades. Since most professors stick to their rules once they are established, however, *you* have almost total control over what that grade will be. But wishing doesn't make it so: you have to know how to make it happen. The trick is to take a management attitude toward your grades.

Taking charge and managing your grade involves six steps: (1) Understand your inner motivation concerning grades, to guard against self-sabotage. (2) Understand the details and logic of your professor's grading system. (3) Keep accurate records of your scores and grades (all of them, including any assignments or quizzes you missed). (4) Project your final grade from your current performance. (5) Determine what immediate steps you must take. (6) Make whatever adjustments seem necessary for effective pursuit of your goal.

Don't underestimate the importance of grades to your mental health. Rightly or wrongly, we interpret grades, like earnings, as powerful messages about our effectiveness.

You can passively allow your grades to happen to you, as many students do, or you can take charge and make them what you want.

Your response...

How important are grades to you? How much control do you seem to have over the grades you get?

Learning Objectives

1. Understand remembering and forgetting as related processes that are indispensable in navigating our way through the barrage of information and complexity of tasks we face literally from moment to moment.

2. Learn the basic theories, mechanisms, and research methods in the field of remembering and forgetting.

3. Learn how neuroscience is investigating the biology of memory in the brain and bringing psychology closer to a physical explanation of how the processes of remembering and forgetting work.

4. Apply the lessons of remembering and forgetting, such as encoding, reasons for forgetting, and combating forgetting with mnemonics, to your college learning tasks.

5. Appreciate the power of cultural differences, even in something as fundamental as memory, through an example of Aborigine and white learning and memory abilities.

6. Consider the legal and social implications of recent research on false memories and how they can be created and implanted.

7. Reconsider the reputation of eyewitness testimony in light of research on the accuracy of eyewitnesses and how they can be mislead by factors like how questions are worded.

Key Terms

These key terms touch on an area of psychology that researchers are just beginning to understand. But what could be more important than the way we orient ourselves to time and place?

---

amnesia	mnemonic methods	recognition
cognitive interview	network hierarchy	repression
eyewitness testimony	network theory	retrieval cues
forgetting	neural assemblies	retroactive interference
forgetting curve	nodes	source misattribution
interference	peg method	state-dependent learning
long-term potentiation (LTP)	proactive interference	tip-of-the-tongue phenomenon
method of loci	recall	

Outline

- *Introduction*
    1. Watching a crime (Mugged!)
    ☐ Were you surprised when you tried Rod Plotnik's quiz about the assault?
    2. **Recall** versus **recognition** (Remembering)
    ☐ Can you see how essay exams and multiple-choice exams require different study techniques?
    3. Eyewitness testimony (Lineup)

A. Organization of Memories

1. Filing and organizing 87,967 memories: **network theory**
2. Network theory of memory organization
   a. Nodes
   b. Associations
   c. Network
3. Organization of network hierarchy
   a. **Nodes**
   b. **Network hierarchy**
   c. Searching nodes
4. Categories in the brain

B. Forgetting Curves

1. Early memories
2. Unfamiliar and uninteresting
   a. **Forgetting curve** (Hermann Ebbinghaus)
   b. Nonsense syllables
3. Familiar and interesting

C. Reasons for Forgetting

1. Overview: **forgetting**
   a. **Repression** (Freud)
   b. Poor **retrieval cues**/poor encoding
   c. **Interference**
   d. **Amnesia**
   e. Distortion
2. **Interference**
   a. **Proactive interference**
   b. **Retroactive interference**
   c. Why did viewers forget the mugger's face?
3. **Retrieval cues**
   a. Forming effective retrieval cues
   b. **Tip-of-the-tongue phenomenon**
4. **State-dependent learning**

D. Biological Bases of Memory

1. Location of memories in the brain
   a. Cortex: short-term memories
   b. Cortex: long-term memories

      c. Amygdala: emotional memories

      d. Hippocampus: transferring memories

      e. Brain: memory model

    2. Making a short-term memory: **neural assemblies**

    3. Making a long-term memory: **long-term potentiation (LTP)**

    4. Making memory better or worse (genetically altered mice)

E. Mnemonics: Memorization Methods

    1. Improving your memory: **mnemonic methods**

    2. **Method of loci**

    3. **Peg method**

    4. Effectiveness of methods

F. Cultural Diversity: Aborigines versus White Australians

    1. Retrieval cues

    2. Visual versus verbal memory

      a. Using visual cues

      b. Performance

      c. Culture and retrieval cues

G. Research Focus: False Memories

    1. Can false memories be implanted?

    2. Research method to create false memories

      a. Procedure

      b. Results

      c. Conclusions

    ☐ What are the implications of this research for psychologists and legal professionals?

H. Application: Eyewitness Testimony

    1. How accurate is **eyewitness testimony**?

    2. Can an eyewitness be misled?

    3. Can questions change the answers? (Elizabeth Loftus)

    4. Is what you say, what you believe? (**source misattribution**)

    5. Which interview technique works best? (**cognitive interview**)

Language Workout

What's That?

p. 261   tried to **ward off** the oncoming threat = push away
with a **menacing** gesture = threatening
the **mugger's** jacket = attacking thief's

p. 262   Norman's **train of thought** = direction of thinking

p. 264   He **got around** the fact = avoided the problem
the ticking of a **metronome** = (for a picture of a metronome, see p. 12)
He used only **rote** memory = mechanical, routine

p. 265   **prominent** memory researchers = well-known
if you study primarily by **cramming** = studying the night before the exam
While **showing off** her new pair of skates = attract attention

p. 271   **at my fingertips** = easily available (in memory)

p. 273   **stammering** = stopping-and-starting speech, stuttering

p. 274   a series of **armed** robberies = using guns
The police had few **leads** = clues, information
After being **prompted** to look = encouraged
wearing a **clerical** collar = for priests or religious leaders

p. 275   a **hit-and-run** accident = driver escapes, does not stop to help
police **interrogation** = questioning

p. 278   Kim **stuck by her** = stayed with her
against all odds = despite little chance of success
they **courted** = dated
I was **crushed** = extremely disappointed
surroundings might **jog** her memory = stimulate
fingering her **china** = dishes
Nothing **clicked** = was recognizable

Build Your Word Power

eyewitnesses made **mistakes** (p. 274) = identifying the **wrong** person
subjects **misremembered** what they saw (p. 275) = remember **wrong**ly
people may believe **misinformation** = **wrong** information
the questions were deliberately **mis**leading = questions leading in the **wrong** direction
source **misattribution** = giving credit to the **wrong** cause
So, **mis-** means _____.

Here are some more words that begin with **mis-**. On the right side of the page are definitions of
these words, but they are **misordered**. Draw a line connecting the correct word to its definition.

misclassify	identify illness wrongly
miscount	send in the wrong direction
misdiagnose	put in wrong category
misfit	write 223 when the answer is 227
misguide	person who is in the wrong group

mishandle	give the wrong name
misuse	give the wrong fact
misidentify	apply talent for criminal (wrong) purpose
misinform	use resources in the wrong way
mismanage	treat in the wrong way

What's the Difference?

Look at these two sentences and see if you can find the difference in the meaning of **while**: While showing off her new pair of skates, my sister fell down. (p. 265) Aborigines used visual retrieval cues, **while** the white Australians used verbal retrieval cues. (p. 272) The **while** in the first sentence tells the reader that it is happening at the same time. The **while** in the second sentence is used to show a difference.

The most common use of **while** is to show that two things are occurring at the same time:

Romeo washed the dishes **while** Juliet dried them.
While Bob was studying Module 12, he was watching a kung fu film.

Notice how there is a comma when the sentence starts with **while** because it is not the main subject and verb, but no commas if **while** comes after the main subject and verb. (See Module 5.)

The comma is used differently when **while** shows a difference:

His father is a smoker, **while** Luis is not.

The sentence above shows a difference with *exactly* the same meaning as <u>but</u> and <u>although</u> sentences. So, we have three ways to show a difference:

His father is a smoker, **while** Luis is not. His father is a smoker, **but** Luis is not.
Although his father is a smoker, Luis is not.

We can also use this form of **while** at the beginning of the sentence:

While Yang Li can speak Chinese, she is unable to read it.

The sentence above shows a difference in the same way as <u>but</u> and <u>although</u> sentences. TRY IT:

While Yang Li can speak Chinese, she is unable to read it. _____, **but** she is unable to read it. **Although** Yang Li can speak Chinese, _____.

Answers

misclassify	=	put in wrong category
miscount	=	write 223 when the answer is 227
misdiagnose	=	identify illness wrongly
misfit	=	person who is in the wrong group
misguide	=	send in the wrong direction
mishandle	=	treat in the wrong way
misuse	=	apply talent for criminal (wrong) purposes
misidentify	=	give the wrong name
misinform	=	give the wrong facts
mismanage	=	use resources in the wrong way

Yang Li can speak Chinese, but she is unable to read it. Although Yang Li can speak Chinese, **she is unable to read it.**

The Big Picture

Which statement below offers the best summary of the larger significance of this module?

A   Research has demonstrated that eyewitness testimony is not very reliable and that false memories can be implanted. These discoveries throw our whole understanding of memory up for grabs.

B   We may be stuck with the cognitive models that now describe remembering and forgetting, since a biological understanding of the neural basis of memory appears to be beyond the reach of neuroscience.

C   The subtle operations of acquiring (and then sometimes losing) memories suggest that remembering and forgetting work together in a reciprocal balance to meet the changing demands of our environments.

D   The fact that Aborigines remember in a different way than white Australians suggests that the mechanisms of memory are mainly cultural, and have little common biological or evolutionary basis.

E   Would a psych instructor *dare* expect us to remember all this complicated stuff for an exam? We think not!

True-False

_____   1. Of the two ways to remember, recall is easier than recognition.

_____   2. According to network theory, memory is organized like a gigantic map on which roads connect cities of related information.

_____   3. Forgetting curves measure the length of time that pieces of information will remain in long-term memory.

_____   4. Rod Plotnik says Freud's theory of repression best explains why his sister can't remember what she did on her 9th birthday — something very embarrassing happened!

_____   5. Amnesia is the loss of memory that may occur following drug use, damage to the brain, or after severe psychological trauma.

_____   6. Proactive interference occurs when you are trying too hard to remember new information.

_____   7. Although it is the brain that does the "thinking," the spinal cord stores the actual memories.

_____   8. Both the method of loci and the peg method are mnemonic strategies.

_____   9. It turns out that people *are* different in mental ability — Aborigines, for example, score lower than white Australians on intelligence tests.

_____ 10. Psychologists have discovered that introducing misleading information during questioning can distort eyewitness testimony.

Flashcards 1

_____ 1. amnesia

_____ 2. forgetting

_____ 3. interference

_____ 4. long-term potentiation (LTP)

_____ 5. network theory

_____ 6. nodes

_____ 7. recall

_____ 8. recognition

_____ 9. repression

_____ 10. retrieval cues

a. memory files that contain related information organized around a specific topic or category

b. mental reminders we create by forming vivid mental images or creating associations between information

c. identifying previously learned information with the help of more external cues

d. a common reason for forgetting; recall of a particular memory is blocked by other related memories

e. says we store related ideas in separate categories or files called nodes, all linked together in a network

f. the inability to retrieve, recall, or recognize information that was stored in long-term memory

g. loss of memory caused by a blow or damage to the brain or by drug use or by severe psychological stress

h. a neuron becoming more sensitive to stimulation after it has been repeatedly stimulated

i. retrieving previously learned information without the aid of or with very few external cues

j. a Freudian mental process that automatically hides emotionally threatening information in unconscious

Flashcards 2

_____ 1. cognitive interview

_____ 2. forgetting curve

_____ 3. method of loci

_____ 4. network hierarchy

_____ 5. peg method

_____ 6. proactive interference

_____ 7. retroactive interference

_____ 8. source misattribution

_____ 9. state-dependent learning

_____ 10. tip-of-the-tongue phenomenon

a. when new information (learned later) blocks the retrieval of related old information (learned earlier)

b. encoding technique that creates visual associations between memorized places and items to memorize

c. a technique for questioning eyewitnesses by having them imagine and reconstruct details of event fully

d. encoding technique that creates associations between number-word rhymes and items to be memorized

e. when old information (learned earlier) blocks the remembering of new information (learned later)

f. despite great effort, temporary inability to recall information we absolutely know is in our memory

g. easier to recall information when in same emotional or physiological state or setting as when first learned

h. a memory error that results when a person has difficulty in deciding where a memory came from

i. measures amount of previously learned information that subjects can recall or recognize across time

j. arranging nodes so concrete information is at bottom of hierarchy, with abstract ideas at top level

Multiple-Choice

_____   1. Rod Plotnik begins this module with a scene from a campus mugging. His point is to show that
   a. crime is so scary that we are likely to remember every detail
   b. crime is a special situation, in which the everyday rules of memory do not apply
   c. remembering and forgetting are automatic in dramatic situations like this one
   d. remembering and forgetting are not as simple as most people think

_____   2. Your brow beading with perspiration, you struggle to answer this question, desperately summoning your best powers of
   a. recall
   b. reflection
   c. recognition
   d. recollection

_____   3. If you only glanced through the module, pray that the snap quiz will be
   a. essay
   b. multiple-choice
   c. short essay
   d. oral

_____   4. According to network theory, memory is organized by
   a. nodes, associations, and links among pieces of information
   b. most important to least important information
   c. chronological order, according to when information was acquired
   d. "programs" of information, similar to a TV "network"

_____   5. Memory files containing related information organized around a specific topic are called
   a. network hierarchies
   b. nodes
   c. network theories
   d. modules

_____   6. Recent brain scan research shows that the brain has
   a. prewired categories for processing information
   b. specific, tiny locations for each individual bit of information you remember
   c. hundreds, or even thousands, of different nodes for filing information
   d. identifiable networks that are like well traveled highways connecting nodes

_____   7. Which of the following groups of items would provide the best material for scientific research on memory over time?
   a. names and faces of childhood friends
   b. commonly studied facts, such as state capitals
   c. foreign language vocabulary
   d. nonsense syllables

_____ 8. Analysis of the data yielded by such research (above) would yield
   a. rates of retention
   b. memory percentages
   c. forgetting curves
   d. cognitive charts

_____ 9. A friend says you did something terribly embarrassing at the party, but you can't remember it — this is an example of
   a. repression
   b. poor retrieval cues
   c. amnesia
   d. interference

_____ 10. You were introduced to your friend's professor recently, but there was no time to chat and now you can't recall the professor's name — this is an example of
   a. repression
   b. poor retrieval cues
   c. amnesia
   d. interference

_____ 11. Amnesia is usually caused by
   a. forcing a painful memory out of consciousness
   b. being blocked or prevented by other related memories
   c. a blow or damage to the brain
   d. failing to create vivid mental images or associations

_____ 12. Sometimes we misremember something (like our grades!) due to memory distortions caused by
   a. low intelligence
   b. sleep deprivation
   c. recreational drug use
   d. bias or suggestibility

_____ 13. Proactive interference is when
   a. information learned later now disrupts retrieval of information learned earlier
   b. learning positive information interferes with the retrieval of negative information
   c. information learned earlier now disrupts retrieval of information learned later
   d. retrospective thinking interferes with potential learning

_____ 14. Retroactive interference is when
   a. information learned later now disrupts retrieval of information learned earlier
   b. learning positive information interferes with the retrieval of negative information
   c. information learned earlier now disrupts retrieval of information learned later
   d. retrospective thinking interferes with potential learning

_____ 15. Darn! I know it as well as I know my own name, but I just can't remember it right now — sounds like a case of
   a. false memory
   b. source misattribution
   c. state-dependent learning
   d. tip-of-the-tongue phenomenon

_____ 16. An example of state-dependent learning would be when you
   a. become so emotional you can't remember something you are sure you know
   b. get angry at someone and suddenly recall related past annoyances
   c. become so emotional you completely forget something painful
   d. get better grades in psychology after transferring to a school in another state

_____ 17. Brain scans are advancing our knowledge of remembering and forgetting by identifying the
   a. struggle of the cortex to control the amygdala and hippocampus
   b. neural assemblies that form long-term memories
   c. brain areas involved in processing and storing different thoughts and memories
   d. precise synapses where new memories are formed

_____ 18. The process in which a neuron becomes more sensitive to stimulation after it has been repeatedly stimulated is called
   a. long-term potentiation (LTP)
   b. state dependent learning
   c. neural assembly formation
   d. interference

_____ 19. Long-term potentiation (LTP) works by
   a. stimulating the amygdala
   b. changing the structure and function of neurons
   c. adding short-term memories together
   d. not repeating new information too many times

_____ 20. Both the method of loci and the peg method work by
   a. causing learning to be strengthened through repeated practice
   b. creating strong associations that will serve as effective retrieval cues
   c. connecting material to be learned to the purpose it will be used for
   d. considering material to be memorized as easy and pleasant to learn

_____ 21. Bulletin from the front in research on memory enhancing products:
   a. the popular herbal supplement ginkgo does not help
   b. concentrating on encoding techniques such as making good associations does not help
   c. listening to an audiocassette program on photographic memory does help
   d. using marijuana in sufficient quantities does help

_____ 22. Aborigine children performed significantly better than white Australian children on memory tasks when
   a. only Aborigine objects were used
   b. the task involved auditory cues
   c. testing was done outdoors in a natural setting
   d. the task involved visual cues

_____ 23. Recent research on false memories of abuse in young children has shown that
   a. children can be coached to lie about trivial matters, but not about sexual abuse
   b. false memories can be created through repeated suggestions
   c. children make things up because they really can't remember very well at that age
   d. children tend to lie about most things if they can get something out of it

_____ 24. When evaluating eyewitness testimony, pay close attention to
    a. whether the eyewitness has anything to gain or lose by testifying
    b. how confident the eyewitness appears to be
    c. how the questions to the eyewitness are worded
    d. whether the eyewitness seems biased in favor of or against the defendant

_____ 25. Because of research on eyewitness testimony, police now use a technique called the
    a. cognitive interview
    b. good cop/bad cop strategy
    c. bait-and-switch method
    d. skeptical questioning interview

Short Essay

1. Summarize the current psychological explanation for how memory works.

2. What are the main reasons for forgetting and how do they work?

3. What is the main lesson of this module for you as a college student?

4. Why did Aborigines do better than white Australians on a memory test.

5. What are the implications of research on false memories for the legal system and for psychotherapy?

Test-Taking Tips 4

More hints:

- Be on the lookout for any *part* of an answer that makes the *whole* answer untrue.

- When you find an answer that sounds correct, you must also check the others — to make sure there isn't another answer that is even *more* true.

Answers for Module 12

The Big Picture (explanations provided for incorrect choices)

A Actually these discoveries reinforce the model of the mind as constructive and flexible.
B A biological understanding of the neural basis of memory is rapidly approaching.
C Correct! You see the "big picture" for this Module.
D An unwarranted deduction. The example shows that our common biology can be influenced by cultural factors.
E It's just a joke!

True-False (explanations provided for False choices; page numbers given for all choices)

1	F	261	Recognition is easier than recall because cues are available.
2	T	262	
3	T	264	
4	F	265	Plotnik uses this example to explore four theories of forgetting.
5	T	265	
6	F	266	Proactive interference occurs when old information interferes with learning new information.
7	F	268	The brain controls both thinking and memory.
8	T	271	
9	F	272	In tasks involving visual retrieval cues, Aborigine children did better than white Australian children.
10	T	274	

Flashcards 1

1 g   2 f   3 d   4 h   5 e   6 a   7 i   8 c   9 j   10 b

Flashcards 2

1 c   2 i   3 b   4 j   5 d   6 e   7 a   8 h   9 g   10 f

Multiple-Choice (explanations provided for incorrect choices)

1 a Well, how did you do on the quiz?
   b The rules have to apply to crime, too, or they cannot be considered rules.
   c More likely it is just the opposite.
   d Correct! See page 261.

2 a Recall refers to retrieving previously learned material without the aid of any external cues.
   b Reflection is not a correct technical term in the psychology of memory.
   c Correct! See page 261.
   d Recollection is not a correct technical term in the psychology of memory.

3 a Think about which is easier — recall or recognition?
   b Correct! See page 261.
   c Think about which is easier — recall or recognition?
   d Think about which is easier — recall or recognition?

4 *a Correct! See page 262.*
   b How would "importance" be determined?
   c Then we would always have to remember *when* we acquired the information.
   d This analogy misunderstands the meaning of "network."

5 a Network hierarchies are arrangements of nodes into a certain order, like blue jay – bird – animal.
   b Correct! See page 263.
   c Network theory is a larger idea built on the concepts of nodes and hierarchies.
   d Plotnik uses the term modules for the sections of his textbook.

6 *a Correct! See page 263.*
   b Sounds logical, but brain scans can't show that much yet.
   c Even if brain scans could identify nodes, the number of them would be vastly greater than thousands.
   d Even if brain scans could identify networks, they would be more like associations than highways.

7   a   Memory of these items would be influenced by a subject's life history.
    b   Memory of these items would be influenced by a subject's general knowledge.
    c   Memory of these items would be influenced by what language a subject speaks.
    d   *Correct! See page 264.*

8   a   This is not a correct technical term in the psychology of memory.
    b   This is not a correct technical term in the psychology of memory.
    c   *Correct! See page 264.*
    d   This is not a correct technical term in the psychology of memory.

9   *a*   *Correct! See page 265.*
    b   No, because you didn't make a special effort to remember it.
    c   No, because you remember other things about the party.
    d   No, because no related memories interfered.

10 a   No, because there was nothing threatening about the name or the professor.
    b   *Correct! See page 265.*
    c   No, because you didn't receive a blow or damage to the brain.
    d   No, because related memories did not interfere with remembering the professor's name.

11 a   That would be repression.
    b   That would be interference.
    c   *Correct! See page 265.*
    d   That would be poor retrieval cues.

12 a   Intelligence was not a variable in this research.
    b   Forgetting perhaps, but not *mis*-remembering.
    c   Forgetting perhaps, but not *mis*-remembering.
    d   *Correct! See page 265.*

13 a   This is retroactive interference.
    b   There is no evidence that this occurs in memory.
    c   *Correct! See page 266.*
    d   This is a nonsense statement.

14 *a*   *Correct! See page 266.*
    b   There is no evidence that this occurs in memory.
    c   This is proactive interference.
    d   This is a nonsense statement.

15 a   False memories refer to things you never knew.
    b   Source misattribution refers to a memory error.
    c   State-dependent learning refers to a situation that aids remembering.
    d   *Correct! See page 267.*

16 a   Sounds more like tip-of-the-tongue phenomenon.
    b   *Correct! See page 267.*
    c   Sounds more like Freud's repression.
    d   It's just a joke! (Kind of lame, I admit!)

17 a   All three of these areas of the brain are involved in forming long-term memories.
    b   Neural assemblies are involved in the work of short-term memory.
    c   *Correct! See page 268.*
    d   Brain scans, valuable as they are, can't begin to approach such precision.

18 *a*   *Correct! See page 269.*
    b   State dependent learning refers to a situation that aids remembering. See page 267.
    c   Neural assemblies refer to short-term memory processes.
    d   Interference refers to situations that make remembering more difficult. See page 265.

19 a   The amygdala is involved in emotional memories.
    b   *Correct! See page 269.*
    c   LTP involves long-term, not short-term, memory.
    d   Just the opposite is true.

20   a   Practice alone, as in rote learning, is slow and difficult.
      b   *Correct! See page 271.*
      c   This is a possible learning strategy, but not the same as the methods in question.
      d   This is a possible motivational approach, not the same as the methods in question.

21   *a*   *Correct! See page 271.*
      b   On the contrary, it's the only thing that does help.
      c   Research says it doesn't.
      d   You wish!

22   a   Non-Aborigine objects were also used.
      b   It is the type of cue that is important, but the cues weren't auditory.
      c   The testing was not done outdoors.
      d   *Correct! See page 272.*

23   a   There is no such research finding.
      b   *Correct! See page 273.*
      c   There is no such research finding.
      d   There is no such research finding.

24   a   What about eyewitnesses with nothing to gain or lose?
      b   An eyewitness can be completely confident . . . and also mistaken.
      c   *Correct! See page 274.*
      d   What about eyewitnesses with no apparent biases either way?

25   *a*   *Correct! See page 275.*
      b   On TV shows they still use it!
      c   That is a deceptive sales technique in business.
      d   This is not an actual term in psychology.

Short Essay (sample answers)

1. Network theory is the currently most popular model for how we file and organize memories. According to this theory, we store related ideas in separate categories or memory files called nodes. Through associations, we link thousands of nodes into a gigantic interconnected network. We can navigate through the network because the nodes are organized in hierarchies around specific topics or categories. We work our way up or down through the appropriate network hierarchy, from concrete to more specific to abstract information.

2. There are four main reasons for forgetting. Repression is Freud's idea that emotionally threatening or anxiety-producing information is buried in the unconscious. Poor retrieval cues are failures to make useful associations during encoding. Interference is caused by related information blocking recall. Amnesia is the temporary or permanent loss of memories caused by a blow or brain damage. A fifth possible reason for forgetting is distortion caused by bias or suggestibility, which interferes with the accuracy of remembering.

3. Becoming aware of memory dynamics, like why we remember and forget, and learning mnemonic strategies, like the method of loci and the peg method, may be of some help in becoming a more successful student. But the main lesson is that better long-term memory is made up of good encoding through powerful retrieval cues. Forming vivid mental images or creating associations between new information and information we already know sets the stage for effective retrieval of information when it is needed.

4. The test involved remembering where objects had been placed on a board divided into 20 squares. Aborigine adolescents did better than white Australian adolescents. The task capitalized on traditional Aborigine culture and learning, which emphasizes reliance on visual retrieval cues for survival in a harsh desert environment. On the other hand, white adolescents, raised in an industrial culture, did better on tests that emphasized verbal learning cues.

5. Research shows that, through repeated suggestions, obviously false memories (getting one's hand caught in a mousetrap and having to go to the hospital to have it removed!) can be implanted in children's minds. Apparently, both district attorneys and psychotherapists were convinced of the accuracy of such wildly false memories, with harmful consequences to those involved. Legal authorities must be aware that children can become convinced that false memories are true; psychotherapists must be careful not to encourage them.

Module 13

Intelligence

The Social Psychology of Psychology

Perhaps no single topic reveals the interconnectedness of psychology and society more clearly than the complicated issue of intelligence. Delineating the nature and quality of human thought, captured in the concept of intelligence, has always been a primary goal of psychology. Yet few other subjects have entangled the science of psychology more controversially in the needs and passions of society.

Few would argue the importance of addressing the special needs of the super bright and the severely retarded. It seems obvious that something real is going on in both cases. But what about the rest of us, the great majority? How real are the differences among us that psychology measures with such precision, and, until recently, with such confidence? Questions like these evoke the central question of the social sciences.

The Nature-Nurture Debate in the Social Sciences

Heredity or environment? Personality or experience? Are we best explained by reference to our nature (what is built in) or to our nurture (how we are raised)? This is the essence of the nature-nurture debate, an old argument over basic assumptions that continues to rage in the social sciences. Two controversies illustrate the nature-nurture debate: (1) How important is what we inherit (genetics) compared to what we experience (learning)? (2) To what extent can we control our thoughts, feelings, and actions (free will) compared to control over us by outside forces (determinism).

You will find echoes of the nature-nurture debate in almost everything you read about psychological research and theory. Your basic orientation toward nature or nurture will influence what major theories in psychology you find most convincing, what giants of psychology you like and dislike, what research you believe or doubt, and even what "facts" you accept or reject. Whenever you come across an idea in psychology that arouses your strong interest, whether positive or negative, try examining the idea from the perspective of the nature-nurture debate. Odds are, the idea strongly supports or challenges your basic assumptions about life.

In the long run, thoughtful study of psychology will drive us more and more toward a middle position, an 'interactionist' point of view that sees humans as products of the interplay of heredity and environment, individual uniqueness and group pressure, rational choice and force of habit. Still, I am willing to bet that most of us will continue to feel the pull of our basic adherence either to the argument of nature or the argument of nurture.

Effective Student Tip 13

Risk a New Idea

You didn't come to college to stay the same. You intend to be a better and more fully developed person when you leave. You hope to grow in many ways, and one of the most important is mental. Intellectual growth requires a spirit of openness to change, of willingness to risk new ideas.

If you don't try out a new idea in college, you probably never will. As time goes on, work, family, and responsibility all conspire to make most of us more cautious and more conservative. Never again will you encounter as many new and different ideas as in college. In one sense, the very mission of colleges and universities is to hit us with new ideas. If everything was dandy just the way it is now, we really wouldn't need colleges and universities.

When a professor or student throws out a challenging idea, seriously consider whether it might be true. If true, how would it change what you believe? If false, how do your own beliefs disprove it?

Accepting intellectual challenges will strengthen your ideas and your ability to defend them. You might even solve a problem you have been puzzling over. Most of the time, however, you will augment and improve your understanding of the world and yourself only slightly. This is a great victory. We call it growth.

Your response...

What startling new idea have you encountered recently? What was your reaction to that idea?

Learning Objectives

1. Understand intelligence as an awesome set of skills and abilities that should serve to unite all humans but that have often divided and alienated us.

2. Learn how different definitions of intelligence have led to three different theories of what it is and how it affects our lives.

3. Explain how intelligence has been measured, how intelligence tests were developed, how IQ scores are distributed and used.

4. Appreciate the individual and social problems inherent in attempts to measure intelligence and use IQ scores in everything from education to employment.

5. Consider the fundamental importance of the nature-nurture question in psychology and the social sciences and attempt to determine where you stand on this issue.

6. Appreciate the subject of intelligence as an example of the complex interaction between science and culture, as illustrated by the social history of IQ tests and immigration.

7. Learn what psychological research suggests about the value of intervention programs like Head Start and whether they should be continued.

Key Terms

Understanding the controversies over intelligence will make these key terms easier to learn.

Binet-Simon Intelligence Scale
cultural bias
cultural-familial retardation
fraternal twins
Gardner's multiple-
   intelligence theory
gifted
heritability
identical twins
intelligence quotient

intervention program
mental age
mental retardation
nature-nurture question
non-intellectual factors
normal distribution
organic retardation
psychometric approach
psychometrics
reaction range

reliability
Sternberg's triarchic theory
two-factor theory (Spearman)
validity
Wechsler Adult Intelligence
   Scale (WAIS-III)
Wechsler Intelligence Scale for
   Children (WISC-III)

Outline

- *Introduction*
    1. Mirror, mirror, on the wall, who is the most intelligent of them all? (Five winners)
        a. How would you rank these five unusual people on intelligence?
        b. What were the reasons for your rankings?
    2. **Psychometrics** (Most intelligent?)

A. Defining Intelligence

1. Problem: definition

☐ Consider both the advantages and disadvantages of the following definitions of intelligence. Which theory makes the most sense to you?

2. Two-factor theory (Charles Spearman)

   a. **Psychometric approach**

   b. **Two-factor theory**

   c. Advantages and disadvantages

3. Multiple-intelligence theory (Howard Gardner)

   a. **Gardner's multiple-intelligence theory**

   b. Advantages and disadvantages

4. Triarchic theory (Robert Sternberg)

   a. **Sternberg's triarchic theory**

   b. Advantages and disadvantages

5. Current status

B. Measuring Intelligence

1. Earlier attempts to measure intelligence

   a. Head size and intelligence (Francis Galton)

   b. Brain size and intelligence (Paul Broca)

   c. Brain size and achievement

   d. Brain size, sex differences, and intelligence

   e. Measuring intelligence

2. Binet's breakthrough (Albert Binet)

   a. **Binet-Simon Intelligence Scale**

   b. **Mental age**: measure of intelligence

3. Formula for IQ (Lewis Terman)

☐ What is the essential difference between Binet's and Terman's approach to intelligence?

   a. **Intelligence quotient**

   b. Ratio IQ replaced by deviation IQ

4. Examples of IQ tests

   a. **Wechsler Adult Intelligence Scale (WAIS-III)**

   b. **Wechsler Intelligence Scale for Children (WISC-III)**

5. Two characteristics of tests

☐ The two terms below are absolutely essential to an understanding of science, and therefore to an appreciation of the basis of psychology. Can you define each term? Give an example of each?

   a. **Validity**

   b. **Reliability**

C. Distribution and Use of IQ Scores

1. **Normal distribution** of IQ scores
2. **Mental retardation**: IQ scores
   a. Borderline mentally retarded
   b. Mild/moderately mentally retarded
   c. Severely/profoundly mentally retarded
   d. Causes
      (1) **Organic retardation**
      (2) **Cultural-familial retardation**
3. Vast majority: IQ scores
   a. Do IQ scores predict academic achievement?
   b. Do IQ scores predict job performance?
4. Gifted: IQ scores
   a. **Gifted**
   b. How do gifted individuals turn out? (Lewis Terman)

D. Potential Problems of IQ Testing

1. Binet's two warnings
   a. Intelligence tests do not measure innate abilities or natural intelligence
   b. Intelligence tests, by themselves, should not be used to label people
2. Racial discrimination
   a. Definition of mental retardation
   b. Educational decisions
3. **Cultural bias**
4. Other cultures
5. **Non-intellectual factors**

E. Nature-Nurture Question

1. Definitions: the **nature-nurture question**
2. Twin studies
   a. **Fraternal twins** and **identical twins**
   b. Genetic factors
   c. Definition of intelligence
   d. Interaction of nature and nurture
   e. Interaction
3. Adoption studies

4. Interaction: nature and nurture

    a. **Heritability**

    b. **Reaction range**

5. Racial controversy (*The Bell Curve* by Richard Herrnstein and Charles Murray)

    a. Difference between IQ scores

    b. Cause of IQ differences

F. *Cultural Diversity: Races, IQs, and Immigration*

  1. Misuse of IQ tests

    a. Innate intelligence (Lewis Terman)

    b. Classifying races (Robert Yerkes)

  2. Immigration laws

    a. Immigration Law of 1924

    b. Mismeasurement examined (Stephen Jay Gould)

G. *Research Focus: New Approaches*

  1. Can genius be found in the brain?

  2. Can Spearman's "g" be found in the brain?

H. *Application: Intervention Programs*

  1. Definition of **intervention program**

    a. Abecedarian Project

    b. Head Start

  2. Raising IQ scores

  3. Need for intervention programs

The Language Workout Marathon

If you have been using Eric Bohman's "Language Workout" sections, you know how helpful they are. Eric also wrote a summary test so you can see how much you have learned.

Eric calls this special test "The Language Workout Marathon" (to suggest how far you have come!). It is in the Language Workout section of Module 25. Try it!

Language Workout

What's That?

p. 281 she **made a big stir** = caused excitement
in **classical music circles** = an informal group of people in the same profession

p. 283 **spatial** intelligence = ability to perceive differences in terms of space

p. 284 Efforts to measure intelligence began in **earnest** = with serious work
Galton **switched gears** = changed methods

p. 285 Binet was very **pessimistic** = doubtful
By a strange **twist of fate** = unexpected result

p. 286 on a **one-to-one basis** = one examiner with one student (not group)
from a **deprived** environment = without such things as money, home, food, etc.
rule out other cultural or educational problems = exclude

p. 287 this characteristic **makes or breaks** a test = decides the success of

p. 288 a greatly **impoverished** environment = very limited, without necessities

p. 289 labeled as **nerds** and **geeks** = unfashionable people, often working with computers
2% actually **flunked out** = left school because of bad grades

p. 290 considered a **dead end** = hopeless, with no hope of success
a **class action suit** = lawsuit with group of people suing one company
on behalf of = for the benefit of
people **of color** = non-white

p. 292 **written in stone** = cannot be changed, permanent

p. 296 a **meager** 13 years = very small number
unconstrained breeding = uncontrolled, unlimited
feebleminded = with weak mental ability
The **fair** peoples = with blond hair and light skin
congressmen **sought** a way = looked for (were seeking)
Yerkes's data were so **riddled** with errors = overloaded

p. 299 below the **poverty line** = standard of income that classifies people as poor or not-poor

p. 302 police have **seized** $700,000 = taken control of
he was **committed** to a state school = placed (by legal order)
that's a **sure thing** = a gambling term for a likely winning bet

Making Connections

We can use **which** to connect two sentences that have the same word in common:

Americans like to eat <u>fast food</u>. <u>Fast food</u> can be unhealthy.
Americans like to eat fast food, which can be unhealthy.

In the same way, we can use which to connect and to measure with words like **some**, **all**, **many**, or any number.

Marcella has a lot of <u>work</u> tonight. <u>Some of the work</u> is important.
Marcella has a lot of work tonight, some of which is important.

In this example, we replaced the subject of the second sentence, <u>some of the work</u>, with **some of which**. Notice how it is used in the text:

Along with using IQ scores to label individuals came racial and cultural discrimination, **some of which** continue to the present. (p. 290)

As the reader, we know that **some of which** in this sentence means that some racial and cultural discrimination still continues.

Try to connect the following sentences

Sharella bought a dozen eggs. Three of them were cracked.
Sharella _____.

The library has 85,000 books. Most of them are about technical subjects.
The library _____.

Did you remember to put in the comma after the first sentence? You need the comma to show that the two are connected, not joined into one.

Try some more:

Mr. and Mrs. Smith have a lot of problems. 90% of them can be solved.
Mr. and Mrs. Smith _____.

Chang-Woo had ten math problems to solve. All ten of them required a calculator.
Chang-Woo _____.

Now look at the following example:

Marcella has a lot of <u>work</u> tonight. She has finished <u>some of the work</u>.
Marcella has a lot of work tonight, **some of which** she has finished.

In this example, <u>some of the work</u> is the object of the sentence, but we can still replace it with **some of which**. The difference is that we have to move the word that connects to the first sentence (<u>some of the work</u>) to the beginning of the second sentence we are connecting.

Try to connect the following sentences:

Jenny has a lot of research to do. The professor wants all of it tomorrow.
Jenny _____.

Ernie wrote a 27-page paper. His dog ate half of it.
Ernie _____.

Marco read 135 pages of the textbook. He remembered none of it the next morning.
Marco _____.

Answers

Sharella bought a dozen eggs, **three of which** were cracked.
The library has 85,000 books, **most of which** are about technical subjects.
Mr. and Mrs. Smith have a lot of problems, **90% of which** can be solved.
Chang-Woo had ten math problems to solve, **all ten of which** required a calculator.
Jenny has a lot of research to do, **all of which** the professor wants tomorrow.
Ernie wrote a 27-page paper, **half of which** his dog ate.
Marco read 135 pages of the textbook, **none of which** he remembered the next morning.

The Big Picture

Which statement below offers the best summary of the larger significance of this module?

A   Intelligence is a real dimension along which people do vary, but it must be measured and used with great sensitivity because we do not know with certainty how it is formed and how it influences a person's life.

B   From Binet to the present, psychology has refined the measurement of intelligence to a degree of precision where IQ scores can and should be used in a wide variety of personal and social decisions.

C   Psychology has wasted great energy and resources pursuing the nature-nurture question, when it should have been obvious all along that we get our smarts from an irreversible throw of the genetic dice.

D   The measurement of intelligence has been so riddled with bias and discrimination that most psychologists are ready to abandon the concept of intelligence altogether.

E   My psych instructor must think I'm real stoopid. She just handed out a page of questions and thought I wouldn't notice there are no answers on it!

True-False

_____   1. The key issue in defining intelligence is whether it is essentially cognitive abilities or a combination of cognitive abilities and other skills.

_____   2. It is generally true that the larger the brain the more intelligent the person.

_____   3. Alfred Binet gave us the concept of an intelligence quotient (IQ).

_____   4. Lewis Terman's formula for determining IQ was mental age divided by chronological age times 100.

_____   5. If you use a precise doctor's scale in an attempt to measure your intelligence, your results will be reliable, but not valid.

_____   6. As a result of protest movements, the major intelligence tests are now independent of culture.

_____   7. Twin studies suggest that we inherit only a small percentage of our intelligence.

_____   8. Adoption studies suggest that environment plays a significant role in determining intelligence.

_____   9. Measurements of intelligence have been used to support racial and ethnic discrimination.

_____   10. Research shows that intervention programs like Head Start, while well meaning, have few long-term benefits.

Flashcards 1

_____ 1. Binet-Simon Intelligence Scale

_____ 2. Gardner's multiple-intelligence theory

_____ 3. intelligence quotient

_____ 4. mental age

_____ 5. nature-nurture question

_____ 6. psychometrics

_____ 7. reliability

_____ 8. Sternberg's triarchic theory

_____ 9. two-factor theory

_____ 10. validity

a. says intelligence is three skills — analytical thinking, problem solving, practical thinking

b. says there can be at least seven different kinds of intelligence: verbal, musical, logical, spatial, body…

c. estimating intellectual progress by comparing child's score on an IQ test to average children of same age

d. computed by dividing a child's mental age (MA) by the child's chronological age (CA) then times 100

e. degree to which a test measures what it is supposed to measure

f. says that intelligence is based on a general mental abilities factor (g) plus specific mental abilities (s)

g. asks how much genetic and environmental factors each contribute to the development of intelligence

h. area of psychology concerned with developing tests that assess abilities, skills, beliefs, and traits

i. consistency; a person's test score on a test at one time should be similar to score on a similar test later

j. first intelligence test; items of increasing difficulty measured vocabulary, memory, common knowledge

Flashcards 2

_____ 1. cultural bias

_____ 2. gifted

_____ 3. heritability

_____ 4. intervention program

_____ 5. mental retardation

_____ 6. non-intellectual factors

_____ 7. psychometric approach

_____ 8. normal distribution

_____ 9. organic retardation

_____ 10. reaction range

a. substantial limitation in functioning characterized by sub-average intellectual functioning, other limits

b. question wording and background experiences more familiar to some social groups than to others

c. measures or quantifies cognitive abilities or factors that are thought to be involved in intellectual performance

d. extent to which traits, abilities, or IQ scores increase or decrease as result of interaction with environment

e. a statistical arrangement of scores so that they resemble the shape of a bell; the bell shaped curve

f. amount or proportion of some ability, characteristic, or trait that can be attributed to genetic factors

g. impressive cognitive abilities; moderate defined by IQ scores of 130 to 150, profoundly by 180 and above

h. factors such as attitude, experience, and emotional functioning that may help or hinder performance on tests

i. creates environment that offers more opportunities for intellectual, social, personal development

j. mental deficits resulting from genetic problems or brain damage

Multiple-Choice

_____ 1. Rod Plotnik challenged you to rank five unusual people according to intelligence to show that
   a. although Bill Gates dropped out of Harvard, he is clearly the smartest of the group
   b. intelligence is related to gender, race, and social class
   c. although they were all high achievers, only Steve Lu had truly high intelligence (IQ 194)
   d. intelligence could be defined in several different ways

_____ 2. Solving scientific puzzles like the one above is the goal of a branch of psychology called
   a. genetics
   b. psychometrics
   c. twin studies
   d. psychodynamics

_____ 3. Charles Spearman's two-factor theory says that intelligence is a
   a. general factor (g) plus specific mental abilities (s)
   b. group of separate and equally important mental abilities
   c. set of processes for solving problems
   d. combination of biological functions of the brain and nervous system

_____ 4. An advantage of both Howard Gardner's multiple-intelligence theory and Robert Sternberg's triarchic theory is that they
   a. yield a single score that is useful for predicting academic performance
   b. measure each of the five known areas of intelligence
   c. take into account abilities not covered by standard IQ tests
   d. define intelligence in a way that is completely free of cultural influence

_____ 5. _____ theory would best take account of Serena William's tennis and Midori's music achievements
   a. Spearman's two factor theory of intelligence
   b. Gardner's multiple-intelligence theory of intelligence
   c. Sternberg's triarchic theory of intelligence
   d. Gates' "wealth rules" theory of intelligence

_____ 6. All of the following _except_ _____ size have been proposed as indications of intelligence
   a. head
   b. skull
   c. brain
   d. neuron

_____ 7. The first intelligence test was devised by
   a. Charles Spearman
   b. Louis Terman
   c. Alfred Binet
   d. Howard Gardner

_____ 8. The original purpose of Binet's Intelligence Scale was to
    a. differentiate children of normal intelligence from those who needed extra help
    b. identify specially gifted children who could benefit from government scholarships
    c. isolate those children who were so slow nothing would help them
    d. replace the much criticized SAT in college admissions

_____ 9. The formula for computing IQ (developed by Lewis Terman) is
    a. level of schooling divided by actual age
    b. mental age divided by chronological age times 100
    c. test score divided by grade in school plus 100
    d. chronological age divided by mental age

_____ 10. The most widely used intelligence test for adults is the
    a. Wechsler Adult Intelligence Scale (WAIS-III)
    b. Binet-Simon Intelligence Scale
    c. Gardner Multiple Tasks Scale
    d. Sternberg Triarchic Scale

_____ 11. Ten times your sister jumps on the scale and ten times it reads 115 pounds. "Wow," she exclaims, "I'm taller than the average American woman!" Her results are
    a. both reliable and valid
    b. neither reliable nor valid
    c. reliable, but not valid
    d. valid, but not reliable

_____ 12. If you measured the intelligence of everyone in the United States, a distribution of all the scores would look like a
    a. curve sloping gently upward to the right
    b. bell-shaped curve
    c. flat horizon line with a skyscraper in the middle
    d. curve that rises and falls at regular intervals

_____ 13. Research suggests that gifted children, like those in Terman's famous study, grow up to be
    a. not as greatly different from other children as high intelligence might predict
    b. plagued by the mental instability that goes with high intelligence
    c. much lonelier, sadder, and more eccentric than average
    d. far more healthy, happy, and successful than children of average intelligence

_____ 14. The problem with IQ tests is that they are
    a. completely free of cultural bias
    b. seldom used to get children into the right classes in school
    c. sometimes used to label people and discriminate against them
    d. unable to predict how well a child will do in school

_____ 15. In intelligence testing, cultural bias refers to
    a. whether tests are both valid and reliable
    b. intellectual factors like honors classes and high IQ
    c. distrust of non-western cultures
    d. how questions are worded and what experiences they are based on

_____ 16. Attitudes, experience, and emotions that may help or hinder performance on tests are called
   a. cognitive factors
   b. invalidating variables
   c. nonintellectual factors
   d. racial variables

_____ 17. In the matter of intelligence, the answer to the nature-nurture question is that
   a. twin studies prove the predominance of nurture
   b. adoption studies prove the predominance of nature
   c. intervention programs show that intelligence is fixed at birth
   d. both nature and nurture contribute about equally to the formation of intelligence

_____ 18. Twin studies suggest that intelligence is
   a. about 90% inherited
   b. only slightly influenced by heredity
   c. about 50% determined by genetics
   d. a random phenomenon unaffected by heredity

_____ 19. Adoption studies suggest that intelligence
   a. can be positively affected by improved environmental conditions
   b. is essentially fixed at birth by heredity
   c. is lessened by the loss of one's biological parents
   d. does not change much, regardless of family environment

_____ 20. The _____ indicates the extent to which traits, abilities, or IQ scores may increase or decrease as a result of interaction with environmental factors
   a. nurture rating
   b. genetic research index
   c. heritability factor
   d. reaction range

_____ 21. One problem with the racial conclusions drawn by the authors of _The Bell Curve_ is that
   a. Blacks and Whites consistently score the same on intelligence tests
   b. the APA prohibits collecting data about race in research on intelligence
   c. skin color is not reliable in identifying racial makeup
   d. Richard Herrnstein and Charles Murray did not say IQ differences were genetic

_____ 22. The story of IQ tests and immigration shows that
   a. good research can be used for bad purposes
   b. scientific research often reflects the prejudices of the times
   c. good research can be used to right injustice
   d. scientific research is politically neutral

_____ 23. Can genius, such as Einstein possessed, be found in the brain?
   a. yes, because studies of Einstein's brain show enlarged areas (compared to the average brain)
   b. no, because genius is composed of variables that can't be measured scientifically
   c. possibly, but as yet neuroscience cannot answer this question
   d. unlikely, because once a person is deceased the brain can no longer be studied

_____ 24. Studies of the effectiveness of intervention programs like Head Start suggest that
   a. however well-intentioned, intervention programs don't work
   b. there are many social needs and benefits that justify continuing these programs
   c. the short-term benefits fail to justify the high costs of these programs
   d. the main benefits of these programs go to the middle-class professionals they employ

_____ 25. When you look back at how you rated the intelligence of the five unusual people described on the first page of this module, you might well conclude that intelligence is
   a. a topic that can offend, but people should just get over it
   b. like politics and religion, a subject that is beyond scientific discussion
   c. a topic psychology would be better off to drop
   d. one of the most complicated and controversial topics in psychology

Short Essay

1. Why is "intelligence" so difficult to define and measure?

2. Describe the main theories of intelligence and how they differ.

3. Why have IQ scores been criticized as a faulty invention of psychology?

4. Why are psychologists who investigate intelligence so interested in studying twins and adopted children?

5. Intervention programs, like Head Start, are well intentioned, but also costly and of limited effectiveness in raising IQ scores. Should such programs be ended, or continued and even expanded?

Test-Taking Tips 5

More hints:

- Trust your common knowledge and don't choose an answer that is obviously not the way the world really works.

- Often the question itself contains a strong hint about the right answer.

Answers for Module 13

The Big Picture (explanations provided for incorrect choices)

A *Correct! You see the "big picture" for this Module.*
B Despite improvements in the measurement of IQ, applying IQ scores to practical decisions is far from easy or obvious. Psychologists are not yet agreed on exactly what IQ is, or how to use it.
C Think about all the research on how environmental conditions can affect IQ.
D Not true. Most psychologists believe the concept is valid, but must be defined more carefully.
E It's just a joke!

True-False (explanations provided for False choices; page numbers given for all choices)

1	T	282	
2	F	284	Brain size has no practical relation to intelligence.
3	F	285	The mathematical intelligence quotient was devised by Lewis Terman.
4	T	285	
5	T	287	
6	F	291	Every intelligence test is affected by culture, but most are now free of obvious cultural bias.
7	F	292	Twin studies suggest that we inherit up to 50 percent of our intelligence.
8	T	293	
9	T	296	
10	F	298	Research finds long-term benefits, although perhaps not as many as program advocates hoped for.

Flashcards 1

1 j   2 b   3 d   4 c   5 g   6 h   7 i   8 a   9 f   10 e

Flashcards 2

1 b   2 g   3 f   4 i   5 a   6 h   7 c   8 e   9 j   10 d

Multiple-Choice (explanations provided for incorrect choices)

1 a He is fabulously wealthy, but does that prove he is the most intelligent?
   b These five accomplished people would seem to disprove that notion.
   c He has an incredibly high measured IQ, but does that prove he is "smarter" than the others?
   d Correct! See page 281.

2 a Genetics refers to the biology of inheritance.
   b Correct! See page 281.
   c Twin studies are a specific strategy for studying intelligence.
   d Psychodynamics refers to the psychoanalytic method pioneered by Sigmund Freud.

3 *a Correct! See page 282.*
   b Check the name of Spearman's theory again.
   c Check the name of Spearman's theory again.
   d Psychometricians study how intelligence works more than its biological components.

4 a Both theories see intelligence as several abilities.
   b Psychologists do not agree that there are exactly five areas of intelligence.
   c Correct! See page 283.
   d Since all measures of intelligence are based on language and experience, none is independent of culture.

5 a Spearman's theory emphasizes mental abilities.
   b Correct! See page 283.
   c Sternberg's theory emphasizes three different kinds of reasoning processes.
   d This connection of wealth and intelligence isn't really serious, but we often act like it is.

6 a There is no significant relationship between head size and intelligence.
   b There is no significant relationship between skull size and intelligence.
   c There is no significant relationship between brain size and intelligence.
   d Correct! See page 284.

7 a   Spearman is known for his definition of intelligence.
   b   Terman invented the concept of the Intelligence Quotient (IQ).
   c   *Correct! See page 285.*
   d   Gardner is a contemporary psychologist with a new theory of intelligence.

8 *a*   *Correct! See·page 285.*
   b   That's the point — giftedness wasn't an original focus of intelligence testing.
   c   That's the point — discrimination wasn't an original focus of intelligence testing.
   d   Hint: think early twentieth-century France!

9 a   This is close to Binet's formula for mental age.
   b   *Correct! See page 285.*
   c   This is a nonsense formula.
   d   Then lower numbers would indicate higher intelligence.

10 *a*   *Correct! See page 286.*
   b   This was the original intelligence test, now replaced by the Stanford-Binet test.
   c   Gardner has not developed a generally accepted overall intelligence test.
   d   Sternberg has not been able to develop a test that works according to his theory.

11 a   This is half right (check the definition of valid).
   b   This is half right (check the definition of reliable).
   c   *Correct! See page 287.*
   d   A valid test measures what it is supposed to measure.

12 a   Would that mean most people have very high intelligence?
   b   *Correct! See page 288.*
   c   Would this mean almost everyone has the same intelligence?
   d   Such a curve would show changes over time, not absolute amounts.

13 *a*   *Correct! See page 289.*
   b   Mental instability does not go with high intelligence.
   c   If anything, it tends to be the opposite.
   d   Sounds logical, but the differences are not great.

14 a   Even if true, how would that be a problem?
   b   They are often used for this purpose (but how fairly does it work?)
   c   *Correct! See page 290.*
   d   IQ tests do predict school success to some extent.

15 a   Validity might be indirectly involved, but not reliability.
   b   *Non*-intellectual factors can be involved, but not these intellectual factors.
   c   It is not distrust, but failure to take account of cultural differences that is a problem.
   d   *Correct! See page 291.*

16 a   *Non*-cognitive factors might have been somewhat correct.
   b   This is not an actual term in psychology.
   c   *Correct! See page 291.*
   d   Some of these factors may involve race, but most do not.

17 a   Twin studies have strengthened the nature side, but they have not ended the debate.
   b   Adoption studies have strengthened the nurture side, but they have not ended the debate.
   c   Intervention programs strengthen the nurture side, but they do not end the debate.
   d   *Correct! See page 292.*

18 a   If this were true, many of our democratic ideas might have to change.
   b   Twin studies suggest just the opposite.
   c   *Correct! See page 292.*
   d   Twin studies suggest just the opposite.

19 *a*   *Correct! See page 293.*
   b   Adoption studies suggest just the opposite.
   c   Adopted children do not suffer drops in intelligence.
   d   Adoption studies do show changes in intelligence.

20 a   Sounds right, but this is not a correct term in psychology.
    b   It wouldn't be genetic research as much as environmental research.
    c   Heritability is the amount of some ability, characteristic, or trait that can be attributed to genetic factors.
    d   Correct! See page 293.

21 a   There are racial differences in IQ scores — the question is why.
    b   It does not.
    c   Correct! See page 294.
    d   That is exactly what they said.

22 a   In this case, neither the research nor the purpose was good.
    b   Correct! See page 296.
    c   In this case, research contributed to injustice.
    d   This research had a definite, and deplorable, political purpose.

23 a   But are those areas the key ones, and are they enlarged in other geniuses?
    b   It is complicated, but science has the potential to measure anything that can be defined objectively.
    c   Correct! See page 297.
    d   There are many studies that can be conducted on preserved brains (like Einstein's).

24 a   Definite benefits have been identified — the question is cost and long-range effectiveness.
    b   Correct! See page 298.
    c   The short-term benefits probably do justify the costs.
    d   This cynical view is not supported by the research.

25 a   No one needs to accept being offended, and psychology should take care not to do so.
    b   No subject should be beyond careful and sensitive scientific investigation.
    c   As a science, psychology must pursue the truth wherever it leads.
    d   Correct! See page 281.

Short Essay (sample answers)

1. Rod Plotnik introduced us to five unusual people. Each of them is accomplished, but in different ways. Could we devise a single test that would show just how they differ from others? Wouldn't a test that showed any of them as "average" be untrue to their special abilities? How could their different talents be reduced to a single score that would correctly place them in a hierarchy of all people? Finally, how would we take account of both the inherited characteristics and unique experiences that went into making them who they are?

2. There are three main theories of intelligence. The traditional definition, entirely cognitive, is Charles Spearman's two-factor theory, in which there is a general mental ability factor (g) plus many specific mental abilities. A broader idea of intelligence is Howard Gardner's multiple-intelligence theory, in which there are at least seven different kinds of intelligence, not all cognitive. Finally, Robert Sternberg's triarchic theory bases intelligence on analytical thinking skills, problem-solving skills, and practical thinking skills.

3. IQ scores can be harmful. Alfred Binet sought to identify children who needed special help. But when Lewis Terman invented a numerical score to summarize intelligence, IQ scores became labels with the power to glorify or stigmatize individuals and whole groups. Examples of the misuse of IQ scores range from the Immigration Act of 1924 to the misplacement of minority children in remedial classes. Intelligence tests themselves have been shown to contain cultural bias in their wording or the experiences they reflect.

4. Intelligence may be the best example of the nature-nurture question. How much comes from heredity and how much from environmental experience? It is very difficult to separate out these variables in individual cases. But twins, exactly (identical) or strongly (fraternal) alike in heredity, and children adopted into different circumstances, constitute a natural experiment in the effects of nature and nurture. Twins can be compared to each other and adopted children can be compared to their siblings and natural parents.

5. The aim of the original intervention program was to give disadvantaged children a "head start" by providing early IQ-raising experiences that would help them later in school. But initial increases in IQ did not last after children left the program. Still, follow-up research shows other long-term benefits. Take account of these facts in your answer about ending or extending these programs. You might also refer to the current social and economic needs of many people, as well as the budget constraints faced by governmental agencies.

Module 14

Thought & Language

Can We Study Ourselves Scientifically?

Historians of science have pointed out that the accumulation of human knowledge seems backwards. We understood the far-away phenomena of astronomy centuries ago, gradually grasped the principles of physics and biology in modern times, but only now are beginning to penetrate the mysteries of the brain and the mind. The closer we are to something, the harder it is to study it objectively. Add to this difficulty an even greater one — we *are* the very thing we want to study. Natural scientists say this problem alone dooms the social sciences to be inherently subjective and therefore not really scientific. Social scientists disagree, of course, but they admit that being objective about ourselves presents enormous challenges.

Processes That Make Us Human

As an animal lover, I welcome every discovery of animals engaging in behavior (like tool-using) previously thought to be the exclusive property of *Homo sapiens*. Those of us who observe animals in the wild know they communicate very effectively. New research shows that elephants communicate at a decibel level we can't even hear. Still, is it really language? (See Rod Plotnik's fascinating review of whether apes can acquire language.)

In our efforts to win greater respect for the rights and inherent value of other animals, some of us argue that we humans aren't so different and shouldn't consider ourselves morally superior. Nevertheless, we have to admit that humans have strikingly unique skills and abilities in three areas that perhaps define our species. We have unmatched intellectual potential, unrivaled flexibility in exploiting that potential, and a system of communication that preserves and extends those mental powers. In this module, Rod Plotnik continues the story of these quintessential human properties, helping us appreciate how interrelated they are.

Science is never easy, however. We all know what thought and language are, yet how do we describe and explain them? Our own subjective experience seems to get in the way of objective understanding. We have to fight for every piece of knowledge. Further complicating matters is the sad fact that science is not always neutral. In the previous module, Rod Plotnik described times in our history when racial prejudice distorted the measurement of intelligence. After weighing all the evidence on whether other primates can acquire language, most psychologists have concluded that, however remarkable, the linguistic abilities of apes are not true language. So says science. Or is it our human prejudice?

Effective Student Tip 14

What Can You Do?

Some students freeze up when they get an assignment, fearing that, unless they instantly know what to do and how to do it, they're dead. The solution, if only they realized it, is right at hand. One of the best ways to tackle a new challenge is to draw on what you already do well. Step away from the course for a moment. What can you do competently right now?

Perhaps your work relates to the course (a business student at a bank, or a psychology student in a day-care center). Your experiences and observations would make great examples to use in class discussion or in written reports. Most professors delight in having students relate the subject matter of the course to the realities of the working world. If you learned how to operate a word processor at work, can you use it after hours to prepare papers so beautiful they will knock your professor's socks off? If you are an athlete, can you use your knowledge of effective training techniques to work out a schedule for gradually building up your academic skills?

You only start from square one once, and that was years ago. By now you have acquired many competencies, some quite special. Don't hesitate to use them.

Your response...

What are you really good at? Could that skill be used in your schoolwork? (Don't say "no" too quickly!)

Learning Objectives

1. Understand thought and language as related achievements that make humans the most adaptive and accomplished species on earth.

2. Learn the basic mechanisms of concept formation, problem solving, and creativity.

3. Learn the four basic rules that define language and the four basic stages in acquiring language.

4. Explain how thought and language are united in two kinds of reasoning.

5. Understand dyslexia as an illustration of the difficult skill of reading.

6. Consider your position on the role of cultural and gender influences on thinking.

7. Review the research on the controversy over whether animals have language.

Key Terms

Oh, oh... another tough set of key terms. This module covers two areas of psychology, thought and language, which are related but also separate and complete fields of study in their own right. Both are complicated and offer some highly technical facts and concepts [that's one of the terms]. Buckle down!

algorithms
analogy
availability heuristic
babbling
basic rules of grammar
Chomsky's theory of language
cognitive approach
communication
concept
convergent thinking
creative individual
creative thinking
critical language period
deductive reasoning
deep structure
divergent thinking
dyslexia

environmental language
  factors
exemplar model
functional fixedness
grammar
heuristics
inductive reasoning
innate language factors
insight
language
language stages
morpheme
morphology
overgeneralization
parentese (motherese)
phonemes
phonology

problem solving
prototype theory
reasoning
savants
semantics
sentences
single words
social cognitive learning
subgoals
surface structure
syntax or grammar
telegraphic speech
theory of linguistic relativity
thinking
transformational rules
two-word combinations
word

Outline

- *Introduction*
    1. Concepts (4-year-old Jeff)
    2. Creativity (Gordon Parks)
    3. **Cognitive approach** (Information processing)
        a. **Thinking**
        b. **Language**

A. *Forming Concepts*
    1. **Concept**
    ☐ "Concept" is another of those deceptively simple common terms. Can you define it formally?
    2. **Exemplar model** — problems
        a. Too many features
        b. Too many exceptions
    3. **Prototype theory** — advantages
        a. Average features
        b. Quick recognition
    4. Early formation
    5. Categories in the brain
    6. Functions of concepts
        a. Organize information
        b. Avoid relearning

B. *Solving Problems*
    1. **Problem solving**
    2. Different ways of thinking
        a. **Algorithms**
        b. **Heuristics (availability heuristic)**
        c. Artificial intelligence
    3. Three strategies for solving problems
        a. Changing one's mental set
            (1) **Functional fixedness**
            (2) **Insight**
        b. Using an **analogy**
        c. Forming **subgoals**

C. *Thinking Creatively*

   1. How is creativity defined?

☐   Do you consider yourself a creative person? How do you express your creativity?

      a. **Creative thinking**

      b. **Creative individual**

      c. Psychometric approach

         (1) **Convergent thinking**

         (2) **Divergent thinking**

      d. Case study approach

      e. Cognitive approach

   2. Is IQ related to creativity (**savants**)?

   3. How do creative people think and behave?

      a. Focus

      b. Cognition

      c. Personality

      d. Motivation

   4. Is creativity related to mental disorders?

D. *Language: Basic Rules*

   1. **Language**

      a. **Word**

      b. **Grammar**

   2. Four rules of language

      a. **Phonology** and **phonemes**

      b. **Morphology** and **morpheme**

      c. **Syntax** or **grammar**

      d. **Semantics**

   3. Understanding language (Noam Chomsky)

      a. Mental grammar

      b. Innate program

   4. Different structure, same meaning

      a. **Surface structure**

      b. **Deep structure**

      c. **Transformational rules**

      d. **Chomsky's theory of language**

E. *Acquiring Language*

   1. Four stages in acquiring language (**language stages**)

      a. **Babbling**

      b. **Single words** and **parentese (motherese)**

      c. **Two-word combinations**

      d. **Sentences**

         (1) **Telegraphic speech**

         (2) **Basic rules of grammar**

         (3) **Overgeneralization**

      e. Going through the stages

   2. Learning a particular language

      a. What are innate factors?

         (1) **Innate language factors**

         (2) **Critical language period**

      b. What are environmental factors?

         (1) **Environmental language factors**

         (2) **Social cognitive learning**

F. *Reason, Thought, & Language*

   1. Two kinds of **reasoning**

      a. **Deductive reasoning**

      b. **Inductive reasoning**

   2. Why reasoning fails

   3. Words and thoughts: **theory of linguistic relativity** (Benjamin Whorf)

      a. Inuit versus American words for snow

      b. Thinking in two languages

G. *Research Focus: Dyslexia*

   1. What kind of problem is **dyslexia**?

   2. Cognitive approach plus physiological approach

      a. What's involved in reading?

         (1) Phoneme (sound) producer

         (2) Word analyzer

         (3) Automatic detector

      b. Why can't dyslexics read?

      c. Can training help?

H. Cultural Diversity: Influences on Thinking

1. Differences in thinking

2. Male-female differences

   a. Men and women use language differently (Deborah Tannen)

   b. Brains process words differently

I. Application: Do Animals Have Language?

1. Criteria for **language** (**communication**)

☐ What is the difference between *communication* and *language*?

   a. Learning a set of abstract symbols

   b. Using abstract symbols to express thoughts

   c. Learning complex rules of grammar

   d. Generate an endless number of meaningful sentences

2. Dolphins (Louis Herman)

3. Gorilla and chimpanzee

   a. Koko (Francine Patterson)

   b. Washoe (Beatrice and Allan Gardner)

   c. Criticisms (Herbert Terrace)

4. Bonobo chimp: star pupil

   a. Kanzi (Sue Savage-Rumbaugh)

   b. "Language" gene (FOXP2)

Language Workout

What's That?

p. 305   No one thought Parks would **amount to much** = be successful
He was **out on the streets** at age 15 = living alone (without family)
you're gonna be **porters** = laborers who carry luggage or packages
worst of all, **lynchings** = illegal hangings (murders)
That man didn't want to **take me on** = take responsibility for me
lived in **flophouses** = cheap hotels

p. 306   would **tax** the best of memories = be difficult for

p. 308   **novices** become too focused = newcomers
Heuristics are **rules of thumb** = quick rules

p. 309   the sudden **grasp** of a solution = understanding

p. 310   a time of **segregation** = forced separation of different races in public

p. 311   **unconventional** = outside ordinary behavior
their creative **fires are fueled** = energies are powered, stimulated
achieved creative **breakthroughs** = new solutions

p. 312   A word is an **arbitrary** pairing = random, without a reason

p. 315   shows **warmth** = friendly, loving quality

p. 316   father **strapped** her to a potty chair = tied
period of social deprivation **left its mark** = had long-lasting effects

p. 318   there is only one correct conclusion to **draw** = make
provided you're aware of their **pitfalls** = weak points
it often **runs counter to** our experiences = opposes, goes against

p. 319   Whorf's story **lives on** = continues (is not forgotten)
very **temperamental** = moody, sensitive, unpredictable

p. 322   the answer **hinges on** the difference = depends on
to **probe** the sea = explore, investigate
Frisbee = plastic disk used in game

p. 326   **singsong crooning** = making sounds with definite rhythm (like singing a song)
patronizing **gibberish** = nonsense words

Build Your Word Power

You have probably noticed the shorter **in**, **im** or **ex** at the beginnings of words. They are similar in meaning to the longer **Intro**, meaning inward, and **extro**, meaning outward, that you met in the Language Workout for Module 8. See if you can provide the missing definitions.

Example: **intrinsic** means coming from inside, while **extrinsic** means coming from outside.

   internal means inside, while **external** means _____.
   include means _____ ,while **exclude** meets to not put in.
   import means to bring into the country, while **export** means _____.
   implicit means _____, while **explicit** means clearly stated.

What's the Difference?

As Plotnik explains on p. 313, most of us can see the difference between **active** sentences ("You picked up a caterpillar") and **passive** sentences ("A caterpillar was picked up by you"). But how can we choose which one to use? It depends on the focus of your sentence, the main subject.

Most sentences are active: someone does/did something. For example: **Darwin wrote the first book about evolution.** So, if your focus is Darwin, his many actions and achievements, then you will want to keep Darwin **active** in your sentence: you will have the person writing.

On the other hand, sometimes you will want to write about an object. For example: **The first book about evolution was written by Darwin.**

If your focus is evolution, the development and importance of the idea, then you will want to make your reader think about evolution and the first book about it. In this case, you will probably choose to keep Darwin **passive** in your sentence.

Another reason to use a passive sentence is when the writer wants to hide the active part. It's better to say, "The copy machine is broken," than "I broke the copy machine," to avoid trouble.

Look at how Plotnik uses a passive sentence in this way to introduce his next topic: The exemplar model has generally been replaced by a different theory of how we form concepts: the prototype theory. (p. 306)

TIP: When you see the word **by** in a sentence, there is a good chance it's a **passive** sentence. Moreover, the word after **by** is probably the doer of the action in the sentence. If the word after **by** can do the action in the verb, you have a passive sentence.

Sometimes, in an active sentence, the person or force performing the action is obvious or not important, so we choose to use a passive sentence. So, instead of writing **People often use heuristics in daily life**, Plotnik writes **Heuristics are often used in daily life**. (p. 308)

Look at these sentences from the text and decide if they are active or passive sentences. Think about the verb in the sentence. Is the subject doing the action in the verb (active) or is someone or something else doing the action to the subject (passive)?

1) Researchers have studied creative individuals. (p. 311)
2) They are driven by internal values or personal goals. (p. 311)
3) Their creative fires are fueled by psychological or mental problems. (p. 311)
4) A commonly used heuristic is called the availability heuristic. (p. 308)
5) Studies show that savants lack verbal intelligence. (p. 311)

Answers

internal means inside, while external means outside.
include means to put in, while exclude meets to not put in.
import means to bring into the country, while export means to bring out of the country.
implicit means not clearly stated, while explicit means clearly stated
1) Researchers have studied creative individuals. *Active:* The researchers study
2) They are driven by internal values or personal goals. *Passive:* The values and goals drive them.
3) Their creative fires are fueled by psychological or mental problems. *Passive:* The problems fuel the fires.
4) A commonly used heuristic is called the availability heuristic. *Passive:* People call the commonly used heuristic the availability heuristic.
5) Studies show that savants lack verbal intelligence. *Active:* The studies show

The Big Picture

Which statement below offers the best summary of the larger significance of this module?

A   There you go again, Rod Plotnik! You didn't have enough space in your textbook, so you crammed two subjects into this module even though they don't have much in common.

B   Both subjects are interesting, but the material on thought is essentially philosophical while the material on language is truly psychological. Therefore, the section on thought could have been omitted from a textbook in general psychology.

C   Thought and language, while technically separate topics in psychology, are intimately connected. In their sophisticated human form, each would be impossible without the other. It is likely that they developed together.

D   Rod Plotnik included material on both language and thought in the same module because language is learned in childhood and thought explains adult psychology. Together, they show precisely how childhood and adulthood are connected.

E   What do I think about this module? Gee, I don't know…, I can't put it into words.

True-False

_____   1. According to prototype theory, we form a concept by constructing a complete list of all the properties that define an object, event, or characteristic.

_____   2. Today computer programs can beat all but the very best human chess players because they employ such powerful heuristics.

_____   3. Good thinking: insight, analogy, subgoals. Bad thinking: functional fixedness.

_____   4. Divergent thinking is a popular psychometric measure of creativity.

_____   5. There is no scientific data to back up the common belief that creativity is related to an increased risk of mental instability.

_____   6. Noam Chomsky bases his theory of language on the premise that humans have inborn language capabilities.

_____   7. Children complete the essential tasks of learning language during the three-word stage.

_____   8. It is easier to learn a foreign language in grade school than in college.

_____   9. Inuit people (Eskimos) probably think differently about snow because they have so many more words for it than other people do.

_____   10. Despite the fascinating research on communication in dolphins, gorillas, and chimpanzees, so far it appears that only humans clearly meet the four criteria for true language.

Flashcards 1

_____ 1. concept

_____ 2. convergent thinking

_____ 3. creative thinking

_____ 4. deductive reasoning

_____ 5. divergent thinking

_____ 6. exemplar model

_____ 7. functional fixedness

_____ 8. heuristics

_____ 9. inductive reasoning

_____ 10. prototype theory

a. says you form a concept by creating a mental image based on the average characteristics of an object

b. flexibility in thinking plus reorganization of thought to produce innovative ideas and solutions

c. a mental set characterized by inability to see an object having a function different from its usual one

d. beginning with a problem and coming up with a single correct solution

e. drawing a specific conclusion from a general assumption believed to be true; general to particular

f. rules of thumb or clever short-cuts that reduce the number of operations needed to solve a problem

g. beginning with a problem and coming up with many different solutions

h. a way to group objects, events, etc., on the basis of some characteristics they all share in common

i. says you form a concept of an object or event by making a mental list of its essential characteristics

j. making particular observations then drawing a broader conclusion from them; particular to general

Flashcards 2

_____ 1. critical language period

_____ 2. dyslexia

_____ 3. morpheme

_____ 4. overgeneralization

_____ 5. parentese (motherese)

_____ 6. phonemes

_____ 7. semantics

_____ 8. telegraphic speech

_____ 9. theory of linguistic relativity

_____ 10. transformational rules

a. the smallest meaningful combination of sounds in a language

b. applying a grammatical rule to cases where it should not be used ("I goed to store")

c. a way adults speak to young children; slower, higher than normal voice, simple sentences, repeats words

d. procedures for converting our ideas from surface structures into deep structures and back again

e. the basic sounds of consonants and vowels (any word can be broken down into these units)

f. a distinctive pattern of speaking in which the child omits articles, prepositions, and parts of verbs

g. specifies the meaning of words or phrases when they appear in various sentences or contexts

h. reading, spelling, and writing difficulties that may include reversing or skipping letters and numbers

i. says differences among languages result in similar differences in how people think and perceive world

j. the time from infancy to adolescence when language is easier to learn; more difficult to learn after period

Multiple-Choice

_____ 1. For Rod Plotnik, this module illustrates the importance of the _____ approach to psychology
   a. behavioral
   b. cognitive
   c. humanistic
   d. psychodynamic

_____ 2. Concepts are crucial to effective thinking because without concepts we would
   a. not know the rules for logical thought
   b. forget most of what we learn
   c. be overwhelmed by apparently unrelated pieces of information
   d. lose our motivation to think

_____ 3. Most psychologists favor the _____ explanation of concept formation because it _____
   a. exemplar model / is based on good, sound definitions
   b. exemplar model / accounts for the exceptions to the rule
   c. prototype theory / is based on complete listings of essential properties
   d. prototype theory / accounts for more objects using fewer features

_____ 4. Children quickly form and develop concepts because the human brain
   a. is set up to store different categories in different areas
   b. is made up of a sponge-like material that easily sops up new information
   c. operates at the conscious level
   d. places each new bit of information in a separate category

_____ 5. A computer program finally has defeated a top human chess player, primarily because
   a. increasingly more powerful algorithms finally won
   b. good heuristics finally won
   c. computers don't have to take breaks for food and drink
   d. there is an element of luck in any game

_____ 6. When your friend remarks pessimistically that crime is increasing ("Did you see that gruesome murder on the news last night?"), you recognize the operation of the
   a. accuracy algorithm
   b. availability heuristic
   c. prototype theory
   d. subgoal strategy

_____ 7. If you were not able to solve the nine-dot problem, it probably was because of
   a. functional fixedness
   b. lack of insight
   c. using poor analogies
   d. failure to establish subgoals

_____ 8. Remember how Sultan figured out how to get a banana that was out of reach (Module 10)? That was a classic example of solving problems by using
   a. subgoals
   b. analogies
   c. insight
   d. functional fixedness

_____ 9. One of the best ways to finish your assignment on time is to
   a. have the problem in the back of your mind, and wait for a sudden flash of insight
   b. use the analogy of other, similar assignments you have done before
   c. fix your thoughts on the function that is involved in the assignment
   d. break the assignment down into subtasks and subgoals

_____ 10. A serious problem with too many college courses is that they place all the emphasis on _____ thinking
   a. creative
   b. convergent
   c. divergent
   d. brainstorm

_____ 11. The existence of autistic savants shows that the link between creativity and intelligence is
   a. strong, because savants always have high IQ scores
   b. moderate, because savants typically have normal IQ scores
   c. nonexistant, because savants seldom show creativity
   d. weak, because savants usually have low IQ scores

_____ 12. From most *particular* to most *general* in the rules of language, the correct order is
   a. morpheme – phoneme – syntax – semantics
   b. syntax – phoneme – semantics – morpheme
   c. phoneme – morpheme – syntax – semantics
   d. semantics – syntax – morpheme – phoneme

_____ 13. According to Noam Chomsky, language operates at two levels:
   a. spoken words and censored words
   b. surface structure and deep structure
   c. obvious meaning and implied meaning
   d. sentences and telegraphic speech

_____ 14. Chomsky's theory of language says that children
   a. learn those words and phrases that are reinforced by the environment
   b. learn those sentences that are spoken by their parents
   c. inherit a special ability to understand the language spoken by their parents
   d. inherit a mental program for learning a universal grammar

_____ 15. Which is the correct sequence of stages in children's acquisition of language?
   a. crying, begging, asking, reasoning
   b. senseless noises, listening, imitation, original productions
   c. babbling, one-word, two-word, three-word, four-word, etc.
   d. babbling, single word, two-word combinations, sentences

_____ 16. "I goed to store" is an example of
   a. babbling
   b. parentese
   c. overgeneralization
   d. telegraphic speech

_____ 17. The debate over how we acquire language concerns _____ versus _____
   a. innate language abilities / environmental language factors
   b. universal abilities / different skills from one cultural group to another
   c. superficial / deep-seated
   d. individual / common to the group

_____ 18. Bad news if you are planning to take a foreign language in college: the existence of
   a. transformational rules
   b. telegraphic speech
   c. the critical language period
   d. parentese

_____ 19. When you use particular observations in order to draw a broader conclusion, you are using
   a. deductive reasoning
   b. inductive reasoning
   c. convergent thinking
   d. divergent thinking

_____ 20. Benjamin Whorfs' theory of linguistic relativity might be proved by the observation that Inuit people (Eskimos) have many more words for snow... except for the fact that
   a. they also have fewer words for rain
   b. snow is obviously such a crucial factor in their lives
   c. there is no relationship between language and thought
   d. the claim turned out to be untrue

_____ 21. Which one of the following is _not_ a brain area involved in learning to read?
   a. dyslexic arranger
   b. phoneme (sound) producer
   c. word analyzer
   d. automatic detector

_____ 22. When American and Japanese students looked at an underwater scene, cultural differences in thinking were revealed by
   a. Americans seeing the fish as food and Japanese as works of art
   b. American analytical thinking versus Japanese holistic thinking
   c. Japanese studious observation versus American casual observation
   d. Japanese interest in the large fish and American interest in the background

_____ 23. Male-female differences in using language may be explained by new research showing that
   a. men and women are raised according to different rules and standards
   b. men have developed a better style of speaking
   c. women prefer to attack problems while men prefer to listen, give support, or be sympathetic
   d. male and female brains process language differently

_____ 24. When Rod Plotnik says he talks to his dog "Bear," his point is that
    a. Bear can communicate, but only Rod has language
    b. Bear has learned hundreds of words and can understand sentences
    c. Bear has learned the dog version of language, but he isn't really communicating
    d. Bear has mastered the four criteria for communication

_____ 25. The bottom line in the debate over whether animals can acquire true language seems to be that
    a. dolphins may possess a system of communication far superior to human language
    b. pygmy chimps are the only animals able to learn true language
    c. only humans clearly meet the four criteria for true language
    d. several of the higher primates can acquire the language skills of five-year-old children

Short Essay

1. How do the topics of thought and language illustrate the importance and power of the cognitive approach to psychology?

2. Describe the prototype theory of concept formation and explain why is it considered superior to the exemplar model of concept formation.

3. In what ways did Noam Chomsky change the way we understand language abilities and language acquisition?

4. Are male-female differences in thinking real, or mainly stereotypes? What evidence supports your position?

5. Do animals have language?

Test-Taking Tips 6

More hints:

- Use everything you know. Even if you can't recall the specific information needed, think about what you *do* remember concerning the subject.

- Don't jump to the conclusion that an answer is correct just because it uses the right word. The entire statement must be true.

Answers for Module 14

The Big Picture (explanations provided for incorrect choices)

A There are powerful connections between thought and language. Think about what I am saying!
B The study of thought is highly philosophical, but what is closer to the essence of humanness?
C Correct! You see the "big picture" for this Module.
D Close, since language is an essential part of child psychology, but thought applies to both children and adults.
E It's just a joke!

True-False (explanations provided for False choices; page numbers given for all choices)

1	F	306	Concept formation relies on relationships between ideas.
2	F	308	Computer programs play chess by comparing thousands of rules or algorithms.
3	T	309	
4	T	310	
5	F	311	Some evidence exists, but it is possible that mood disorders may be sources of artistic inspiration.
6	T	313	
7	F	315	There is no "three-word" stage.
8	T	316	
9	F	319	New research finds that Inuit people (Eskimos) *do not* have more words for snow.
10	T	322	

Flashcards 1

1 h   2 d   3 b   4 e   5 g   6 i   7 c   8 f   9 j   10 a

Flashcards 2

1 j   2 h   3 a   4 b   5 c   6 e   7 g   8 f   9 i   10 d

Multiple-Choice (explanations provided for incorrect choices)

1 a The behavioral approach stresses the power of the environment in conditioning.
   b Correct! See page 305.
   c The humanistic approach stresses self-concept and human potential.
   d The psychodynamic approach stresses unconscious processes and conflicts.

2 a Concepts are not the same as rules.
   b Concepts are not the main factor in memory.
   c Correct! See page 306.
   d Why should concepts and motivation to think be linked? This is a nonsense statement.

3 a Wrong theory.
   b Wrong theory.
   c Right theory, but specification of advantages goes with the other theory.
   d Correct! See page 306.

4 *a Correct! See page 307.*
   b The brain does not operate like a sponge (more like an electrical signaling system).
   c The processes involved in concept formation go on at an unconscious level.
   d If that were true, the brain would be overwhelmed by separate bits of unrelated information.

5 *a Correct! See page 308.*
   b Humans employ heuristics better than computers can.
   c True, but human needs did not explain the loss.
   d Wake up! You aren't paying attention!

6 a This is not a correct technical term in the psychology of problem solving.
   b Correct! See page 308.
   c Prototype theory refers to concept formation rather than perception.
   d The strategy of using subgoals refers to problem solving.

7	*a*	*Correct! See page 309.*
	b	The question is, what prevented insight from occurring?
	c	Analogies would not be of much help in this problem.
	d	Subgoals would not be of much help in this problem.

8	a	Sultan did not break the task down into separate parts.
	b	Sultan did not relate the new situation to an old, familiar situation.
	c	*Correct! See page 309.*
	d	Functional fixedness hinders, not aids, problem solving.

9	a	Waiting is the worst thing to do.
	b	Sounds good, but that wouldn't be the strongest strategy.
	c	This is a nonsense statement that alludes to the term functional fixedness.
	d	*Correct! See page 309.*

10	a	That will be the day!
	b	*Correct! See page 310.*
	c	Divergent thinking refers to coming up with many possible answers.
	d	Brainstorming refers to a group "thinking out loud" together.

11	a	Savants usually have low IQ scores.
	b	Savants usually have low IQ scores.
	c	Savants often show remarkable creativity.
	d	*Correct! See page 311.*

12	a	Ask yourself, which is the smallest unit of speech?
	b	Ask yourself, which is the smallest unit of speech?
	c	*Correct! See page 312.*
	d	Ask yourself, which is the smallest unit of speech?

13	a	The concept of censoring is not part of Chomsky's theory.
	b	*Correct! See page 313.*
	c	The concepts of obvious and implied meaning are not part of Chomsky's theory.
	d	Correct terms, but not what Chomsky meant.

14	a	Chomsky's theory downplays the importance of the environment.
	b	That would not explain why children can produce sentences they have never heard before.
	c	That would not explain how children adopted from other countries learn language.
	d	*Correct! See page 313.*

15	a	These are not the technical terms used in psychology.
	b	These are not the technical terms used in psychology.
	c	Close, but there is no three-word (or more) stage.
	d	*Correct! See page 314.*

16	a	Babbling refers to the sounds six-month old infants make.
	b	Parentese refers to how adults talk to children who are learning to speak.
	c	*Correct! See page 315.*
	d	Telegraphic speech refers to the first sentences, in which parts are left out.

17	*a*	*Correct! See page 316.*
	b	The debate is not over the effects of culture.
	c	Both sides agree that language abilities are profoundly important.
	d	The debate is not over individual or group factors.

18	a	This is Chomsky's term for procedures of converting ideas from surface structure to deep structure.
	b	Telegraphic speech is a childhood pattern of speech in which elements are left out.
	c	*Correct! See page 316.*
	d	Hopefully, your parents stopped talking to you like that after infancy.

19	a	Just the opposite is true.
	b	*Correct! See page 318.*
	c	This term applies to creativity, not reasoning.
	d	This term applies to creativity, not reasoning.

20 a   They do not have fewer words for rain.
    b   This fact tends to support the linguistic relativity theory.
    c   This statement is obviously untrue.
    d *Correct! See page 319.*

21 *a* *Correct! See page 320.*
    b   This brain function is the first step in reading.
    c   This brain function is the second step in reading.
    d   This brain function is the third step in reading.

22 a   This was not a difference between the two groups.
    b *Correct! See page 321.*
    c   This was not a difference between the two groups.
    d   Just the opposite was true.

23 a   Language differences may be rooted more in physiology than in culture.
    b   Deborah Tannen says male and female styles are different, but not necessarily better or worse.
    c   Wouldn't that be wonderful!
    d *Correct! See page 321.*

24 *a* *Correct! See page 322.*
    b   Bear understands what Rod is communicating, but he does not know words or understand sentences.
    c   Oh, he's communicating all right (just look at the cute picture)!
    d   The four criteria relate to language, which is a special form of communication.

25 a   Fascinating theory, but can they acquire what we consider language?
    b   Do pygmy chimps meet the four criteria for true language?
    c *Correct! See page 322.*
    d   None even comes close.

Short Essay (sample answers)

1. The cognitive approach to psychology emphasizes processing, storing, and using information, and it studies the effect of information on human abilities and activities. Thinking, or reasoning, involves forming concepts, solving problems, and engaging in creative activities. Language, a special form of communication, involves complex rules to form and manipulate symbols and generate meaningful sentences. These mental activities, the heart of the cognitive approach, are the processes that differentiate humans from other animals.

2. Nothing is more important to thinking than concepts, but how do we form them? According to the exemplar model, we build up lists of essential characteristics of things. But there are too many characteristics to remember and too many exceptions to the lists. According to prototype theory, we create mental images based on the average characteristics of things. It is easier to match new things to existing prototypes than to long lists of characteristics. Prototype theory is a better explanation of our power to form new concepts.

3. Chomsky changed the way we think about language. Instead of language learning through experience, Chomsky proposed that the human brain is already wired for language. A mental grammar allows language production and an innate brain program guides language learning. Below the surface structure of language (the wording of a sentence) lies the deep structure (the underlying meaning of the sentence). All languages share a common universal grammar and children inherit a mental program to learn this universal grammar.

4. The idea that men and women think differently is popular, but are such supposed differences real or mainly stereotypes? If there are differences, are they inherent? And are they important? However you argue in your answer, you should consider Deborah Tannen's research and the recent findings from brain scans that on the same language tasks men and women are using different areas of their brains. Even if you agree that there are differences, are they important? As Tannen says, different does not necessarily mean better.

5. There is a fascinating history of attempts to prove that at least some animals have language. Louis Herman's dolphins learned 50 hand signals, Francine Patterson's Koko has a vocabulary of 800 signs, and Sue Savage-Rumbaugh's Kanzi uses symbols and knows 200 spoken English words. Are these impressive accomplishments language, or imitation? So far, no animal has met the four criteria for true language: learning and using abstract symbols, learning rules of grammar, and constructing meaningful sentences.

Module **15**

Motivation

Does Learning Interest You?

Studying psychology offers a wonderful extra payoff: learning how to become a more effective student. Sometimes Rod Plotnik gives you an outright suggestion and sometimes you have to make the connection yourself, but each module contains a fact or an insight you can apply to becoming more effective in your college work. One of the most important ideas concerns motivation.

Module 15 introduces the idea of intrinsic motivation, the kind of motivation that goes beyond working for a specific, immediate, tangible payoff. Not that there's anything wrong with motivation through rewards. That's what gets us to work and makes us meet specific goals. In the long run, however, sustained pursuit of complex goals requires that extrinsic reinforcement be replaced by intrinsic motivation. That's why you get smiley faces on your papers in grade school, but not in college.

It is important to understand your motivation for attending college. If the real reason you enrolled was to please your parents or because all your friends went, you may have a difficult time mustering the energy and finding the time college work demands. If you find the activity of learning itself interesting, however, your college studies should be exciting and fun.

Our Motivation to be Effective

I think the most significant of all motivations may be the need to be effective. Oh sure, thirst, hunger, and sex are more immediate and can be insanely demanding, but what is it that we want all the time? We want to be effective in our dealings with the world, in our interactions with other people, and in managing our personal lives. Some call this a sense of mastery or control, but I like the word "effectiveness" to convey our broad need to do things that work.

The idea comes from Robert W. White, who wrote persuasively about "competence motivation" forty years ago. Unfortunately, his idea of competence has become so deeply woven into the fabric of modern psychology that we tend to overlook it. I think effectiveness is such a significant need that it deserves explicit recognition.

Perhaps you see why it is so important to do well in college. Success in college is the crucial measure of effectiveness at this point in your life. Examine your thoughts, feelings, and behavior. Doing something well — being effective — makes you pleased and happy, but when you are ineffective, you feel awful. Everything in your psychological makeup says you want to be effective in college.

Effective Student Tip 15

The One Day You Must Not Miss Class

The day the term paper is due? The day a surprise quiz is likely? The big exam? All these are important days to attend, but there is one day when you absolutely must not miss class. That's the day you don't have the assigned paper ready or aren't prepared for the test.

Of course this is exactly the day you are most tempted to cut. The embarrassment! The humiliation! Yet that's the very day when you can profit most from attending.

What you dread probably won't happen. Turns out you weren't the only one who goofed, and no one is taken out and shot. Not planning to read the papers until the weekend anyway, the professor may take yours later. Some professors will reassign a tough paper, reschedule an exam, or even allow a retake.

One especially good thing can happen when you attend on that agonizing day: you learn more about yourself. Why did you procrastinate? Why did you trip yourself up by not leaving enough time? What are your true feelings about the teacher, and how did they come into play? If you go to class and discuss it, all of this becomes more clear, your relationship becomes more honest, and you take an important step toward becoming a more effective student. If you stay in bed, everything just gets worse.

Your response...

Have you ever avoided a class when there was a problem? What happened?

Learning Objectives

1. Understand motivation as the force (or forces) driving those actions that make us human and keep us alive and emotionally vibrant.

2. Learn the basic theories that have been proposed in order to explain our biological and social needs.

3. Understand the biology and psychology of hunger and the special problems we face in contemporary society as we attempt to regulate this absolutely essential motivating force.

4. Understand the biology and psychology of sexual behavior and the special problems we face in contemporary society as we attempt to understand this essential yet complex motivating force.

5. Consider your position on the clash of cultures over the tradition of genital cutting.

6. Appreciate achievement as a unique human need that is revealed in striving for success, fear of failure, and the remarkable accomplishments of immigrant children.

7. Apply the findings and ideas of psychology to one of the most pressing issues of the day: eating problems and treatment.

Key Terms

There are lots of key terms in this module because Rod Plotnik discusses several major areas of motivation, like hunger, sex, and aggression. But many of these terms are already part of your general knowledge.

achievement need
AIDS (Acquired Immune Deficiency Syndrome)
anorexia nervosa
biological hunger factors
biological needs
biological sex factors
biosocial theory
bulimia nervosa
central cues
double standard for sexual behavior
evolutionary theory
extrinsic motivation
fat cells
fear of failure
female hypothalamus
fixed action pattern
gender identity
gender identity disorder

gender roles
genetic hunger factors
genetic sex factors
genital cutting
high need for achievement
HIV positive
incentives
inhibited female orgasm
instincts
interactive model of sexual orientation
intrinsic motivation
male hypothalamus
Maslow's hierarchy of needs
metabolic rate
motivation
obesity
optimal or ideal weight
organic factors
overweight

paraphilias
peripheral cues
premature or rapid ejaculation
psychological factors
psychological sex factors
psychosocial hunger factors
reward/pleasure center
self-handicapping
set point
sex chromosome
sex hormones
sexual dysfunctions
sexual orientation or preference (heterosexual, bisexual, homosexual)
social needs
Thematic Apperception Test (TAT)
underachievers
weight-regulating genes

Outline

- *Introduction*

    1. **Motivation** (Mark Wellman)

    2. Achievement (Victor)

    ☐ What was the hardest thing you have ever done? The greatest victory you have ever achieved? How do you explain your behavior in these extreme situations?

A. *Theories of Motivation*

1. Instinct

    a. **Instincts**

    b. **Fixed action pattern**

2. Brain: **reward/pleasure center**

3. **Incentives**

4. Cognitive factors

    a. **Extrinsic motivation**

    b. **Intrinsic motivation**

5. Explaining human motivation

    a. Reward/pleasure center of the brain, incentives, and cognitive or intrinsic factors (this Module)

    b. Emotional and personality factors (Modules 16, 19, and 20)

B. *Biological & Social Needs*

1. **Biological needs**

2. **Social needs**

3. Satisfying needs: **Maslow's hierarchy of needs** (Abraham Maslow)

4. Maslow's hierarchy of needs (arranged as a pyramid)

    a. Level 5: self-actualization

    b. Level 4: esteem needs

    c. Level 3: love and belonging needs

    d. Level 2: safety needs

    e. Level 1: physiological needs

C. *Hunger*

1. Optimal weight

    a. **Optimal or ideal weight**

    b. Natural regulation

2. Overweight

    a. **Overweight**

    b. **Obesity**

3. Three hunger factors

   a. **Biological hunger factors**

   b. **Psychosocial hunger factors**

   c. **Genetic hunger factors**

4. Biological hunger factors

   a. **Peripheral cues**

   b. **Central cues**

5. **Genetic hunger factors**

   a. **Fat cells**

   b. **Metabolic rate**

   c. **Set point**

   d. **Weight-regulating genes**

6. **Psychosocial hunger factors**

   a. Learned associations

   b. Socio-cultural influences

   c. Personality traits

D. *Sexual Behavior*

   ☐ Does sex, which Freud claimed was central to human psychology, cause any particular concerns or problems in your life? Good…, I thought not!

1. Three factors

   a. **Genetic sex factors**

   b. **Biological sex factors**

   c. **Psychological sex factors**

2. Genetic influences on sexual behavior

   a. **Sex chromosome**

   b. Differentiation

   c. Male sex organ and male brain

   d. Female sex organs and female brain

   e. Importance of testosterone

3. Biological influences

   a. **Sex hormones**

   b. **Male hypothalamus**

   c. **Female hypothalamus**

   d. Sexual motivation

4. **Psychological sex factors**

   a. 1st step: gender identity

      (1) **Gender identity**

      (2) **Gender identity disorder**

   b. 2nd step: gender roles

      (1) **Gender roles**

      (2) Stereotypic or traditional expectations

   c. 3rd step: **sexual orientation or preference**

      (1) **Homosexual orientation, bisexual orientation,** and **heterosexual orientation**

      (2) **Interactive model of sexual orientation**

5. Male-female sex differences

☐ Is the "double standard" still operating among the people you know?

   a. **Double standard for sexual behavior**

   b. **Biosocial theory**

   c. **Evolutionary theory**

6. Homosexuality

   a. Genetic/biological factors

   b. Psychological factors

7. Sexual response, problems, and treatments

   a. **Paraphilias**

   b. **Sexual dysfunctions**

   c. **Organic factors**

   d. **Psychological factors**

   e. Four-stage model of sexual response (William Masters and Virginia Johnson)

      (1) Excitement

      (2) Plateau

      (3) Orgasm

      (4) Resolution

   f. **Premature or rapid ejaculation**

   g. **Inhibited female orgasm**

8. AIDS: Acquired Immune Deficiency Syndrome

   a. **HIV positive**

   b. **AIDS (Acquired Immune Deficiency Syndrome)**

      (1) Risk for AIDS

      (2) Progression of disease

      (3) Treatment

E. *Cultural Diversity: Genital Cutting*

   1. Good tradition or cruel mutilation?

□ If you value the ideal of cultural diversity, can you still condemn the practice of genital cutting in those cultures that believe in it?

  2. Issues involved in **genital cutting**

      a. What is its purpose?

      b. Are there complications?

      c. Is there a solution?

F. *Achievement*

  1. Kinds of achievement

□ Do you feel a strong need for achievement? How does achievement influence your life?

      a. **Social needs**

      b. **Achievement need** (David McClelland and John Atkinson)

      c. How is the need for achievement measured? **Thematic Apperception Test (TAT)**

      d. What is **high need for achievement**?

  2. **Fear of failure: self-handicapping**

  3. Underachievement

      a. **Underachievers**

      b. Characteristics

  4. Three components of success

  5. Cognitive influences

      a. **Cognitive factors in motivation**

      b. **Intrinsic motivation**

      c. **Extrinsic motivation**

  6. Intrinsic motivation

G. *Research Focus: Immigrant Students*

  1. Why did immigrant children do well?

  2. A study of academic performance

      a. Procedure and results

      b. Conclusions

H. *Application: Eating Problems & Treatment*

  1. Dieting: problems, concerns, and benefits

□ Why are eating problems so common?

      a. Overweight and dieting

      b. Diet program/life style

  2. Serious eating disorders: risk factors and treatment

      a. **Anorexia nervosa**

      b. **Bulimia nervosa**

Language Workout

What's That?

p. 332 biological needs to **run amuck** = to be out of control

p. 333 we face **roadblocks** = setbacks, obstacles

p. 336 after birth and **reared** in adopted family = raised

p. 337 Examples may be **cited** = given as proof

p. 339 you are **destined** to be = forced

p. 340 **exerts** a powerful influence = presents, gives off
mannerisms of the other sex = ways of moving and speaking
rough and tumble play = not polite, with possible violence

p. 342 **extramarital affairs** = sex outside the marriage relationship
offspring of low quality = children

p. 344 using a **vibrator** = device used to stimulate sexual feeling

p. 345 through **casual** contact = common, ordinary (not close)
1,000 times more **infectious** = able to spread disease

p. 346 men want to marry **virgins** = women who have never had sex
ancient **rite of passage** = custom to mark new stage of life
Muslim **clerics** = religious leaders
serves no **hygienic** purpose = health, cleanliness
amputation of the male's penis = removal, cutting off
bleeding, and even **hemorrhaging** = losing large amounts of blood
cysts = abnormal growths on the body
maintain female **chastity** = pure state (without sexual experience)
organizations have **endorsed** anti-circumcision laws = approved

p. 348 people in **ambiguous** situations = without clear meaning

p. 349 The **paradox** of underachievement = puzzle, contradiction

p. 350 very little **charitable work** = unpaid volunteer helping poor

p. 351 making teachers more **accountable** = responsible for results

p. 356 scientists figured out the **plumbing** = physical system

Making Connections

Maybe your English teacher made you practice using **whom** in sentences like the following:

The rock star whom I interviewed has a new hit song.

This sentence is perfectly correct, but modern grammar experts agree that this way to use **whom** is dying. Why? Because it is hard to use it correctly, so it slows down our communication. Most grammar teachers now believe that it is perfectly acceptable to write:

The rock star who I interviewed has a new hit song.

Still, this doesn't mean that **whom** is completely dead! We still <u>must</u> use **whom** after a preposition like **of, for, with, to,** and **from**. This is a very useful way to join sentences together that have the same person in both sentences (we'll look at the same things, places, and time in the next Language Workout module). For example, look at the following two sentences:

The <u>man</u> works for the government. Ludmila is married **to him.**

Since **him** in the second sentence refers to the man, we can place the second sentence starting with the preposition and **whom** for **him** right after the word <u>man</u> to create the following single sentence:

The man **<u>to whom</u>** <u>Ludmila is married</u> works for the government.

You probably wouldn't hear someone say this in everyday conversation. Instead, you would hear a shorten form like this:

The man <u>Ludmila is married to</u> works for the government.

Although this sentence is easier, it's important to understand the use of the more formal **to whom** sentence because textbooks and professional work use this language like this example from the text:

After we have acquired a gender identity, gender role, and sexual orientation, there remain sometimes difficult decisions about when, where, and **with whom** sexual behavior is appropriate. (p. 342)

NOW YOU TRY IT. See if you can put together sentences in the same way. Read the following sentences, and then use the preposition/**whom** form to make one sentence:

Example: The tourists spent a lot of money. Jin traveled with them to Korea.
The tourists **with whom Jin traveled** spent a lot of money.

Don't bother with commas here. You are joining these two sentences together and not interrupting the main idea like in Module 6. Try some now. If you're not sure of your answers, you can always check the Answers at the end.

The new nurse never smiles. All the patients are complaining about her.
The _____.

The fat man is called Santa Claus. Many children believe in him.
The _____.

The model will arrive in five minutes. The photographer is waiting for her.
The _____.

The grandmother comes from Norway. Claus inherited his blue eyes from her.
The _____.

The dancer injured her leg. The ballet cannot start without her.
The _____.

Answers

The new nurse about whom all the patients are complaining never smiles.
The fat man in whom many children believe is called Santa Claus.
The model for whom the photographer is waiting will arrive in five minutes.
The grandmother from whom Claus inherited his blue eyes comes from Norway.
The dancer without whom the ballet cannot start injured her leg.

The Big Picture

Which statement below offers the best summary of the larger significance of this module?

A   One day we may have a single explanation of human motivation, but for now there seem to be several useful ways of looking at it. These different approaches to motivation parallel the general approaches to psychology.

B   Rod Plotnik gives us several different areas of motivation (hunger, sex, achievement) to show that each area of human behavior has its own particular kind of motivation. There is no overall theory of motivation.

C   In areas like hunger, sex, and achievement, human motivation is radically different from animal motivation. Thus the study of motivation shows that humans are far above the lower animals, a fact psychology should recognize.

D   After years of exploring the reasons how and why humans pursue their goals, it seems to come down to "mind over matter." Once again, cognitive psychology is shown to be superior to the other approaches.

E   Oh sure, I *could* learn all the stuff in this module. But why bother?

True-False

_____   1. Animals have instincts; humans have fixed action patterns.

_____   2. The concept of homeostasis supports the drive reduction theory.

_____   3. The concept of intrinsic motivation rests on a recognition of the importance of external factors.

_____   4. Maslow's hierarchy of needs nicely brings together both biological and social needs.

_____   5. Humans are the only animal for whom learned cues to eating are more powerful than biological cues.

_____   6. As one might expect, the male lion gets sex whenever he wants it.

_____   7. The percentage of people who are homosexual is rising rapidly.

_____   8. A sexual attraction to particular articles of clothing, such as shoes, is classified as a paraphilia.

_____   9. Researchers believe they will find a cure for AIDS in the next year or two.

_____   10. The dull truth is that the only realistic solution to weight problems is a combination of better eating habits and exercise.

Flashcards 1

_____ 1. achievement need

_____ 2. extrinsic motivation

_____ 3. fear of failure

_____ 4. fixed action pattern

_____ 5. incentives

_____ 6. instincts

_____ 7. intrinsic motivation

_____ 8. Maslow's hierarchy of needs

_____ 9. self-handicapping

_____ 10. underachievers

a. innate tendencies or biological forces that determine behavior

b. goals that can be either objects or thoughts, which we learn to value and which we are motivated to obtain

c. engaging in certain behaviors because the behaviors are personally rewarding or fulfill our beliefs

d. a motivation to avoid failure by choosing easy, nonchallenging tasks where failure is unlikely

e. individuals who score relatively high on tests of ability but perform more poorly than scores predict

f. an ascending order in which biological needs are placed at the bottom and social needs at the top

g. engaging in certain behaviors that either reduce biological needs or help us obtain external rewards

h. an innate biological predisposition toward a specific behavior in a specific environmental condition

i. a tendency to do things that contribute to failure and then to use these things as excuses for failure

j. your desire to set challenging goals and to persist in pursuing those goals in the face of obstacles

Flashcards 2

_____ 1. anorexia nervosa

_____ 2. bulimia nervosa

_____ 3. double standard for sexual behavior

_____ 4. gender identity

_____ 5. gender roles

_____ 6. genital cutting

_____ 7. inhibited female orgasm

_____ 8. paraphilias

_____ 9. set point

_____ 10. sexual dysfunctions

a. problems of sexual arousal or orgasm that interfere with adequate functioning during sexual behavior

b. traditional or stereotypic behaviors, attitudes, and personality traits designated masculine or feminine

c. a set of beliefs, values, or expectations that subtly encourages sexual activity in males (not females)

d. a certain level of body fat that our body strives to maintain constant throughout our lives

e. characterized by binge-eating and purging and an excessive concern about body shape and weight

f. a serious eating disorder characterized by refusing to eat, an intense fear of fat, and a distorted body image

g. sexual deviations characterized by repetitive or preferred sexual fantasies about nonhuman objects

h. a persistent delay or absence of orgasm after becoming aroused and excited

i. the individual's subjective experience and feelings of being either a male or a female

j. practice in some traditional African cultures of cutting away the female's external genitalia

Multiple-Choice

_____ 1. Rod Plotnik tells the story of Mark Wellman's incredible climb to illustrate the fact that
   a. you can do anything you really put your mind to
   b. you should take risks in life, but also have strong ropes!
   c. the causes of human actions are complex, yet important to understand
   d. there must be a single source of motivation, as yet undiscovered

_____ 2. Early in this century, most psychologists believed that motivation was explained by
   a. will power
   b. instincts
   c. environmental incentives
   d. beliefs and expectations

_____ 3. What were once called instincts are now called
   a. fixed action patterns
   b. incentives
   c. rewards
   d. energizers

_____ 4. Brain scans have revealed a new source of motivation, the
   a. instinct
   b. fixed action pattern
   c. reward/pleasure center
   d. incentive

_____ 5. The newest theory of motivation places greatest emphasis on
   a. will power
   b. instincts
   c. environmental incentives
   d. beliefs and expectations

_____ 6. The key idea of Maslow's hierarchy of needs is that
   a. unless social needs like esteem are satisfied, one cannot deal effectively with biological needs like safety
   b. basic biological needs must be satisfied before higher social needs can be dealt with
   c. unless you achieve level five, you are a defective person
   d. the higher needs are essential; the lower needs are incidental

_____ 7. The highest level need (at the top of the pyramid) in Maslow's hierarchy is
   a. safety needs
   b. love and belonging needs
   c. esteem needs
   d. self-actualization

_____ 8. Which one of the following is *not* a biological cue for hunger?
   a. glucose in the blood
   b. the hypothalamus
   c. learned associations
   d. the walls of the stomach

_____ 9. Which one of the following is *not* a genetic factor that influences body weight?
   a. fat cells
   b. metabolic rate
   c. set point
   d. responsiveness to food cues

_____ 10. The best explanation of the common tendency of dieters to regain the weight they lose is the
   a. fat cell
   b. metabolic rate
   c. set point
   d. weight-regulating gene

_____ 11. All of the following are examples of psychosocial hunger factors *except*
   a. striving to maintain a constant level of body fat
   b. large portions and tasty junk foods high in calories
   c. mass media images of the ideal woman as thin
   d. depression, anxiety, markedly low self-esteem, and being overly sensitive to rejection

_____ 12. Lions never go on talk shows; their sexual behavior is kept in line by the fact that
   a. females do most of the hunting
   b. hormones and pheromones prevail
   c. social roles and rules predominate
   d. a lioness's bite can be fatal

_____ 13. Gender identity disorder is commonly referred to as
   a. bisexuality
   b. homosexuality
   c. sexual disorientation
   d. transsexualism

_____ 14. The term "double standard" means the
   a. social expectation that men will be more sexually active than women
   b. biological fact that women want one man but men want more than one woman
   c. added burden modern women face of both working and caring for their families
   d. new idea that a woman can ask a man out and still expect him to pick up the check

_____ 15. What makes a person homosexual? Much of the new evidence points to
   a. social factors like having homosexual teachers
   b. biological factors like genetic and hormonal influences
   c. family factors like overbearing mothers
   d. intellectual factors like fascination with art

_____ 16. Which one of the following is the correct order of human sexual response?
   a. excitement – plateau – orgasm – resolution
   b. plateau – excitement – orgasm – resolution
   c. excitement – orgasm – plateau – resolution
   d. orgasm – excitement – resolution – plateau

_____ 17. The most effective treatment for AIDS is to
   a. take a drug "cocktail" daily until the symptoms are gone
   b. take a drug "cocktail" daily for the rest of one's life
   c. cease all sexual activity for an indefinite period
   d. cease all intravenous drug use immediately

_____ 18. The influence of culture in sexuality is clearly seen in the debate over
   a. celibacy
   b. paraphilias
   c. genital cutting
   d. sexual dysfunctions

_____ 19. In the story of Victor, who was teased about being a "White boy," we see a
   a. determination to have White friends even if his schoolmates disapproved
   b. triumph of the achievement need over peer pressure not to succeed in school
   c. refusal to be ashamed of being White in a mostly Black school
   d. fear of failure causing him to take only easy, unchallenging courses

_____ 20. The best motivation for superior academic performance is having a
   a. high need for achievement
   b. high fear of failure
   c. very efficient self-handicapping strategy
   d. reasonable excuse for occasional failure

_____ 21. Which of the following is the best example of self-handicapping?
   a. choosing easy, nonchallenging tasks where failure is unlikely
   b. performing more poorly on an exam than IQ scores would predict
   c. getting plenty of sleep before the exam, but doing poorly anyway
   d. having a hangover during the exam, then blaming drug use for poor results

_____ 22. Is extrinsic motivation or intrinsic motivation more effective in getting people to donate blood?
   a. extrinsic, because people need something tangible when pain is involved
   b. it depends on how the rewards are offered and how they are perceived
   c. intrinsic, because people want to feel good about doing unselfish deeds
   d. neither should be involved in behavior that is our civic duty

_____ 23. Immigrant children, who did not even know English when they came here, did better in school than native-born students because they
   a. adopted their parents' hopeful values about education
   b. rejected the old culture and relentlessly pursued Americanization
   c. were provided extra tutoring and books that native-born students did not get
   d. insisted on speaking English everywhere, even at home

_____ 24. Oprah Winfrey, who has fought being overweight for years, now realizes that she
   a. suffers from an unconscious tendency toward bulimia nervosa
   b. needs to cut back on her daily running because it only causes greater hunger
   c. needs a maintenance program that involves eating less and exercising more
   d. suffers from a serious lack of will power

_____ 25. Girls with anorexia nervosa and those with bulimia nervosa have in common
   a. upper-class family backgrounds
   b. regularly engaging in vomiting or use of laxatives
   c. histories of sexual abuse in childhood
   d. distorted thinking about body image and weight

Short Essay

1. Describe the three hunger factors that control eating behavior and regulate weight.

2. Is the double standard for sexual behavior still in operation? Illustrate your answer with examples from your own experience.

3. What are the issues in the controversy over genital cutting?

4. Is intrinsic motivation superior to extrinsic motivation?

5. Whether you are overweight, underweight, or just right, what did you learn about hunger motivation in this module that you can apply to your own life?

Our Need for Effectiveness

Go back to page 250 and re-read what I wrote about effectiveness. I really think I have an important message here, even though I may not have explained it well. Can you see what I am getting at? Could the key to a happier and more successful life begin with recognition of our universal need to be effective?

Answers for Module 15

The Big Picture (explanations provided for incorrect choices)

 A *Correct! You see the "big picture" for this Module.*
 B There are several overall theories of motivation, each seeking to explain all areas of behavior.
 C There are too many similarities between animal and human motivation to justify the statement.
 D The idea of "mind over matter" is not supported by most psychological theories.
 E It's just a joke!

True-False (explanations provided for False choices; page numbers given for all choices)

 1 F 330 Instincts and fixed action patterns are the same; humans have few of them.
 2 T 330
 3 F 331 Intrinsic motivation refers to internal factors in motivation.
 4 T 333
 5 T 334
 6 F 338 The male lion gets sex only when the female lion is receptive and interested.
 7 F 343 The small percentage of people who are homosexual remains constant.
 8 T 344
 9 F 345 Sadly, there is no cure for AIDS in sight.
 10 T 352

Flashcards 1

 1 j   2 g   3 d   4 h   5 b   6 a   7 c   8 f   9 i   10 e

Flashcards 2

 1 f   2 e   3 c   4 i   5 b   6 j   7 h   8 g   9 d   10 a

Multiple-Choice (explanations provided for incorrect choices)

 1 a An inspiring slogan, but, as a psychologist, Rod Plotnik cannot be satisfied with slogans.
    b This answer, which does not show much understanding of Mark Wellman, is at best funny, at worst silly.
    c *Correct! See page 329.*
    d A mysterious single source of motivation would mean there is no scientific way to explain it.

 2 a Will power is not a widely accepted concept in psychology.
    b *Correct! See page 330.*
    c Environmental incentives refers to a modern behavioral explanation of motivation.
    d Beliefs and expectations refers to a relatively recent cognitive explanation of motivation.

 3 a *Correct! See page 330.*
    b Incentives are learned goals; instincts are inborn.
    c Rewards are learned goals; instincts are inborn.
    d This is not a correct term in psychology.

 4 a Instincts cannot be precisely located in the brain.
    b Fixed action patterns cannot be precisely located in the brain.
    c *Correct! See page 330.*
    d Incentives cannot be precisely located in the brain.

 5 a Will power is not a widely accepted concept in psychology.
    b Instincts refers to the original biological theory of motivation.
    c Environmental incentives refers to a modern behavioral explanation of motivation.
    d *Correct! See page 331.*

 6 a Maslow's theory says exactly the opposite.
    b *Correct! See page 332.*
    c Maslow doubts that many people in contemporary society can achieve the highest need level.
    d Maslow says almost the opposite (although he does value the higher needs).

7   a   Safety needs are at level 2 (of 5).
    b   Love and belonging needs are at level 3 (of 5).
    c   Esteem needs are at level 4 (of 5).
    d   *Correct! See page 333.*

8   a   Glucose is a peripheral biological cue for hunger.
    b   The hypothalamus is a central biological cue for hunger.
    c   *Correct! See page 334.*
    d   The stomach walls are peripheral biological cues for hunger.

9   a   Fat cells are genetically influenced.
    b   Metabolic rates are genetically influenced.
    c   The set point probably is genetically influenced.
    d   *Correct! See page 336.*

10 a   This genetic factor would not explain regaining the weight lost.
    b   This genetic factor would not explain regaining the weight lost.
    c   *Correct! See page 336.*
    d   This factor, by itself, would suggest a continual weight gain.

11 *a*   *Correct! See page 337.*
    b   These are examples of learned associations to foods.
    c   These are examples of socio-cultural influences on eating.
    d   These are examples of personality traits associated with eating problems.

12 a   What would that have to do with sexual behavior?
    b   *Correct! See page 338.*
    c   Felines are not highly social animals — other factors control their sexual behavior.
    d   It's just a joke!

13 a   Bisexuality refers to a pattern of sexual arousal by persons of both sexes.
    b   Homosexuality refers to a pattern of sexual arousal by persons of the same sex.
    c   This is not a correct term in psychology.
    d   *Correct! See page 340.*

14 *a*   *Correct! See page 342.*
    b   This commonly believed statement (not the definition) is probably untrue.
    c   The term refers to sexual attitudes and behavior.
    d   Sounds like this answer (not the definition) was written by a man!

15 a   There is no evidence that children are influenced to be homosexual by role models.
    b   *Correct! See page 341.*
    c   This is an old idea that never had much research support.
    d   This idea reflects a common and unsupported prejudice

16 *a*   *Correct! See page 344.*
    b   Ask yourself, which one obviously comes first?
    c   Would orgasm come immediately after excitement?
    d   Ask yourself, which one obviously comes first?

17 a   No drugs we have today kill the virus.
    b   *Correct! See page 345.*
    c   That wouldn't affect the disease that already exists.
    d   That wouldn't affect the disease that already exists.

18 a   Culture does not play a large part in the American debate over celibacy.
    b   There is no real debate over paraphilias.
    c   *Correct! See page 346.*
    d   There is no real debate over sexual dysfunctions.

19 a   The story of Victor was not about having White friends.
    b   *Correct! See page 348.*
    c   The story of Victor was not about a White student.
    d   The story of Victor was not about fear of failure (just the opposite).

20 **a** *Correct! See page 348.*
    b   Positive motives are stronger than negative motives.
    c   Self-handicapping strategy refers to making up excuses for failure.
    d   Excuses are never as useful as realistic appraisals.

21 a   This could be fear of failure.
    b   This would be underachievement.
    c   Being rested is a good strategy, not an example of self-handicapping.
    d *Correct! See page 349.*

22 a   Just the opposite has been suggested (besides, giving blood is not painful).
    b *Correct! See page 350.*
    c   That was the assumption, but it turned out not to be so simple.
    d   All behavior is motivated; even "our civic duty" supposes the intrinsic motivation of good citizenship.

23 **a** *Correct! See page 351.*
    b   They did not have to reject their old culture, and what they pursued was success through education.
    c   They did not get much extra help.
    d   They probably spoke their parents' language at home, but they studied hard!

24 a   Oprah did not say she had been bulimic.
    b   Oprah has a good exercise program that includes daily runs.
    c *Correct! See page 352.*
    d   Will power is not a useful concept in weight management.

25 a   They can come from any social class.
    b   This applies mainly to bulimics.
    c   A few do, but most do not.
    d *Correct! See page 353.*

Short Essay (sample answers)

1. Three factors interact to influence weight. Biological hunger factors come from physiological changes in blood chemistry and signals from digestive organs that provide feedback to the brain. Psychosocial hunger factors come from learned associations between food and other stimuli. Genetic hunger factors come from inherited instructions found in our genes. Together, these three factors influence the brain to ask for more calories or fewer, and to expend energy that burns more calories or less.

2. The double standard for sexual behavior refers to a set of beliefs, values, and expectations that subtly encourages sexual activity in males but discourages the same behavior in females. He is a lover; she is a slut! Is this double standard still in force? Or has your generation risen above such outdated beliefs? Support your answer with evidence from your observations of society at large as well as from the interactions you personally see among your acquaintances and fellow students.

3. Genital cutting involves cutting away the female's external genitalia and sewing together the remaining edges. This ancient rite of passage, practiced in traditional cultures in parts of Africa and the Arabian Peninsula, is extremely painful and inhibits later sexual satisfaction. Does the acceptance of this practice in traditional cultures justify its continuation? Are Westerners justified in condemning the practices of other cultures? The United Nations opposes the practice, but has had only limited success in eliminating it.

4. Are people more likely to give blood to obtain a material reward or to enjoy the satisfaction of helping others? Research suggested that offering money actually decreased volunteering. This finding supported the idea that intrinsic motivation is superior to extrinsic motivation. But later research showed the issue to be more complex, emphasizing how people perceive rewards. Phony praise for doing little work actually discourages students. Perhaps the distinction between kinds of motivation is not entirely useful.

5. Most animals in nature maintain an optimal weight in favorable conditions, but we humans enjoy few natural constraints on eating behavior. It is so easy to eat too much, or too little, and so difficult to eat just right. Even for those of you whose weight is optimal, good health is constantly threatened by social and political (price supports for sugar!) considerations. And you won't be young forever. From the wealth of information Rod Plotnik gives us about hunger, what did you learn that could help you live better?

Module 16

Emotion

A Gift of Nature

If visitors from outer space dropped in for a visit, what would impress them most about us? Not our powers of logic and reason (theirs would be superior). Perhaps our emotions, which add the vitality to our life experience, would impress them as truly marvelous. "What a wonderful gift nature has given you," they might tell us. We would be surprised, because feelings seem to create such problems for us.

In this module, Rod Plotnik carefully unravels the most important theories about what emotion is and how it works. All the theories keep coming back to two questions: (1) Does the body's reaction to a stimulus cause an emotion, or does an emotion trigger a physiological response? (2) Does a thought cause an emotion, or does an emotion trigger a thought? Plotnik shows us the competing answers psychology has offered.

Still, something seems to be missing. No one of these classic theories of emotion has triumphed, and none seems fully satisfying, no matter how intriguing the research findings are. What if the *answers* are correct, but the *questions* are wrong? What if emotion is not separate from the mental process, but an integral part of it?

A Different View of Emotion

New discoveries in neuroscience are beginning to suggest that sensory data doesn't really become thought until it is charged by the force of emotion. A dual mental system both transforms sensory experience to tell us what's out there and also uses emotion to tell us how important it is. Feelings and thoughts are inseparable.

The new discoveries fit nicely with a different view of emotion, discovered by psychotherapist and writer Kenneth Isaacs. In *Uses of Emotion: Nature's Vital Gift* (Praeger: 1998), Isaacs says feelings are always benign and potentially useful parts of mental activity. Emotion comes and goes almost instantaneously, and therefore cannot build up in us. We may remember a feeling, but the actual emotion is already gone and cannot possibly harm us. The mistaken idea that feelings are dangerous entities that must be "gotten out," or at least controlled, robs many people of a rich emotional life and cripples others with extreme fear of emotion expressed in a wide variety of symptoms. The real danger is our misunderstanding and fear of emotion.

Instead of fighting to control emotion, says Isaacs, we should welcome feelings as useful sources of information. We couldn't get along without our emotions any more than we could do without other information. If Kenneth Isaacs is correct, many ideas in psychology will have to be reconsidered.

Effective Student Tip 16

How to Beat Test Anxiety

In a famous experiment, dogs that received shocks in a closed box did not even try to escape when given shocks in an open box. The experimenter called it "learned helplessness." If we could ask them, the dogs might tell us that 'test anxiety' made them fail to jump over to the safe side.

Sometimes school can be like the shock box. Too many painful defeats, and you learn to accept failure as a normal part of life. You don't like it, but you have no experience of escaping it. So don't be too quick to say you are no good at tests. You may have learned to think so, but you can't really know until you take a test *for which you have prepared effectively*.

Scratch the surface of most test anxiety and you find ineffective techniques. The first thing to do is stop blaming yourself. Next, discard the idea that you simply have to try harder. Finally, dissect your weaknesses in note-taking, studying, and test-taking and replace them with better techniques.

You will begin to feel effective when you begin to be effective. As your sense of effectiveness increases, your ability to work out winning strategies will also increase. You may still experience some jitters (phobic effects linger), but who cares? Test anxiety will no longer rule your life.

Your response...

If you were brutally honest with yourself, what steps could you take to improve your test preparation?

Learning Objectives

1. Understand emotion as a vital force that, through the intensity and variety of feelings, helps us interpret the world around us and make decisions on everything from simple daily activities to significant delights or dangers.

2. Learn the basic theories that psychology has devised in attempting to explain emotion.

3. Learn how the brain produces feelings and uses them to promote our welfare.

4. Appreciate the significance of universal facial expressions of emotions and the functions of emotions like happiness.

5. Learn how cultural rules governing the display of emotions differ around the world.

6. Consider what research says about the new concept of emotional intelligence.

7. Understand the strengths and weaknesses of lie detectors.

Key Terms

Try to understand the battle of psychological theories of emotion that is reflected in many of these key terms.

adaptation level theory
affective neuroscience approach
amygdala
cognitive appraisal theory of emotions
cognitive appraisal theory
Control Question Technique

display rules
emotion
emotional intelligence
evolutionary theory of emotions
facial expressions
facial feedback theory
galvanic skin response

happiness
happiness set point
James-Lange theory
lie detector (polygraph)
peripheral theory of emotions
universal emotional expressions
Yerkes-Dodson law

Outline

- *Introduction*
    - You will see that psychologists do not agree on how emotion works. What is *your* understanding of emotion?
    1. Emotional experience: **emotion** (Surfer Rick)
        a. Interpret or appraise the stimulus
        b. Subjective experience or feeling
        c. Physiological responses
        d. Overt or observable behaviors
    2. Staying happy (Lottery winners)

A. Peripheral Theories

1. Sequence for emotions
    a. **Peripheral theory of emotions**
    b. **Cognitive appraisal theory of emotions**
    3. **Affective neuroscience approach**

☐ In both of the two famous peripheral theories of emotion (below), the key is the sequence. Be sure to work it out for each theory. What do modern research findings say about each of the two theories?

2. **James-Lange theory**
    a. Sequence for emotional components
    b. Criticisms

3. **Facial feedback theory**
    a. Sequence for emotional components
    b. Criticisms

B. Cognitive Appraisal Theory

1. Thoughts and emotions?

2. Schachter-Singer experiment
    a. Procedure
    b. Sequence for emotional components

3. **Cognitive appraisal theory**

☐ Can you work out the sequence for emotions in this theory?

    a. Thought then emotion
    b. Emotion without conscious thought

C. Affective Neuroscience

1. Four qualities of emotion
    a. Felt and expressed in facial expressions and physiological responses
    b. Less controllable, may not respond to reason
    c. Influence many cognitive processes
    d. Hard-wired in the brain
    e. Study of emotions: **affective neuroscience approach**

2. Emotional detector and memorizer
    a. Detecting stimuli
    b. Emotional detector: **amygdala**
    c. Emotional memorizer

3. Brain circuits for emotions
    a. Thalamus
    b. Amygdala

    c. Prefrontal cortex

  4. Fear and the amygdala

D. *Universal Facial Expressions*

  ☐ What does it mean when someone says, "I can read you like a book"?

  1. Definition of universal

    a. **Universal emotional expressions**

    b. Number of expressions

  2. Cross-cultural evidence

  ☐ Why are some emotions universal? Why doesn't each culture have its own unique emotions?

  3. Genetic evidence

E. *Functions of Emotions*

  1. Social signals: **facial expressions**

  2. Survival, attention, and memory: **evolutionary theory of emotions**

    a. Attention

    b. Memory

  3. Arousal and motivation: **Yerkes-Dodson law**

F. *Happiness*

  1. Positive emotions

    a. **Happiness**

    b. **Reward/pleasure center**

  2. Long-term happiness

    a. **Adaptation level theory**

    b. Genetic differences in happiness: **happiness set point**

G. *Cultural Diversity: Emotions Across Cultures*

  1. Showing emotions

    a. **Display rules**

    b. Cultural difference in display rules

  2. Perceiving emotions

    a. Display rules about intensity

    b. Power of culture

H. *Research Focus: Emotional Intelligence*

  1. What is **emotional intelligence**? (Daniel Goleman)

    a. How do we measure emotional intelligence?

    b. Is emotional intelligence important?

  2. Preliminary findings about emotional intelligence

I. Application: Lie Detection

1. What is the theory?
    a. **Lie detector (polygraph)**
    b. **Galvanic skin response**

2. What is a lie detector test?
    ☐ Have you ever taken a lie detector test? Would you do so willingly if asked?
    a. **Control Question Technique**
    b. Assessing galvanic skin responses

3. How accurate are lie detector tests?
    a. Innocent or faking
    b. Restrictions
    c. New tests

For Psych Majors Only...

Emotion — Myths and Actualities: Which statements about emotion are true and which are false? Don't worry about your score, because these statements are more the foundation of a theory than a quiz. When you check the "answers," see if you can understand the theory (it was described in my module introduction).

_____   1. Emotions can be dangerous.

_____   2. Emotions have no constructive function.

_____   3. Emotions, once evoked, remain in a kind of pressured storage until discharged.

_____   4. Emotions, while in storage, become a source of damage to the person.

_____   5. The necessary discharge of emotions must be accomplished very carefully so as to cause the least amount of damage.

_____   6. Emotions are vital aspects of human functioning.

_____   7. Emotions are automatic subjective responses to internal and external events.

_____   8. Emotions serve the vital function of informing us of qualities of internal and external events.

_____   9. Emotions are fleeting and in their initial reactive form are impossible to store or accrue.

_____   10. Because emotions are fleeting, their discharge is not mandatory and their expression is optional.

Answers to "Emotion — Myths and Actualities" Quiz

The first five items (all False) represent what Kenneth Isaacs calls _myths_ about feelings, false beliefs that cause us to misunderstand emotion. The second five items (all True) represent what Isaacs sees as _actualities_ of emotion, truths that could make us healthier and happier.

Language Workout

What's That?

p. 359   **appraise** some stimulus = judge, estimate the effect
frantic swimming = very nervous, out of control
playing **poker** = card game
the emotional **high** = experience of pleasure
such an enormous **windfall** = unexpected good fortune

p. 366   **holding down** two jobs = working
going on a **buying spree** = burst of activity (buying)
I thought I'd **drop everything** = change all my plans
hang out at my brother's house = spend time, visit
a **daily diet of little highs** = small experiences of pleasure every day

p. 369   the chance to **come up with** new ideas = create
this book **sparked** tremendous interest = stimulated
I couldn't think **straight** = clearly

p. 370   Ames **pleaded** guilty = answered in court
espionage = spying
skin **conductance** = ability to transmit
They had a **warrant** and arrested him = court order, permission to arrest
the **prosecutor** offered = lawyer responsible for starting lawsuit
Floyd **jumped at the chance** = eagerly agreed to cooperate
several years **behind bars** = in prison
his lawyer **tracked down** the real robbers = found

p. 371   one **field** study = practical (not in a laboratory)

p. 374   **bucking** cultural traditions = opposing, breaking
customers are getting **choosy** = selective, hard to satisfy
a **radical** change = extreme, serious
Japanese salespeople are very **reserved** = do not show emotions
smiling was totally **frowned upon** = not approved, discouraged
racking up the most sales = making
such a high **premium** on smiling = value

Making Connections

In the last Language Workout Module, we looked at connecting sentences with a preposition and whom, but the word <u>whom</u> can only be used with people. We can use the same principle with all other things by using **which** as follows:

> **Abraham Lincoln was born in a house. The house no longer exists.**
> **The house <u>in which Abraham Lincoln was born</u> no longer exists.**

Notice how **in which** comes right after the house, the word that they had in common. Notice the order of the rest of the sentence. This is somewhat different from speaking. We would probably say:

> **The house <u>where Abraham Lincoln was born</u> no longer exists.**

This sentence is easier to make, but students have to practice the more formal **in which** sentence because this is the language of textbooks and professional work. Did you notice the following sentence in this textbook? Thousands of people train for months to run grueling 26-mile-long marathons, **in which** only the top two or three receive any prize money. (p. 331)

This is really two sentences. The first sentence is: Thousands of people train for months to run grueling 26-mile-long **marathons.** The second one is: **In these marathons** only the top two or three receive any prize money.

Notice that the word **marathons** is repeated. We don't want to repeat the same word, so we replace the second **marathons** with **which.** We can join two sentences with any preposition and **which** in combinations like **with which, at which, for which, to which, from which,** and many others.

NOW YOU TRY IT. See if you can put together sentences in the same way. Read the following sentences, and then use the preposition + **which** form to make one sentence:

> Example: The strength surprised me. The child shook my hand with strength.
> The strength **with which the child shook my hand** surprised me.

Don't bother with commas here. You are joining these two sentences together and not interrupting the main idea like in Module 6. Try some now. If you're not sure of your answers, you can always check the Answers at the end.

1) The temperature is zero degrees centigrade. Water freezes below this temperature.
   The _____.

2) The factory is closed for repairs. Miguel's father works at the factory.
   The _____.

3) The letter never arrived. Anya was waiting for the letter.
   The _____.

4) The company went out of business. We bought our computers from the company.
   The _____.

5) The land lies in an earthquake zone. The nuclear power plant is built on the land.
   The _____.

Now let's work backwards. See if you can take this sentence from the text and make it into two.

> These data come from less realistic laboratory settings that use simple tasks, such as identifying some object **about which** the subject — often a college student — has been told to lie. (p. 371)

Answers

1) The temperature **below which water freezes** is zero degrees centigrade.
2) The factory **at which Miguel's father works** is closed for repairs.
3) The letter **for which Anya was waiting** never arrived.
4) The company **from which we bought our computers** went out of business.
5) The land **on which the nuclear power plant is built** lies in an earthquake zone.
"These data come from less realistic laboratory settings that use simple tasks, such as identifying some object."
"The subject — often a college student — has been told to lie about it (identifying a some object, a simple task)."

The Big Picture

Which statement below offers the best summary of the larger significance of this module?

A   There is a reason why Rod Plotnik talks about sharks, primitive peoples, and greed in this module: emotion almost seems to be left over from an earlier period in our evolution, something we would be better off without.

B   Nothing is more basic to our common psychological experience than emotion processes, yet science has not yet agreed on how to explain emotion. In science, that which is closest to us is often the last to be understood.

C   Emotions provide startling evidence for the cultural and environmental side of the nature-nurture debate. All over the world people treat emotions very differently, with little evidence of commonality.

D   Emotions are not terribly important in human affairs, but they add a much-needed drama and spice to life. The best way to handle emotions is not to pay too much attention to them.

E   Sheesh! This $&!# module really ticks me off! All those %!$# theories to learn! Why is emotion important, anyhow?

True-False

_____   1. Psychologists now agree that the James-Lange theory provides the best explanation of how emotions work.

_____   2. The amygdala monitors and evaluates whether stimuli have positive or negative emotional significance for our well-being and survival.

_____   3. People all over the world recognize the expression of a few universal emotions.

_____   4. The evolutionary theory of emotions says one function of emotions is to help us evaluate objects, people, and situations in terms of how good or bad they are for our well-being and survival.

_____   5. Emotions are essential to our survival.

_____   6. Human emotions, like the human appendix, are left over from our primitive past and are not really needed today.

_____   7. The reason the joy of winning the lottery doesn't last is that taxes soon take most of the winnings.

_____   8. Display rules are cultural expectations that govern the presentation and control of emotional expression in specific situations.

_____   9. People all over the world rate happiness as the most intense emotion.

_____   10. Lie detector tests determine whether a statement is true or false.

Flashcards 1

_____ 1. affective neuroscience approach

_____ 2. cognitive appraisal theory of emotions

_____ 3. emotion

_____ 4. emotional intelligence

_____ 5. evolutionary theory of emotions

_____ 6. facial feedback theory

_____ 7. happiness

_____ 8. lie detector (polygraph)

_____ 9. peripheral theory of emotions

_____ 10. universal emotional expressions

a. has four components: (1) appraisal (2) subjective feeling (3) physiological responses (4) overt behaviors

b. based on theory that a person telling a lie feels guilt or fear and exhibits involuntary physical responses

c. feeling a positive emotion, being satisfied with one's life, and not experiencing negative emotions

d. emphasize how your interpretations or appraisals of situations give rise to your emotional feelings

e. emphasize how physiological changes in the body give rise to your emotional feelings

f. says sensations from movement of facial muscles and skin are interpreted by brain as different feelings

g. a number of specific inherited facial patterns or expressions that signal specific feelings

h. ability to perceive emotions accurately, to take feelings into account, and to understand and manage emotions

i. studies the underlying neural bases of mood and emotion by focusing on the brain's neural circuits for emotion

j. says we evolved basic emotional patterns to adapt and solve problems important for our survival

Flashcards 2

_____ 1. adaptation level theory

_____ 2. amygdala

_____ 3. cognitive appraisal theory

_____ 4. Control Question Technique

_____ 5. display rules

_____ 6. facial expressions

_____ 7. galvanic skin response

_____ 8. James-Lange theory

_____ 9. happiness set point

_____ 10. Yerkes-Dodson law

a. communicate state of your personal feelings and provide different social signals to others around you

b. specific cultural norms that regulate how, when, and where we should express emotion (and how much)

c. changes in sweating of fingers (or palms) that accompany emotional experiences and are independent of perspiration

d. says performance on a task is an interaction between the level of arousal and the difficulty of the task

e. monitors and evaluates whether stimuli have positive or negative emotional significance for our well-being

f. each individual has a genetically determined level for experiencing happiness, some more and some less

g. says we quickly become accustomed to receiving some good fortune (winning lottery), so the initial joy fades

h. says your interpretation of situation, object, or event can contribute to experiencing different feelings

i. says brain interprets specific physiological changes as feelings or emotions (see bear – run – feel fear)

j. lie detection procedure that utilizes both neutral questions and critical (emotional) questions

Multiple-Choice

_____   1. Rod Plotnik tells us about the surfer who was attacked by a shark to show that
       a. sometimes you can feel all the emotions at once
       b. emotions play a major role in our lives
       c. sometimes survival depends on having no emotions
       d. emotions (like the joy of surfing) can get in the way of common sense

_____   2. Which one of the following is *not* a component of an emotion?
       a. appraising a stimulus
       b. physiological responses
       c. overt behaviors
       d. genetic variation

_____   3. Rod also suggests that instant lottery millionaires make a good case study of the
       a. emotional foundations of risk taking
       b. gender differences in joy over winning
       c. duration of happiness over time
       d. feelings of guilt that accompany winning while others are losing

_____   4. The _____ theory says emotions result from specific physiological changes in the body
       a. shark bite
       b. James-Lange
       c. facial feedback
       d. cognitive appraisal

_____   5. The _____ theory says emotions result from our brain's interpretation of muscle and skin movements that occur when we express an emotion
       a. Schacter-Singer
       b. James-Lange
       c. facial feedback
       d. cognitive appraisal

_____   6. The _____ theory says that your interpretation of a situation, object, or event can contribute to, or result in, your experiencing different emotional states
       a. Charles Darwin
       b. James-Lange
       c. facial feedback
       d. cognitive appraisal

_____   7. The most recent explanation of emotions is the
       a. affective neuroscience approach
       b. cognitive appraisal theory
       c. facial feedback theory
       d. James-Lange theory

_____   8. Among the main functions of the amygdala are
    a. suppressing feelings of fear and covering over memories of fear
    b. maintaining calm and promoting a meditative state
    c. sensing feelings of hunger and maintaining a set weight
    d. detecting threats and storing memories with emotional content

_____   9. The affective neuroscience approach to understanding fear studies all of the following *except* the
    a. thalamus
    b. visual cortex
    c. amygdala
    d. prefrontal cortex

_____   10. Evidence for the universality of emotional expression comes from the fact that people all over the world
    a. consider happiness to be the most intense emotion
    b. follow the same rules about how to show emotions
    c. recognize facial expressions of certain basic emotions
    d. make up rules about how to show emotions

_____   11. Which one of the following is *not* a universally recognized emotion?
    a. indecision
    b. happiness
    c. surprise
    d. anger

_____   12. The fact that blind infants begin to smile around 4–6 weeks shows that
    a. they are socially delayed, because sighted infants smile almost immediately
    b. blind children can learn anything sighted children can
    c. some facial expressions are biologically programmed
    d. at least in the beginning, humans have a cheerful disposition

_____   13. Which one of the following is *not* something emotions do for us?
    a. help us attain well-being and survival
    b. help us answer questions of fact
    c. motivate and arouse us
    d. help us send social signals

_____   14. The relationship between emotional arousal and performance on a task is explained by the
    a. Yerkes-Dodson law
    b. James-Lange theory
    c. Schacter-Singer law
    d. Darwinian law of survival

_____   15. At the most basic level, the feeling of happiness is best explained by the
    a. realization that we possess more than others
    b. speed with which we adapt to good fortune
    c. facial muscles that produce smiles
    d. reward/pleasure center in the brain

_____ 16. Adaptation level theory explains why people who win big in the lottery
     a. don't come forward to claim their prizes right away
     b. often spend lavishly until they are right back where they started
     c. don't feel much happier than anyone else after a while
     d. often report that winning permanently changed them from discontented to happy persons

_____ 17. Can money buy happiness? Psychology suggests that the answer is
     a. yes, because once a person climbs above the poverty level worries tend to disappear
     b. no, because humans appear to have a genetically determined happiness set point
     c. yes, money raises us above the adaptation level
     d. no, but it sure finances the illusion

_____ 18. Cultural rules that govern emotional expression in specific situations are called
     a. display rules
     b. feelings guides
     c. emotion set points
     d. intensity rules

_____ 19. Cross-cultural research reveals that the most intense emotion is
     a. happiness
     b. disgust
     c. anger
     d. (it differs from culture to culture)

_____ 20. The new concept of emotional intelligence includes all of the following *except*
     a. excluding emotions when making crucial decisions
     b. perceiving emotions accurately
     c. taking feelings into account when reasoning
     d. managing emotions in oneself and others

_____ 21. Results from programs attempting to teach and improve emotional intelligence suggest that the concept may be
     a. the breakthrough in teaching that education has been waiting for
     b. confirmed by the many new tests developed to measure it
     c. the answer to the problem of test anxiety
     d. more hype than substance

_____ 22. Lie detector tests measure
     a. whether a statement is true or false
     b. how much physiological arousal the subject feels
     c. whether the subject is basically honest or dishonest
     d. how much character a person has

_____ 23. The purpose of the Control Question Technique is to
     a. eventually eliminate the need for trial by jury
     b. control for the effect of the polygraph
     c. eliminate the contaminating effect of the galvanic skin response
     d. compare responses to neutral questions and critical questions

_____ 24. In most courtrooms, lie detector test results are
   a. admissible, because they give scientifically derived evidence
   b. admissible, because the jury must hear any evidence available
   c. inadmissible, because of their potential for error
   d. inadmissible, because they would put lawyers out of work

_____ 25. [*For Trekkies only*] The subject matter of this module helps us understand why, in a perverse way, we find the character of _____ so fascinating
   a. Spock
   b. Uhuru
   c. Kirk
   d. Scotty

Short Essay

1. Summarize the three different explanations through which psychology has tried to understand emotion.

2. Why are universal facial expressions of emotion recognized around the world?

3. What are the functions of emotions?

4. What are display rules for the expression of emotion and what do they tell us about emotion in general?

5. If you were accused of committing a crime, would you be willing to take a lie detector test?

Answers for Module 16

The Big Picture (explanations provided for incorrect choices)

A Emotion is vital to human adaptation and functioning. We need emotion to live.
B Correct! You see the "big picture" for this Module.
C Just the opposite is true. Read the material on universal emotions.
D Just the opposite is true. Most psychologists agree that emotions provide vital clues to our inner life and motivation.
E It's just a joke!

True-False

1	F	360	Psychologists do not agree on which theory of emotions is correct.
2	T	362	
3	T	364	
4	T	365	
5	T	365	
6	F	365	Emotion is crucial to human functioning and survival.
7	F	366	The joy doesn't last because even winners get used to their new advantages.
8	T	367	
9	F	367	Different cultures vary in which emotion they see as most intense.
10	F	370	Lie detector tests measure physiological arousal, not lying.

Flashcards 1

1 i 2 d 3 a 4 h 5 j 6 f 7 c 8 b 9 e 10 g

Flashcards 2

1 g 2 e 3 h 4 j 5 b 6 a 7 c 8 i 9 f 10 d

Multiple-Choice (explanations provided for incorrect choices)

1 a This statement is untrue.
   b Correct! See page 359.
   c Emotions are very important to survival.
   d It's just a joke!

2 a Conscious experience is one of the three components of emotion.
   b Physiological arousal is one of the three components of emotion.
   c Overt behavior is one of the three components of emotion.
   d Correct! See page 359.

3 a Risk taking is not the research interest here.
   b Gender differences were not involved in happiness over winning.
   c Correct! See page 359.
   d Guilt feelings are not the research interest here.

4 a Stop worrying! There is no shark bite theory of emotions.
   b Correct! See page 360.
   c The facial feedback theory says emotions result from how our brain interprets movement of facial muscles.
   d This theory says emotions result from appraising situations as having positive or negative impact on our lives.

5 a This famous experiment supports the cognitive appraisal theory.
   b The James-Lange theory says emotions result from specific physiological changes in the body.
   c Correct! See page 361.
   d This theory says emotions result from appraising situations as having positive or negative impact on our lives.

6 a Charles Darwin's work supports the facial feedback theory of emotions.
   b The James-Lange theory says emotions result from specific physiological changes in the body.
   c The facial feedback theory says emotions result from how our brain interprets movement of facial muscles.
   d Correct! See page 362.

7   *a*   *Correct! See page 362.*
    b   The cognitive appraisal theory goes back to the Schacter-Singer experiment in 1962.
    c   The facial feedback theory is several decades old.
    d   The James-Lange theory dates back to the late 1800s.

8   a   Just the opposite is true.
    b   Just the opposite is true.
    c   Hunger and eating is controlled by the hypothalamus, not the amygdala.
    d   *Correct! See page 362.*

9   a   The thalamus is involved in gathering information about a threat.
    b   *Correct! See page 363.*
    c   The amygdala is involved in identifying and warning about a threat.
    d   The prefrontal cortex is involved in analyzing and remembering a threat.

10 a   There are cultural variations in ranking the intensity of emotions.
    b   There are cultural variations in rules about showing emotions.
    c   *Correct! See page 364.*
    d   True, but this would not be evidence of the universality of emotions.

11 *a*   *Correct! See page 364.*
    b   Happiness is one of the basic emotions.
    c   Surprise is one of the basic emotions.
    d   Fear is one of the basic emotions.

12 a   Sighted infants also being to smile at 4–6 weeks.
    b   Smiling is not learned, the potential to smile is built in.
    c   *Correct! See page 364.*
    d   Early smiling is more about social bonding than disposition.

13 a   Emotions do help us adapt and survive.
    b   *Correct! See page 365.*
    c   Emotions do motivate and arouse us.
    d   Emotions do express social signals.

14 *a*   *Correct! See page 365.*
    b   The James-Lange theory says body changes lead to emotional feelings.
    c   The Schacter-Singer experiment (not law) supports the cognitive appraisal theory of emotion.
    d   Darwin was the first to propose the existence of universal emotions.

15 a   Shame on you! (OK, that's a small part of it, but it's not the main explanation for happiness.)
    b   Wouldn't that be an explanation for the decline of feelings of happiness?
    c   That's what the facial feedback theory implies, but facial muscles can't be more basic than brain functions.
    d   *Correct! See page 366.*

16 a   Some do, some don't (they see their lawyers first).
    b   Most use their winnings wisely.
    c   *Correct! See page 366.*
    d   The point is that this rarely happens . . . but why not?

17 a   Don't quit school, but people experience unhappiness at every income level.
    b   *Correct! See page 366.*
    c   This answer is a confusion of the meaning of the adaptation level theory.
    d   It's just a joke!

18 *a*   *Correct! See page 367.*
    b   This is not a correct technical term in psychology.
    c   This is not a correct technical term in psychology.
    d   This is not a correct technical term in psychology.

19 a   There are cultural variations in ranking the intensity of emotions.
    b   There are cultural variations in ranking the intensity of emotions.
    c   There are cultural variations in ranking the intensity of emotions.
    d   *Correct! See page 367.*

20   **a**   *Correct! See page 369.*
      b   This is one of the components of the definition of emotional intelligence.
      c   This is one of the components of the definition of emotional intelligence.
      d   This is one of the components of the definition of emotional intelligence.

21   a   Emotional intelligence relates to education, but is not a teaching method.
      b   There is not yet an established test to measure emotional intelligence.
      c   Test anxiety is not the main focus of the concept of emotional intelligence.
      d   *Correct! See page 369.*

22   a   Lie detector tests do not actually measure truth or falsity.
      b   *Correct! See page 370.*
      c   Lie detector tests do not actually measure truth or falsity.
      d   Character is an intangible factor no machine could measure easily.

23   a   What about the constitutional guarantee of trial by a jury of your peers?
      b   The polygraph is the lie detector machine.
      c   The galvanic skin response is what is measured and compared.
      d   *Correct! See page 371.*

24   a   Because lie detector tests measure arousal rather than lying, they can be unreliable.
      b   Because lie detector tests measure arousal rather than lying, they can be unreliable.
      c   *Correct! See page 371.*
      d   It's just a joke!

25   **a**   *Correct! See page 359.*
      b   Uhuru shows the full range of emotional responses, but Spock exhibits little emotion.
      c   Kirk shows the full range of emotional responses, but Spock exhibits little emotion
      d   Scotty shows the full range of emotional responses, but Spock exhibits little emotion

Short Essay (sample answers)

1. Does emotion come from bodily changes, thoughts and evaluations, or brain processes? Peripheral theories say that changes in the body, like running or smiling, cause changes in emotion. The cognitive appraisal theory says that changes in thoughts or evaluation of situations cause changes in emotion. More recently, the affective neuroscience approach says that the brain's neural circuits, especially the amygdala, evaluate stimuli and produce or contribute to experiencing different emotional states. Bet on brain processes!

2. There are seven facial expressions for emotion (anger, happiness, fear, surprise, disgust, sadness, and contempt) that are universally recognized across cultures. They probably evolved because they served adaptive and survival functions for our ancestors. All infants develop facial expressions in a predictable order, even blind infants who are not copying adults. These universal facial expressions, present from infancy, suggest that emotion is natural, ever-present, and beneficial. We should welcome it and use it.

3. Emotions have three basic functions. First, through signals conveyed by facial expressions, emotions send powerful social signals about our feelings or needs. Second, the evolutionary theory of emotions says they help us adapt and survive by evaluating objects, people, and situations in terms of how good or bad they are for our well-being. Emotions also focus our attention and increase memory and recall. Third, emotions arouse and motivate many behaviors that prepare the body for some action.

4. We are learning in this textbook that culture has a powerful effect on psychology. Display rules are a good example. Although there are universal emotions and universal facial expressions that accompany them, each culture works out rules for how these emotions are displayed. American culture encourages public display of emotion, such as open-mouth laughing, but Japanese culture discourages showing much emotion in public, so the mouth is often covered when laughing in public. Emotion is universal; display is particular.

5. It is often suggested that if you "have nothing to hide" you should agree to take a lie-detector test to exonerate yourself. But lie-detector tests exonerated the spy Aldrich Ames, and researchers estimate that the polygraph is wrong anywhere from 25–75% of the time! The problem is that the polygraph measures galvanic skin responses (physiological changes), not "lies." Until lie detection methods are improved, perhaps with brain scans of neural activity, the courts will be right not to admit polygraph results.

Module 17

Infancy & Childhood

The Competent Child

One of the most striking changes in psychological thinking about child development in recent years has been the emerging view of the child as a competent person, right from the beginning. It had been thought that human infants were essentially helpless, completely dependent on the care of adults. Rod Plotnik shows how current research on newborns' abilities, and better understanding of how children interact with adult caregivers, has given us a fresh picture of childhood. We now see children as incredibly active, responsive persons who spend much of their day "working" at building relationships and creating environments most conducive to growth. If the little rugrats could talk, they would probably even claim that *they* are in charge, not us.

The Importance of Childhood in Psychology

One of psychology's most important contributions to modern knowledge is the idea of childhood as a separate, special phase of human life, with processes of development crucial for the rest of life. That idea seems obvious today, but not long ago most people thought of children simply as small adults, not really different in any special way, or as happy innocents enjoying a carefree period of freedom before the onset of adult concerns.

Once psychology recognized the importance of childhood, every comprehensive theory had to attempt to explain it. Not surprisingly, most of the 'big' theories in psychology are also theories of childhood. Sigmund Freud argued that in the first five years children struggle through a series of conflicts that essentially shape personality. Erik Erikson placed the most fundamental developmental tasks in the early years and showed how they affected all later growth. Jean Piaget claimed that mature thinking evolves just as obviously as the physical body, and illustrated the many ways in which children think differently than adults. Albert Bandura demonstrated that children learn even from the simple act of observing, and have a powerful tendency to imitate what they see around them. If you can master this module, with its heavy involvement of psychology's most famous names, you can congratulate yourself on learning the major theories of modern psychology.

Thinking about childhood inevitably leads to ideas about psychology in general. In order to explain what children are like, it is necessary to say what humans are like. In no time at all, we are back debating the nature-nurture question. If we find a strong urge in children to be competent, must that not mean we all have a need to be effective?

Effective Student Tip 17

Overstudy!

My favorite myth about tests is the often-heard lament, "I studied too hard!" The idea seems to be that what you learn has only a fragile and temporary residence in your head, and studying too much disorganizes it or knocks it right back out again. A sadder myth is the belief so many students have that they are "no good at tests," when the truth is that, for whatever reasons, they have not yet *done* well. No less misguided is the teeth-clenching determination to "do better next time," with no idea of what specific steps to take to bring that about.

A closer look would reveal that each of these misguided students is making the same mistake: not studying hard enough, or effectively enough. When I am able to persuade students to read the assigned chapters three or four times (they thought once was enough), the results amaze them. Almost invariably, their test grades go from 'D' or 'C' to 'B' or 'A.' Why? Because with more study, and better study, they are really mastering the material.

Determine how much studying you think will be enough for the next test. Then do more. Lots more. The single best way to improve your test scores is to overstudy the material.

Your response...

Have you ever studied much harder for a test than seemed necessary? What happened?

Learning Objectives

1. Understand infancy and childhood as closely related periods in a sequence of development that leads to adolescence and adulthood.

2. Appreciate the crucial importance of the nature-nurture question in psychology and social science through investigation of genetic and environmental influences on infancy and childhood.

3. Learn the basic biology of prenatal influences, the prenatal period, newborn's abilities, and the principles of sensory and motor development.

4. Understand emotional development in infancy and childhood through the psychology of temperament, emotions, and attachment.

5. Learn the classic theories of cognitive and social development: Piaget's cognitive development, Freud's psychosexual stages, Erikson's psychosocial stages, and Bandura's social cognitive theory.

6. Consider your position on the origin, meaning, and significance of gender differences and gender roles.

7. Explore the problem of child abuse — its causes, treatment, and prevention.

Key Terms

The inclusion of four major psychological theories in this module brings in many key terms. Group the terms by the famous psychologists who used them to build their theories.

accommodation
amniocentesis
anal stage
assimilation
attachment
cephalocaudal principle
child abuse and neglect
cognitive development
cognitive developmental
   theory
conception or fertilization
concrete operations stage
conservation
cross-sectional method
developmental norms
developmental psychologists
Down syndrome
egocentric thinking
embryonic stage
emotional development

evolutionary theory
fetal alcohol syndrome (FAS)
fetal stage
formal operations stage
gender identity
gender roles
gender schemas
genital stage
germinal stage
inhibited/fearful children
insecure attachment
latency stage
longitudinal method
maturation
motor development
nature-nurture question
object permanence
oral stage
ovulation
phallic stage

Piaget's cognitive stages
placenta
prenatal period
preoperational stage
principle of bidirectionality
prodigy
proximodistal principle
psychosexual stages
psychosocial stages
resiliency
secure attachment
sensorimotor stage
separation anxiety
social cognitive theory
social development
social role theory
temperament
teratogen
visual cliff
vulnerability

Outline

- *Introduction*
  - ☐ The nature-nurture question may be the most fundamental issue in the social sciences. It comes up again and again in psychology. Do you understand the basic issues?
  1. **Nature-nurture question** (Baby Jessica by *nature*)
  2. **Developmental psychologists** (Baby Jessica by *nurture*)

A. *Prenatal Influences*

  1. Nature and nurture
     a. **Prodigy**
     b. Nature-nurture interaction
  2. Genetic and environmental factors
     a. Parents, daughters, and son
     b. Interaction
  3. **Prenatal period**: three stages
     a. **Germinal stage**
        (1) **Ovulation**
        (2) **Conception or fertilization**
     b. **Embryonic stage**
     c. **Fetal stage**
  4. Placenta and teratogens
     a. **Placenta**
     b. **Teratogen**
  5. Birth defects and amniocentesis
     a. **Amniocentesis**
     b. **Down syndrome**
  6. Drugs and prenatal development
     a. Drug usage during pregnancy
        (1) Cocaine plus other drugs
        (2) Smoking and nicotine
        (3) Lead
     b. Alcohol
        (1) Heavy drinking: **fetal alcohol syndrome (FAS)**
        (2) Moderate drinking: fetal alcohol effects (FAE)

B. *Newborn's Abilities*

 1. Genetic developmental program

    a. Genetic program

    b. Brain growth

 2. Sensory development

    a. Faces

    b. Hearing

    c. Touch

    d. Smell and taste

    e. Depth perception: **visual cliff**

 3. **Motor development**

    a. **Proximodistal principle**

    b. **Cephalocaudal principle**

    c. **Maturation**

    d. **Developmental norms**

    e. Neural connections: interaction of genetic program and environmental stimulation

C. *Emotional Development*

 1. Definition: **emotional development**

 2. **Temperament** and emotions

    a. Study of infant temperament (Thomas and Chess)

       (1) Easy babies (40%)

       (2) Slow-to-warm-up babies (15%)

       (3) Difficult babies (10%)

       (4) No-single-category babies (35%)

    b. Genetic influence and environmental influence

 3. **Attachment** (John Bowlby)

    a. How does attachment occur? **separation anxiety** (Mary Ainsworth)

    b. Are there different kinds of attachment?

       (1) **Secure attachment**

       (2) **Insecure attachment**

    c. What are the effects of attachment?

D. *Research Focus: Temperament*

 1. Are some infants born fearful?

    a. **Longitudinal method**: disadvantages and advantages

    b. **Cross-sectional method**: advantages and disadvantages

2. Research methods for studying developmental changes (Jerome Kagan)

   a. Procedure: **inhibited/fearful children**

   b. Results

      (1) How many were fearful/inhibited?

      (2) How many changed temperaments?

      (3) What happens in the brain?

   c. Conclusions: how to help fearful children?

E. *Cognitive Development*

   ☐ When you are with young children, does their thinking seem like ours, except less developed, or does it seem quite different from adult thought?

1. Piaget's theory: **cognitive development**

   a. **Assimilation**

   b. **Accommodation**

2. **Piaget's cognitive stages**

   a. **Sensorimotor stage**

      (1) Hidden objects

      (2) **Object permanence**

   b. **Preoperational stage**

      (1) Symbols

      (2) **Conservation**

      (3) **Egocentric thinking**

   c. **Concrete operations stage**

      (1) Conservation

      (2) Classification

      (3) New abilities

   d. **Formal operations stage**

      (1) Adult thinking and reasoning

      (2) Abstract ideas and hypothetical constructs

   e. Piaget's key ideas (about children and cognitive development)

      (1) Gradually develop reasoning through assimilation and accommodation

      (2) Naturally curious, intrinsically motivated to explore, develop cognitive skills

      (3) Acquire different kinds of thinking and reasoning abilities through different stages

3. Evaluation of Piaget's theory

   a. Impact and criticisms

      (1) Impact of Piaget's theory

      (2) Criticisms

       (3) Current status

   b. New information

       (1) Genetic factors

       (2) Brain development

F. *Social Development*

   1. **Social development**

   2. Freud's **psychosexual stages** (and potential conflicts)

   ☐ The heart of Sigmund Freud's theory is the sexual conflict at each stage. Do you buy his descriptions?

     a. **Oral stage**

     b. **Anal stage**

     c. **Phallic stage**

     d. **Latency stage**

     e. **Genital stage**

   3. Erikson's **psychosocial stages** (and potential problems) [Stages 1–5 here, 6–8 in Module 18.]

   ☐ The heart of Erik Erikson's theory is the potential social problem at each stage. Do his ideas make sense?

     a. Stage 1: trust versus mistrust

     b. Stage 2: autonomy versus shame and doubt

     c. Stage 3: initiative versus guilt

     d. Stage 4: industry versus inferiority

     e. Stage 5: identity versus role confusion

     f. Evaluation of Erikson's and Freud's theories

   4. Bandura's **social cognitive theory**

   ☐ Albert Bandura, originally a behaviorist, wanted to bring thinking into learning (see Module 10). Can you see why his theory is called both "social" and "cognitive"?

   5. Resiliency

     a. **Vulnerability**

     b. **Resiliency**

   6. Gender differences

     a. Social development

        (1) **Gender identity**

        (2) **Gender roles**

     b. **Social role theory**

     c. **Cognitive developmental theory: gender schemas**

   7. Differences in gender traits

     a. Social role theory: outside pressures

     b. Cognitive developmental theory: inside pressures

8. Male and female differences

☐ What position do you take in the debate over gender differences?

  a. Career choices

  b. Aggression

  c. Different brains

8. Review: the Big Picture

  a. Newborn's abilities

  b. Motor development

  c. Emotional development

  d. Cognitive development

  e. Social development

  f. Importance of childhood

G. *Cultural Diversity: Gender Roles*

  1. Identifying gender roles

  2. Gender roles across cultures

  3. Two answers

    a. **Social role theory**

    b. **Evolutionary theory**

H. *Application: Child Abuse*

  1. Kinds of abuse: **child abuse and neglect**

  2. Who abuses children? **principle of bidirectionality**

  3. What problems do abused children have?

  4. How are abusive parents helped?

A Day in the Nursery

You know that little brat who gets in the way and makes it difficult for you to study? Instead of muttering "rugrat" under your breath, think "research subject" instead! The theories you are studying are somewhat abstract when presented in a textbook, but you've got the real article right in front of you. Put on your mental lab coat and look at this child coolly and dispassionately (i.e., scientifically). Does the behavior you observe support or contradict the theories you are studying? All right! Now psychology is getting real.

Language Workout

What's That?

p. 377   **put** Jessica **up** for adoption = offered
          courts have **sided with** biological parents = agree with
          they have **a good bond** in the home = a strong relationship
          the **age-old** question = long-time

p. 378   He **walks on the waves** = He makes miracles

p. 379   the ovum is **sloughed off** = separated, removed
          when most **miscarriages** occur = death of fetus inside mother

p. 381   short **stature** = height
          gets a **pat on the backside** = slap from the doctor at birth (see photo on p. 395)
          ready **to take on the world** = for the future

p. 382   very **keen** hearing = good, well-developed

p. 383   they can control their **trunks** = bodies (from shoulders to hips)

p. 387   **fretting** = worrying behavior

p. 388   an infant is soon ready to **creep** = move on the floor

p. 390   computer **hackers** = users who break into private information
          if **going steady** is a good idea = dating only one person exclusively

p. 392   being very neat, **stingy** = unwilling to share or spend money

p. 393   she is **bound** to get into conflict = sure

p. 396   not **mutually exclusive** = unable to exist together
          armed forces = soldiers, army
          society rewards boys for **acting out** = expressing their impulses

p. 400   all the **trappings** of being perfect = outward signs
          a **pillar** of the Denver community = leader

p. 404   **bullying** = forcing others to do what you want
          truancy = avoiding school
          no **putdowns** = hurtful or critical remarks

What's the Difference?

NON-COUNT NOUNS

You have certainly learned that some nouns in English are non-count, which means that we cannot count them directly. Many second-language students are surprised that we cannot count the following words in English because these words can be counted in their languages.

    research / **advice** / **equipment** / **information** / **knowledge** / **evidence**

So, we can *never* use "a" or "an" with any of these words.

Also, we can *never* add an "s" to make a plural with any of the words above.

But isn't there some way to count research? Yes, but we need to use another word: it's possible to say **a piece of research** or **a research project**. We can also say: The professor assigned **some**

research or **a lot of research** or **too much research** or **several pieces of research** or **three research projects**.

If you think that you are hearing people say "researches," you are right. But they are not counting their research. Instead, they are reporting an action: What does she do? <u>She researches</u> the influence of alcohol on fetal development.

To practice these non-count nouns, read the following sentences. Choose the correct form of the <u>underlined word</u> and circle it. In the Answers, you will find possible replacement nouns that can be counted.

> Grandpa enjoys giving <u>advice</u> / <u>advices</u> to young people.
> Maryam is spending hours in the library on her <u>research</u> / <u>researches</u>.
> Willard stopped at the Tourist Office to get some <u>information</u> / <u>informations</u>.
> The failed business sold all its <u>equipment</u> / <u>equipments</u> to pay its bills.
> The team of lawyers presented surprising <u>evidence</u> / <u>evidences</u> about the crime.
> A lot of <u>knowledge</u> / <u>knowledges</u> disappeared when the library burned down.

Flex Your Word Power with Plurals

Check out this sentence:

> In most cases, only a single **ovum** is released during ovulation, but sometimes two **ova** are released. (p. 379)

Notice the ending of the word **ov<u>um</u>** is quite different in the plural form **ov<u>a</u>**. Here are some other words you may have encountered recently with unusual plural forms

> one **cris<u>is</u>**, two **cris<u>es</u>**
> one **criteri<u>on</u>**, several **criteri<u>a</u>**

Now try to test yourself with the correct form below and then check the Answers.

> The president has had to solve many public **cris____** , but the problem of global warming may be the most difficult **cris____**.

> Cost and convenience are two of the **criteri____** used by most students when they are choosing a college, yet a more important **criteri____** should be the program of studies.

> One of the world's most expensive foods is caviar, which is actually the **ov____** from a large fish called a sturgeon. Each **ov____** is so small that a spoon can hold fifty or more.

Answers

Grandpa enjoys giving <u>advice</u> to young people. (You could say "recommendations" or suggestions.")
Maryam is spending hours in the library on her <u>research</u>. (You could say "projects.")
Willard stopped at the Tourist Office to get some <u>information</u>. (You could say "facts.")
The failed business sold all its <u>equipment</u> to pay its bills. (You could say "machines.")
The team of lawyers presented surprising <u>evidence</u> about the crime. (You could say "facts.")
A lot of <u>knowledge</u> disappeared when the library burned down. (You could say "facts" or "ideas.")
The president has had to solve many public **crises**, but the problem of global warming may be the most difficult **crisis.**
Cost and convenience are two of the **criteria** used by most students when they are choosing a college, yet a more important **criterion** should be the program of studies.
One of the world's most expensive foods is caviar, which is actually the **ova** from a large fish called a sturgeon. Each **ovum** is so small that a spoon can hold fifty or more.

The Big Picture

Which statement below offers the best summary of the larger significance of this module?

A   It is in areas like infancy and childhood that psychology risks losing the respect of the general public. If we present theories as outrageous as Freud's and as strange as Piaget's, how can we expect to be taken seriously?

B   The fact this module ends with a section on child abuse is sad testimony to the state of childhood today. If you read it carefully, you realize that this module is mostly about the injuries and misfortunes suffered by children.

C   In the ongoing argument over nature and nurture, the pendulum is clearly swinging toward nurture. All the major theories (Freud, Erikson, Piaget) say that our personalities are shaped mainly by our environment.

D   The processes of development that take place during infancy and childhood reveal the complex and subtle interaction of the forces of nature and nurture, suggesting that this interplay probably continues throughout life.

E   This theory of Freud's about an oral stage is really a crock! Say, get me another brewski, would you?

True-False

_____   1.   The nature-nurture question asks how much development owes to inheritance and how much to learning and experience.

_____   2.   The "visual cliff" is the distance beyond which infants cannot see clearly.

_____   3.   The cephalocaudal principle of motor development says that the parts closer to the head develop before the parts closer to the feet.

_____   4.   The concept of maturation is closer to "nurture" than to "nature."

_____   5.   Attachment is the close emotional bond that develops between infant and parent.

_____   6.   In Piaget's first stage of cognitive development, the child relates sensory experiences to motor actions.

_____   7.   When Piaget used the word "operations," he meant behaviors such as walking and talking that accomplish important tasks for the child.

_____   8.   In Erikson's scheme, each stage of life contains a "test" that, if failed, prevents you from entering the next stage.

_____   9.   Studies of "resilient" children tend to support Erikson's idea that later positive experiences can compensate for early traumas.

_____   10.   Ninety percent of abusive parents were themselves abused children.

Flashcards 1

_____   1. anal stage

_____   2. concrete operations stage

_____   3. formal operations stage

_____   4. genital stage

_____   5. latency stage

_____   6. nature-nurture question

_____   7. oral stage

_____   8. phallic stage

_____   9. preoperational stage

_____   10. sensorimotor stage

a. Freud's 1st stage; age 0-18 mo; infant's pleasure seeking is centered on the mouth

b. Freud's 2nd stage; age 1-3; infant's pleasure seeking centered on anus and its functions of elimination

c. Freud's 3rd stage; age 3-6; child's pleasure seeking is centered on the genitals

d. Piaget's 4th stage; from age 12; adolescents develop ability to think about and solve abstract problems

e. Piaget's 2nd stage; age 2-7; children learn to use symbols like words to think about things not present

f. Piaget's 3rd stage; age 7-11; children perform logical mental operations on physically present objects

g. Freud's 4th stage; age 6-puberty; child represses sexual thoughts and engages in nonsexual activities

h. Freud's 5th stage; after puberty; individual has renewed sexual desires fulfilled through relationships

i. asks how much genetic factors and environmental factors each contribute to a person's development

j. Piaget's 1st stage; birth-age 2; infant interacts with environment by sensory experience and motor action

Flashcards 2

_____   1. attachment

_____   2. cephalocaudal principle

_____   3. gender schemas

_____   4. maturation

_____   5. proximodistal principle

_____   6. resiliency

_____   7. separation anxiety

_____   8. temperament

_____   9. teratogen

_____   10. visual cliff

a. any environmental agent (such as a disease, drug, or chemical) that can harm a developing fetus

b. personality, family, other factors that compensate for increased life stresses to prevent expected problems

c. states that parts closer to center of infant's body develop before parts farther away

d. an infant's distress (loud protests, crying, and agitation) whenever the parents temporarily leave

e. a close fundamental emotional bond that develops between the infant and the parent or caregiver

f. developmental changes that are genetically or biologically programmed rather than learned

g. states that parts of the body closer to the infant's head develop before parts closer to the feet

h. stable behavioral and emotional reactions that appear early and are influenced largely by genetics

i. a glass tabletop with checkerboard and clear glass surfaces to create the illusion of a drop to the floor

j. sets of information and rules organized around how either a male or a female should think and behave

Multiple-Choice

_____ 1. Rod Plotnik begins the module with the heart-wrenching story of little Jessica, who was taken from her potential adoptive parents and given to her birth mother, to illustrate
  a. the danger that adoptive parents will not love children as much as birth parents
  b. the mischief that arises when developmental psychologists are brought in
  c. a tragic failure of the foster parent program
  d. a real-life application of the nature-nurture question

_____ 2. Applying the nature-nurture question to Yehudi Menuhin, the child violin prodigy, we would ask whether his special abilities
  a. are a gift of God or an accident of nature
  b. are inborn or the product of learning and experience
  c. will stay with him or fade as he gets older
  d. are genuine or the result of good publicity

_____ 3. The briefest period of prenatal development is the
  a. germinal stage
  b. embryonic stage
  c. fetal stage
  d. baby-making stage [just kidding!]

_____ 4. The medical test called _____ is performed to indicate genetic problems like _____
  a. teratogen identification / lead poisoning
  b. placentosis / fetal alcohol syndrome (FAS)
  c. fetal stage assessment / brain damage
  d. amniocentesis / Down syndrome

_____ 5. If you believe what the textbook says about teratogens, you would tell pregnant women to
  a. watch their weight gain very carefully
  b. get plenty of rest — even more as they approach delivery
  c. avoid alcohol entirely
  d. avoid becoming overly stressed

_____ 6. Infants first use their more developed arms, and then their fingers, whose control develops later — this is the
  a. cephalocaudal principle
  b. proximodistal principle
  c. principle of maturation
  d. principle of normal development

_____ 7. The term temperament refers to
  a. contrary behavior that is typical of the "terrible twos"
  b. emotional characteristics that are largely influenced by environmental factors
  c. relatively stable individual differences in mood and emotional behavior
  d. the formal name in psychology for childhood temper tantrums

_____ 8. A longitudinal study of infant temperament found that
     a. infants develop a distinct temperament in the first two to three months
     b. infants' temperaments tend to mirror their parents' temperaments
     c. temperament is determined by the emotional state of the mother during pregnancy
     d. temperament fluctuates widely during infancy

_____ 9. The research on infant temperament tends to support the
     a. prenatal influences theory
     b. nature side of the nature-nurture question
     c. concept of gradual maturation
     d. nurture position in child development

_____ 10. The fearful or inhibited temperament is probably caused by
     a. an overactive amygdala in the brain
     b. overprotective parental care
     c. nutritional deficiencies in infancy
     d. an unacceptably high number of frightening experiences during infancy

_____ 11. For Jean Piaget, children deal with and adjust to the world through twin processes he called
     a. conservation and revisionism
     b. motor learning and cognitive learning
     c. egocentric thinking and magical thinking
     d. assimilation and accommodation

_____ 12. The essence of Piaget's theory of cognitive development is that
     a. through thousands and thousands of mistakes, the child gradually builds a factual picture of the world
     b. a child's picture of the world is slowly, gradually shaped by a steady succession of learning experiences
     c. each stage is characterized by a distinctly different way of understanding the world
     d. the mind of a child is like the mind of an adult — there just isn't as much information in it

_____ 13. The concept of object permanence develops during the _____ stage
     a. sensorimotor
     b. preoperational
     c. concrete operations
     d. formal operations

_____ 14. Watching juice poured from a short, wide glass into a tall, narrow glass, the child cries, "I want [the tall] glass!" thus illustrating the problem of
     a. object permanence
     b. egocentric thinking
     c. classification
     d. conservation

_____ 15. Piaget said adult thinking is finally achieved in the _____ stage
     a. preoperational
     b. sensorimotor
     c. formal operations
     d. concrete operations

_____ 16. If there is a single idea that Erik Erikson's theory clearly modifies, it is
   a. Freud's emphasis on the critical importance of the first five years
   b. the idea that childhood development takes place in stages
   c. Piaget's emphasis on how children see the world
   d. Bandura's idea that children learn through social interaction

_____ 17. All of the following are positive outcomes in Erikson's first four stages, but which list is in the correct chronological order?
   a. trust – autonomy – industry – initiative
   b. trust – initiative – industry – autonomy
   c. trust – autonomy – initiative – industry
   d. autonomy – initiative – industry – trust

_____ 18. Perhaps the most attractive aspect of Erikson's theory is that he sees development as
   a. packed into the formative years, so a happy child almost automatically becomes a happy adult
   b. biologically predetermined in a positive direction, so only extreme trauma results in negative personality traits
   c. arising from a foundation of essential human goodness and positiveness
   d. continuing throughout life, with many opportunities for reworking and rebuilding personality traits

_____ 19. Albert Bandura's social cognitive theory emphasizes the importance of
   a. thinking about the social interaction going on around you
   b. extrinsic motivation over intrinsic motivation
   c. learning through observation
   d. performing observable behaviors and receiving external rewards

_____ 20. Which one of the following is _not_ an essential ingredient of resiliency?
   a. a positive temperament
   b. parents free from mental and financial problems
   c. a substitute caregiver
   d. social support from peers

_____ 21. When do you know whether you're a boy or a girl? The answer is
   a. early in the first year
   b. between the ages of 2 and 3
   c. when you first observe other kids (as in bathing) and notice the obvious anatomical differences
   d. it's never really "learned" — it's something you always know

_____ 22. New research suggests that girls and women may develop traits of being concerned, sensitive, and nurturing because
   a. as victims of discrimination, they know hurt and suffering intimately
   b. generations of women have found that sticking together is a good strategy
   c. their brains are wired for processing, coding, and remembering emotional experiences
   d. their smaller size and lesser strength means they have to rely on other abilities

_____ 23. Why are gender roles similar across cultures? Social role theory points to _____ while evolutionary theory emphasizes _____
   a. women's natural friendliness / men's natural shyness
   b. developing from different divisions of labor / continuations of early survival mechanisms
   c. differences in size and strength / differences in nurturance and sociability
   d. competition over access to mates / assigning different work to males and females

_____ 24. Do children who suffer abuse grow up to be child abusers themselves?
   a. about 30% do, but there are compensatory factors that can prevent this from happening
   b. a few do, but not because they were abused themselves
   c. about 85% do, which means we can identify the future abusers
   d. almost none do — the abuse–abuser link is a popular myth

_____ 25. Treatment for child abuse involves at least two goals:
   a. arresting the abusing parent and removing the child from the home
   b. placing the child in a temporary foster home and enrolling the parent in counseling
   c. teaching the parent to substitute verbal for physical punishment and helping the child learn how to read the parent's moods
   d. overcoming the parent's personal problems and changing parent–child interactions

Short Essay

1. Describe the two sides of the nature-nurture question and explain why this debate is so important in psychology and social science.

2. What is attachment and how is it crucial to emotional development in infancy and childhood?

3. Summarize Piaget's four stages of cognitive development.

4. How are Freud's and Erikson's theories of development similar and how do they differ?

5. What is your answer to the question of differences in gender traits and gender roles, and the social significance of such differences?

Answers for Module 17

The Big Picture (explanations provided for incorrect choices)

A   Part of the enduring value of theories like Freud's and Piaget's is that they provoke us to see human behavior in new ways. Education is about intellectual change and growth.
B   The module also offers many ideas about the resiliency and strengths of childhood.
C   The pendulum is swinging back toward the nature. The theories cited place more emphasis on nature than nurture.
D   *Correct! You see the "big picture" for this Module.*
E   It's just a joke!

True-False

1	T	377	
2	F	382	The visual cliff is an experimental device to test depth perception.
3	T	383	
4	F	383	Maturation refers to changes that are genetically or biologically programmed — that's "nature."
5	T	385	
6	T	389	
7	F	390	For Piaget, "operations" are mental manipulations of information.
8	F	393	It's not pass or fail; each stage presents a problem each person solves in a slightly different way.
9	T	394	
10	F	401	Some abused children (about 30%) grow up to become abusive parents, but most do not.

Flashcards 1

1 b	2 f	3 d	4 h	5 g	6 i	7 a	8 c	9 e	10 j

Flashcards 2

1 e	2 g	3 j	4 f	5 c	6 b	7 d	8 h	9 a	10 i

Multiple-Choice (explanations provided for incorrect choices)

1   a   Jessica was fully loved by the parents who wanted to adopt her.
   b   Developmental psychologists did not cause any mischief.
   c   It was not a foster parent case, nor was it a failure for Jessica.
   d   *Correct! See page 377.*

2   a   This is a misstatement of the nature-nurture question.
   b   *Correct! See page 378.*
   c   This is a misstatement of the nature-nurture question.
   d   This is a misstatement of the nature-nurture question.

3   **a**   *Correct! See page 379.*
   b   The embryonic period spans the 2 to 8 weeks after conception.
   c   The fetal period covers most of the nine months after conception.
   d   It's just a [bad] joke!

4   a   Not a correct term / not a genetic problem.
   b   Not a correct term / not a genetic problem.
   c   Not a correct term / not a genetic problem.
   d   *Correct! See page 380.*

5   a   Teratogens do not refer to weight.
   b   Teratogens do not refer to rest.
   c   *Correct! See page 380.*
   d   Teratogens do not refer to stress.

6   a   The cephalocaudal principle says parts of the body closer to the head develop before parts closer to the feet.
   b   *Correct! See page 383.*
   c   Maturation refers to the pattern according to which development unfolds.
   d   This is not a correct technical term in developmental psychology.

7   a   The term is much broader than the narrow meaning of "temper."
      b   Temperament is thought to be mainly influenced by genetic factors.
      c   *Correct! See page 384.*
      d   The term is much broader than the narrow meaning of "temper tantrums."

8   *a*   *Correct! See page 384.*
      b   Each individual comes into the world with a unique temperament.
      c   Temperament probably is genetically influenced.
      d   Temperament is relatively constant.

9   a   This is not a correct technical term in developmental psychology.
      b   *Correct! See page 384.*
      c   Temperament appears to be present at birth.
      d   Nurture refers to the influence of experience and the environment.

10   *a*   *Correct! See page 387.*
      b   Research does not suggest overprotection as the cause.
      c   Research does not suggest nutritional deficiencies as the cause.
      d   Research does not suggest frightening experiences as the cause.

11   a   Although they reflect some of Piaget's thinking, these are not his overall processes.
      b   Although they reflect some of Piaget's thinking, these are not his overall processes.
      c   Although they reflect some of Piaget's thinking, these are not his overall processes.
      d   *Correct! See page 388.*

12   a   Piaget's theory is not based on trial and error learning.
      b   This would be more true of a behavioral approach to learning.
      c   *Correct! See page 388.*
      d   Piaget believed that children's and adults' minds are qualitatively different.

13   *a*   *Correct! See page 389.*
      b   Remember that object permanence is the first cognitive achievement.
      c   Remember that object permanence is the first cognitive achievement.
      d   Remember that object permanence is the first cognitive achievement.

14   a   Object permanence means understanding that objects still exist even if they can no longer be seen, etc.
      b   Egocentric thinking refers to seeing the world only from your own viewpoint.
      c   Classification refers to the ability to organize objects mentally according to some dimension.
      d   *Correct! See page 389.*

15   a   This is the second stage.
      b   This is the first stage.
      c   *Correct! See page 390.*
      d   This is the third stage.

16   *a*   *Correct! See page 393.*
      b   Erikson's theory is a stage theory.
      c   Erikson's theory doesn't emphasize cognitive development, but doesn't reject the importance of mental life.
      d   Erikson also emphasizes social interaction.

17   a   This is almost right. Review *industry* and *initiative*.
      b   This is almost right. Review the importance of *autonomy*.
      c   *Correct! See page 393.*
      d   Is it reasonable that an infant would develop a sense of autonomy first?

18   a   Erikson assumes that development continues throughout the life span.
      b   Erikson notes that many difficulties, large and small, occur in life.
      c   Erikson does not assume that humans are basically good.
      d   *Correct! See page 393.*

19   a   No doubt important, but not what Bandura emphasized.
      b   Just the opposite is true.
      c   *Correct! See page 394.*
      d   Just the opposite is true.

20 a   This is one of the three factors that characterize resilient children.
    b *Correct! See page 394.*
    c   This is one of the three factors that characterize resilient children.
    d   This is one of the three factors that characterize resilient children.

21 a   Gender roles are complicated and take some time to learn.
    b *Correct! See page 396.*
    c   Knowing about anatomical differences does not automatically convey an understanding of gender roles.
    d   Gender roles are learned.

22 a   Possible, but the new research comes from brain scans.
    b   Possible, but the new research comes from brain scans.
    c *Correct! See page 396.*
    d   Possible, but the new research comes from brain scans.

23 a   The distinction is neither true nor the basis of the differences in theories.
    b *Correct! See page 399.*
    c   Just the opposite is true.
    d   Just the opposite is true.

24 *a* *Correct! See page 401.*
    b   Sadly, there is a strong link between being abused and abusing.
    c   It is nowhere near this automatic.
    d   Unfortunately, it is not a myth.

25 a   These are extreme measures used in cases of imminent danger to the child.
    b   Such a recommendation would be costly and extreme.
    c   Such a recommendation would accept the idea that abuse would continue.
    d *Correct! See page 401.*

Short Essay (sample answers)

1. The nature-nurture question asks how much genetic factors (nature) and environmental factors (nurture) contribute to a person's biological, emotional, cognitive, personal, and social development. This question is one of the most fundamental issues in understanding others and ourselves. It is involved in almost every problem in psychology, from intelligence to temperament to gender differences. As we saw in the story of baby Jessica, the nature-nurture question is often at the heart of real-life situations.

2. Attachment is a close, fundamental emotional bond that develops between an infant and his or her parents or caregiver. John Bowlby believed that attachment behavior evolved due to its adaptive value in our species. Mary Ainsworth discovered separation anxiety (when parents temporarily leave) and two kinds of attachment, secure (parents as a home base for exploration) and insecure (ambivalence or resistance toward parents). Secure attachment is the foundation for successful adult relationships.

3. Jean Piaget said that by means of an interaction of assimilation and accommodation children advance through four stages of cognitive development. (1) Sensorimotor: relate their sensory experiences to their motor actions, attain object permanence. (2) Preoperational: learn to use symbols to think about things that are not present, attain conservation. (3) Concrete operations: perform a number of logical mental operations on concrete objects. (4) Formal operations: think about and solve abstract problems in a logical manner.

4. Psychoanalysts Sigmund Freud and Erik Erikson saw development as the progression through a series of stages, each with a special conflict or problem. For Freud, each of five "psychosexual" stages, completed by age five, presented a sexual conflict to resolve. For Erikson, each of eight "psychosocial" stages, from birth to death, presented a social need to satisfy. These influential personality theories are complete philosophies of human nature, but are more descriptive than explanatory, and difficult to verify or test experimentally.

5. Psychology has always been fascinated (obsessed?) with gender differences, which have been noted again and again, most recently in differing brain activity. Children are not all alike, but are the differences sexual, or temperamental? Where there are apparent differences, such as in career choice or aggression, are the differences better explained by social role theory or evolutionary theory? Your answer should consider these factors, but should also take account of your own accumulating experience in the world of men and women.

Module 18

Adolescence & Adulthood

All About You

If there is one module in the textbook that clearly is about *you*, this is it. If you are in college, you've just been an adolescent and now you're an adult. Therefore, it will be the hardest module to learn.

Say what?

When studying something like the brain or memory or language, even though it's all right on top our shoulders, it seems removed from our everyday knowledge. In a way, that makes it easier to objectify, and hence to learn.

The facts and theories of adolescence and adulthood, on the other hand, are so close to our everyday experience that it is difficult to obtain sufficient distance to allow getting a handle on them. As you read, you say "yes…," "yes…," yes…," but later it's hard to remember what ought to stand out as important to learn.

I suggest a three-step process in studying this material. First, give yourself credit for what you have learned from your own experience. Don't expect every idea in the module to be new to you. Second, recognize that many of the new ideas discussed in the module may be interesting, but have not yet been accepted as permanent contributions to knowledge. Find out from your professor what to master. Third, have one simple question in mind as you read and study: is this idea helpful? In other words, does what you are reading seem true about yourself, add to your knowledge, and deepen your understanding? Pay special attention to those facts and ideas that do.

The Elegance of Erik Erikson

In this module Rod Plotnik concludes his review of Erik Erikson's fascinating theory of development across the lifespan. (Erikson, considered a "neo-Freudian," does appear again in Plotnik's discussion of psychoanalytic personality theories in Module 19.)

To win a place in the educated public's understanding, a theory needs sharp edges and distinctive, even shocking, premises. We all remember Pavlov's confused dog, Freud's obsession with sex, Piaget's surprising ideas about how children think, and Skinner's untiring lever-pressing rats. Erik Erikson's elegant, almost poetic saga of human life lacks all that. Consequently, although psychologists respect Erikson highly, the educated public does not know his outlook very well. That's a shame, because it might be the most true-to-life theory of all.

Re-read Rod Plotnik's thoughtful discussion of Erikson in Modules 17 and 18. Put Erikson on your list of authors to read in the original.

Effective Student Tip 18

What the Professor Wants

I remember a student who would walk me to class and offer an admiring comment on my shirt, or some such, but then fail to turn in the assignment. Professors love compliments and admiring students. They're human, after all. That isn't what they really want, though.

Every professor wants to be an effective teacher. What your professor wants from you personally is that you really do *learn*. The best thing you can do for your professor is also the best thing you can do for yourself: learn, achieve your goals, and be successful.

Professors sometimes deceive themselves and each other by saying, "If I can help just one student, it's all worth while…," but they don't really believe it. Deep down, they wish *every one* of their students would learn and progress. Then they would know what they are doing is right, which would satisfy their own urge to be effective.

Like you, your professor wants to be effective, but because the measure of that effectiveness is your learning, only you can bring it about. Does it occur to you that you and the professor really need each other? Both of you want to be effective in life, and you can help each other achieve that effectiveness. Don't underestimate your power. The professor's fate is in your hands!

Your response…

Of all the teachers you have known, which one meant the most to you? Explain why.

Learning Objectives

1. Understand adolescence and adulthood as the continuation and completion of the four-stage human life cycle: infancy, childhood, adolescence, and adulthood.

2. Learn the basic biology of puberty and sexual behavior in adolescent girls and boys, and the kinds of changes that come with aging later in adulthood.

3. Explore cognitive and emotional changes through examining Jean Piaget's theory of cognitive development, new discoveries in brain development, Lawrence Kohlberg's theory of moral reasoning, and studies of parenting styles.

4. Learn about personality and social changes through consideration of the psychology of self-esteem, Erik Erikson's adult psychosocial stages, and personality change in adulthood.

5. Understand gender roles and gender expectations, the different kinds of love, choosing a partner, and the success or failure of long-term relationships.

6. Explore the research on happy marriages, why marriages succeed or fail, and cultural differences in preferences for partners and reasons for marrying.

7. Refine your understanding of teenage suicide and explore the issue of doctor-assisted suicide in the elderly.

Key Terms

The key terms for this module show great variety. Some are crucial terms from famous theories, while others denote biological facts or interesting concepts from new research and thinking about adolescence and adulthood. You probably already know some of these terms, since more and more they are appearing in newspaper and magazine articles about adolescence and adulthood, sex and love, and self-identity and aging.

adolescence
aging by chance theory
aging by design theory
authoritarian parents
authoritative parents
BioPsychoSocial model
cognitive development
companionate love
conventional level
estrogen
female secondary sexual
  characteristics

formal operations stage
gender roles
personal identity or self-
  identity
male secondary sexual
  characteristics
menarche
menopause
normal aging
passionate love
pathological aging
perceptual speed

permissive parents
personality and social
  development
postconventional level
preconventional level
processing speed
puberty
reaction time
schema
self-esteem
testosterone
triangular theory of love

Outline

- *Introduction*
    1. **Adolescence** (Teenager Branndi)
    □ What was your own adolescence like? Was it the best of times or the worst of times?
    2. Adulthood (Prom queen Susan)

A. *Puberty & Sexual Behavior*
    1. Definition: **puberty**
    □ Do you remember a time when you were confused or troubled by how your body was changing? What were your thoughts and feelings about it at the time?
    2. Girls during puberty
        a. Physical growth
        b. Female sexual maturity: **menarche** and **estrogen**
        c. **Female secondary sexual characteristics**
        d. Early versus late maturing
    3. Boys during puberty
        a. Physical growth
        b. Male sexual maturity: **testosterone**
        c. **Male secondary sexual characteristics**
        d. Early versus late maturing
    4. Adolescents: sexually mature
        a. Conflicting answers
            (1) Advise
            (2) Approach: **BioPsychoSocial model**
        b. Decisions about becoming sexually active
            (1) Abstinence
            (2) Problems

B. *Cognitive & Emotional Changes*
    1. Definition: **cognitive development**
    2. Piaget's cognitive stages: continued
        a. Stage 4: **Formal operations stage**
        b. Thinking abstractly
    3. Brain development: reason and emotion
        a. Prefrontal cortex: executive functions
            (1) Vulnerability
            (2) Risk-taking behavior

    b. Limbic system: emotional behaviors

        (1) Moody, emotional, and impulsive behaviors

        (2) Conclusion

4. Kohlberg's theory of moral reasoning

    a. Three levels of moral reasoning

        (1) **Preconventional level**

        (2) **Conventional level**

        (3) **Postconventional level**

    b. Evaluating Kohlberg's theory

        (1) Stages

        (2) Thinking versus behaving (Carol Gilligan)

        (3) Brain or neural factors

5. Parenting styles and effects

☐ Which of Diana Baumrind's parenting styles describes your family?

    a. Personal experiences

    b. Different styles of parenting (Diana Baumrind)

        (1) **Authoritarian parents**

        (2) **Authoritative parents**

        (3) **Permissive parents**

    c. Effects of parenting styles

6. Adolescence: Big Picture

    a. Girls during puberty

    b. Boys during puberty

    c. Sexual maturity

    d. Piaget's stages: continued

    e. Brain development: reason and emotion

    f. Kohlberg's theory of moral reasoning

7. Beyond adolescence

    a. Changes in cognitive speed

        (1) **Processing speed**

        (2) **Perceptual speed**

        (3) **Reaction time**

    b. Changes in memory

        (1) Memory differences

        (2) Normal forgetting

       (3) Brain changes

       (4) Memory-enhancing products

C. *Personality & Social Changes*

  1. Definition

    a. **Personality and social development**

    b. **Personal identity or self-identity**

  2. Development of **self-esteem**

    a. High self-esteem

    b. Low self-esteem

    c. Reversals

    d. Forces shaping self-esteem

    e. Importance of self-esteem

  3. Adulthood: Erikson's psychosocial stages

    a. Stage 5: Identity versus Role Confusion

    b. Stage 6: Intimacy versus Isolation

    c. Stage 7: Generativity versus Stagnation

    d. Stage 8: Integrity versus Despair

  4. Personality change

D. *Gender Roles, Love, & Relationships*

  1. Definition: **gender roles**

    a. Current gender roles: U.S. and worldwide

    b. Gender roles: development and function

  2. Expectations

  3. Kinds of love

    a. **Passionate love**

    b. **Companionate love**

    c. **Triangular theory of love** (Robert Sternberg)

       (1) Passion

       (2) Intimacy

       (3) Commitment

    d. Brain in love

  4. Choosing a partner: **schema**

  5. Long-term relationship: success or failure? (John Gottman)

    a. Critical factors

    b. Happy relationships

    c. Happiness graph

E. *Research Focus: Happy Marriages*

    1. Why do marriages succeed or fail?

    2. "Love Lab" study (John Gottman)

        a. Method

            (1) Facial responses

            (2) Physiological responses

            (3) Longitudinal method

        b. Results and conclusions

            (1) Unsuccessful relationships

            (2) Successful relationships

            (3) Advice

F. *Cultural Diversity: Preferences for Partners*

    1. Measuring cultural influences

    2. Desirable traits

        a. What is considered desirable in a potential partner?

        b. How much is virginity valued around the world?

    3. Reasons for marrying

        a. How much is love valued?

        b. How do women decide?

        c. How do men decide?

G. *Physical Changes: Aging*

    1. Kinds of aging

        a. **Normal aging**

        b. **Pathological aging**

    2. Reasons for aging

        a. **Aging by chance theory**

        b. **Aging by design theory**

    3. Sexual changes with aging

        a. Sexual changes in women: **menopause**

        b. Sexual changes in men

H. *Application: Suicide*

    1. Teenage suicide

    ☐ If you are like most of us, you know someone who committed suicide (or tried to). What happened?

    2. Problems related to teenage suicide

        a. Problems and symptoms

        b. Precipitators

3. Preventing teenage suicide

   a. Identify risk factors

   b. Crisis management

   c. Hotline services

4. Suicide in the elderly

☐ Do you oppose or support doctor-assisted suicide? What are your reasons?

   a. Risk factors

   b. Assisted suicide

   c. Legal suicide

   d. Opponents and proponents of doctor-assisted suicide

Flashcards *for the fun of it...*

A Special Rock 'n' Roll Quiz on Adolescence: Teenagers have always been aware of living in an emotional pressure cooker, and the music they listen to reflects their concerns. Can you match these worries of adolescence with the Golden Oldies that expressed them so memorably? After you try this quiz, how about making up one of your own? Perhaps you could base it on current hits.

_____	1. masculinity	a.	Why Do Fools Fall in Love?
_____	2. femininity	b.	Fifty Ways to Leave Your Lover
_____	3. self-esteem	c.	Walk Like a Man
_____	4. vulnerability	d.	Get a Job
_____	5. chastity	e.	Big Girls Don't Cry
_____	6. intimacy	f.	Sweet Little Sixteen
_____	7. romantic love	g.	Lonely Girl
_____	8. career	h.	Where Did My Baby Go?
_____	9. marriage	i.	Under the Boardwalk
_____	10. commitment *(not!)*	j.	Going to the Chapel

Answers to "A Special Rock 'n' Roll Quiz on Adolescence"

1 c   2 e   3 g   4 h   5 f   6 i   7 a   8 d   9 j   10 b

Language Workout

What's That?

p. 407   **Stay in there** = keep trying
elected **prom** queen = yearly dance in high school
levelheaded person = with good judgment
cocky-type person = happy, risk-taking
she did not **figure on** a divorce = predict

p. 408   this growth **spurt** begins = sudden increase

p. 409   not using **contraceptives** = devices to prevent pregnancy

p. 410   I'm very **outspoken** = open, not afraid to give opinion

p. 411   getting a tongue pierced **on a dare** = because of a challenge from friend

p. 412   may involve **making bargains** = balancing good and bad effects

p. 413   I **get around** them = avoid the rules
I'm asking for **the world** = too much
My parents never **make** their punishments **stick** = enforce
I play right into it = I use their feelings to my advantage
different **costs** and benefits = disadvantages

p. 419   a friend **fixed me up with** Charlie = arranged a date with

p. 420   **stonewalling** = rejecting any discussion (like a stone wall)

p. 422   his claim is **nothing but** amazing = completely, totally
a known **sore point** = cause of disagreement
husbands who were **autocratic** = controlling

p. 423   simply **out of the question** = not considered

p. 425   results in **cessation** of ovulation = ending, stopping of a process
baby boomers = people born soon after Second World War, from 1945 to 1960.
women experience **hot flashes** = sudden feeling of heat
a society that **glorifies** being young = honors, praises

p. 426   the **class clown** = student known for making jokes
considered teenage **histrionics** = dramatic behavior
listen to **oldies** = old songs
I've finally **slipped over the edge** = moved into dangerous situation
gregarious = friendly, sociable

Making Connections

When you are reading, it's helpful to understand all the transition words that writers give you. These transition words tell you what to expect next.

What do you expect when you see these transition words?

   however / **nevertheless** / **still** / **on the other hand** / **conversely** / **in contrast**

These words tell you that the sentence that follows will be opposite from the previous sentence. Here are some examples:

I think English grammar is hard. **On the other hand**, the Language Workout makes it easy. These transitions help the reader anticipate the next sentence. **However,** not all transitions are equal.

However is the most commonly used of these transitions because we can use it in any situation to warn the reader of a change from the first sentence. **On the other hand**, transitions like **conversely, in contrast,** and **on the other hand** can only be used to illustrate a direct opposite from the sentence before, so you couldn't use them in sentence 2.

Look at the examples from the text and notice the difference in how they are used.

Teenage girls report that sex and pregnancy are the number one issues they face today. **However,** curiosity, media coverage, and peer pressure play a large role in motivating sexual activity. (p. 409)

happy marriages had husbands who were good at not immediately rejecting their wives' advice… **In contrast**, unhappy marriages had husbands who were autocratic. (p. 422)

How would you complete the following sentence with this transition?

Esmeralda just signed a contract to play in a movie.
Nevertheless, _____.

You probably wrote a sentence similar to one of these:

Nevertheless, she is not at all excited.
Nevertheless, she will probably not move to Hollywood.
Nevertheless, she is not giving up her job at the bank.

These are not directly opposite from the sentence before, but these sentences are opposite from what you would expect. **Nevertheless** and **Still** work best in these cases.

Practicing this kind of thinking will help you understand what you read more quickly and more deeply. Read the following sentences and fill in with what transitions would work best.

Faysal never eats meat. _____, he sometimes eats fish.

Bogdana works hard during the week. _____, she relaxes all weekend.

Arthur's father is a strict disciplinarian. _____, Arthur's mother is not.

She has no acting experience. _____, Esmeralda just signed a contract to play in a movie.

Some teenagers get their tongues pierced. _____, I think this is disgusting.

Answers

Faysal never eats meat. **Still / Nevertheless / However,** he sometimes eats fish.
Bogdana works hard during the week. **Conversely / On the other hand / In contrast / However,** she relaxes all weekend.
Arthur's father is a strict disciplinarian. **Conversely / On the other hand / In contrast / However,** Arthur's mother is not.
She has no acting experience. **Still / Nevertheless / However,** Esmeralda just signed a contract to play in a movie.
Some teenagers get their tongues pierced. **Still / Nevertheless / However,** I think this is disgusting.

The Big Picture

Which statement below offers the best summary of the larger significance of this module?

A   There is at least one compensation for the physical, cognitive, and emotional upheaval of adolescence — it is followed by adulthood, a period of calm and psychological smooth sailing while waiting for the end.

B   Although psychological theories of development tend to place great importance on infancy and childhood, it must be remembered that adolescence and adulthood are also periods of great change.

C   Rod Plotnik wants us to understand that Erikson's psychosocial stage theory of human development is the best, because it is the only one that takes into account adolescence, adulthood, and old age.

D   Once again psychology challenges the popular notion that men and women are equal. Discoveries in every area — physical, cognitive, and personality — reveal significant differences between the way men and women function.

E   Have you noticed that your parents are getting smarter as you get older?

True-False

_____   1. Contrary to the traditional view, new research suggests that adolescence is not necessarily a period of great psychological turmoil and severe emotional stress.

_____   2. Girls normally experience the physical changes of puberty about two years earlier than boys.

_____   3. For obvious reasons, early maturing girls are more confident and outgoing than late maturing girls.

_____   4. The good news (too late for you) is that the happiest, best adjusted adolescents come from families using the permissive style of parenting.

_____   5. Enjoy it while you can! The sad fact is that *all* cognitive abilities decline with age.

_____   6. Erik Erikson saw the key developmental issue of adolescence as the acquisition of a positive sense of identity.

_____   7. According to Erikson, the main task of young adulthood is to find intimacy by developing loving relationships.

_____   8. Robert Sternberg's triangular theory of love explains why romantic love doesn't last — it has passion and intimacy, but it lacks commitment.

_____   9. Regardless of culture, young adults all over the world ranked traits desirable in a potential mate in almost exactly the same way.

_____   10. Most women report a kind of relief after menopause — at least they don't have to endure sex anymore.

Flashcards 1

_____ 1. adolescence	a. the major male hormone; stimulates growth of genital organs and development of sexual characteristics
_____ 2. estrogen	b. the first menstrual period; a signal that ovulation may have occurred; potential to conceive child
_____ 3. formal operations stage	c. the last of Piaget's cognitive stages (age 12–adulthood), when adolescents develop the ability to think logically
_____ 4. personal identity or self-identity	d. how we describe ourselves; includes our values, goals, traits, interests, and motivations
_____ 5. menarche	e. how much one likes oneself; includes feelings of self-worth, attractiveness, and social competence
_____ 6. normal aging	f. may be caused by genetic defects, physiological problems, or diseases, all of which accelerate the aging process
_____ 7. pathological aging	g. a developmental period (age 9–17) of significant biological changes resulting in secondary sexual characteristics
_____ 8. puberty	h. a gradual and natural slowing of our physical and psychological processes from middle to late adulthood
_____ 9. self-esteem	i. one of the major female hormones; at puberty, stimulates development of sexual characteristics
_____ 10. testosterone	j. a developmental period (age 12–18) during which many characteristics change from childlike to adult-like

Flashcards 2

_____ 1. aging by chance theory	a. traditional or stereotypic behaviors, attitudes, and personality traits adults expect of males and females
_____ 2. aging by design theory	b. continuously thinking about loved one: accompanied by warm sexual feelings and powerful emotions
_____ 3. authoritarian parents	c. less controlling; nonpunishing and accepting attitude; make few demands on their children
_____ 4. authoritative parents	d. having trusting and tender feelings for someone whose life is closely bound up with one's own
_____ 5. companionate love	e. attempt to control behavior of their children in accordance with an absolute standard of conduct
_____ 6. gender roles	f. says our bodies age because of preset biological clocks that are like blueprints controlling cell death
_____ 7. menopause	g. says your body ages because of naturally occurring problems or breakdowns in the body's cells
_____ 8. passionate love	h. gradual stoppage in secretion of estrogen, causing cessation of ovulation, menstrual cycle
_____ 9. permissive parents	i. says love has three components: passion, intimacy, and commitment
_____ 10. triangular theory of love	j. attempt to direct their children's activities in a rational way; supportive, loving; discuss their rules and policies

Multiple-Choice

_____ 1. Rod Plotnik introduces us to the ambitious teen Branndi and the divorced former prom queen Susan in order to show that
   a. teen Brandi lives a more turbulent life than adult Susan
   b. Brandi's personality is all over the place, while Susan's is calmer and more stable
   c. adolescence and adulthood are both periods of great change, as was childhood
   d. most change occurs in childhood, less in adolescence, and even less in adulthood

_____ 2. Experts now believe that adolescence is *not* a period of
   a. great psychological turmoil
   b. considerable biological, cognitive, and social changes
   c. searching for personal identity
   d. dramatic positive or negative changes in self-esteem

_____ 3. When you compare the development of sexual maturity in girls and boys during puberty, you find that the changes are
   a. radically different in girls and boys
   b. gradual in girls but sudden in boys
   c. essentially the same, but occur about two years earlier in girls
   d. somewhat similar, except that the difference between a boy and a man is far greater than the difference between a girl and a woman

_____ 4. In terms of enjoying a psychological advantage in adjustment, it is better to be a/n
   a. early maturing girl
   b. late maturing girl
   c. early maturing boy
   d. late maturing boy

_____ 5. For today's biology lesson, we will be discussing adolescent
   a. estrogen in girls and testosterone in boys
   b. female secondary sexual characteristics and male primary sexual characteristics
   c. varying rates of menarche in girls and boys during puberty
   d. puberty results: female sexual maturity and male sexual immaturity

_____ 6. According to the BioPsychoSocial approach, problems of adolescent sexual behavior
   a. dominate adolescents' biology, their psychology, and their social lives
   b. cannot be discussed independently of hormonal, cognitive, personality, or emotional factors
   c. tend to be overrated, although they do have a minor effect on many parts of adolescents' lives
   d. (there is no "BioPsychoSocial" approach; this is a nonsense term)

_____ 7. The stage during which adolescents develop the ability to think about abstract or hypothetical concepts and solve problems in a logical way is
   a. Freud's stage three: the phallic stage
   b. Erikson's stage eight: integrity versus despair
   c. Piaget's stage four: formal operations
   d. Kohlberg's stage two: conventional level

_____ 8. New research suggests that teenagers engage in irresponsible, risky behaviors because their
   a. beliefs include an irrational confidence in their invulnerability
   b. limbic systems are still at a primitive level of development
   c. brains are often "rewired" by alcohol and drug use
   d. brains have underdeveloped executive functions but a well-developed emotional center

_____ 9. Lawrence Kohlberg based his theory of moral development on research into the
   a. behaviors that children of different ages listed as "good" or "bad"
   b. stories children made up when asked to illustrate good and bad behavior
   c. correlation between how children rated their own behavior and how their teachers rated it
   d. reasoning children used to solve problems that posed moral dilemmas

_____ 10. One of the main criticisms of Kohlberg's theory of moral reasoning is that
   a. his theory describes moral behavior more than moral thinking
   b. Carol Gilligan showed that men and women think alike on moral questions
   c. new findings show how brain and neural factors influence moral thinking
   d. only Stage 6, the highest stage of moral reasoning, has firm research support

_____ 11. Your new friend seems to be competent, independent, and achievement oriented; you guess that she had _____ parents
   a. authoritarian
   b. authoritative
   c. permissive
   d. protective

_____ 12. Which one of the following cognitive abilities does _not_ decrease with aging?
   a. processing speed
   b. perceptual speed
   c. reaction time
   d. interpretation

_____ 13. Grandmother forgets a name and worries that she is "losing it" — you should reassure her that
   a. some memory problems often occur in people 60 and over
   b. her memory may be slipping, but her reaction time will speed up
   c. if she lives long enough, it is likely she will get Alzheimer's disease
   d. daily intake of the supplement ginkgo biloba should improve her memory

_____ 14. Probably the most disturbing finding about self-esteem during adolescence is that
   a. boys' self-esteem plunges unless they are good at athletics
   b. girls are more likely to show declining or low self-esteem
   c. both boys' and girls' self-esteem rises rapidly, then falls during adulthood
   d. once self-esteem declines, it almost never recovers or increases

_____ 15. In Erik Erikson's psychosocial stage theory, an adolescent who does not develop a positive sense of identity is likely to suffer from
   a. role confusion
   b. stagnation
   c. a sense of inferiority
   d. isolation

_____ 16. According to Erik Erikson's Stage 8, what we need in late adulthood is
   a. recognition, respect, and honor from our family and colleagues
   b. a sense of pride in our acquisitions and our standing in the community
   c. a sense of contentment about how we lived and what we accomplished
   d. mainly good health — without it there is despair

_____ 17. What is this thing called love? Robert Sternberg's triangular theory says love is a mix of
   a. romantic love, respect, and companionship
   b. romance, sharing, and loyalty
   c. infatuated love plus companionate love
   d. passion, intimacy, and commitment

_____ 18. You feel euphoria and intense passion when you find your "one true love," probably because
   a. your relationship has advanced from infatuated love to companionate love
   b. you are experiencing what Sternberg calls "companionate love"
   c. the reward/pleasure center of your brain is experiencing increased activity
   d. (you can't explain it, because love is too mysterious for scientific study)

_____ 19. John Gottman has identified four major problems between couples that often lead to divorce:
   a. criticism, defensiveness, contempt, stonewalling
   b. poverty, impulsive spending, lack of savings, unemployment
   c. age differences, religious differences, political differences, language differences
   d. physical attractiveness, flirting, jealousy, lack of inhibitions

_____ 20. Which one of the following is *not* a procedure used in John Gottman's "Love Lab"?
   a. recording each partner's facial expressions during while they discuss marriage sore points
   b. recording each partner's physiological responses during discussions of marriage problems
   c. longitudinal methods (retesting the same couples regularly during 14 years)
   d. learning better sexual performance, but in the lab with a professional sex surrogate

_____ 21. Culture influences preferences for marriage partners — we know that because
   a. women express more stringent standards in deciding whom to marry
   b. the value placed on female virginity varies from country to country
   c. the importance of love in choosing a spouse is about the same from country to country
   d. women tend to marry younger men who are physically attractive

_____ 22. According to the _____, our bodies age because of naturally occurring problems or breakdowns in the body's cells
   a. aging by chance theory
   b. aging by design theory
   c. triangular theory (middle, late, and very late adulthood)
   d. chronological aging theory

_____ 23. The most significant gender difference in aging is that at about age 50
   a. men lose the ability to have erections
   b. men experience a sudden increase in sexual desire
   c. women experience menopause
   d. women lose all sexual desire

_____ 24. When a young person commits suicide, our typical reaction is an anguished "Why? Why?"… but the truth is that
   a. nothing can stop a person who has decided to commit suicide
   b. there probably were signs of psychological problems and behavioral symptoms long before
   c. psychology has no answer to the riddle of why adolescents, with their whole lives before them, sometimes take their own lives
   d. adolescents who are contemplating suicide go to great lengths to disguise their intentions

_____ 25. Perhaps the main reason why the debate over assisted suicide is intensifying is that
   a. a doctor has invented a machine that makes it relatively easy
   b. psychologists, as scientists, are unwilling to become involved in a moral question
   c. morals in our country are breaking down
   d. the population of the elderly will almost double in the next 35 years

Short Essay

1. Which of the three basic styles of parenting described by Diana Baumrind (authoritarian, authoritative, or permissive) best describes how your parents tried to raise you? How successful were their efforts? Give examples from your adolescence.

2. How does Erik Erikson describe the basic task or social problem of adolescence and the possible outcomes of attempts to resolve it?

3. What is Robert Sternberg's triangular theory of love and why is it so useful?

4. What has psychology learned about why marriages succeed or fail?

5. What is your position on the controversial topic of doctor-assisted suicide?

More about My Mother

I love the story my mother recalled from her college days way back in the 1920's (see "How Behaviorism Revolutionized Psychology" in Module 9). My mother is a remarkable person in many ways. Very much in the spirit of Erik Erikson's life span development theory, she and others like her are redefining our understanding of old age. After retirement, my mother discovered the joys of running. She goes out every day for a run/walk of two or three miles. Once a year, to celebrate her birthday, she goes five miles, although in the last few years she has split the five miles between morning and afternoon outings. As I write this, we have just celebrated her 99th birthday! (And yes, she did her five miles!) I hope that you, too, have the good fortune to continue learning wonderful lessons from your parents.

Answers for Module 18

The Big Picture (explanations provided for incorrect choices)

A Adolescence is neither so tumultuous nor adulthood so stagnant as this gloomy statement suggests.
B Correct! You see the "big picture" for this Module.
C Although the emphasis on the entire life cycle is a strength of Erikson's theory, Plotnik does not advocate adherence in any one approach to psychology.
D Evolution seems to have created some gender differences, but how significant they are today remains debatable.
E It's just a joke!

True-False

1	T	407	
2	T	408	
3	F	408	Early maturing girls tend to be less confident and outgoing. (Can you see why this might happen?)
4	F	413	Happiness and good adjustment are related to the authoritative style of parenting.
5	F	415	Not all cognitive abilities decline with aging (some even improve).
6	T	417	
7	T	417	
8	T	419	
9	F	420	There is considerable cultural variation in desirable characteristics of potential mates.
10	F	425	Menopause is a stressful life change for many women.

Flashcards 1

1 j	2 i	3 c	4 d	5 b	6 h	7 f	8 g	9 e	10 a

Flashcards 2

1 g	2 f	3 e	4 j	5 d	6 a	7 h	8 b	9 c	10 i

Multiple-Choice (explanations provided for incorrect choices)

1 a Brandi may be more exuberant, but Susan has experienced divorce and the death of her son.
   b Brandi has the energy of adolescence, but Susan has experienced both the joys and pains of adulthood.
   c Correct! See page 407.
   d All three of these stages bring great change in a person's life.

2 *a Correct! See page 407.*
   b These changes, especially the biological ones, are obvious.
   c Searching for identity continues to be seen as a key factor in adolescence.
   d Research points to the importance of changes in self-esteem in adolescence.

3 a Adolescent boys and girls go through the same developmental processes.
   b The same things happen, but not at the same times.
   c Correct! See page 408.
   d Does this statement really make sense?

4 a It turns out they have problems. (Can you see why?)
   b This situation is neither very good nor very bad.
   c Correct! See page 408.
   d It turns out they have problems. (Can you see why?)

5 *a Correct! See page 408.*
   b Both girls and boys show development of secondary sexual characteristics in adolescence.
   c Menarche only occurs in girls.
   d Puberty results in sexual maturity in both females and males (although sometimes it doesn't seem like it!).

6 a Dominate is too strong, and not the focus of the BioPsychoSocial approach.
   b Correct! See page 409.
   c Problems like sexual behavior are real; the question is how best to understand them.
   d Like it or not, there is such a term.

7   a   Too young — this would refer to the kindergarten period.
     b   Too old — this would refer to old age.
     c   *Correct! See page 410.*
     d   Too young — this would be the middle stage of moral reasoning.

8   a   The "invulnerability" explanation has been replaced by new findings about brain development.
     b   The limbic system is well developed; it is the executive functions that are still developing.
     c   Alcohol and drug use are dangerous, but do not rewire the brain.
     d   *Correct! See page 411.*

9   a   Kohlberg did not use the survey method.
     b   Kohlberg used stories in his research, but the children did not make them up.
     c   Kohlberg did not use teachers in his research.
     d   *Correct! See page 412.*

10   a   Kohlberg has been criticized for just the opposite emphasis.
     b   Gilligan attempted to show just the opposite.
     c   *Correct! See page 412.*
     d   Stage 6 has now been omitted because so few people reach it.

11   a   Authoritarian parents tend to produce hostile boys and dependent girls.
     b   *Correct! See page 413.*
     c   Permissive parents tend to produce less assertive and less achievement-oriented children.
     d   This is not one of Diana Baumrind's three parenting styles.

12   a   Research shows that processing speed declines with age.
     b   Research shows that perceptual speed declines with age.
     c   Research shows that reaction time declines with age.
     d   *Correct! See page 415.*

13   *a*   *Correct! See page 415.*
     b   Reaction time also slows down beginning in the late fifties.
     c   So far, her memory loss seems natural and not the sign of worse to come.
     d   Researchers found that ginkgo biloba did not improve memory or concentration.

14   a   Athletics are important for boys in our culture, but not all important.
     b   *Correct! See page 416.*
     c   There is no such predictable rise and fall in self-esteem.
     d   Fortunately, this is not true. It depends on circumstances like earned successes, or therapy.

15   *a*   *Correct! See page 417.*
     b   Stagnation is an outcome of poor development in middle adulthood.
     c   A sense of inferiority is an outcome of poor development in middle and late childhood.
     d   Isolation (instead of intimacy) is an outcome of poor development in young adulthood.

16   a   This answer assumes that we are mainly egotistical.
     b   This answer assumes that we are mainly vain.
     c   *Correct! See page 417.*
     d   Many people live satisfying lives even with health problems.

17   a   Romantic love lacks one of Robert Sternberg's three components of love.
     b   These factors are not among Robert Sternberg's three components of love.
     c   Wouldn't a triangular theory require *three* elements?
     d   *Correct! See page 419.*

18   a   That would involve a decline in euphoria and passion.
     b   Companionate love is a combination of intimacy and commitment without any sexual passion.
     c   *Correct! See page 419.*
     d   Tell that to Robert Sternberg, John Gottman, and various researchers in neuroscience!

19   *a*   *Correct! See page 420.*
     b   These economic factors are less important than a couple's social interactions.
     c   These personal factors are less important than a couple's social interactions.
     d   These sexual factors are less important than a couple's social interactions.

20 a   This was an important part of Gottman's Love Lab procedure.
    b   This was an important part of Gottman's Love Lab procedure.
    c   This was an important part of Gottman's Love Lab procedure.
    d *Correct! See page 422.*

21 a   Men express more stringent standards.
    b *Correct! See page 423.*
    c   If true (it's not), this would refute the importance of cultural influences.
    d   This tendency is truer of men than of women.

22 *a* *Correct! See page 424.*
    b   Just the opposite is true.
    c   There is no triangular theory of aging (but see theories of love).
    d   This is a nonsense phrase, not a correct term in the psychology of aging.

23 a   No need for worry — they don't.
    b   Some men might act like it, but there is no physiological basis for such a change.
    c *Correct! See page 425.*
    d   Some women might act like it, but there is no physiological basis for such a change.

24 a   If you believe this, you must learn more about suicide prevention. A friend may need your help one day.
    b *Correct! See page 426.*
    c   Psychology does not have all the answers, but it does have some good advice and prevention techniques.
    d   Just the opposite is true — they usually give signals. (But are we sensitive enough to recognize them?)

25 a   This fact gives the media something to focus on, but doesn't explain the debate.
    b   Even if true, why would that intensify the debate?
    c   This is too broad a generalization to prove anything.
    d *Correct! See page 427.*

Short Essay (sample answers)

1. If you said *authoritarian*, you need examples of attempts to shape, control, and evaluate your behavior in accordance with a set standard of conduct that comes from religious or respected authorities. If you said *authoritative*, you need examples of attempts to direct your activities in a rational and intelligent way, being supportive, loving, and committed, and discussing rules. If you said *permissive*, you need examples of less controlling, nonpunishing, accepting attitudes, using reason, making few demands. How well did it work?

2. For Erikson, adolescents (12–20) are going through Stage 5, "Identity versus Role Confusion." They are leaving behind the carefree, irresponsible, and impulsive behaviors of childhood and developing the more purposeful, planned, and responsible behaviors of adulthood. If adolescents successfully resolve this problem, they will develop a healthy and confident sense of identity. If unsuccessful, they will experience role confusion, which results in having low self-esteem and becoming unstable or socially withdrawn.

3. It turns out love is *not* a many-splendored thing! Sternberg says there is a love triangle with three sides, intimacy, passion, and commitment. You feel love in passion, share emotional and material love in intimacy, and form a serious relationship in commitment. The genius of Sternberg's theory is that the three sides can be arranged in different combinations, explaining passionate love and companionate love, and answering questions about love at first sight, quick marriage, love without sex, and why romantic love doesn't last.

4. There is a kind of contradiction in marriage right from the beginning. Couples are brought together by passionate feelings generated by the reward/pleasure center of the brain, but kept together by deeper social and personal satisfactions. In his "Love Lab" [Note to Professor: I'll volunteer!] John Gottman has discovered four major problems in interaction that couples face: (1) giving too many criticisms, (2) becoming too defensive, (3) showing contempt of a partner, and (4) stonewalling on disagreements.

5. As the population of elderly people almost doubles over the next 35 years, the pros and cons of doctor-assisted suicide will only be argued more intensely. Whichever side you support, you should also take account of the opposite view. Opponents argue that allowing people to take their own lives opens the door to many abuses, from poor decisions by the mentally ill to abuses from the profit motive. Proponents argue that it would end unbearable suffering in incurable patients. Give examples from family or friend's experiences.

Freudian & Humanistic Theories

Big Theories to Answer Big Questions

In Modules 19 and 20, Rod Plotnik discusses personality theory, one of the most absorbing areas in all of psychology. Personality theories tackle the big questions, the questions we think about when we try to understand who we are and what meaning and purpose our lives have. We feel that we are unique individuals, but aren't we essentially like everyone else? We know we are growing and developing, but aren't we also somehow very much the same from year to year? We would like to change some things about ourselves, but why does that seem so difficult to do?

A theory of personality is necessarily comprehensive. The better it is, the more of our questions about ourselves it answers. As you study these two modules, pay attention to each theory's basic assumptions about human nature. Do you agree with them? To what extent can you see yourself in each theory? Does it describe you and explain your life?

But Do They Explain You?

I've said it before, but it's especially true for the two modules on personality: *challenge every new idea you meet.* Ask yourself, is that idea really true? Does that concept explain my own experience accurately? Does this theory capture how I feel about myself and life in general?

When Sigmund Freud says you have inborn sexual and aggressive tendencies, do you find them in yourself? When Abraham Maslow and Carl Rogers portray humans as fundamentally good, does that square with people as you know them? When Albert Bandura (next module) suggests that we are what we have learned to expect ourselves and the world to be, ask yourself if you are something more than a collection of past experiences. When Gordon Allport (also next module) paints your personality as a complex mosaic of tendencies to behave in certain ways, ask yourself if that captures all you are.

Finally, you might think about your own theory of personality. You do have one, even though you probably haven't tried to work it out in any detail. Anyone who studies psychology inevitably comes to have some sort of theory of personality — a global view of how all the facts and ideas in psychology fit together, and how they apply to everyday life. Reflecting on your own ideas about human nature will help you understand psychology's famous theories of personality.

Effective Student Tip 19

Three Secrets of Effective Writing

Too many students think the ability to write well is something you have to be born with. The truth is just the opposite. Any student can become a good writer. The *art* of writing requires curiosity and creativity, but we all have those qualities. The *craft* of writing is as learnable as cooking or carpentry. Three secrets of effective writing reveal how any serious student can get started on becoming a better writer.

Secret #1: Tell a *story* that is important to you. We organize our memory around stories. A well-told story is the most effective way to convey information.

Secret #2: Paint *word pictures*. We understand best what we can visualize. A beautifully worded description is the most effective way to create understanding in writing.

Secret #3: Think of writing as a *craft* (the artistry will come naturally, flowering as you work). One by one, learn the skills of good writing. Start by learning how to type a beautiful paper, the easiest procedure to learn and the one that has the most immediate effect on your reader.

When you think of writing as a craft, you realize that the goal is progress, not perfection. It doesn't really matter how good your next paper is, as long as it is a little bit better than the last one. That's progress.

Your response...

What was the best paper you ever wrote? What made it so good?

Learning Objectives

1. Understand Freudian and humanistic theories, which emphasize our inner life, as the first half of four major approaches to personality [social cognitive and trait theories are covered in the next module].

2. Learn the basic concepts of the psychodynamic approach to the understanding of personality through mastering the basic concepts of Sigmund Freud.

3. Appreciate Freud's psychoanalytic theory, with its ideas of motivation, divisions of the mind, and developmental stages, as a comprehensive approach to human nature

4. Learn the basic concepts of the humanistic approach to the understanding of personality through mastering the basic concepts of Abraham Maslow and Carl Rogers.

5. Appreciate the cultural factors that help account for the unexpected academic success of the Indo-Chinese boat people who fled to the United States after the Vietnam conflict.

6. Study shyness as an example of personality problems and how they are understood and treated.

7. Understand the most important projective tests as basic assessment tools in the study of personality.

Key Terms

Many of the key terms for this module have crossed over into the general vocabulary of the educated person.

ability tests
anal stage
anxiety
cognitive unconscious
collective unconscious
conditional positive regard
conscious thoughts
defense mechanisms
deficiency needs
denial
displacement
dream interpretation
ego
fixation
free association
Freud's psychodynamic theory of personality
Freudian slips
genital stage
growth needs
holistic view

humanistic theories
id
ideal self
implicit or nondeclarative memory
latency stage
Maslow's hierarchy of needs
Oedipus complex
oral stage
personality
personality tests
phallic stage
phenomenological perspective
pleasure principle
positive regard
projection
projective tests
psychological assessment
psychosexual stages
rationalization
reaction formation

real self
reality principle
reliability
repression
Rogers' self-actualizing tendency
Rorschach inkblot test
self theory or self-actualization theory
self or self-concept
self-actualization
shyness
sublimation
superego
Thematic Apperception Test (TAT)
theory of personality
unconditional positive regard
unconscious forces
unconscious motivation
validity

Outline

- *Introduction*
    1. Personality (Kurt Cobain)
        a. **Personality**
        b. **Theory of personality**
    2. Changing personality (Charles Dutton)

A. *Freud's Psychodynamic Theory*
    1. Definition
        a. **Freud's psychodynamic theory of personality**
        b. Childhood
        c. A method of psychotherapy (Module 24) plus a theory of personality (this module)
    2. Conscious versus unconscious forces
        a. **Conscious thoughts**
        b. **Unconscious forces**
        c. **Unconscious motivation**
    3. Techniques to discover the unconscious
        a. **Free association**
        b. **Dream interpretation**
        c. **Freudian slips**

B. *Divisions of the Mind*
    1. Id, ego, and superego
    ☐ How do Freud's twin concepts of the pleasure principle and the reality principle make conflict inevitable in his personality theory?
        a. **Id**: pleasure seeker (**pleasure principle**)
        b. **Ego**: executive negotiator between id and superego (**reality principle**)
        c. **Superego**: regulator (conscience)
    2. **Anxiety**
    3. **Defense mechanisms**
    ☐ Freud didn't mean that defense mechanisms are bad. Can you think of an everyday life example for each defense mechanism that also shows how it promotes our adaptation and survival?
        a. **Rationalization**
        b. **Denial**
        c. **Repression**
        d. **Projection**
        e. **Reaction formation**
        f. **Displacement**

    g. **Sublimation**

C. *Developmental Stages*

    1. Development: dealing with conflicts

        a. **Psychosexual stages**

        b. Conflict

    2. Fixation: potential personality problems

        a. **Fixation**

        b. Too little or too much gratification

    3. Five psychosexual stages

    ☐ For this theory to make any sense, you must appreciate the conflict in each stage. Think about children you have known (including yourself!) and try to come up with examples for each stage.

        a. **Oral stage**

        b. **Anal stage**

        c. **Phallic stage** and the **Oedipus complex**

        d. **Latency stage**

        e. **Genital stage**

D. *Freud's Followers & Critics*

    ☐ Why did Freud's most creative followers eventually become critics?

    1. Carl Jung and the **collective unconscious**

    2. Alfred Adler

    3. Karen Horney

    4. Neo-Freudians (Erik Erikson)

    5. Freudian theory today

        a. How valid is Freud's theory?

            (1) Too comprehensive

            (2) Difficult to test

            (3) Must be updated

        b. How important are the first five years?

        c. Are there unconscious forces? (**implicit or nondeclarative memory**)

        d. What was Freud's impact?

E. *Humanistic Theories*

    1. Three characteristics of **humanistic theories**

        a. **Phenomenological perspective**

        b. **Holistic view**

        c. **Self-actualization**

    2. Abraham Maslow: need hierarchy and self-actualization

      a. **Maslow's hierarchy of needs**

          (1) **Deficiency needs**

          (2) **Growth needs**

      b. **Self-actualization**: characteristics of self-actualized individuals

  3. Carl Rogers: self theory

      a. **Self theory or self-actualization theory**

          (1) **Rogers' self-actualizing tendency**

          (2) **Self or self-concept**

      b. **Real self** versus **ideal self**

      c. **Positive regard**

      d. **Conditional positive regard** and **unconditional positive regard**

      e. Importance of self-actualization

  4. Applying humanistic ideas

  5. Evaluation of humanistic theories

      a. Impact

      b. Criticisms

F. *Cultural Diversity: Unexpected High Achievement*

  1. Boat people: remarkable achievement

  2. Values and motivation

  3. Parental attitudes

G. *Research Focus: Shyness*

  1. What is **shyness** and what causes it? (Philip Zimbardo)

  2. Psychodynamic approach

  3. Social cognitive theory

H. *Application: Assessment — Projective Tests*

  1. Definition of projective tests

      a. **Psychological assessment**

      b. **Personality tests**

      c. **Ability tests**

  2. Examples of **projective tests**

      a. **Rorschach inkblot test**

      b. **Thematic Apperception Test (TAT)**

  3. Two characteristics

      a. **Validity**

      b. **Reliability**

  4. Usefulness of projective tests: advantages and disadvantages

Language Workout

What's That?

p. 433   I feel guilty **beyond words** = cannot be expressed
reform schools = semi-prison for troubled young people
punished with **solitary confinement** = imprisoned alone in cell
after his **parole** = release from prison
his inner **demons** = serious emotional problems (devils)

p. 434   as a **backhanded** response = sarcastic, bitterly backward

p. 435   more truth than **jest** = joking

p. 436   one of those **narcissists** = people fascinated by their own selves
analogous to an iceberg = similar to

p. 438   **lays the groundwork** for personality growth = prepared the basis

p. 439   fears of **castration** = removal of sexual organs

p. 445   **grouchy** = irritable
foster the development = encourage

p. 446   **hang out** on the streets = spend time

p. 450   interpretation of **slips of the tongue** = accidentally speaking your true thoughts

p. 454   a **loner** = person who avoids other people, prefers to be alone
an aggressive **hothead** = person who quickly becomes angry
had no **run-ins** with the law = experiences, problems

What's the Difference?

CONCEPT / PRINCIPLE / THEORY

About now you might be a little uncertain about the difference between a **concept** and a **principle** and a **theory**. Yes, all three are kinds of thoughts, the result of thinking, but how are they different?

A concept is an idea: Before Darwin, few people believed that biology had a direction. Then, Darwin produced **the concept of evolution**. In the same way, before Freud, few people believed that our behavior might be influenced or controlled by hidden drives and feelings. Then, Freud formulated his **concept of the unconscious**. These two contributions were new ideas, claims that such forces really exist.

A principle is a law: It says that some behavior always happens or usually happens. For example, Darwin took his concept of evolution and described how it works in nature. This resulted in the **principle of natural selection**: this said that evolution works to preserve useful attributes and eliminates ones that are not useful. Thus, when Darwin took his concept and showed how it works, he was describing a principle.

A theory is a system: It explains how principles work together, in relation to each other in a bigger framework. So, Freud put together his concept of the unconscious and his belief that unresolved sexual conflicts are stored in the unconscious, with his idea that anxiety arises from such unexpressed conflicts and that psychoanalysis can be useful to resolve these problems. All of this interaction can be described as Freud's **theory of the unconscious**.

Be careful, though: different writers can use these words differently, and certain subject areas — like philosophy or physics — can give them special meanings.

Making Connections

WHY A COLON?

Did you notice this heading in the text? <u>Superego : Regulator</u>. (p. 436)

The punctuation mark between the words is a **colon**. When you see a colon, you are seeing a kind of **equal sign**. It has the same meaning as <u>Superego = Regulator</u>.

The colon tells you that both sides — the words before the colon and the words after the colon — are the same. When you see the colon, the words that follow will **define or explain**. Look at the definitions in these examples from the text:

> She reached her lifelong dream **:** a gold medal in figure skating at the Winter Olympics. (p. 442)
>
> Equally noteworthy was the children's overall performance in math **:** almost 50% of the children earned A's, while another 33% earned B's. (p. 448)

A colon also can introduce a **list**, as in the following examples:

> Maslow divided our needs into two general categories **:** deficiency and growth needs. (p. 443)
>
> We'll describe each of the three characteristics unique to humanistic theory **:** having a phenomenological perspective, a holistic view, and a goal of self-actualization. (p. 442)

Try it yourself. Read the following sentences. Each one needs a colon to make the meaning clear. Decide where the colon is needed and write it in. You can check your answers in the Answers.

> The airline offered three drink choices coffee, tea, and juice.
> To open a childproof bottle, you must do the following actions push down on the cap, align the arrows, and then turn the cap.
> The coach explained that there were only two ways to play the game his way and the wrong way.
> Anorexics have a disturbed body image they are thin but see themselves as fat.
> When asked if she was a person or an animal, Koko the gorilla used sign language to answer with three words "fine animal gorilla."
> Vietnamese culture values respect for elders a child should never show disrespect for adults.
> One symbol of America is now found throughout the world blue jeans.
> In her magazine, Oprah Winfrey started a new idea in publishing she puts her own picture on the cover of every issue.

Answers

The airline offered three drink choices: coffee, tea, and juice.
To open a childproof bottle, you must do the following actions: push down on the cap, align the arrows, and then turn the cap.
The coach explained that there were only two ways to play the game: his way and the wrong way.
Anorexics have a disturbed body image : they are thin but see themselves as fat.
When asked if she was a person or an animal, Koko the gorilla used sign language to answer with three words: "fine animal gorilla."
Vietnamese culture values respect for elders: a child should never show disrespect for adults.
One symbol of America is now found throughout the world: blue jeans.
In her magazine, Oprah Winfrey started a new idea in publishing: she puts her own picture on the cover of every issue.

The Big Picture

Which statement below offers the best summary of the larger significance of this module?

A   The space problems of any textbook are evident in this module. Humanistic psychology has nothing in common with psychoanalytic psychology and belongs in a separate module. These theories are completely different.

B   Behaviorists have always been skeptical about the concept of personality, and the two theories in this module show why. Many Freudian ideas are outlandish and humanistic ideas often seem naive and idealistic.

C   Psychoanalytic and humanistic personality theories are essentially the same. Freud talks about ego, Rogers about self. Freud's unconscious motivation is like Maslow's hierarchy of needs. Superego could be self-actualization, etc.

D   Both psychodynamic and humanistic theories of personality describe processes that go on inside us. But where Freud finds childhood all important, Maslow and Rogers emphasize the challenges of the future.

E   "I made an awful Freudian slip when I was having dinner at my mother's house the other day," one psychologist told another. "I meant to say 'Please pass the butter,'" but what I actually said was, 'You [rhymes with witch], you ruined my life!'"

True-False

_____ 1. Freud's key concept is the idea of conscious processes — how we understand reality.

_____ 2. Free association is necessary because we cannot know the unconscious directly.

_____ 3. For Freud, most personality development takes place during the first five years of life.

_____ 4. Because almost all of Freud's main followers broke with him, today his ideas have little influence.

_____ 5. Freud's famous personality theory is provocative, but hard to test scientifically.

_____ 6. Maslow and Rogers are pessimistic about the degree to which personality can change.

_____ 7. The hierarchy of needs helps explain why children who come to school hungry don't learn well.

_____ 8. Self-actualization means honestly recognizing your actual faults and weaknesses.

_____ 9. Rogers warns that a child who receives only unconditional positive regard will grow up spoiled and unrealistic about life.

_____ 10. For a personality test to be scientifically useful, it must possess the twin characteristics of reliability and validity.

Flashcards 1

_____	1. dream interpretation	a. operates to satisfy drives and avoid pain, without concern for moral restrictions or society's regulations
_____	2. ego	b. the influence of repressed thoughts, desires, or impulses on our conscious thoughts and behaviors
_____	3. fixation	c. this term could serve as the heading for all the other terms in Flashcards 1 (they all relate to this one)
_____	4. Freud's psychodynamic theory of personality	d. being locked into an earlier psychosexual stage because wishes were overgratified or undergratified
_____	5. id	e. assumes that dreams contain underlying, hidden meanings and symbols that provide clues to unconscious thoughts
_____	6. Oedipus complex	f. contains biological drives of sex and aggression that are the source of all psychic or mental energy; goal is pleasure
_____	7. pleasure principle	g. goal is to find safe and socially acceptable ways of satisfying id's desires and superego's prohibitions
_____	8. reality principle	h. develops from ego; goal is to apply the moral values and standards of parents and society in satisfying one's wishes
_____	9. superego	i. process where child competes with same-sex parent for affections and pleasures of opposite-sex parent
_____	10. unconscious motivation	j. has a policy of satisfying a wish or desire only if there is a socially acceptable outlet available

Flashcards 2

_____	1. conditional positive regard	a. our inherent tendency to develop and reach our true potentials; fulfillment of one's unique human potential
_____	2. holistic view	b. according to Rogers, is based on our hopes and wishes and reflects how we would like to see ourselves
_____	3. humanistic theories	c. love, sympathy, warmth, acceptance, and respect, which we crave from family, friends, and people important to us
_____	4. ideal self	d. the warmth, acceptance, and love others could show you as a valued human being, even when you disappoint them
_____	5. phenomenological perspective	e. according to Rogers, is based on our actual experiences and represents how we really see ourselves
_____	6. positive regard	f. this term could serve as the heading for all the other terms in Flashcards 2 (they all relate to this one)
_____	7. real self	g. how we see or describe ourselves; made up of many self-perceptions, abilities, and personality characteristics
_____	8. self or self-concept	h. personality is more than the sum of its parts; the individual parts form a unique and total entity that functions as a unit
_____	9. self-actualization	i. the positive regard we receive if we behave in certain, acceptable ways, such as meeting the standards of others
_____	10. unconditional positive regard	j. your perception or view of the world, whether or not it is accurate, becomes your reality

Multiple-Choice

_____ 1. Rod Plotnik tells the stories of musician Kurt Cobain and actor Charles Dutton to illustrate _____ and _____
   a. the self-destructiveness of greed / the power of religious faith
   b. drug use / crime
   c. wasted lives / lucky breaks
   d. the mysteries of personality / the possibility of personality change

_____ 2. In psychology, the term personality means
   a. a fixed way of responding to other people that is based on our inherited emotional makeup
   b. a combination of long-lasting and distinctive behaviors, thoughts, motives, and emotions that typify how we react to other people and situations
   c. favorable and unfavorable personal characteristics
   d. how interesting and attractive we are to other people

_____ 3. In Sigmund Freud's psychodynamic theory of personality, the unconscious contains
   a. everything we are aware of at a given moment
   b. feelings and thoughts we remember from long ago
   c. material that can easily be brought to awareness
   d. repressed wishes, desires, or thoughts

_____ 4. Saying whatever comes to mind, even if it seems senseless, painful, or embarrassing, is part of the Freudian technique known as
   a. a defense mechanism
   b. a Freudian slip
   c. free association
   d. projection

_____ 5. Which _one_ of the following is an example of a Freudian slip?
   a. you can't remember the name of a person you just met
   b. you call your Honey by the name of your old sweetheart
   c. you call your boss "an old grouch" behind his back
   d. you guess that your friend is taking chemistry but it is actually biology

_____ 6. Freud's three mental processes develop in the following order:
   a. superego – id – ego
   b. ego – id – superego
   c. id – ego – superego
   d. (all three are present at birth)

_____ 7. The ability to create feelings of guilt gives the _____ its power
   a. superego
   b. ego
   c. id
   d. unconscious

_____ 8. If you told Freud you were experiencing anxiety, he would suggest that you are suffering from
  a. nervousness resulting from sleep deprivation due to studying
  b. inner conflicts between the primitive desires of your id and the moral goals of your superego
  c. a conscious dislike of the courses you are taking
  d. open tension between the demands of your id and what you really want to do

_____ 9. A student who blames poor test performance on "tricky questions" — rather than admit to poor preparation — is using the defense mechanism of
  a. compensation
  b. denial
  c. projection
  d. rationalization

_____ 10. The defense mechanism in which unacceptable wishes are turned into their opposites is known as
  a. projection
  b. reaction-formation
  c. compensation
  d. rationalization

_____ 11. Which one of the following shows the correct order of Freud's psychosexual stages?
  a. oral, anal, phallic, latency, genital
  b. anal, latency, phallic, oral, genital
  c. genital, phallic, oral, anal, latency
  d. latency, anal, oral, phallic, genital

_____ 12. The concept of the collective unconscious was proposed by
  a. Carl Jung
  b. Alfred Adler
  c. Karen Horney
  d. B. F. Skinner

_____ 13. Cognitive neuroscientists have developed the concept of _____ to take the place of Freud's theory of repressed unconscious forces
  a. conscious thoughts
  b. the collective unconscious
  c. implicit or nondeclarative memory
  d. the phenomenological perspective

_____ 14. Unlike psychodynamic theories, humanistic theories of personality emphasize
  a. the continual operation of contradictory forces buried deep in our unconscious minds
  b. our capacity for personal growth, the development of our potential, and freedom to choose our destiny
  c. how difficult it is — even with therapy — to change personality significantly
  d. the importance of perceptions and beliefs

_____ 15. The key concept of the humanistic approach to personality is
  a. self-actualization
  b. the phenomenological perspective
  c. the holistic view
  d. deficiency needs

_____ 16. At the first level of Abraham Maslow's hierarchy, we find _____ needs
   a. self-actualization
   b. esteem
   c. love and belongingness
   d. physiological

_____ 17. By self-actualization, Maslow meant
   a. fulfillment of our unique human potential
   b. having our deficiency needs satisfied
   c. being loved and loving someone in return
   d. gaining recognition and status in society

_____ 18. Rogers's concept of our self-actualizing tendency is most clearly a rejection of
   a. Maslow's growth needs and self-actualization
   b. Freud's id and pleasure principle
   c. Jung's collective unconscious
   d. Dutton's humanistic theory

_____ 19. Why are so many people unhappy? Carl Rogers says it is because
   a. happiness is only possible when we become self-actualized
   b. happiness is only an illusion
   c. we have both a real self and an ideal self, and often they are in conflict
   d. we have a positive self and a negative self, and one always dominates

_____ 20. National appreciation days and the popularity of pets illustrate Rogers's concept of
   a. shyness
   b. self theory
   c. conditional positive regard
   d. positive regard

_____ 21. The old warning, "Of course Mommy loves you… when you're good!" is an example of Rogers' concept of
   a. self-actualization
   b. self-esteem needs
   c. conditional positive regard
   d. unconditional positive regard

_____ 22. An evaluation of humanistic theories of personality would emphasize their
   a. positive, hopeful philosophy of human nature rather than scientific explanation of personality development
   b. rational, scientific assessment of the biological strengths and limitations of our species
   c. addition to psychology of new research in personality from genetics and neuroscience
   d. demonstration of how human personality is driven by unconscious irrational forces

_____ 23. The remarkable academic achievement of children of the Indo-Chinese boat people is best explained by the
   a. political values of anti-communism they shared with their new neighbors
   b. restrictive immigration policy that allowed in only well-educated families
   c. high value Protestantism places on school achievement
   d. personal and cultural values concerning education transmitted by their parents

_____ 24. Because they use _____ , projective tests often bring out unconscious material
  a. pictures of people
  b. simple materials
  c. ambiguous stimuli
  d. computer analysis

_____ 25. One of the *disadvantages* of projective tests is that
  a. disagreements often arise over interpretations and classifications
  b. they are difficult to fake because there are no correct or socially desirable answers
  c. they assess a client's hidden and unrecognized unconscious thoughts and desires
  d. you get ink all over your shirt when you try to make the inkblots

Short Essay

1. Describe Freud's divisions of the mind, showing how the three parts interact in governing our behavior.

2. Defense mechanisms are often presented as crutches or excuses, but they are also essential to our healthy functioning. Give examples that illustrate this point.

3. Describe Maslow's hierarchy of needs and explain how it helps us understand human personality.

4. Explain Rogers' twin ideas of conditional and unconditional positive regard.

5. Which concept of personality seems closer to the truth — Freud's psychoanalytic approach or the humanistic approach of Maslow and Rogers? Explain the reasons for your choice.

A Freudian Slip

I have heard (and made) some dandy Freudian slips, but I'm not going to tell them, not here! They can be so revealing. A Freudian slip is saying something you didn't mean to say, breaking something, losing something, etc. The trick is to interpret the hidden meaning lying beneath the actual mistake. Treat the slip as you would a dream: carefully examine the manifest content and try to decipher the latent content (see introductory page of Study Guide Module 24). Start listening for the Freudian slips people make. Listen for your own, too! You may be amazed by what you discover!

Answers for Module 19

The Big Picture (explanations provided for incorrect choices)

A Humanistic psychology borrows from psychoanalytic psychology, and both emphasize the importance of inner life.
B Both psychoanalytic and humanistic approaches are standing the test of time. The statement may have some justice as a criticism, but few would endorse it entirely.
C Humanistic and psychoanalytic theories differ significantly over motivation, childhood, past and future, change, etc.
D Correct! You see the "big picture" for this Module.
E It's just a joke!

True-False

1	F	434	Freud's key concept is unconscious processes.
2	T	435	
3	T	439	
4	F	440	Freud's ideas continue to influence modern psychology.
5	T	441	
6	F	442	Maslow and Rogers are optimistic about human change.
7	T	443	
8	F	443	Self-actualization refers to fulfilling one's unique human potential.
9	F	445	Rogers believes the more unconditional positive regard the better.
10	T	451	

Flashcards 1

1 e   2 g   3 d   4 c   5 f   6 i   7 a   8 j   9 h   10 b

Flashcards 2

1 i   2 h   3 f   4 b   5 j   6 c   7 e   8 g   9 a   10 d

Multiple-Choice (explanations provided for incorrect choices)

1 a Neither greed nor religious faith were prominent features of the lives of Cobain and Dutton.
   b Fits, in a simple way, but Plotnik's stories have a larger purpose and illustrate broader themes.
   c Both lives were wasted at times, but lucky breaks does not apply to either Cobain or Dutton.
   d Correct! See page 433.

2 a Personality is neither fixed nor totally inherited.
   b Correct! See page 433.
   c This is a common meaning of personality, not the psychological definition.
   d This is a common meaning of personality, not the psychological definition.

3 a This statement fits Freud's idea of the conscious mind, not the unconscious.
   b This statement fits Freud's idea of the conscious mind, not the unconscious.
   c This statement fits Freud's idea of the conscious mind, not the unconscious.
   d Correct! See page 434.

4 a Defense mechanisms are unconscious distortions of the truth that protect our favorable sense of self.
   b A Freudian slip is saying something one did not intend to say.
   c Correct! See page 435.
   d Projection is a defense mechanism in which unacceptable thoughts are attributed to others.

5 a Instead of an unconscious mistake, this is a case of failing to memorize the name of the person you just met.
   b Correct! See page 435.
   c Instead of an unconscious mistake, this is a case of intentional but hidden hostility.
   d Instead of an unconscious mistake, this is a case of simply not possessing the correct information.

6 a Which process is most basic? That would have to be first.
   b Which process is most basic? That would have to be first.
   c Correct! See page 436.
   d Since they develop in a sequence, they can't all be present at birth.

7 **a** *Correct! See page 436.*
    b The ego is based on mainly realistic appraisals of the world, not on guilt.
    c The id represents basic biological urges, not feelings of guilt.
    d The unconscious is a state of mind, in which feelings of guilt may reside.

8 a Freud would look for a mental, not physiological, cause for anxiety.
    b *Correct! See page 437.*
    c Anxiety must relate to unconscious thoughts and feelings.
    d From the Freudian point of view, everything about this statement is backwards.

9 a Compensation is making up for deficiencies in one area by overemphasizing attainments in another.
    b Denial is refusing to recognize some anxiety-provoking event or idea.
    c Projection is attributing unacceptable thoughts to others rather than to oneself.
    d *Correct! See page 437.*

10 a Projection is attributing unacceptable thoughts to others rather than to oneself.
    b *Correct! See page 437.*
    c Compensation is making up for deficiencies in one area by overemphasizing attainments in another.
    d Rationalization is making up acceptable excuses for behaviors that make us feel anxious.

11 **a** *Correct! See page 439.*
    b How does a baby deal with the world? That has to be the *first* stage.
    c How does a baby deal with the world? That has to be the *first* stage.
    d How does a baby deal with the world? That has to be the *first* stage.

12 **a** *Correct! See page 440.*
    b Adler developed a theory called "individual psychology."
    c Horney challenged Freud's concept of penis envy.
    d Skinner was a behaviorist (and therefore doubted that the unconscious even exists).

13 a Cognitive neuroscientists are not denying unconscious activity, but changing its explanation.
    b This is Carl Jung's theory of unconscious activity.
    c *Correct! See page 441.*
    d This is humanistic psychology's explanation of how we understand the world.

14 a This is the basic assumption of psychodynamic theories of personality.
    b *Correct! See page 442.*
    c Humanistic theories are optimistic about the possibility of change.
    d This is the basic assumption of cognitive theories of personality.

15 **a** *Correct! See page 442.*
    b Important, but by itself does not explain what drives personality.
    c Important, but by itself does not explain what drives personality.
    d Deficiency needs are the lower-level needs, like food and safety, in Maslow's hierarchy.

16 a Of the four choices, which is the one you absolutely could not live without?
    b Of the four choices, which is the one you absolutely could not live without?
    c Of the four choices, which is the one you absolutely could not live without?
    d *Correct! See page 443.*

17 **a** *Correct! See page 443.*
    b Self-actualization comes from satisfying growth needs, not deficiency needs.
    c Love is important, but (this may come as a shock) not all-important.
    d Recognition and status are temporary and shallow values.

18 a Maslow's and Rogers's ideas of self-actualization are similar.
    b *Correct! See page 444.*
    c Jung disagreed with Freud about the importance of the sex drive, as did later humanistic psychologists.
    d Charles Dutton is an actor (not a psychologist) whom Plotnik used as an example of personality change.

19 a Self-actualization is a higher goal we should strive for, but happiness does not depend on achieving it.
    b This statement is far too cynical for Rogers.
    c *Correct! See page 444.*
    d These are not the two selves Rogers described.

20   a   Shyness is a personality problem addressed more clearly by psychodynamic than humanistic psychology.
     b   Self theory is partly correct, in that it includes positive regard, but it also refers to self-actualization.
     c   Unconditional positive regard would be closer to correct, but positive regard is more general.
     d   *Correct! See page 445.*

21   a   What is Mommy saying about her love for you?
     b   What is Mommy saying about her love for you?
     c   *Correct! See page 445.*
     d   What is Mommy saying about her love for you?

22   ***a***   *Correct! See page 446.*
     b   This would be more true of psychodynamic theories.
     c   Humanistic theories have not yet been much influenced by research in genetics and neuroscience.
     d   This would be true of psychodynamic theories.

23   a   That feeling may have been there, but it does not explain the high academic achievement.
     b   There was no such policy; the boat people were a diverse group.
     c   Most boat people were not members of protestant churches.
     d   *Correct! See page 448.*

24   a   Think about the materials used in the Rorschach (a projective test).
     b   Think about the materials used in the Rorschach (a projective test).
     c   *Correct! See page 450.*
     d   Think about the materials used in the Rorschach (a projective test).

25   ***a***   *Correct! See page 451.*
     b   This is an *advantage* of projective tests.
     c   This is an *advantage* of projective tests.
     d   It's just a joke!

Short Essay (sample answers)

1. For Freud, human personality is a war between the desire for pleasure and the need to be realistic. At birth, the child is all id (pleasure principle), the biological drives of sex and aggression. As the demands of the real world intrude, part of the id becomes the ego (reality principle), attempting to satisfy id desires in safe and socially acceptable ways. Finally, through interaction with parents, part of the ego becomes the superego, a conscience that forces obedience to social and moral demands through the power of guilt feelings.

2. We usually think of defense mechanisms as excuses, like "rationalizing" poor test performance as caused by tricky questions. But our ability to be "rational" is also our greatest human achievement. In the same manner, "denial" can help us be courageous, "repression" can help us escape domination by unacceptable ideas, "projection" can help us understand threatening thoughts, "reaction formation" and "displacement" can help us focus on problems we can solve, and "sublimation" can help us avoid forbidden desires.

3. Every theory of personality must explain motivation, what makes us go. Maslow's hierarchy of needs has the unique strength of stressing higher needs while not underrating the importance of basic needs. Maslow's five levels are (1) physiological needs, essential for life, followed by (2) safety needs and (3) love and belonging needs. Higher needs are (4) esteem and achievement and finally (5) self-actualization. The higher needs are most important for full development, but you can't get there unless the lower needs are met first.

4. When good old Spot happily greets you after the test, you understand why Rogers thinks positive regard is what we want and need. Trouble is, you need more than Spot: you need other people, and they are much less accepting than Spot. You rightly think you deserve unconditional positive regard: warmth, acceptance, and love simply because you are valued as a human being. But all too often, what you get is *conditional* positive regard: warmth, etc., when you behave as others expect. Only Spot loves you unconditionally.

5. This is a hard choice. Don't decide too quickly. The humanists seem so much nicer and more positive than the sour and negative Freudians. But when you actually evaluate other people and make decisions about them, are you a sunny humanist or a cynical Freudian? Today we know more about human nature and human behavior than the Freudians or humanists did. What does our accumulated scientific knowledge, as well as your own self-understanding and experience with others, suggest about which approach is truer?

Module 20

Social Cognitive & Traits

The Story of a Cold-Blooded Killer

Did you know that you are reading the work of a cold-blooded killer? One who could take out a long-bladed knife and charge at an enemy screaming "Kill!... Kill!..."? Of course the enemy in this case was a sack of straw and the killer was a draftee whose only real concern, in a time when our country was totally at peace, was how to get out of KP duty. An ironic twist: when it began raining half-way through the exercise, the officer in charge blew his whistle, loaded us into our trucks, and took us back to our dry barracks. The last thing our Commanding Officer needed was a complaint from some concerned parents' congressperson about how he was treating their boy!

The point of my "war story" is that I wasn't a killer at all (far from it!) and the officer who let us off easy was actually a good soldier. But what if there had been a real war? Maybe I would have acted on my army training. Then what would I have been?

The Genius and Fault of Modern Psychology

In Module 20 Rod Plotnik continues his survey of four dominant personality theories (psychoanalytic, humanistic, social cognitive, and trait) and raises one of the most fundamental questions in psychology: how stable is personality? (See Rod's discussion of person-situation interaction.) If the concept of personality is real, people must show a certain degree of consistency over a wide range of situations. But if people exhibit significantly different behavior in varying situations, how real is the idea of personality?

The genius of modern psychology is to help us see inside. You might say that psychoanalytic theory reveals the dark side of human nature and humanistic the positive, but both place the truth inside. They assume that inner tendencies guide our behavior. On the other hand, social cognitive theories and trait theories assume that our experience in the external world guides our behavior. Experience leads to the development of expectancies and traits. This focus on the outside world introduces a dangerous question: could it be the other way around, with the situation determining the person?

The tendency to find the problem inside is also one of the main faults of modern psychology. We become so good at digging out the "real" reasons for psychological problems, as Freud taught us, that we often overlook obvious situational causes like unemployment or discrimination or even environmental pollution. We learn to manage stress, discover dysfunctions, and blame ourselves. Sometimes we miss the real problem.

By the way, I fudged at that bayonet drill years ago. I was too embarrassed to actually scream "Kill!... Kill!...," so I just pretended to yell. Does that added detail ruin the point I was trying to make? Or does it remind us that psychology is a complicated and fascinating science?

Effective Student Tip 20

What Moves You?

When Delores scored her exam paper, she marked down how many questions she got right (32) and the corresponding letter grade ('D'). She handed me her answer sheet and fled. I began recording her score and grade, and then it hit me: by the grading standards I had written on the board, 32 was a 'C', not a 'D'.

A classmate chased her down the hall and when I showed Delores her mistake and asked her why, she said, "I guess because I always get a 'D'."

Like many students, Delores never did quite as well as I thought she would. Was her "slip of the pen" an indication of mixed motivation? Many students are not really sure why they are in school, why they have taken a certain class, or why they aren't doing as well as their abilities would suggest. All of these questions involve motivation, the basic forces that account for our actions.

Are you in college for your parents? Taking a course to "get it out of the way?" Cutting class without much idea why? These are common cases of mixed or poorly understood motivation. Don't let it happen to you. Try to discover your true motivation. Watch for clues that alert you to possible confusion. You will become more successful, and do it more easily, when you get your motivations and your goals in line. Honesty is the best policy.

Your response...

Try making a totally honest [and private] list of the reasons why you are in college.

Learning Objectives

1. Understand social cognitive and trait theories, which emphasize environmental forces of experience and learning, as the other half of the four basic approaches to personality.

2. Learn the basic concepts of the social cognitive approach to understanding personality through exploring the work of Albert Bandura, Julian Rotter, and Walter Mischel.

3. Learn the basic concepts of the trait approach to understanding personality through exploring the work of Gordon Allport and research leading to the Big Five supertraits.

4. Appreciate the new contributions to personality theory from behavioral genetics and the concept of heritability.

5. Consider the effect of culture on personality through the example of suicide bombers.

6. Review the founders and key concepts of the four main personality theories presented this and the previous modules.

7. Explore the role of objective tests in personality assessment and revisit the concepts of reliability and validity.

Key Terms

These key terms from personality theory are somewhat less common that those in the previous module, but look how few of them there are to learn. Piece of cake!

Bandura's social cognitive
  theory
Barnum principle
behavioral genetics
cognitive factors
delay of gratification
environmental factors
factor analysis
five-factor model
heritability

locus of control
  (internal/external)
longitudinal method
Minnesota Multiphasic
  Personality Inventory
  (MMPI-2)
objective personality tests or
  self-report questionnaires
person-situation interaction
personal factors

quantum personality change
reliability
self-efficacy
social cognitive theory
structured interviews
trait
trait theory
validity

Outline

- *Introduction*
    1. Power of beliefs (Nelson Mandela's strength and persistence)
    2. Determination (Beverly Harvard's skills and resolve)
    □ How do Rod Plotnik's two examples illuminate the concept of personality and questions about it?

A. *Social Cognitive Theory*

   1. Review and definition: **social cognitive theory** (Albert Bandura)

   2. Interaction of three factors

      a. Cognitive-personal factors

         (1) **Cognitive factors**

         (2) **Personal factors**

      b. Behaviors

      c. **Environmental factors**

   3. **Bandura's social cognitive theory**

      a. Four cognitive factors

         (1) Language ability

         (2) Observational learning

         (3) Purposeful behavior

         (4) Self-analysis

      b. **Locus of control: internal/external** (Julian Rotter)

         (1) Internal locus of control

         (2) External locus of control

      c. **Delay of gratification**

         (1) Preferred rewards and delay

         (2) Important to delay gratification?

      d. **Self-efficacy** (Albert Bandura)

         (1) Sources of information

         (2) Influence of self-efficacy

   4. Evaluation of social cognitive theory

      a. Comprehensive approach

      b. Experimentally based

      c. Programs for change

      d. Criticisms and conclusions

B. *Trait Theory*

   1. Definition

      a. **Trait theory**

      b. **Trait**

   2. Identifying traits

      a. How many traits can there be? (Gordon Allport)

         (1) Original list of 18,000 terms

         (2) Reduced to 4,500 traits

    b. Aren't some traits related?

        (1) **Factor analysis** (Raymond Cattell)

        (2) Reduced list to 35 traits

  3. Finding traits: Big Five (supertraits)

    a. **Five-factor model** (OCEAN)

        (1) **Openness**

        (2) **Conscientiousness**

        (3) **Extraversion**

        (4) **Agreeableness**

        (5) **Neuroticism**

    b. Importance of the Big Five

    c. Big Five in the real world

  4. Person versus situation (Walter Mischel)

    a. Experiment: person-situation

        (1) Failure of traits to predict behaviors across different situations

        (2) **Person-situation interaction**

    b. Conclusions

        (1) Descriptions

        (2) Predictions

  5. Stability versus change: **longitudinal method**

    ☐ What is your age, relative to the Big Three-Oh? What does this suggest about your personality?

    a. 13 to 18 years old

    b. 20 to 80 years old

C. *Genetic Influences on Traits*

  1. **Behavioral genetics**

  2. Studying genetic influences: **heritability** (Thomas Bouchard)

  3. Data from twin studies

  4. Influences on personality

    a. Genetic factors (40%)

    b. Nonshared environmental factors (27%)

    c. Error (26%)

    d. Shared environmental factors (7%)

D. *Evaluation of Trait Theory*

  1. How good is the list? (Big Five supertraits)

  2. Can traits predict? (person-situation interaction)

  3. What influences traits? (shared and nonshared factors)

E. *Research Focus: 180 Degree Change*

1. How much can people change in a day (**quantum personality change**)?

2. A study of personality change

   a. Method: **structured interviews**

   b. Results

   c. Conclusions

F. *Cultural Diversity: Suicide Bombers*

1. Story of a suicide bomber

2. Cultural and personal reasons

   a. What conditions lead to suicide attacks?

   b. What motivates a suicide bomber?

   c. Do suicide bombers share certain traits?

   d. What does the future hold?

G. *Four Theories of Personality*

☐ Rod Plotnik gives you a beautiful summary of the important but complex material of Modules 19 and 20. Take advantage of his chart (summarized on the next page). Use the chart as a study tool. Can you describe each theory and its key concepts? This would be a good exercise for a study group or for studying with a friend.

H. *Application: Assessment — Objective Tests*

1. Definition

   a. **Objective personality tests or self-report questionnaires**

   b. Structured (specific questions and answers)

2. Examples of objective tests

   a. Integrity tests

   b. **Minnesota Multiphasic Personality Inventory (MMPI-2)**

3. Reliability and validity

   a. **Barnum principle**

   b. **Validity**

   c. **Reliability**

4. Usefulness

   a. Disadvantages

   b. Advantages

Rod Plotnik's Magic Personality Theory Chart (see pages 472–473 in the textbook)

1. Psychodynamic theory (Sigmund Freud)

   a. Unconscious motivation

      (1) Free association

      (2) Dream interpretation

      (3) Slips of the tongue

   b. Divisions of the mind

      (1) Id (pleasure principle)

      (2) Ego (reality principle)

      (3) Superego (conscience and sense of guilt)

   c. Psychosexual stages

      (1) Oral

      (2) Anal

      (3) Phallic (Oedipus and Electra complexes)

      (4) Latency

      (5) Genital

2. Humanistic theories (Abraham Maslow and Carl Rogers)

   a. Phenomenal perspective, holistic view, and self-actualization

   b. Abraham Maslow's humanistic theory

      (1) Capacity for growth

      (2) Hierarchy of needs

   c. Carl Rogers' self theory

      (1) Self-actualization tendency

      (2) Need for positive regard

3. Social cognitive theory (Albert Bandura)

   a. Cognitive factors

   b. Locus of control

   c. Delay of gratification

   d. Self-efficacy

4. Trait theory (Gordon Allport)

   a. Basic traits

   b. Five-factor model (Big Five supertraits or OCEAN)

      (1) Person-situation interaction

      (2) Changeable and stable

      (3) Genetic factors

Language Workout

What's That?

p. 457   guilty of **plotting** against the government = secretly planning harm
         provided that he make no public speeches = with this condition
         lost no time in resuming = immediately returned to
         they have **what it takes** to be good cops = the necessary qualities

p. 462   **domestic abuse** = violent fighting within family
         street **thugs** = criminals
         this **elusive** list = hard to find

p. 464   The best-known, **right wing** talk-radio host = politically conservative
         Our priorities are **out of whack** = not correct
         whites are **getting away** with drug use = not penalized
         send them up the river, too = send them to jail
         caught in a drug **ring** = criminal group
         you might very well **draw the line** = refuse to continue
         you must **take into account** = consider, judge

p. 465   **thrill seekers** = people who value excitement and danger

p. 466   **chain-smoked** = smoked one cigarette after another without stopping
         they were **flabbergasted** = shocked, very surprised

p. 468   should not be **blown out of proportion** = emphasized too much

p. 470   **Alcoholics Anonymous** = organization to help alcoholics stop drinking
         the **battery** of personality tests = group, set
         relieved of a mental **burden** = worry

p. 471   culture considers them to be **martyrs** = people who die for political or religious reasons

p. 472   **go after** one's dream = pursue, work to achieve
         a socially acceptable **outlet** = way to release pressure

p. 474   has become **big business** = profitable, resulting in new companies
         a **parole board** = official group who decide if a prisoner is ready for release

p. 478   **white collar** workers = business managers, not laborers
         landing a job = winning, being hired for
         medical malpractice insurance = lawsuits by patients against doctors
         intangible skills = difficult to see
         a good **reality check** = comparison of one's judgment with objective conditions

Flex Your Word Power

If someone asks you for the **plot** of a movie you just saw, what does she want to know? She wants to know what the story is about. This is just one meaning for the word **plot**. Look at these sentences from the text in which **plot** is used as a verb.

> The MMPI-2 asks about and identifies a variety of specific personality traits and **plots** whether these traits are in the normal or abnormal range. (p. 474)
> I believe I am being **plotted** against. (p. 474)

In the first sentence, the verb **plots** means to identify or decide a position. This use is common in mathematics and the sciences especially when you **plot** a graph to represent your research. In the second sentence, the verb **plotted** means to plan. For example, you can **plot** your future. However, we most often use it in negative situations such as **plotting** against someone.

What's the Difference?

PROVIDED or EVEN IF

Provided means if, with a positive result: Provided Rob changes his religion, Tanya will marry him. This means that Rob *must* change his religion if Rob wants to marry Tanya. It is a necessary condition. Take a look at the example from the text. Many times [Mandela] was offered his release from prison provided that he make no public speeches public speeches and cease his freedom-fighting activities. (p. 457)

Even if means even though, usually with a negative result: Even if Rob changes his religion, Tanya won't marry him. This means that *nothing* Rob does will change Tanya's decision: She refuses to marry him. Changing religion is *not* enough: it is useless for changing the result. Here's an example from your text. Notice how being an extravert has no effect on the situation below.

> The person-situation interaction explains that even if you were an extravert, you would behave differently at a wedding than at a funeral because each of these situations creates different cues to which you respond. (p. 464)

Test Yourself

Will or **won't**? Write in the word that fits in the sentences below. EXAMPLE: Jack **will** go to the movie with you **provided** you buy the ticket. Jack **will not** go **even if** you buy the ticket.

Sigmund _____ pass the exam even if he cheats.
Sigmund _____ pass the exam provided he cheats.
That alligator _____ bite you, provided you don't step on its tail.
That toothless old alligator _____ bite you, even if you step on its tail.

Provided or **even if**? Try it yourself. Write in the word/words that fit in the sentences below:

The store agreed to sell Dan a case of beer _____ he had proof of his age.
Misha refuses to listen to his boss _____ his job is in danger.
Aisha can get her driver's license _____ she passes the driving test.
_____ our plane arrives on time, Jun can meet us at the airport.
_____ an earthquake destroys the college, the professor will never postpone the midterm exam.

Answers

Sigmund **won't** pass the exam even if he cheats.
Sigmund **will** pass the exam provided he cheats.
That alligator **won't** bite you, provided you don't step on its tail.
That toothless old alligator **won't** bite you, even if you step on its tail.
The store agreed to sell Dan a case of beer **provided** he had proof of his age.
Misha refuses to listen to his boss **even if** his job is in danger.
Aisha can get her driver's license **provided** she passes the driving test.
Provided our plane arrives on time, Jun can meet us at the airport.
Even if an earthquake destroys the college, the professor will never postpone the midterm exam.

The Big Picture

Which statement below offers the best summary of the larger significance of this module?

A   Social cognitive and trait theories of personality are coming together in a single, persuasive description of human behavior. The central idea of this new, unified theory is well represented in the acronym OCEAN.

B   For all the efforts of psychology to work out a convincing explanation of personality, the newly discovered phenomenon of quantum personality change (often in a single day) makes nonsense of any single theory of personality.

C   The most important fact presented in this module is the "cultural diversity" discussion of collectivistic and individualistic cultures (Japan and the United States). The point is that all important personality variables are cultural.

D   This module must be read in conjunction with the previous one. Together they describe the four major theoretical approaches to our understanding of personality. The study of personality shows how we are alike, yet individuals.

E   So what if I have no will power. I don't like marshmallows anyway!

True-False

_____   1. Social cognitive theory combines learning and behavior with ideas about how we think.

_____   2. Gordon Allport and Raymond Cattell were early pioneers of social cognitive theory.

_____   3. One of the key ideas of Albert Bandura's social cognitive theory is observational learning.

_____   4. College students who think they "can't beat the system" ought to study the concept of locus of control.

_____   5. The most important measure of self-efficacy is the ability to delay gratification.

_____   6. A trait is a personal quirk — something that makes you different from everyone else in the world.

_____   7. After a long search, researchers now believe that there are as many as 4,500 different personality traits.

_____   8. One problem with the concept of traits is that traits are not always consistent across situations.

_____   9. Most changes in personality occur before the age of thirty.

_____   10. Genetic influences can determine physical factors like height, but not psychological factors like personality.

Flashcards 1

_____	1. behavioral genetics	a. a statistical measure that estimates how much of a trait is influenced by genetic factors
_____	2. delay of gratification	b. beliefs concerning how much control (internal or external) we have over situations or rewards
_____	3. factor analysis	c. your personal belief concerning how capable you are in controlling events and situations in your life
_____	4. five-factor model	d. voluntarily postponing an immediate reward to continue a task for the promise of a future reward
_____	5. heritability	e. says personality is shaped by environmental conditions, cognitive-personal factors, and behavior
_____	6. locus of control	f. a relatively stable and enduing tendency to behave in a particular way
_____	7. self-efficacy	g. a complicated statistical method; finds relationships among many diverse items and groups them
_____	8. social cognitive theory	h. personality categories: openness, conscientiousness, extraversion, agreeableness, and neuroticism
_____	9. trait	i. an approach for analyzing structure of personality by measuring, identifying, and classifying similarities
_____	10. trait theory	j. study of how inherited or genetic factors affect personality, intelligence, emotions, behavior

Flashcards 2

_____	1. Barnum principle	a. asking each individual same set of focused questions so same information is obtained from everyone
_____	2. cognitive factors	b. consistency; a person's test score at one time should be similar to score on a similar test later
_____	3. longitudinal method	c. our behavior results from an interaction between our traits and the effects of being in a particular situation
_____	4. Minnesota Multiphasic Personality Inventory	d. those cognitive factors that include our beliefs, expectations, values, intentions, and social roles`
_____	5. objective personality test self-report questionnaire	e. sudden (in a single day) and radical or dramatic shift in one's personality, beliefs, or values
_____	6. person-situation interaction	f. studying the same group of individuals repeatedly at many different points in time
_____	7. quantum personality change	g. listing a number of traits in such a general way (like a horoscope) that every reader sees himself or herself in it
_____	8. reliability	h. degree to which a test measures what it is supposed to measure
_____	9. structured interviews	i. true-false self report questionnaire (567 items) describing normal and abnormal behaviors
_____	10. validity	j. specific written statements requiring subjects to respond ("true" or "false") about applicability

Multiple-Choice

_____ 1. Rod Plotnik tells the stories of leader Nelson Mandela and police chief Beverly Harvard to illustrate the
   a. beliefs and traits that motivate human personality
   b. powerful personalities that have been produced by the peoples of Africa
   c. key role of prisons and law enforcement in maintaining social stability
   d. unconscious forces that are the foundation of all personality

_____ 2. Which one of the following forces is _not_ a component of social cognitive theory?
   a. environmental conditions (learning)
   b. cognitive-personal factors
   c. traits
   d. behavior

_____ 3. One of the key concepts in Albert Bandura's social cognitive theory is
   a. need for social approval
   b. observational learning
   c. self-actualization
   d. unconscious conflict

_____ 4. The only statement below that shows _internal_ locus of control is
   a. often exam questions are so unrelated to course work that studying is useless
   b. no matter how hard you try, some people just don't like you
   c. it is not always wise to plan too far ahead, because many things just turn out to be a matter of good or bad fortune
   d. when I make plans, I am almost certain I can make them work

_____ 5. Children and marshmallows were used in a classic study of
   a. observational learning
   b. locus of control
   c. delay of gratification
   d. traits

_____ 6. When the 4-year-olds in the delay of gratification experiment were retested 10 years later,
   a. high delay and low delay children were now about the same
   b. being good at delay was related to many other positive characteristics
   c. high delay children had become anxious, worrywart teens
   d. many had become Scouts, but, curiously, refused to make s'mores

_____ 7. Which one of the following is _not_ included by Bandura in the keys to determining your sense of self-efficacy?
   a. previous experiences of success or failure on similar tasks
   b. comparing your capabilities with those of others
   c. listening to what others say about your capabilities
   d. the power of our conscience to make us feel guilty

_____ 8. One of the major contributions of social cognitive theory to understanding personality is
  a. going beyond symptoms to the deeper emotional or unconscious causes of problems
  b. the development of successful programs for changing behavior and personality
  c. explaining the emotional and genetic causes of behavior
  d. offering a complete theory of personality and human nature

_____ 9. Do women make better cops? Evidence suggests that the answer is
  a. yes, at least for now, because women have a greater determination to succeed
  b. no, because women in our society tend to have a lower sense of self-efficacy
  c. yes, because personality traits shared by many women are useful in police work
  d. no, because the performance of male and female officers is about the same

_____ 10. A trait is defined as a
  a. relatively stable and enduring tendency to behave in a particular way
  b. personal idiosyncrasy that distinguishes us from all others
  c. behavioral tendency that is genetically determined
  d. specific belief about the world that influences our personality

_____ 11. For years, research in personality has tried to identify the
  a. single trait that all humans share
  b. particular traits that make up a healthy personality
  c. most complete list of terms that deal with personality differences
  d. fewest number of traits that cover the largest range of human behaviors

_____ 12. The result of this effort (above) is the current belief that human personality is best described by
  a. five supertraits
  b. 35 basic traits
  c. 4,500 personality traits
  d. 18,000 descriptive terms

_____ 13. The five-factor model of personality gets its range and depth from the fact that
  a. if we know just five things about a person, we can produce a complete picture of him or her
  b. each of the factors is set by age five
  c. each of the factors is determined by the culture in which the person was raised
  d. each factor is actually a continuum, with many related traits at the hot and cold ends

_____ 14. One of the sharpest attacks on the concept of traits was
  a. Mischel's argument that behavior changes in different situations
  b. Bandura's theory that we learn by observing others
  c. Cattell's discovery that needs are arranged in a hierarchy
  d. Allport's list of 18,000 terms that deal with personality differences

_____ 15. In Walter Mischel's classic study of conscientious behavior by college students across different situations, the trait of conscientiousness was found to
  a. govern student behavior with high consistency across different situations
  b. be poor predictors of student behavior in both old and new situations
  c. fail to predict how students would behave in different situations
  d. correctly predict student behavior in each of the five supertraits (OCEAN)

_____ 16. When are you most likely to make changes in your personality? Research says
     a. by age five
     b. before age 30
     c. after age 30
     d. when the end is near

_____ 17. The new area of psychology called behavioral genetics is providing evidence that
     a. twins are very different from single-birth children
     b. twins may appear outwardly similar, but in most respects they are quite different
     c. sharing a family environment is the major influence on personality
     d. inheritance sets a range of behaviors for many aspects of personality

_____ 18. The statistical measure called heritability is a significant scientific advance in the study of personality because it
     a. reveals that environmental factors have far more influence on personality than genetic factors
     b. uses research to estimate how much a trait is influenced by genetic factors
     c. eliminates the need for traditional personality tests and measures
     d. means that if we know a person's genetic code, we know his or her personality

_____ 19. It is now believed that _____ of the development of personality traits is explained by genetics
     a. about half
     b. about one-fifth
     c. almost all
     d. almost none

_____ 20. In evaluating trait theory, critics raise all of the following questions _except_
     a. how good is the list of traits?
     b. can traits predict behaviors?
     c. how much do genetic factors influence traits?
     d. how many supertraits traits are there?

_____ 21. Some people experience a very sudden (in a single day) and radical or dramatic shift in personality, beliefs, or values; psychology calls this a
     a. flash of insight, or "ah ha" experience
     b. born again spiritual experience
     c. quantum personality change
     d. quantitative personality change

_____ 22. What motivates a suicide bomber like the young Palestinian woman described in the text?
     a. a cluster of distinct traits, such as being quick to anger
     b. a combination of personal reasons (death of a friend) and cultural influences (power)
     c. most appear to have been motivated by an external locus of control
     d. they aren't really motivated (most don't know they have been wired with a live bomb)

_____ 23. A good example of a highly structured objective personality test is the
     a. Thematic Apperception Test (TAT)
     b. Rorschach Inkblot Test
     c. Minnesota Multiphasic Personality Inventory (MMPI-2)
     d. traditional psychological interview

_____ 24. The Barnum principle explains how horoscopes predict your future (but ignore validity):
    a. the traits listed are so general that they apply to almost everyone
    b. there is a specific astrological constellation for the date of your birth
    c. astrological signs have been worked out over many millennia
    d. life is a circus — who knows what will happen?

_____ 25. It's so important that it bears repeating: reliability = _____ and validity = _____
    a. truth / consistency
    b. being on target / being correct time after time
    c. hucksterism (Barnum principle) / scientific truth
    d. scores are consistent over time / measures what it claims to measure

Short Essay

1. How might the concept of locus of control help explain both successful and unsuccessful students?

2. Describe the experiment that tested the concept of delay of gratification.

3. Describe the "hot" and "cold" ends of the categories (OCEAN) in the Big Five trait theory of personality (okay, this is hard!).

4. In what ways are suicide bombers examples of cultural diversity?

5. Describe how the Barnum principle explains the popularity of horoscopes.

For Psych Majors Only...

Pioneers in Personality Theory: Psych majors should know the famous pioneers of personality theory discussed Modules 19 and 20. Can you match these psychologists to the phrase that fits their work or ideas?

_____	1. Sigmund Freud	a.	individual psychology
_____	2. Carl Jung	b.	"penis envy" is nonsense
_____	3. Alfred Adler	c.	hierarchy of needs
_____	4. Karen Horney	d.	personality traits
_____	5. Abraham Maslow	e.	delay of gratification
_____	6. Carl Rogers	f.	locus of control
_____	7. Albert Bandura	g.	collective unconscious
_____	8. Walter Mischel	h.	unconditional positive regard
_____	9. Gordon Allport	i.	observational learning
_____	10. Julian Rotter	j.	unconscious motivation

Answers to "Pioneers in Personality Theory" Quiz

1 j   2 g   3 a   4 b   5 c   6 h   7 i   8 e   9 d   10 f

Answers for Module 20

The Big Picture (explanations provided for incorrect choices)

A There are significant differences between social cognitive and trait theories of personality.
B If quantum personality change holds up, each approach will have its own explanation of this kind of change.
C Common personality variables explain the United Nations, the Olympics, world trade, etc. Humans are more alike than different.
D *Correct! You see the "big picture" for this Module.*
E It's just a joke!

True-False

1	T	458	
2	F	458	Allport and Cattell were pioneers of the trait approach to personality.
3	T	459	
4	T	459	
5	F	460	Self-efficacy refers to belief in one's ability to accomplish goals.
6	F	462	A trait is a tendency to act in a consistent manner (not a quirk).
7	F	463	Current research has reduced all traits to five supertraits.
8	T	464	
9	T	465	
10	F	466	Current research suggests that there is a significant genetic component in personality.

Flashcards 1

1 j   2 d   3 g   4 h   5 a   6 b   7 c   8 e   9 f   10 i

Flashcards 2

1 g   2 d   3 f   4 i   5 j   6 c   7 e   8 b   9 a   10 h

Multiple-Choice (explanations provided for incorrect choices)

1 **a** *Correct! See page 457.*
   b The stories of these two remarkable people involve Africa, but more general personality factors are the point.
   c The main point of these twin stories concerns beliefs and determination, not social stability.
   d Just the opposite is true for the personality theories in this module.

2 a This is one of the three forces that social cognitive theory says shape personality development.
   b This is one of the three forces that social cognitive theory says shape personality development.
   c *Correct! See page 458.*
   d This is one of the three forces that social cognitive theory says shape personality development.

3 a This general idea is not a key concept in personality.
   b *Correct! See page 459.*
   c Self-actualization belongs to Abraham Maslow and Carl Rogers.
   d Unconscious conflict belongs to Sigmund Freud.

4 a So there is nothing I can do to get a better grade.
   b So my social skills count for nothing.
   c So my individual efforts will not be effective.
   d *Correct! See page 459.*

5 a Observational learning was studied by Albert Bandura.
   b Locus of control was studied by Julian Rotter.
   c *Correct! See page 460.*
   d Traits were studied by Gordon Allport.

6 a High delay children continued to show better adjustment than low delay children.
   b *Correct! See page 460.*
   c High delay children showed many personality strengths 10 years later.
   d It's just a joke!

7   a   Would this influence how effective you believe you are?
    b   Would this influence how effective you believe you are?
    c   Would this influence how effective you believe you are?
    d   *Correct! See page 460.*

8   a   This would fit psychodynamic theories.
    b   *Correct! See page 461.*
    c   No theory combines emotional and genetic factors to explain personality.
    d   This would fit Sigmund Freud's psychoanalytic theory of personality.

9   a   Determination was not the factor indicated by research.
    b   Even if true, this idea did not apply to women cops.
    c   *Correct! See page 462.*
    d   Research indicated some performance differences. What were they?

10   **a**   *Correct! See page 462.*
     b   This is a common definition of a trait, but not the psychological definition.
     c   Traits are not all genetically determined.
     d   Traits are not exclusively cognitive.

11   a   Rather than a single trait, there probably are five basic traits.
     b   This may be a particular concern of some psychologists, but it is not the main research goal.
     c   Allport compiled such a list, but it was only a starting point in defining traits.
     d   *Correct! See page 462.*

12   **a**   *Correct! See page 463.*
     b   This is the result of factor analysis of the 4,500 traits.
     c   This is what the 18,000 descriptive terms became when translated into traits.
     d   This is where Allport started.

13   a   It is far more complicated than five things, because of the continuum each of the five factors represents.
     b   This would be truer of psychoanalytic theories; trait theories do not specify when traits appear.
     c   Research suggests that personality arises from a universal experience or biological basis rather than culture.
     d   *Correct! See page 463.*

14   **a**   *Correct! See page 464.*
     b   Bandura's theory does not exclude the concept of traits.
     c   Maslow's theory does not exclude the concept of traits.
     d   Allport's list helped develop the concept of traits.

15   a   That was the point of the experiment — just the opposite was true.
     b   The trait did predict behavior in old, similar situations.
     c   *Correct! See page 464.*
     d   Conscientiousness is itself one of the five supertraits.

16   a   Then at what age is personality first formed?
     b   *Correct! See page 465.*
     c   The author of the Study Guide only wishes this were true!
     d   At death?

17   a   Twins are studied not because they are different but because they are alike.
     b   Twins are studied not because they are different but because they are alike.
     c   Possibly true, but this is an environmental influence, not a genetic one.
     d   *Correct! See page 466.*

18   a   Current thinking says that personality is about half genetic and half environmental.
     b   *Correct! See page 466.*
     c   Such tests and measures provide the data that genetic information is able to reinterpret.
     d   If this were true, it would mean that experience is irrelevant to personality development.

19   **a**   *Correct! See page 467.*
     b   This idea considerably understates genetic influences.
     c   This statement is far too extreme.
     d   This statement is far too extreme.

20   a   This is one of the three major questions about traits.
     b   This is one of the three major questions about traits.
     c   This is one of the three major questions about traits.
     d   *Correct! See page 468.*

21   a   Insight refers to understanding more than to change.
     b   This is not a term in psychology.
     c   *Correct! See page 470.*
     d   Sounds right, but check the first word.

22   a   No specific personality profile or traits have been identified.
     b   *Correct! See page 471.*
     c   This has not been reported in studies of suicide bombers.
     d   They know what they are doing.

23   a   This is a projective test.
     b   This is a projective test.
     c   *Correct! See page 474.*
     d   An interview is the opposite of a psychological test.

24   *a*   *Correct! See page 475.*
     b   True, but what connection do they have with your future?
     c   True, but what connection do they have with your future?
     d   Maybe science? But certainly not the Barnum principle.

25   a   If anything, just the opposite (but "truth" is too strong for science).
     b   "On target" could refer to validity, but "being correct" isn't right for either term.
     c   An interesting opposition, but not the meaning of reliability and validity.
     d   *Correct! See page 475.*

Short Essay (sample answers)

1. Julian Rotter's concept of locus of control refers to a continuum of beliefs about how much control we have over situations and rewards. Internal locus of control is the belief that we control our destiny, while external locus of control is the belief that events outside ourselves (fate) determine what happens. Students who believe graduation depends on motivation and determination show internal locus of control, while students who believe graduation depends on chance or things outside their control show external locus of control.

2. Young children were told they could have one marshmallow right now or two marshmallows if they waited until the experimenter returned. The children faced the dilemma of taking a less preferred single marshmallow immediately or delaying gratification but obtaining a more preferred reward by waiting. Delay was more difficult if they looked at the marshmallows. When examined 10 years later, children who showed ability to delay gratification now exhibited several desirable personality characteristics.

3. OCEAN stands for the following five supertraits, each representing a continuum. Openness: is open to novel experiences or has narrow interests. Conscientiousness: is responsible and dependable or is impulsive and careless. Extraversion: is outgoing and decisive or is retiring and withdrawn. Agreeableness: is warm and good-natured or is unfriendly and cold. Neuroticism: is stable and not a worrier or is nervous and emotionally unstable. [Count it right if you got the general idea of each category. Exact wording not necessary.]

4. Do suicide bombers share certain traits? They have some traits in common, but only general traits that apply to others who do not become suicide bombers. Instead of common traits, suicide bombers have in common personal reasons, such as the death of a loved one, and cultural influences, such as the conviction that the suicide bombing makes up for the powerlessness of their parents and the humiliations of their group. The extreme example of suicide bombers shows that individual traits can be outweighed by cultural influences.

5. Loads of people (75%) read horoscopes, and many believe they are so correct that they were written especially for them. But examination shows that horoscopes contain general traits, at least a few of which apply to almost everyone (like the horoscope Rod Plotnik wrote that fooled his students). Except for the fake reference to astronomy, horoscopes are no better than fortune cookies. In their failure to identify or predict traits for a particular person, horoscopes lack validity: they do not measure what they claim to measure.

Module 21

Health, Stress, & Coping

This Module Could Save Your Life!

O.K., maybe I'm exaggerating. Then again, maybe not. Remember Rod Plotnik's discussion of the relationship between illness and stress (in the section on psychosomatic symptoms)? Go back and check how much illness doctors estimate results from stress. The percentages are staggering.

It is becoming clear that stress is one of the greatest health hazards we face. We all feel it. Sometimes it seems that modern life not only is more stressful than 'the good old days' were, but that the number of our daily stressors continues to increase.

Does it have to be this way?

Ironically, considering its prevalence, stress is the one health hazard that is not inevitable, at least not in theory. Old age, if nothing else, is going to get each of us. Accidents will happen. We can't eliminate all disease. You won't solve the problem of environmental pollution all by yourself. Yet you are not doomed to be ravaged by stress.

What can you do about it? First, you can adopt a positive attitude and a healthy life style that will tend to protect you against stress. Second, you can learn how to manage the stress you can't escape. Module 21 explains how both of these safeguards work.

Never mind the grade on the test. Study this module to learn how to live a long and healthy life!

Should Stress Be Managed?

What about stress in *your* life? Do you enjoy a good balance between the demands of your environment and your mental and physical abilities to meet them? Or do you see signs in your behavior or your physical health that suggest too much stress in your life?

Often the suggestion of psychology seems to be that in order to avoid physical and psychological problems, we should learn how to "manage" the stress that is causing them. A different approach would be to think of stress as clues to aspects of life that aren't working effectively. While a heart attack certainly qualifies as a "clue," most stress clues are much more commonplace, and therefore are easy to overlook. Search for the small distortions in your everyday behavior (like swearing, irritation, speeding, and headaches) that could be evidence of stress. Look for feelings, thoughts, and actions that may betray problems in your life and suggest connections to pressures from your environment. Meditation and relaxation certainly are valuable, but changing your life and solving your problems, where possible, would be better.

Effective Student Tip 21

No One Is Lazy

All right, go ahead and call yourself "lazy," if it makes you feel better, but it's not good psychology. First, it may be what cognitive psychologists call a self-handicapping strategy, where you excuse yourself in advance for poor performance. ("I probably won't pass the test..., I'm too lazy to study!") Well, at least they can't say you're dumb! Just lazy.

Second, I would argue that no one is lazy. Oh, sure, we humans like to lie around and we goof off a lot, but that probably has more to do with defending our freedom and autonomy against the regimentation of organized work. The natural tendency of all animals is activity. Watch children at play. Look at the time and energy we put into second jobs, hobbies, sports, and social activities. Normally, we prefer to be doing something, because only activity creates the opportunity to feed our constant hunger to be effective.

When we feel lazy we really are feeling ineffective. The task before us seems too difficult, too unrewarding, or too lacking in novelty and challenge. When you feel 'too lazy' to tackle your schoolwork, the real problem is that you haven't figured out how to handle it effectively, or how to make it deliver positive feedback attesting to your effectiveness.

Your response...

Many of my own students violently disagree with me on this Tip. What do you think?

Learning Objectives

1. Understand health, stress, and coping as immediate, important, personal applications of psychological science to your everyday wellbeing and long-term survival.

2. Learn our basic physiological responses to stress and how they have led to a new understanding of the connection between mind and body.

3. Learn the different kinds of stress and stressors and how we react to them and attempt to deal with them.

4. Appreciate the connection between stress and both personality and social factors.

5. Understand different kinds of coping, choosing a coping strategy, and how people cope with severe trauma.

6. Appreciate how the meditation techniques of Tibetan monks turn Western science on its head, but in so doing teach modern psychology a valuable lesson about the connections between mind and body.

7. Learn how to apply stress management programs and techniques to reducing stress in your daily life.

Key Terms

Many of these key terms are as immediate as the morning newspaper, where, in fact, you may find them. Others are psychological terms that take the discussion of stress and coping a bit deeper. All are relevant to your daily life and important to your health and welfare.

alarm stage
anxiety
anxiety (Freud)
approach-approach conflict
approach-avoidance conflict
autonomic nervous system
avoidance-avoidance conflict
biofeedback
burnout
case study
challenge appraisal
conditioned emotional
  response
conflict
emotion-focused coping
exhaustion stage
experiment
fight-flight response

frustration
galvanic skin response
general adaptation syndrome
  (GAS)
hardiness
harm/loss appraisal
hassles
immune system
locus of control
major life events
mind-body connection
mind-body therapy
observational learning
optimism
pessimism
posttraumatic stress disorder
  (PTSD)
primary appraisal

problem-focused coping
progressive relaxation
psychoneuroimmunology
psychosomatic symptoms
relaxation response
resistance stage
secondary appraisal
social support
stress
stress management program
threat appraisal
transcendental meditation
  (TM)
Type A behavior
uplifts

Outline

- *Introduction*
    1. **Stress** (Rod's blood phobia)
    2. Coping (Sandra's stresses)
- A. *Appraisal*
    1. **Primary appraisal**
    2. Three ways to appraise a stressful situation
        a. **Harm/loss appraisal**
        b. **Threat appraisal**
        c. **Challenge appraisal**
    3. Situations and primary appraisals
    4. Appraisal and stress levels
        a. **Galvanic skin response**
        b. Stress experiment
    5. Same situation, different appraisals
    6. Sequence: appraisal to arousal
- B. *Physiological Responses*
    - ☐ Can you explain why the fight-flight response was so valuable in our early evolution but has become such a problem in modern life? (See "For Psych Majors Only..." box.)
    1. **Fight-flight response** (physical and psychological stimuli)
        a. Sequence for activation of the fight-flight response
            (1) Appraisal
            (2) Hypothalamus
            (3) Sympathetic division
            (4) Fight-flight response
        b. Fight-flight: physiological and hormonal responses
            (1) Stress appraisal
            (2) Respiration
            (3) Heart rate
            (4) Liver
            (5) Pupils
            (6) Hair
            (7) Adrenal glands
            (8) Muscle tension
            (9) Male-female difference ("tend and befriend" instead of fight-flight)

2. **Psychosomatic symptoms**

☐ Do you ever experience psychosomatic symptoms? (The truthful answer is "Yes!") Can you describe a typical symptom you sometimes have and relate it to stress in your life?

3. Development of symptoms

   a. Common psychosomatic symptoms

   b. Development of psychosomatic symptoms

4. **General adaptation syndrome (GAS)** (Hans Selye)

   a. **Alarm stage**

   b. **Resistance stage**

   c. **Exhaustion stage**

5. **Mind-body connection: mind-body therapy**

6. **Immune system**

   a. **Psychoneuroimmunology** (Ader and Cohen)

   b. Evidence for psychoneuroimmunology

   c. Conditioning the immune system

      (1) Classical conditioning experiment

      (2) History of psychoneuroimmunology

C. *Stressful Experiences*

   1. Kinds of stressors

      a. **Hassles**

      b. **Uplifts**

      b. **Major life events** (Social Readjustment Rating Scale [SRRS])

   2. Situational stressors

      a. **Frustration**

      b. **Burnout**

      c. Violence: **posttraumatic stress disorder (PTSD)**

   3. **Conflict**

      a. Three common kinds of conflicts

         (1) **Approach-approach conflict**

         (2) **Avoidance-avoidance conflict**

         (3) **Approach-avoidance conflict**

      b. Five styles of dealing with conflict

         (1) Avoidance

         (2) Accommodation

         (3) Domination

(4) Compromise

(5) Integration

4. **Anxiety**

   a. Three ways of developing anxiety

      (1) Classical conditioning: **conditioned emotional response**

      (2) **Observational learning**

      (3) Unconscious conflict: **anxiety (Freud)**

   b. Coping with anxiety

      (1) Extinction (problem-focused, conscious techniques)

      (2) Freudian defense mechanisms (emotion-focused, unconscious coping techniques)

D. *Personality & Social Factors*

1. **Hardiness**

   a. Definition

   b. Function

2. **Locus of control**

   a. External locus of control

   b. Internal locus of control

3. Optimism versus pessimism

   a. **Optimism** (optimists)

   b. **Pessimism** (pessimists)

   c. Personality factors (positive or negative emotions)

4. **Type A behavior** (Friedman and Rosenman)

   a. Personality and heart attacks

   b. Revised definition of Type A behavior over three decades

5. **Social support**

   a. Buffer against stress

   b. Maintaining mental health

E. *Kinds of Coping*

1. Appraisal: **secondary appraisal**

2. Kinds of coping

   a. **Problem-focused coping**

   b. **Emotion-focused coping**

3. Choosing a coping strategy

F. *Research Focus: Coping with Trauma*

1. How do people cope with severe burns?

2. Research methods

   a. **Experiment**

   b. **Case study**

3. Coping with initial stressful effects

4. Coping with long-term stressful effects

5. Conclusions

G. *Cultural Diversity: Tibetan Monks*

1. Monks' amazing abilities

☐ Does Rod Plotnik's example of Tibetan monks mean that modern science is flawed?

2. Voluntary control of **autonomic nervous system**

   a. Voluntary control

   b. Explanation

   c. Studying the mind's abilities

H. *Application: Stress Management Programs*

1. Definition: **stress management program**

☐ Could you apply the basic principles of a stress management program to your own life?

2. Changing thoughts

   a. Use challenge appraisals

   b. Substitute positive self-statements

3. Changing behaviors (emphasize problem-focused over emotion-focused activities)

4. Learning to relax

   a. **Biofeedback**

   b. **Progressive relaxation**

   c. Meditation

      (1) **Transcendental meditation (TM)**

      (2) **Relaxation response**

5. Stopping stress responses

The Language Workout Marathon

You have learned many new things about the English language. To see how much you remember, try the Language Workout Marathon. You can find it in Module 25!

For Psych Majors Only...

It's a Jungle Out There! Imagine two of your prehuman ancestors venturing away from the trees looking for food. Suddenly they hear a low growling and see a huge cat with enormous fangs coming toward them. One (an early scientist) is delighted with the new creature and decides to go up and pet it. The other, feeling awful but also all charged up, makes an instant decision to run for the nearest tree and climb like never before. The survivor, whose makeup contained a little more of what became our fight-flight response, lived to contribute genes to the next generation. The other one made a contribution to the genes of the saber-toothed tiger.

Fast forward to today at the office. Suddenly the boss is standing over your desk saying something about a project that was supposed to be finished. Should you calmly explain that one of the reports you need hasn't arrived yet, or should you run for the nearest tree, like your ancestor did? Is it just another problem, or is it a real saber-toothed tiger? You get all charged up just trying to decide.

The situation in today's jungle of school, work, and relationships is much more complicated than it was for our ancestors. It's hard to tell the real emergencies, so we exhaust ourselves with constant false alerts. The fight-flight response was supposed to be for the rare enemy or tiger, not for the simple problems of daily life.

One Small Step

If this module got to you at all, now might be a good time to take a step toward modifying your lifestyle. Start by making one small change. Nothing big, just something that takes only a few minutes a day. Take a walk around the block. Spend a few minutes in silent contemplation. Munch veggies instead of chips. What could you do that would be the first step toward a healthier and less stressful lifestyle?

Language Workout

What's That?

p. 481   as I **come to** = become conscious again
    grimacing at herself = frowning, making unhappy face
    She **ducks into** the shower = enters
    bundles up the kids = puts coats on, dresses for outdoors
    food stamps = government help for poor people to buy food
    to **make ends meet** = have enough money for all necessities
    husband had **forged** a check = signed false name (crime)
    she had come to the **end of her rope** = limit of her strength
    a homeless **shelter** = temporary housing for homeless people

p. 482   need to **mobilize** your physical energy = gather, activate

p. 483   not to **identify with** the injured = feel sympathy for

p. 484   stomach **knotting** = uncomfortable tight feeling
    situations that are **novel** = new

p. 487   **coed** Joan = college student (female)
    taking a toll on her stomach = hurting, causing harm
    has **given rise to** a new area = produced

p. 488   **coming down with something** = beginning to feel sick from illness
    They **tackled** this question **head-on** = tried to solve it directly
    folk wisdom = popular beliefs

p. 490   **grin and bear it** = smile and do what's necessary (don't resist)

p. 491   **checked into** a hospital = entered, registered as a patient
    a **graphic** example = dramatic, clear
    cynical people = who mistrust other people

p. 492   individuals **go to any lengths** to win = do anything necessary, even bad actions

p. 495   If I study hard and **apply myself** = use my abilities

p. 500   painful changes of their **dressings** = bandages
    going out for football = participating, joining team

p. 506   a lump **turned up** = appeared
    totally **benign** = harmless
    would bet his children's lives = is 100% certain
    explore **my inner drag queen** = possibilities to play with clothing styles
    other **Pollyana** things = overly optimistic
    pass the Kleenex = (I'm going to cry)

Build Your Word Power

Have you **overlooked** some of the earlier workouts? You may want to check the grammar sections **even if** (from Module 20) you didn't have to read them for class. In Module 2, you read about the use of **over** at the beginning of words. See if you can guess the meanings of these words from the sentences.

Millions of others **over**react to the point of fainting? (p. 482)

That triggers a chain of intense mental events and **over**active physiological responses. (p. 482)

It **over**taxes your emotional and physiological recourses. (p. 482)

Making Connections

Do you remember **some of which, all of which,** and **half of which**? We practiced them in Module 13. These forms help us to count and measure objects.

We can join sentences that count and measure persons in the same way with similar forms like **some of whom, all of whom,** and **half of whom**.

Look at the following pair of sentences:

The professor gave a surprise quiz to the students.
None of the students was expecting it.

We can join these sentences together using **none of whom**:

The professor gave a surprise quiz to the students, **none of whom** was expecting it.

We use a comma here because it is extra information about the students. It is not necessary for understanding *which* students.

Look at another example. This one is from the text:

They tackled this question head-on by giving the same amount of cold virus to 394 subjects, **all of whom** were quarantined for a week. (p. 488)

We can tell from this sentence that all 394 subjects were quarantined for a week.

Test Yourself

Join the sentences below using **whom**:

The meeting was attended by all the employees. **Some of them** arrived late.
The meeting _____.

Emma invited 20 people to her birthday party. **All of them** brought gifts.
Emma _____.

The experiment used 324 college students. **Half of them** were given placebos.
The experiment _____.

The United States has elected 43 presidents. **Not one of them** was named "Bob."
The United States _____.

Answers

Overreact = to react too strongly
Overactive = working at higher than normal levels
Overtaxes = takes too much from you
The meeting was attended by all the employees, **some of whom** arrived late.
Emma invited 20 people to her birthday party, **all of whom** brought gifts.
The experiment used 324 college students, **half of whom** were given placebos.
The United States has elected 43 presidents, **not one of whom** was named "Bob."

The Big Picture

Which statement below offers the best summary of the larger significance of this module?

A   With the creation of the new field of psychoneuroimmunology, psychology has at last proved the truth of the old motto "mind over matter." We now know that any physical problem can be solved by using mental processes.

B   Although Western science tends to treat mind and body as separate entities, obviously they are part of the same whole. This module brings together our current understanding of stress and the many new techniques for coping with stress in our lives.

C   The purpose of this module is to alert psychology students to the many misuses of science fostered by the holistic health movement and to warn them not to be fooled by stress management courses, Tibetan monks, meditation tapes, and other mind-body fakery.

D   Psychology is learning how to build stress-resistant people. By using discoveries like hardiness, coping mechanisms, locus of control, Type A behavior, and the fight-flight syndrome, everyone can be free from stress.

E   *Stress! Stress!* You want to talk about *stress!* Just cancel that %$&# exam!

True-False

_____   1. Stress depends partly on how we evaluate a situation.

_____   2. To "appraise" something means to feel very positive about it.

_____   3. The fight-flight response goes back to the earliest days of the human species.

_____   4. Research shows that small daily hassles are far more stressful than major life events.

_____   5. The way we respond to frustration influences our levels of stress.

_____   6. Conflict means the inevitable run-ins that occur when you have to work with someone else.

_____   7. Your personality can influence how well you deal with stress.

_____   8. One of the best prescriptions for successfully handling stress is to have many relationships that confer social support.

_____   9. Some Tibetan monks have developed a type of yoga that allows them to levitate their bodies several inches off the ground.

_____ 10. Biofeedback is a technique for clearing your head of all thoughts, worrisome and otherwise.

Flashcards 1

_____ 1. anxiety

_____ 2. fight-flight response

_____ 3. general adaptation syndrome (GAS)

_____ 4. locus of control

_____ 5. mind-body connection

_____ 6. posttraumatic stress disorder (PTSD)

_____ 7. primary appraisal

_____ 8. psychosomatic symptoms

_____ 9. stress

_____ 10. Type A behavior

a. body reacting to stressful situations by going through three stages: alarm, resistance, exhaustion

b. continuum of beliefs about the extent to which one is in control of one's own future

c. how your thoughts, beliefs, and emotions produce beneficial or detrimental physiological changes

d. anxious or threatening feeling of a situation being more than our resources can adequately handle

e. real, often painful symptoms that are caused by psychological factors such as worry, tension, stress

f. theory that traits of aggressive workaholism, anger, competition, hostility, can lead to a heart attack

g. directs great sources of energy to muscles and brain, creating preparation of body for action

h. result of direct personal experience of an event involving actual or threatened injury or death

i. initial, subjective evaluation of a situation in which you balance demands against your abilities

j. an unpleasant state characterized by feelings of uneasiness and apprehension, physiological arousal

Flashcards 2

_____ 1. burnout

_____ 2. emotion-focused coping

_____ 3. exhaustion stage

_____ 4. hardiness

_____ 5. hassles

_____ 6. major life events

_____ 7. problem-focused coping

_____ 8. psychoneuroimmunology

_____ 9. social support

_____ 10. transcendental meditation (TM)

a. combination of three personality traits (control, commitment, challenge) that protect us from stress

b. moderation of stress by having groups, family, and friends who provide attachment and resources

c. small, irritating, frustrating events we face daily and that we appraise or interpret as stressful experiences

d. feelings of doing poorly at one's job, physical and emotional exhaustion, due to very high demands

e. breakdown in internal organs or weakening of immune system due to long-term, continuous stress

f. primarily doing things to deal with emotional distress, such as seeking support, avoiding, denying

g. study of the relationship between central nervous system, endocrine system, and psychosocial factors

h. potentially disturbing or disruptive situations that we appraise as having significant impact on our lives

i. assuming a comfortable position, eyes closed, and repeating a sound to clear one's head of all thoughts

j. solving the problem by seeking information, changing your behavior, or taking whatever action in necessary

Multiple-Choice

_____ 1. Rod Plotnik uses his problem with having blood drawn in the doctor's office to show that
    a. how we interpret or appraise a situation determines the stress it causes
    b. a bad scare in childhood will stay with you for the rest of your life
    c. some events, like having blood drawn, are stressful to everyone
    d. stress can overcome a person for no apparent reason

_____ 2. Rod's initial, subjective evaluation of the situation in the doctor's office is an example of a
    a. secondary appraisal
    b. challenge appriasal
    c. primary appraisal
    d. tertiary appraisal

_____ 3. Which one of the following is *not* a type of primary appraisal?
    a. harm/loss
    b. threat
    c. challenge
    d. advantage/resource

_____ 4. A good clue to whether a person is experiencing stress is the
    a. potential danger of the situation (like operating a chainsaw)
    b. amount of blood at the scene
    c. galvanic skin response
    d. "deer caught in the headlights" expression

_____ 5. Rod Plotnik lists his students' reactions to a number of common stressors in order to illustrate the point that
    a. modern life has become almost unbearably stressful
    b. not everyone appraises these situations the same way
    c. there is a core of common experiences that everyone considers stressful
    d. the one thing everybody hates is waiting

_____ 6. The reason why the fight-flight response can harm our health is that
    a. every time it is triggered our bodies go through an automatic process of arousal
    b. overuse is a kind of "crying wolf" that eventually results in letting our guard down
    c. biologically, humans were designed for quiet, peaceful lives
    d. psychologically, humans do not tolerate challenge very well

_____ 7. The fact that the fight-flight response is also found in animals such as alligators suggests that
    a. except for a thin layer of civilization, humans are basically the same as reptiles
    b. evolution sometimes creates mechanisms that are harmful to the species (us)
    c. we may desire a peaceful existence, but our basic nature is aggressive and violent
    d. it must be an old and powerful evolutionary mechanism for survival

_____   8. Which one of the following is *not* a common psychosomatic symptom?
  a. intense cramping and nausea due to food poisoning
  b. muscle pain and tension in the neck, shoulders, and back
  c. having either tension or migraine headaches
  d. eating problems like feeling compelled to eat or having no appetite

_____   9. Which one of the following is *not* a stage in the general adaptation syndrome?
  a. alarm
  b. attack
  c. resistance
  d. exhaustion

_____   10. The mind-body connection and mind-body therapy are both based on the idea that
  a. thoughts and emotions come from changes in bodily activity
  b. thoughts and emotions can change physiological and immune responses
  c. when you have a strong feeling or powerful idea, you must express it through bodily action
  d. mind and body are two separate and independent areas of activity

_____   11. "Psychoneuroimmunology" is the study of
  a. the manner in which physical factors create psychological symptoms
  b. how disease can make a person psychotic or neurotic
  c. the interaction of physical and psychological factors in health
  d. (this is a trick question — that is a made-up word)

_____   12. The total score on the Social Readjustment Rating Scale
  a. subtracts positive life events from negative life changes
  b. gives a precise cut-off point for becoming ill or staying well
  c. reflects how well you cope with stress
  d. reflects how many major life events you have experienced in the past year

_____   13. Having feelings of doing poorly, physically wearing out, or becoming emotionally exhausted because of stress at work is called
  a. frustration
  b. burnout
  c. conflict
  d. stress

_____   14. According to Freud's explanation, we try to reduce anxiety by employing
  a. problem-focused coping at the ego level
  b. defense mechanisms at the unconscious level
  c. approach/avoidance choices at the ego level
  d. "snap out of it" coping messages at the superego level

_____   15. Which one of the following is *not* an ingredient of hardiness?
  a. control
  b. commitment
  c. contentment
  d. challenge

_____ 16. The famous "Type A behavior" research attempted to relate certain personality traits to
   a. hardy personality
   b. locus of control
   c. increased risk of cancer
   d. increased risk of heart attack

_____ 17. Today, research into Type A behavior points to the risks of being a
   a. hostile/angry person who would benefit from decreasing negative traits
   b. workaholic person with a habitual sense of time urgency and explosive pattern of speaking
   c. depressed, angry, competitive and easily frustrated worker
   d. Type B person who is too easygoing to be successful

_____ 18. People in Roseto, Pennsylvania didn't follow healthy lifestyles, but they had lower rates of heart attacks, ulcers, and emotional problems — probably because
   a. the steep Pennsylvania hills forced them to exercise whether they wanted to or not
   b. being the home of the University of Pennsylvania, the town had superb medical facilities
   c. families in this small town were all related to each other, which had built up a good genetic background over many generations
   d. relationships with family and neighbors were extremely close and mutually supportive

_____ 19. Secondary appraisal means
   a. deciding what we can do to manage, cope, or deal with the situation
   b. our subjective evaluation of a situation to decide if we can deal with it
   c. the extent to which we appraise a situation as stressful after we have taken time to think about it objectively
   d. the extent to which we find a situation stressful the second time we encounter it

_____ 20. Solving a problem by seeking information, changing your own behavior, or taking whatever action is necessary is called
   a. problem-focused coping
   b. emotion-focused coping
   c. primary appraisal
   d. secondary appraisal

_____ 21. All of the following are sex differences in choosing coping strategies *except*
   a. women tend to use more coping strategies
   b. men are more likely to withdraw or avoid problems
   c. men are more likely to engage in emotion-focused coping in dealing with stressors
   d. women are more likely to use emotion-focused coping to seek emotional support and advice

_____ 22. Our understanding of _____ makes it hard for us to explain the amazing abilities of Tibetan monks
   a. cultural diversity
   b. the autonomic nervous system
   c. biofeedback training
   d. the relaxation response

_____ 23. If Tibetan monks can raise their body temperature through meditation, then perhaps
  a. Western medicine — not Asian — represents the real medical fakery
  b. Western medicine should pay more attention to psychological factors
  c. every culture has a form of medicine that is best for its own members
  d. every culture develops some phenomena that can't be fully explained

_____ 24. A good way to prevent taking an exam from becoming more stressful is to
  a. repeat over and over again that the exam can't be all that bad
  b. use threat appraisals to scare yourself into taking the exam seriously
  c. engage in biofeedback sessions to learn to control physiological responses
  d. work at substituting positive self-statements for negative self-statements

_____ 25. The relaxation technique that involves learning to increase or decrease physiological signals from the body is called
  a. the relaxation response
  b. progressive relaxation
  c. biofeedback
  d. Transcendental Meditation (TM)

Short Essay

1. Why was the fight-flight response good for early humans (and still is for alligators) but not so good for modern humans?

2. Isn't it maddening when you get sick _after_ the semester is over, just as you are ready to kick back and have fun? Describe how the new science of psychoneuroimmunology explains this phenomenon.

3. Are you aware of exhibiting any psychosomatic symptoms? Can you connect any of these symptoms to stresses in your life? Give one good example.

4. Why is it better to be an optimist than a pessimist?

5. People in the small town of Roseto, Pennsylvania, had an awful diet and lifestyle. Yet they suffered fewer heart attacks, had fewer ulcers, and fewer emotional problems than the national average. Why? Showoffs can also tell what happened when people moved to better homes in the countryside.

Answers for Module 21

The Big Picture (explanations provided for incorrect choices)

A   This statement is too extreme. We now see the influence of mental factors, but not a dominance of them.
B   *Correct! You see the "big picture" for this Module.*
C   This statement is too extreme. Caution and common sense are advised, but the new alternative health approaches do deserve our consideration.
D   Stress has a useful function in alerting us to unhealthy aspects of our environment. We can't be entirely stress free.
E   It's just a joke!

True-False (explanations provided for False choices; page numbers given for all choices)

1	T	482	
2	F	482	Appraisal refers to how we evaluate a person or situation.
3	T	484	
4	F	490	It is not that hassles are more stressful, but that there are so many more of them.
5	T	491	
6	F	492	Conflict refers to situations in which there are competing possible solutions.
7	T	494	
8	T	497	
9	F	501	They're good . . . but not *that* good! (Read the statement again!)
10	F	503	Biofeedback is voluntarily learning to control physiological responses such as blood pressure.

Flashcards 1

1 j   2 g   3 a   4 b   5 c   6 h   7 i   8 e   9 d   10 f

Flashcards 2

1 d   2 f   3 e   4 a   5 c   6 h   7 j   8 g   9 b   10 i

Multiple-Choice (explanations provided for incorrect choices)

1   *a*   *Correct! See page 481.*
    b   Not necessarily — it depends on how you come to understand it later.
    c   Many people can have blood drawn without feeling too much stress.
    d   Stress can be predicted, understood, and handled without harmful effects.

2   a   A secondary appraisal involves deciding how to deal with a potentially stressful situation.
    b   A challenge appraisal means you have the potential for gain or personal growth in a situation.
    c   *Correct! See page 482.*
    d   There is no tertiary appraisal.

3   a   If we appraise a situation as causing us harm or loss, it is stressful.
    b   If we appraise a situation as threatening, it is stressful.
    c   If we appraise a situation as challenging, it demands resources, but is usually less stressful.
    d   *Correct! See page 482.*

4   a   Many people would show caution, but not necessarily stress, around a chainsaw.
    b   Some of us would recoil at the sight of blood, but many would feel a desire to help.
    c   *Correct! See page 483.*
    d   That might show surprise, but not necessarily stress (besides, it's too inaccurate a measure).

5   a   Could be true, but this is not Plotnik's point.
    b   *Correct! See page 483.*
    c   Just the opposite is true.
    d   Annoying as waiting is, only 65 percent (not everyone) rated it as stressful.

6   *a*   *Correct! See page 484.*
    b   The body does not let down its guard — that's the point.
    c   Throughout evolution, humans have faced challenge and threat.
    d   Humans seem to thrive on change and actively seek it.

7 a   That is far too extreme an implication; despite this mechanism, we are very different from reptiles.
   b   That is not the way evolution works; the fight-flight response must have helped our species survive.
   c   The fight-flight response is designed to help us in extreme situations, not to govern our general behavior.
   d *Correct! See page 484.*

8 *a* *Correct! See page 486.*
   b   This is a common psychosomatic symptom.
   c   This is a common psychosomatic symptom.
   d   This is a common psychosomatic symptom.

9 a   Alarm is one of the three stages of the general adaptation syndrome.
   b *Correct! See page 487.*
   c   Resistance is one of the three stages of the general adaptation syndrome.
   d   Exhaustion is one of the three stages of the general adaptation syndrome.

10 a   It is not true that ideas and feelings come mainly from changes in the body.
   b *Correct! See page 487.*
   c   Ideas and feelings do not have to be expressed in physical behavior.
   d   The mind-body connection and mind-body therapy assume just the opposite.

11 a   The problem is not one of simple cause and effect.
   b   This statement is basically untrue.
   c *Correct! See page 488.*
   d   It is a real word, and conveys an important new concept.

12 a   This is not how the SRRS works.
   b   The SRRS gives a general indication, but not a precise cut-off point.
   c   The SRRS measures amounts of stress, but not how well you deal with it.
   d *Correct! See page 490.*

13 a   Frustration is the particular feeling that results when our attempts to reach some goal are blocked.
   b *Correct! See page 491.*
   c   Conflict is the feeling we experience when we must decide between two or more incompatible choices.
   d   Stress is a more general feeling of a situation straining or overloading our psychological resources.

14 a   This is a cognitive, not psychoanalytic, explanation.
   b *Correct! See page 493.*
   c   This is a behavioral, not psychoanalytic, explanation.
   d   This is a nonsense statement.

15 a   Control is one of the three personality traits that make up hardiness.
   b   Commitment is one of the three personality traits that make up hardiness.
   c *Correct! See page 494.*
   d   Challenge is one of the three personality traits that make up hardiness.

16 a   The hardy personality is a different factor in stress management.
   b   Locus of control is a different factor in stress management.
   c   Close, but no cigar.
   d *Correct! See page 496.*

17 *a* *Correct! See page 496.*
   b   This is more true of the Type A research of the 1970s.
   c   This is more true of the Type A research of the 1980s.
   d   Type B behavior is just the opposite of the characteristics implicated in heart attacks.

18 a   Sounds logical, but the facts stated are not true.
   b   Sounds logical, but the facts stated are not true.
   c   Sounds logical, but the facts stated are not true.
   d *Correct! See page 497.*

19 *a* *Correct! See page 499.*
   b   Secondary appraisal is an objective process.
   c   It's not a second appraisal of the stressful situation, but a different consideration.
   d   It's not a second appraisal of the stressful situation, but a different consideration.

20   **a**   *Correct! See page 499.*
     b   Emotion-focused coping does not involve taking direct action to change the problem situation.
     c   Primary appraisal does not refer to solving a problem.
     d   Secondary appraisal does not refer to solving a problem.

21   a   Research shows that this is a sex difference in coping strategies.
     b   Research shows that this is a sex difference in coping strategies.
     c   *Correct! See page 499.*
     d   Research shows that this is a sex difference in coping strategies.

22   a   Cultural diversity should make us more sensitive to the amazing abilities the monks possess.
     b   *Correct! See page 501.*
     c   Biofeedback training should help us understand how monks control involuntary responses.
     d   The relaxation response is not directly related to the monks control of involuntary responses.

23   a   Serious medical practices, regardless of culture, should not be regarded as fakery.
     b   *Correct! See page 501.*
     c   Effective medical treatment (if accepted) works regardless of culture.
     d   Science does not, *cannot*, place any physical phenomenon out of bounds for study.

24   a   This will only make you less likely to prepare for the exam by studying.
     b   Using challenge appraisals might help, but not threat appraisals.
     c   This would work for lowering your blood pressure, but how would that help remove the stress of an exam?
     d   *Correct! See page 502.*

25   a   The relaxation response is a method of inducing a relaxed state.
     b   Progressive relaxation is a method of inducing a relaxed state.
     c   *Correct! See page 503.*
     d   Transcendental Meditation (TM) is a method of inducing a relaxed state.

Short Essay (sample answers)

1. Imagine conditions for early humans, living with dangers including larger, stronger, and faster animals. Threat wouldn't be constant, but it could be sudden and deadly. (Ditto for alligators.) Those who could make quick decisions on whether to fight or flee would survive (and pass their genes on to the next generation). The dangers of modern life are not so clear yet seem to come at us constantly. As we gear up for fight or flight over and over again, our immune systems and our health suffer. Better appraisals could help.

2. *Psycho* (mind) *somatic* (body) symptoms are the real and sometimes painful physical symptoms that are caused by increased physiological arousal resulting from psychological factors, such as worry, stress, and anxiety. (Review the list on page 486.) Describe a psychosomatic symptom you are aware of in your own life and explain what stressful conditions seem to bring it about. If you can't come up with one from your own life, talk about a friend's problem — but be aware that you are very unusual, or not looking too deeply!

3. Psychoneuroimmunology is the relatively new science of the relationship between the central nervous system, the endocrine system, and psychosocial factors. During a long, difficult semester, many students go through a cycle of feeling stress, mobilizing strength to resist it, then instead of resting and restoring bodily resources go through the cycle all over again. About the time finals are over, your immune system is badly depleted. Bingo! You get a cold, just when you thought you could relax and have fun.

4. The answer has to do with feeling more or fewer positive or negative emotions, which in turn are involved in increasing or decreasing stress levels and chances of developing psychosomatic symptoms. Optimism leads to believing and expecting that good things will happen, and therefore to experiencing more positive emotions. Pessimism leads to believing and expecting that bad things will happen, and therefore more negative emotions. Both are relatively stable personality traits, not easy to change, but worth working on.

5. The crucial difference in Roseto turned out to be that family relationships were extremely close and mutually supportive, and this wonderful social support system extended to neighbors and to the community as a whole. That the health benefits of social support came as a surprise in a profoundly social species is a telling commentary on modern psychology, with its relentless efforts to look inside. BTW, when prosperous former residents moved out into the countryside, the health benefits of close social support began to decline!

Module 22

Assessment & Anxiety Disorders

What Is Psychological Abnormality?

We can often recognize when a fellow human is psychologically 'abnormal,' but when we try to say exactly what makes the person abnormal, we find that it is not so easy.

Rod Plotnik begins this module with a hard problem for psychology and psychiatry: how to understand and treat mental disorders. In his examples of infamous criminals and everyday problems you will see that psychological science has not yet attained the agreement and precision of medical science. All doctors will agree on the diagnosis of a broken arm, but what about a broken mind? Since psychology has such a long way to go before it can claim a comprehensive and satisfactory definition of abnormality, perhaps I can be forgiven for trying my own definition.

One Try at a Definition of Psychological Abnormality

Psychological abnormality is a typically temporary condition of dysfunction and distress caused by deficits or breakdowns in the universal need to be effective. Lack of effectiveness can occur in any one or more of six areas of human psychological functioning (see Plotnik's six approaches to psychology).

The most damaging results of the loss of effectiveness are the corresponding breakdowns in those processes of regulation and self-regulation that are so crucial to the welfare of human beings, who lack guidance by instincts or reflexes. It is the loss of regulation and self-regulation that seems 'abnormal,' and is so frightening, both to the troubled person and to others.

If we suffer from psychological abnormality, the best thing we can do is begin to take competent action. But this is not so easy. Intervention and treatment may be needed in any one or more of the six realms of psychological functioning. (1) We may need psychoactive drugs to restore the regulation of a biologically based mental function. (2) We may need to explore the past and learn to understand our basic psychological processes, especially emotion. (3) We may need to reverse a negative self-image and learn to think more realistically about ourselves and others. (4) We may need to modify old habits that no longer work and develop new skills and abilities. (5) We may need to project our values and hopes into the future, to discover our true aspirations and real selves. (6) We may need to rebuild and strengthen our ties to others, in order to gain the social support we need to resurrect old competencies and build new ones.

> Check it out! PowerStudy 2.0 includes a 40-50 minute presentation that uses animations, visuals, and interactive activities as well as quizzing to help you understand concepts in this module.

Effective Student Tip 22

What 'Boring' Really Means

Students often complain that they aren't doing well because their classes and schoolwork are boring. I could suggest that *they* are interesting persons, and therefore have a duty to help make their classes interesting, but that wouldn't be fair. It would be more realistic to advise them to reconsider what boring really means.

Most students think certain people (not themselves!) or certain activities are boring, but that is incorrect. Psychologically, boredom means being trapped, not being able to engage in an activity that is good for you. The next time you feel bored, ask yourself if there is anything taking place that allows you to grow and to express what is uniquely you. I'll bet you'll discover that 'boring' means not being able to exercise your urge to be effective.

Nothing is intrinsically boring. Every experienced teacher I've known had something worthwhile to say. Give me any example of activity or knowledge you might consider boring and I'll find someone, somewhere, whose great passion in life is pursuing exactly that activity or acquiring precisely that knowledge. Your schoolwork isn't boring, but perhaps you haven't yet found a way to connect it to the passions in *your* life.

Your response...

Think of something really boring. Now reconsider. Is there a way in which it might *not* be boring?

Learning Objectives

1. Understand *assessment* as a scientific procedure for determining psychological abnormalities and their treatment, and *anxiety disorders* as the more common, less crippling mental disorders (the more debilitating, mood disorders and schizophrenia, are treated in the next module).

2. Learn the causes of abnormal behavior and how it is defined and assessed.

3. Learn how mental disorders are diagnosed and understood with the American Psychiatric Association's *Diagnostic and Statistical Manual of Mental Disorders-IV-Text Revision* or DSM IV-TR.

4. Understand the roots and varieties of anxiety disorders and somatoform disorders.

5. Learn how culture affects mental disorders through the example of taijin kyofusho, or TKS.

6. Explore the research on understanding and preventing teenage school shootings.

7. Learn how common phobias are understood and treated.

Key Terms

The key terms in this module ask you to be part lawyer, part historian, and part doctor. They will require more study than many other modules, but hard study will pay off. The next module is worse!

---

agoraphobia
case study
clinical assessment
clinical diagnosis
clinical interview
cognitive-behavioral therapy
cognitive-emotional-
  behavioral and
  environmental factors
conduct disorder
conversion disorder
*Diagnostic and Statistical
  Manual of Mental Disorders-*

IV-Text Revision or DSM-IV-
  TR
exposure therapy
generalized anxiety disorder
genetic factors
insanity
labeling
maladaptive behavior
  approach
mass hysteria
mental disorder
obsessive-compulsive disorder
panic attack

panic disorder
personality tests
phobia
social norms approach
social phobias
somatization disorder
somatoform disorders
specific phobias
statistical frequency approach
taijin kyofusho or TKS

Outline

- *Introduction*
  1. Mental disorder (Jeffrey Dahmer)
     a. **Insanity**
     b. **Mental disorder**

    2. **Phobia** (Kate Premo's aviophobia)

A. *Factors in Mental Disorders*

  1. Causes of abnormal behavior

    a. Biological factors

      (1) **Genetic factors**

      (2) Neurological factors

    b. **Cognitive-emotional-behavioral and environmental factors**

  2. Definitions of abnormal behavior

    a. **Statistical frequency approach**

    b. **Social norms approach**

    c. **Maladaptive behavior approach**

B. *Assessing Mental Disorders*

  1. Definition of assessment

    a. Case of Susan Smith

    b. **Clinical assessment**

  ☐ Why is assessment of a mental problem more likely to be controversial than assessment of a problem of physical health?

  2. Three methods of assessment

    a. Neurological tests

    b. **Clinical interview**

    c. **Personality tests** (objective tests and projective tests)

C. *Diagnosing Mental Disorders*

  1. Real life assessment: Susan Smith

    a. Her past

    b. Her present

  2. DSM-IV-TR

    a. **Clinical diagnosis**

    b. *Diagnostic and Statistical Manual of Mental Disorders-IV-Text Revision* or **DSM-IV-TR**

  3. Nine major problems: Axis I

    a. Disorders usually first diagnosed in infancy, childhood, or adolescence

    b. Organic mental disorders

    c. Substance-related disorders

    d. Schizophrenia and other psychotic disorders

    e. Mood disorders (Susan Smith: diagnosis — mood disorder)

    f. Anxiety disorders (Kate Premo: diagnosis — specific phobia)

    g. Somatoform disorders

      h. Dissociative disorders

      i. Sexual and gender-identity disorders

   4. Other problems and disorders: Axes II, III, IV, and V

      a. Axis II: Personality Disorders (Jeffrey Dahmer: diagnosis — antisocial personality disorder)

      b. Axis III: General Medical Conditions

      c. Axis IV: Psychosocial and Environmental Problems

      d. Axis V: Global Assessment of Functioning Scale

      e. Using all five Axes

      f. Usefulness of DSM-IV

   5. Potential problems using DSM-IV

      a. **Labeling** mental disorders

      b. Social and political implications

      c. Frequency of mental disorders

D. *Anxiety Disorders*

   1. **Generalized anxiety disorder (GAD)**

   ☐ Do you sometimes experience anxiety? How does it feel?

      a. Symptoms

      b. Treatment

   2. **Panic disorder**

      a. Symptoms (**panic attack**)

      b. Treatment

   3. **Phobia**

      a. **Social phobias**

      b. **Specific phobias**

      c. **Agoraphobia**

   4. **Obsessive-compulsive disorder**

   ☐ No, you don't have the disorder, but what are some of your obsessive-compulsive behaviors?

      a. Symptoms

      b. Treatment

         (1) **Exposure therapy**

         (2) Antidepressant drugs

E. *Somatoform Disorders*

    1. **Somatoform disorders**

    ☐ Do you worry about your body or your health? Are your worries realistic or exaggerated?

        a. **Somatization disorder**

        b. **Conversion disorder**

    2. **Mass hysteria**

F. *Cultural Diversity: An Asian Disorder*

    1. **Taijin kyofusho or TKS**

    ☐ What is taijin kyofusho and what are its implications for psychiatry?

        a. Occurrence

        b. Cultural values

    2. Social customs (cultural differences)

G. *Research Focus: School Shootings*

    1. What drove teens to kill fellow students and teachers **(conduct disorder)**?

    2. **Case study**

    3. Risks shared by adolescent school shooters

        a. Risk factors

        b. Neurological factors

H. *Application: Treating Phobias*

    1. Specific phobia: flying

    ☐ Is there anything you are "phobic" about?

    2. **Cognitive-behavioral therapy**

        a. Thoughts

        b. Behaviors

    3. **Exposure therapy** (virtual reality therapy)

    4. Social phobia: public speaking

        a. Explain

        b. Learn and substitute

        c. Expose

        d. Practice

    5. Drug treatment of phobias

        a. Tranquilizers

        b. Problems with drug treatments

Language Workout

What's That?

p. 509 considered him an **average Joe** = ordinary man
guy who **held down** a job = worked
serial killers = criminals who murder again and again in a pattern
con their victims = cheat or trick people
15 **consecutive** life terms = one after another (not at same time)

p. 511 no **adverse** consequences to society = bad, negative

p. 513 the **defense** = lawyers who prove innocence
and **prosecution** = lawyers who prove criminality
refused to **press charges** = make formal complaint to police
scarred by her father's suicide = emotionally injured
a **heightened** emotional reaction = stronger than normal

p. 514 **enuresis** = bedwetting (associated with childish lack of control)
delirium = state of mental confusion, with possible hallucinations
dementia = madness, loss of all connection with reality
The **cardinal** feature = most important

p. 517 **fidgeting** in his chair = moving nervously

p. 518 a person **goes to great lengths** to avoid = tries unusually hard
characterized by irrational, **marked**, and continuous fears = strong, noticeable
caused **stark** terror = total, harsh

p. 519 **hoarding** = collecting and storing supplies (often hidden)

p. 520 in the **soprano** section = people who sing in the highest voice

p. 522 result in **a loss of face** = dignity, respect in society

p. 523 he wanted to **get back at** a popular boy = take revenge on
I got **beat up** = to be hit and kicked
who are **picked on** and **bullied** = to be abused verbally and physically

p. 524 she was **groggy** for days = weak, unable to think clearly

p. 528 **Hillside Strangler** = famous serial killer
to **throw police off** her sweetheart's trail = distract police
She is **disbarred** = officially prevented from working as lawyer (punishment)
those who **fall for** men = fall in love with
yearnings = feelings of intense desire
the daily **tedium** = boring, routine life

Making Connections

WHY A SEMI-COLON?

When you see a semi-colon, it is probably telling you that one complete sentence has some connection with the next complete sentence.

Look at this example: Jiang isn't Chinese ; he is Korean.

A common example seen in advertisements is: Buy now ; pay later.

Both sides of the semi-colon are strong, complete sentences. Both can stand alone, but the semi-colon links them together. So, the semi-colon **separates**, like a period (full stop), because it ends a complete thought. But it also **connects** like a colon because it shows a relationship.

Did you notice the following examples in the text? Look at how the semi-colon connects the meanings of the two sentences in the following examples:

> An estimated 25 million Americans have a similar irrational and intense fear of flying, which is called *aviophobia*; they refuse to get on a plane. (p. 509)
> In comparison, making eye contact is very common in Western culture; if you did not make eye contact in social interactions, you would be judged as shy or lacking in social skills. (p. 522)

Often transitions are used after a semi-colon. These transitions can let the reader know that the next sentence continues with more information such as <u>in addition</u> or <u>besides</u> (See Language Workout Module 10); they can inform the reader that the next sentence is a result of the first with <u>as a result</u> and <u>consequently</u> (See Language Workout Module 11); and they can even indicate that the next sentence is opposite from the first with transitions like <u>however,</u> <u>on the other hand</u>, and <u>nevertheless</u> (See Language Workout Module 18).

Did you notice how many sentences were connected using semi-colons in the above sentence? Look at how 3 sentences are connected with semi-colons in the text:

> Almost all of us 'people watch'**;** we observe parents, brothers, sisters, peers, friends, and teachers; by doing so, we learn a great deal. (p. 459)
> Most (87%) said that, during the quantum experience, an important truth was revealed to them; 78% said that they were relieved of a mental burden; and 60% said that they felt completely loved. (p. 470)

NOW YOU TRY IT. Where do you think a semi-colon should go in the sentences below? Write in a semi-colon. You may need to change the punctuation in sentences below:

> Jacque's dog doesn't bite in fact, his dog has no teeth.
> The family was flying to Seattle their luggage was sent to Moscow.
> Veronica applied for a job at Big National Bank in addition, she filled out applications at Dollars-R-Us Bank.
> Pedro planned to have a nice, relaxing bike ride in reality Jacque's dog chased him everywhere he went.
> Lily is a big fan of Leonardo Di Caprio for example, she has seen **Titanic** thirty-seven times.

The following passage needs more than one semi-colon. Write them in where they are needed:

> Arnold Schwarzenegger started as a body builder then he moved to Hollywood for a career in acting finally he changed to politics, becoming governor of California.

Answers

Jacque's dog doesn't bite; in fact, his dog has no teeth.
The family was flying to Seattle; their luggage was sent to Moscow.
Veronica applied for a job at Big National Bank; in addition, she filled out applications at Dollars-R-Us Bank.
Pedro planned to have a nice, relaxing bike ride; in reality, Jacque's dog chased him everywhere he went.
Lily is a big fan of Leonardo Di Caprio; for example, she has seen **Titanic** thirty-seven times.
Arnold Schwarzenegger started as a body builder; then he moved to Hollywood for a career in acting; finally he changed to politics, becoming Governor of California.

The Big Picture

Which statement below offers the best summary of the larger significance of this module?

A   A major goal of modern psychology is to apply science to the tasks of understanding the causes of mental disorders, developing methods of assessment, and working out effective techniques of treatment.

B   Psychology is more an art than a science. Lacking specific guidance, each clinical psychologist or psychiatrist must rely on experience, intuition, and sometimes guesswork in assessing and treating suffering people.

C   It is in the area of psychological disorders that modern psychology has encountered its most stubborn difficulties. There are so many specific disorders that it is almost impossible to understand them scientifically.

D   Now that psychology has the new, improved fourth edition of the Diagnostic and Statistical Manual of Mental Disorders (DSM-IV-TR), it has become simple to identify a person's problem and prescribe the correct treatment for it.

E   When asked why he had placed ten-foot poles with a rope at the top all around his yard, the man responded, "To keep out the giraffes." "But there are no giraffes around here," his astonished neighbor replied. "Sure keeps them out, doesn't it!"

True-False

_____   1. The psychiatrists who examined him all agreed that Jeffrey Dahmer was insane.

_____   2. Although no one dreamed she would kill her own children, Susan Smith's neighbors had considered her a ticking bomb likely to explode at any minute.

_____   3. When psychiatrists need to make diagnoses, they turn to DSM-IV.

_____   4. Nearly 50% of all Americans report having had at least one mental disorder during their lifetimes.

_____   5. Anxiety is a general problem that can result in many different disorders.

_____   6. Panic disorder is more common among women than men.

_____   7. Don't waste time worrying about your phobias — they usually disappear in a few months.

_____   8. Experiences like going back inside to check that you turned off the oven show that obsessive-compulsive disorder is quite common.

_____   9. Taijin kyofusho or TKS is a social phobia characterized by a morbid fear of offending others.

_____   10. Research has shown that drug treatment is superior to cognitive-behavior programs for getting rid of phobias.

Flashcards 1

_____ 1. clinical interview

_____ 2. cognitive-behavioral therapy

_____ 3. *Diagnostic and Statistical Manual...* or DSM-IV-TR

_____ 4. exposure therapy

_____ 5. insanity

_____ 6. labeling

_____ 7. maladaptive behavior approach

_____ 8. phobia

_____ 9. social norms approach

_____ 10. statistical frequency approach

a. legal term meaning not knowing the difference between right and wrong

b. says a behavior is abnormal if it deviates greatly from accepted social standards, values, or norms

c. anxiety disorder with intense, irrational fear out of all proportion to possible danger of object or situation

d. one method of gathering information about relevant past and present behaviors, attitudes, emotions

e. changing negative thoughts by substituting positive ones; changing limiting behaviors by learning new behaviors

f. says a behavior is abnormal if it interferes with the individual's ability to function personally or in society

g. says a behavior is abnormal if it occurs rarely or infrequently relative to the general population

h. gradually exposing a person to the real anxiety-producing situations or objects that the person is attempting to avoid

i. naming differences among individuals, placing them in specific categories; possible negative associations

j. describes a uniform system for assessing specific symptoms and matching them to 300 disorders

Flashcards 2

_____ 1. agoraphobia

_____ 2. generalized anxiety disorder

_____ 3. mass hysteria

_____ 4. mental disorder

_____ 5. obsessive-compulsive disorder

_____ 6. panic disorder

_____ 7. social phobias

_____ 8. somatoform disorders

_____ 9. specific phobias

_____ 10. taijin kyofusho or TKS

a. characterized by marked and persistent fears that are unreasonable; fear of an object or situation

b. characterized by a terrible fear of offending others through awkward social or physical behavior

c. problem that seriously interferes with ability to live a satisfying personal life, function in society

d. characterized by recurrent and unexpected panic attacks; continued worry about having more attacks

e. characterized by excessive or unrealistic worry about everything; feeling that something bad will happen

f. characterized by irrational, marked, and continuous fear of performing in social situations

g. characterized by anxiety about being in places or situations from which escape might be difficult

h. process in which a group of people develop similar fears, delusions, behaviors, or physical symptoms

i. persistent, recurring irrational thoughts along with irresistible impulses to perform an act repeatedly

j. complaints of a pattern of recurring, multiple, and significant bodily symptoms; no physical causes

Multiple-Choice

_____ 1. The main issue in the Jeffrey Dahmer trial was whether Dahmer
    a. actually killed 15 young men, or only the one he was arrested for
    b. was under the influence of drugs when he killed
    c. knew the difference between right and wrong when he killed
    d. really intended to kill the five men who said they got away

_____ 2. The difference between the terms insanity and mental disorder is that
    a. insanity is more severe than a mental disorder
    b. insanity is a legal term while mental disorder is a medical term
    c. mental disorders are specific forms of insanity
    d. mental disorders do not qualify for insurance reimbursement

_____ 3. In the attempt to understand the causes of abnormal behavior, the newest area of interest is
    a. biological factors (genetic and neurological)
    b. cognitive-emotional-behavioral factors
    c. environmental factors
    d. serial killers like Jeffrey Dahmer

_____ 4. Which one of the following is _not_ a way of defining abnormal behavior?
    a. statistical frequency approach
    b. deviation from social norms approach
    c. maladaptive behavior approach
    d. slips of the tongue approach

_____ 5. The method most commonly used to assess abnormal behavior is the
    a. Rorschach inkblot test
    b. neurological examination
    c. personality test
    d. clinical interview

_____ 6. Rod Plotnik tells the story of Susan Smith in great detail to make the point that
    a. clinical diagnosis is a complicated yet necessary process
    b. childhood sexual abuse almost always results in adult problems
    c. despite all we know about Susan Smith, we still can't understand why she did it
    d. her friends and neighbors should have seen the tragedy coming

_____ 7. The most widely used system of psychological classification is the
    a. _Freudian Psychoanalytic System (FPS)_
    b. _Diagnostic and Statistical Manual of Mental Disorders-IV-Text Revision_ or DSM-IV-TR
    c. _Disordered Mind Standards-III (DMS-III)_
    d. _Federal Uniform Psychopathology Code (UPC)_

_____ 8. One interesting fact about the official manual of diagnosis is that with each new edition
    a. the Freudian explanation of mental disorders has become more dominant
    b. research findings continue to be ignored in favor of clinical opinions
    c. new findings from genetics and neuroscience are used to identify causes of mental disorders
    d. the number of disorders has increased

_____ 9. When you first read about the DSM, it seems overly complicated (why not just a list?), but the purpose of having all the axes, syndromes, and problems is to
    a. give all kinds of therapists (Freudian, humanistic, behavioral, etc.) the categories they need
    b. give the many clinicians who use it lots of diagnoses to choose from
    c. ensure that nothing important about a person's condition is overlooked
    d. rule out any possible disagreement among clinicians

_____ 10. You're not like the nutcases described in the textbook, are you? *Now don't start cry babying about*
    a. the DSM
    b. labeling
    c. the frequency of mental disorders
    d. assessment

_____ 11. A recent large-scale study showed that _____ of all Americans had at least one mental disorder during their lifetime
    a. only 15%
    b. almost 50%
    c. fully 80%
    d. almost 100%

_____ 12. After substance abuse disorders, the most commonly reported mental disorders are
    a. schizophrenic disorders
    b. mood disorders
    c. anxiety disorders
    d. organic mental disorders

_____ 13. The anxiety disorder that causes the greatest terror and suffering is
    a. panic disorder
    b. simple phobia
    c. generalized anxiety disorder
    d. social phobia

_____ 14. Psychologically, the interesting thing about panic attacks is that
    a. often people who are fearful in one situation are quite brave in others
    b. realistically, the person suffering the attack is not in danger at all
    c. people suffering these attacks have been shown to crave attention and sympathy
    d. they are brief, relatively mild affairs that the person can laugh about later

_____ 15. Rose is so afraid of being out in public that she stays at home all the time now; Rose suffers from
    a. a simple phobia
    b. a social phobia
    c. agoraphobia
    d. claustrophobia

_____ 16. Remember the case of Shirley, who had to do everything precisely 17 times? The theory is that she was trying to
    a. reduce or avoid anxiety associated with feeling or being dirty
    b. obey inner voices which told her God loves cleanliness
    c. cleanse her mind of confusing hallucinations
    d. please her mother, who used to punish her severely whenever she got her clothes dirty while playing

_____ 17. Shirley's obsessive-compulsive disorder might be lessened by a new treatment called
  a. depth therapy
  b. hypnotherapy
  c. stimulant drug therapy
  d. exposure therapy

_____ 18. The key feature of somatoform disorders is
  a. pretending to be sick to avoid school or work
  b. real physical symptoms but no physical causes
  c. imagining physical symptoms that aren't really there
  d. psychological problems but no physical symptoms

_____ 19. Medical doctors need to know psychology, because some of their patients are likely to be suffering from
  a. agoraphobia
  b. antisocial personality disorder
  c. somatization disorder
  d. mass hysteria

_____ 20. When half of the 500 children gathered to perform in a concert suddenly became ill, the cause was determined to be
  a. mass hysteria
  b. mass delusion
  c. somatoform disorder
  d. somatization disorder

_____ 21. Of all the mental disorders we know, it's a good bet you don't have to worry about getting TKS, mainly because you
  a. are in college, and therefore too old to get it
  b. are in college, and therefore too intelligent to get it
  c. got shots for it as a child
  d. don't live in Japan

_____ 22. The community is always shocked, yet most teenage school shooters
  a. gave warning signs of their violent intentions, which were not taken seriously
  b. came from among the poorest families in the community
  c. had fathers, uncles, or cousins who were members of extremist groups
  d. were well know to the local police as habitual lawbreakers

_____ 23. A neurological risk factor for becoming a teenage school shooter is that the
  a. limbic system has not yet learned to control violent behavior
  b. prefrontal cortex in the adolescent brain is still immature
  c. shooters have a history of aggression and discipline problems at school or home
  d. prefrontal cortex is a primitive part of the brain that exhibits emotional and violent impulses

_____ 24. Part of the cognitive-behavioral therapy used to help Kate Premo overcome her fear of flying was
  a. gradually exposing Kate to the real anxiety-producing situations until the anxiety decreased
  b. placing Kate under hypnosis and implanting the message, "You will not be afraid"
  c. simulating actual flying (real airline seats, vibrations, noise) in a virtual reality situation
  d. substituting positive, healthy, realistic thoughts for negative, unhealthy, distorted ones

_____ 25. Which one of the following is *not* a technique for treating phobia?
   a. gradually exposing a client to the feared situation
   b. administering an antidepressant drug to the client
   c. hospitalizing the client until his or her fears begin to diminish
   d. teaching the client to become aware of thoughts about the feared situation

Short Essay

1. What were the psychological issues involved the trial of Jeffrey Dahmer?

2. Describe the scope and the advantages and disadvantages of the *Diagnostic and Statistical Manual of Mental Disorders-IV-Text Revision* or DSM-IV-TR.

3. What are somatoform disorders? Give some examples.

4. Describe the Asian mental disorder called taijin kyofusho, or TKS, and what we can learn from it.

5. How does cognitive-behavioral therapy help people like Kate Premo who suffer from aviophobia?

For Psych Majors Only...

Psychology at its Most Real: Now, boys and girls, can you say "diathesis-stress theory?" You will by the time you are finished with this module and the next.

These two modules are tough partly because the subject involves the technical terminology of medical science and the concept of the medical model of illness. You must learn to think and talk like a doctor. But the main reason is that the subject touches on the most difficult challenge faced by psychology: how to understand why things go wrong for troubled people and how to help them.

Have you noticed how frequently new discoveries about the causes and treatment of mental illnesses are in the news? The field of abnormal psychology is developing right before your eyes. Memorize what you must in these modules, but keep your eyes on the big picture, too.

Yes, these modules are tough, but they present psychology at its most real.

Answers for Module 22

The Big Picture (explanations provided for incorrect choices)

 A *Correct! You see the "big picture" for this Module.*
 B Clinical psychology rests on a considerable foundation of empirical support and shared professional experience.
 C Debate about psychological disorders continues, but a great deal is known about specific disorders and the relationships between them. And research continues.
 D Most psychotherapists see DSM-IV-TR as an advance, but diagnosis is not yet perfect. There is still much to learn.
 E It's just a joke!

True-False (explanations provided for False choices; page numbers given for all choices)

1	F	509	Because of the complexity of Dahmer's symptoms, psychiatrists did not agree about his sanity.
2	F	513	Susan Smith's neighbors thought she was a "good girl" and did not see how troubled she really was.
3	T	514	
4	T	516	
5	T	517	
6	T	517	
7	F	518	Phobias tend to persist and may require therapy.
8	F	519	These everyday experiences don't interfere with normal functioning, and so are not a mental disorder.
9	T	522	
10	F	525	Psychotherapy is at least equally effective in combating phobias.

Flashcards 1

 1 d   2 e   3 j   4 h   5 a   6 i   7 f   8 c   9 b   10 g

Flashcards 2

 1 g   2 e   3 h   4 c   5 i   6 d   7 f   8 j   9 a   10 b

Multiple-Choice (explanations provided for incorrect choices)

 1 a   Dahmer admitted the murders.
    b   Dahmer did not claim diminished capacity because of drug use.
    c   *Correct! See page 509.*
    d   Dahmer admitted his homicidal intent, nor was this the main issue.

 2 a   These two terms describe the same condition, but from different perspectives.
    b   *Correct! See page 509.*
    c   These two terms describe the same condition, but from different perspectives.
    d   Mental disorders do qualify for insurance reimbursement.

 3 *a*   *Correct! See page 510.*
    b   While still important, these are not the newest areas of interest and discovery.
    c   While still important, these were emphasized in the 1960s.
    d   That is only one specific (and rare) aspect of abnormal behavior.

 4 a   Statistical frequency is a way to define abnormal behavior.
    b   Deviation from social norms is a way to define abnormal behavior.
    c   Maladaptive behavior is a way to define abnormal behavior.
    d   *Correct! See page 511.*

 5 a   Is this procedure administered to most mental patients?
    b   Is this procedure administered to most mental patients?
    c   Is this procedure administered to most mental patients?
    d   *Correct! See page 512.*

 6 *a*   *Correct! See page 512.*
    b   This statement might be true, but it is not Plotnik's point.
    c   Accurate diagnosis yields understanding of many apparently baffling cases.
    d   Susan Smith's problems were deep and well hidden from her friends and neighbors.

7   a   This is a made-up title, not a real manual.
         b   *Correct! See page 514.*
         c   This is a made-up title, not a real manual.
         d   This is a made-up title, not a real manual.

8   a   DSM III (1980) dropped the Freudian terminology and orientation in favor of specific symptoms and criteria.
         b   Just the opposite is true.
         c   Rather than a problem, this will be a strength of the next DSM (likely in 2010).
         d   *Correct! See page 513.*

9   a   This is just the opposite of the aim of the DSM.
         b   This is just the opposite of the aim of the DSM.
         c   *Correct! See page 514.*
         d   There is still disagreement, as in the court battles over whether defendants are insane or not.

10   a   That does not describe the slur contained in this question!
         b   *Correct! See page 516.*
         c   That does not describe the slur contained in this question!
         d   That does not describe the slur contained in this question!

11   a   This figure is too small.
         b   *Correct! See page 516.*
         c   This figure is too large.
         d   Does this figure square with your own observations?

12   a   These disorders affect less than 1% of people.
         b   These disorders affect about 20% of people.
         c   *Correct! See page 517.*
         d   These disorders affect only a small number of people.

13   *a*   *Correct! See page 517.*
         b   Simple phobias, like fear of snakes, can be handled relatively easily by avoiding the feared object.
         c   Generalized anxiety disorder is uncomfortable, but not a cause of terror.
         d   Social phobias cause fear and avoidance of groups, but not necessarily terror.

14   a   The point is sudden, unexplained fear, not bravery in the face of real danger.
         b   *Correct! See page 517.*
         c   If anything, sufferers try to hide the fact that they have panic attacks.
         d   Nothing could be farther from the truth.

15   a   Simple phobias, like fear of snakes, can be handled relatively easily by avoiding the feared object.
         b   Social phobia are fears of social situations (not just public places).
         c   *Correct! See page 518.*
         d   Claustrophobia is fear of being in enclosed spaces.

16   *a*   *Correct! See page 519.*
         b   Shirley did not hear voices (more common in schizophrenia).
         c   Shirley did not suffer from hallucinations (more common in schizophrenia).
         d   This was not part of Shirley's case history.

17   a   Talk therapy has not been particularly successful in treating OCD.
         b   This therapy has not been particularly successful in treating OCD.
         c   Drug therapy is used for OCD, but the drugs are antidepressant, not stimulant.
         d   *Correct! See page 519.*

18   a   Sufferers of somatoform disorders are not faking.
         b   *Correct! See page 520.*
         c   The physical symptoms are actually present.
         d   There are physical symptoms.

19   a   This rare disorder (if the patient came to the office at all!) would be obvious to most doctors.
         b   This rare disorder would not disguise itself as a physical complaint.
         c   *Correct! See page 520.*
         d   You wouldn't see mass hysteria in a single, individual patient.

20   *a*   *Correct! See page 520.*
     b   This is not a correct technical term in psychology.
     c   Somatoform disorder applies to single cases of having a symptom without a physical cause.
     d   Somatization disorder is having numerous symptoms with physical causes.

21   a   It can strike college students. (But you will see that this is a misleading clue!)
     b   Intelligent people can get it. (But you will see that this is a misleading clue!)
     c   There are no shots for TKS.
     d   *Correct! See page 522.*

22   *a*   *Correct! See page 513.*
     b   The "facts" stated here are not true.
     c   The "facts" stated here are not true.
     d   The "facts" stated here are not true.

23   a   The executive prefrontal cortex must control the more primitive limbic system.
     b   *Correct! See page 523.*
     c   These are environmental, not neurological, risk factors.
     d   That would be true of the limbic system, not the prefrontal cortex.

24   a   This is exposure therapy.
     b   Hypnotherapy was not used to treat Kate Premo.
     c   Virtual reality therapy is a version of exposure therapy.
     d   *Correct! See page 524.*

25   a   Gradual exposure is a treatment for phobias.
     b   Administering antidepressant drugs is a treatment for phobias.
     c   *Correct! See page 524.*
     d   Teaching clients to become aware of their thoughts is a treatment for phobias.

Short Essay (sample answers)

1. There was no question that Jeffrey Dahmer was a serial killer who committed 15 grisly murders. But was he legally sane at the time of the murders? Did he know the difference between right and wrong? The jury agreed with the prosecution that Dahmer was sane, and convicted him. The question of exactly what mental disorder Dahmer suffered was not a legal issue. Many experts believe Dahmer suffered from antisocial personality disorder, at the least, and perhaps other disorders as well.

2. The DSM has grown to be a large book covering almost 300 mental disorders. It describes the symptoms of nine major clinical syndromes on Axis I, personality disorders on Axis II, and related conditions on three more axes. The advantages of the DSM are objective guidelines and scientific precision in communicating with other professionals, conducting research, and designing treatment programs. The disadvantages are continuing disagreements on diagnoses and potential social, political, and labeling problems.

3. Somatoform disorders are genuine (not faked) ailments consisting of bodily symptoms with no physical causes — the real causes are psychological and related to anxiety. Two kinds are somatization disorder and conversion disorder. Experienced medical practitioners know that many of the complaints their patients present are actually psychological problems disguised as bodily problems. The doctor's advice to "Take two aspirins and call me in the morning" is actually not far from what is needed: sympathy and understanding.

4. Taijin kyofusho, or TKS, is a kind of social phobia characterized by a terrible fear of offending others through awkward social or physical behavior, such as staring, blushing, giving off an offensive odor, having an unpleasant facial expression, or having trembling hands. The fact that TKS is common in Japan but unknown in the United States shows the power of cultural norms to shape the particular expression of a psychological problem, in this case anxiety, the second most common mental disorder in both countries.

5. Aviophobia is the technical term for a type of specific phobia commonly known as fear of flying. Cognitive-behavioral therapy combines two methods. (1) Changing negative, unhealthy, or distorted thoughts ("That noise must mean trouble") by substituting positive, healthy, realistic ones ("It's just the landing gear going down"). (2) Changing limiting or disruptive behaviors by learning and practicing new skills to improve functioning. Breathing, relaxation, and imagery exercises are used to help the person calm down.

Mood Disorder & Schizophrenia

The Story of a Troubled Person

One of the most perplexing and controversial problems of psychology is how to understand and treat human anguish and suffering. The great danger is that we may classify, label, and prescribe, but without really understanding. Modern psychology has come a long way from the unthinking and often cruel 'treatment' in use not so long ago, but we are still far from having a reliable science of diagnosis and therapy.

I want to suggest an exercise that may help you think about the great complexity of emotional disturbance, yet also show you that your own psychological sensitivity and insight into human suffering may be greater than you realize. The exercise is to write a brief paper about a troubled person you know. I think this would be a good paper to use for an assignment in psychology or English.

An Exercise in Understanding

Write about someone you know fairly well, such as a relative or friend, who seems unable to enjoy the normal human satisfactions of love and work (that was Freud's definition of emotional disturbance). The reasons for the troubled person's distress could be anything from the broad spectrum of mental problems: severe depression or schizophrenia, common problems of anxiety, panic, and phobia, or social problems like alcoholism and child abuse. What you already know about the person is enough for this exercise.

Work hard to draw a clear picture of your troubled person. Include a personality description, tell the life history briefly, and look for significant turning points in the person's life. Bring in ideas from the relevant approaches to psychology and famous theories of personality and treatment.

Your conclusion should reinforce three points: (1) your theory about why the person became troubled, (2) how the person could be helped (what might work), and finally (3) what the story of this troubled person teaches us about human behavior in general — what lessons it has for our own lives.

You could use this exercise as an opportunity to think and write about your own life and problems. Even though you probably aren't a troubled person, you may have private doubts and worries or painful experiences you would benefit from exploring.

> Check it out! PowerStudy 2.0 includes a 40-50 minute presentation that uses animations, visuals, and interactive activities as well as quizzing to help you understand concepts in this module.

Effective Student Tip 23

Try, Try Again

I envied my brilliant classmates. I felt guilty when I read about the successes of others. "How did they do it?" I asked when I read about a new book or scientific breakthrough or business achievement. Now (taking nothing away from the few true geniuses among us) I realize that most successful people just kept trying.

Newly famous stars often ruefully acknowledge their "overnight success." They know they have been waiting tables and taking every part they could get for years before their big break. Perhaps they are uncomfortable with fame because they know it is illusory. The reality is the love for their craft that kept them working at it no matter how few the rewards.

Again and again, when you read about a new discovery or a great accomplishment, you find that a previously unheralded person, probably not much different from you or me, has been working at it for years. What these admirable people do have is persistence, a force psychology could do well to study in greater depth.

The moral is simply this: most great achievements result from a combination of an idea that won't let go of the person, sufficient time to work and rework the idea, and persistence in seeing it through. If at first you don't succeed....

Your response...

Looking back at your life, are there goals you wish you had pursued with greater determination?

Learning Objectives

1. Understand mood disorders and schizophrenia as the most serious and life-threatening psychological abnormalities we humans face.

2. Learn the basic kinds, causes, and treatments of mood disorders, including the last-resort treatment called electroconvulsive therapy or ECT.

3. Learn six kinds of personality disorders, including the uncommon but dangerous antisocial personality disorder.

4. Understand the types, symptoms, causes, and treatment of the devastating group of disorders called schizophrenia.

5. Understand the causes and startling symptoms of the rare dissociative disorders.

6. Appreciate how worldwide psychological abnormalities are interpreted differently by particular cultures.

7. Investigate research on the psychologically curative powers of exercise, and learn the steps you can take to deal with the common experience of mild depression.

Key Terms

You're in med school now. You've really got to work to learn all these key terms, but if you can do it you will gain a whole new world of understanding.

antidepressant drugs
antisocial personality disorder
atypical neuroleptic drugs
Beck's cognitive theory of depression
biological factors underlying depression
bipolar I disorder
catatonic schizophrenia
dependent personality disorder
diathesis stress theory
disorganized schizophrenia
dissociative amnesia
dissociative disorder

dissociative fugue
dissociative identity disorder
dopamine theory
dysthymic disorder
electroconvulsive therapy or ECT
genetic marker
hallucinations
histrionic personality disorder
major depressive disorder
mood disorder
negative symptoms of schizophrenia
neuroleptic or antipsychotic drugs

obsessive-compulsive personality disorder
paranoid personality disorder
paranoid schizophrenia
personality disorder
positive symptoms of schizophrenia
psychosocial factors
schizophrenia
schizotypical personality disorder
tardive dyskinesia
Type I schizophrenia
Type II schizophrenia
typical neuroleptic drugs

Outline

- *Introduction*
  1. Mood disorder (Chuck Elliot)
  2. Schizophrenia (Michael McCabe)
  ☐ How do Rod Plotnik's two examples differ greatly from those he used in the previous module?

A. *Mood Disorders*
  1. Kinds of **mood disorder**
  ☐ Do you ever feel depressed? How does it affect you? How do you fight it?
     a. **Major depressive disorder**
     b. **Bipolar I disorder**
     c. **Dysthymic disorder**
  2. Causes of mood disorders
     a. **Biological factors underlying depression**
        (1) Genetic factors
        (2) Neurological factors
        (3) Brain scans
     b. **Psychosocial factors**
        (1) Stressful life events
        (2) Negative cognitive style
        (3) Personality factors
  3. Treatment of mood disorders
     a. Major depression and dysthymic disorder
        (1) **Antidepressant drugs**
        (2) Selective serotonin reuptake inhibitors (SSRIs)
        (3) Effectiveness of antidepressants
        (4) Psychotherapy
        (5) Relapse
     b. Bipolar I disorder
        (1) Treatment: lithium
        (2) Mania
        (3) Relapse

B. *Electroconvulsive Therapy*
  1. Definition and usage
  ☐ Why is ECT, which seems to work, such a controversial form of therapy?
     a. **Electroconvulsive therapy or ECT**

    b. Usage

  2. Effectiveness of ECT

    a. Modern ECT

    b. Memory loss

C. *Personality Disorders*

  1. Definition: **personality disorder**

  ☐ No, you're not sick, but which of these personality disorders is closest to your own personality?

    a. **Paranoid personality disorder**

    b. **Schizotypical personality disorder**

    c. **Histrionic personality disorder**

    d. **Obsessive-compulsive personality disorder**

    e. **Dependent personality disorder**

    f. **Antisocial personality disorder**

  2. Antisocial personality disorder

    a. Delinquent

    b. Serial killer

    c. Two characteristics

  3. Psychopaths: causes and treatment

    a. Causes

      (1) Psychosocial factors

      (2) Biological factors

    b. Treatment

D. *Schizophrenia*

  1. Definition and types of **schizophrenia**

    a. Subcategories of schizophrenia

      (1) **Paranoid schizophrenia**

      (2) **Disorganized schizophrenia**

      (3) **Catatonic schizophrenia**

    b. Chance of recovery

      (1) **Type I schizophrenia**

      (2) **Type II schizophrenia**

  2. Symptoms

    a. Disorders of thought

    b. Disorders of attention

    c. Disorders of perception: **hallucinations**

    d. Motor disorders

    e. Emotional (affective) disorders

3. Biological causes

    a. Genetic predisposition (the Genain quadruplets)

    b. **Genetic marker**

        (1) Breakthrough

        (2) Environmental factors

4. Neurological causes

    a. Ventricle size

    b. Frontal lobe: prefrontal cortex

5. Environmental causes

    a. Environmental risk factors

    b. **Diathesis stress theory** of schizophrenia

6. Treatment

    a. Symptoms

        (1) **Positive symptoms of schizophrenia**

        (2) **Negative symptoms of schizophrenia**

        (3) **Neuroleptic or antipsychotic drugs**

    b. *Typical* neuroleptics

        (1) **Typical neuroleptic drugs**

        (2) **Dopamine theory**

    c. *Atypical* neuroleptics

        (1) **Atypical neuroleptic drugs**

        (2) Newer atypical neuroleptics

7. Evaluation of neuroleptic drugs

    a. *Typical* neuroleptics

        (1) Side effects: **tardive dyskinesia**

        (2) Effectiveness

        (3) Relapse

    b. *Atypical* neuroleptics

        (1) Side effects

        (2) Effectiveness and relapse

        (3) Different nervous system, different drugs

E. *Dissociative Disorders*

  1. Definition: **dissociative disorder**

  ☐ What features do all the dissociative disorders have in common? (And don't say you forgot!)

  2. **Dissociative amnesia** [Who am I?]

3. **Dissociative fugue** [Where am I?]

4. **Dissociative identity disorder** [formerly called multiple personality disorder]

   a. Definition

   b. Occurrence and causes

      (1) Explanations

      (2) Treatment

F. *Cultural Diversity: Interpreting Symptoms*

   1. Spirit possession

   2. Cultural differences in occurrence

   3. Cultural differences in gender roles

G. *Research Focus: Exercise versus Drugs*

   1. Choices of therapy for depression: **major depressive disorder**

   2. Exercise experiment: seven rules [of scientific experimentation]

      a. Method and results

      b. Relapse

      c. Conclusion

H. *Application: Dealing with Mild Depression*

   1. Mild versus major depression

      a. Continuum

      b. Similarities

      c. Vulnerability

   2. Beck's theory of depression

      a. **Beck's cognitive theory of depression**

      b. Specific negative, maladaptive thoughts (overgeneralization, selective attention)

   3. Overcoming mild depression

      a. Improving social skills

         (1) Problem: poor social skills / program: positive steps

         (2) Problem: low self-esteem / program: thought substitution

      b. Eliminating negative thoughts

         (1) Problem: negative thoughts

         (2) Program: substituting positive thoughts

      c. Power of positive thinking

         (1) Brain scans

         (2) Altering brain functioning by talk therapy

Language Workout

What's That?

p. 531   the boss fired him **on the spot** = immediately
no better off than he had been before = not improved at all
Marsha was **at her wit's end** = upset, desperate for a solution

p. 535   causing a **grand-mal seizure** = very strong attack, involving entire body
as if I've just **downed** a frozen margarita = drunk (cocktail
No more **egregious** highs or lows = terrible
I'm clearheaded and **even-keeled** = balance
medication **keeps** my illness **in check** = controls

p. 536   **Don't judge a book by its cover** = Look more deeply, go below the surface
cold-blooded killers = with no sympathy or mercy for victims
being submissive and **clingy** = dependent on other people

p. 537   developed into **full-blown** psychopaths = with complete range of symptoms

p. 538   I was so **high on life** = happy, optimistic

p. 539   How in the hell **were we dealt this hand**? = How did this happen to us?

p. 544   Gene-**alias**-Burt = also called

p. 548   **scrape up enough bucks** to pay my rent = find enough money
tired of my **moping around** = acting unhappy, not being active
I should just **get over him** = stop thinking about him
what do I do to get out of **my funk** = my feelings of depression
making a **blanket** judgment = too general

p. 549   we **get down in the dumps** = feel depressed
I've got a lot going for me = I have many advantages and possibilities

p. 552   the disease begins to **warp** reality = distort
Dishing out meds = giving pills (medicines)
the nation **bemoans** the **dearth** of reintegration services = complain about lack
vocational as well as social skills training = career preparation
still **wrongheadedly** regards = wrongly
Get me to Supercuts = Take me to a hair salon.

Making Connections

COMMAS (A Second Look)

In Module 6, we learned that commas could be used to interrupt the main idea of the sentence with some extra information. Remember that this information has a comma at the beginning and a comma at the end so that you can remove the information and it would not affect the sentence. There are many different reasons why a writer might want to use interrupters. Let's look at some of those reasons in examples from Module 23.

Interrupters

Interrupters allow the writer to provide several **examples**.

Stressful events, **such as having hostile parents, poor social relations, the death of a parent or loved one, and career or personal problems**, can contribute to the development and onset of schizophrenia. (p. 540)

They can allow the writer to **identify** a word within the sentence.

Researchers found that a group of neurotransmitters, called the monoamines (**especially serotonin and norepinephrine**) are known to be involved in mood problems. (p. 533)

The interrupter can identify **time**.

We discussed how, **after treatment for a mental disorder**, a certain percent of patients relapse or again return to having serious symptoms. (p. 547)

They can **specify** details within the sentence.

Researchers concluded that, **for more than two-thirds of the patients**, antisocial personality disorders are an ongoing, relatively stable, long-term problem that may need continual treatment. (p. 537)

Interrupters can also help the writer **classify** a word.

Unlike Sheryl Crow's problem, **which was major depressive disorder**, Chuck Elliot has bipolar I disorder, which means that he cycles between episodes of depression and mania.

They are useful when the writer wants to **emphasize** a part.

These studies on the living brains of depressed patients suggest that faulty brain structure or function, **especially in the prefrontal cortex**, contributes to the onset and/or maintenance of mood disorders. (p. 533)

If the writer really wants to draw attention to the extra information, he may use **dashes** (—) instead of **commas** (,). We find dashes more often in newspaper and magazine writing and less in academic writing. Look at the following two examples from the text. Notice how the sentence with the dashes draws your eyes more to the information inside the interrupter than the commas.

The psychiatrist was pointing out three major factors — biological, neurological, and environmental — that interact in the development of schizophrenia. (p. 539)
The psychiatrist was pointing out three major factors, such as biological, neurological, and environmental, that interact in the development of schizophrenia. (p. 539)

When you are reading your textbook, you are going to notice the first sentence with the dashes more. Notice also that the writer would need to add a transitional word when using commas.

NOW YOU TRY IT. Underline the interrupter in this sentence from the text. Include the missing commas, all four of them.

In other cases, mental disorders may involve a relatively common behavior or event that through some learning observation or other process has the power to elicit tremendous anxiety and becomes a phobia. (p. 509)

Answers

In other cases, mental disorders may involve a relatively common behavior or event that, <u>through some learning, observation, or other process</u>, has the power to elicit tremendous anxiety and becomes a phobia.

The Big Picture

Which statement below offers the best summary of the larger significance of this module?

A   When you see the wide variety of psychological illnesses affecting people, you are tempted to conclude that consciousness may be the fatal weakness of the human species. We think too much, and torture ourselves with fears.

B   With every additional discovery in neuroscience, it becomes more obvious that "psychological" disorders are essentially biological. There is not much we can do to prevent or cure these disorders. You either have good genes or you don't.

C   There is a class of psychological disorders that are characterized by their crippling effect on a person's ability to function in society. In their extreme forms, they may interfere with a person's contact with reality.

D   Psychiatry has discovered a definite hierarchy of disorders. From *least* harmful to *most* harmful, they are: dissociative disorders, schizophrenia, personality disorders, and mood disorders.

E   Every time the psychiatrist held up a new Rorschach ink blot card, the subject gave an interpretation that was more disgusting and more vulgar than the last. When the exasperated psychiatrist remarked on this, the subject protested, "But Doc, you're the one showing the dirty pictures!"

True-False

_____   1. The most serious mood disorder is major depression.

_____   2. Dysthymic disorder is characterized by fluctuations between episodes of depression and mania.

_____   3. Sheryl Crow was famous and successful, so she was able to get over her depression fairly easily.

_____   4. The most common treatment for major depression is electroconvulsive therapy (ECT).

_____   5. People suffering from antisocial personality disorder are extremely shy and attempt to avoid other people.

_____   6. People suffering from Type I schizophrenia (more positive symptoms) have a better chance for recovery than those suffering from Type II schizophrenia (more negative symptoms).

_____   7. The importance of the Genain quadruplets is that they provided evidence for a genetic component in schizophrenia.

_____   8. Antipsychotic drugs are effective, but they also have serious side effects.

_____   9. Dissociative disorders work like this: dissociative amnesia, forget; dissociative fugue, flee; dissociative identity disorder, split off.

_____   10. Although many people experience occasional mild depression, there is not much they can do except tough it out.

Flashcards 1

_____ 1. antisocial personality disorder

_____ 2. bipolar I disorder

_____ 3. catatonic schizophrenia

_____ 4. disorganized schizophrenia

_____ 5. dysthymic disorder

_____ 6. histrionic personality disorder

_____ 7. major depressive disorder

_____ 8. obsessive-compulsive personality disorder

_____ 9. paranoid personality disorder

_____ 10. paranoid schizophrenia

a. being chronically but not continuously depressed for a period of two years; poor appetite, insomnia, fatigue

b. a pattern of disregarding or violating the rights of others without feeling guilt or remorse (usually male)

c. characterized by excessive emotionality and attention seeking

d. characterized by periods of wild excitement or periods of rigid, prolonged immobility; frozen posture

e. a pattern of distrust and suspiciousness and perceiving others as having evil motives

f. continually being in a bad mood, having no interest in anything, or getting no pleasure from activities

g. an intense interest in being orderly, achieving perfection, and having control

h. characterized by fluctuating between episodes of depression and mania

i. characterized by auditory hallucinations or delusions of being persecuted or delusions of grandeur

j. marked by bizarre ideas (often about body), confused speech, childish behavior, great emotional swings

Flashcards 2

_____ 1. diathesis stress theory

_____ 2. dissociative amnesia

_____ 3. dissociative fugue

_____ 4. dissociative identity disorder

_____ 5. dopamine theory

_____ 6. electroconvulsive therapy or ECT

_____ 7. genetic marker

_____ 8. mood disorder

_____ 9. schizophrenia

_____ 10. tardive dyskinesia

a. says that some people have a genetic predisposition interacting with life stressors to cause schizophrenia

b. says dopamine neurotransmitter system is somehow overactive and causes schizophrenic symptoms

c. suddenly, unexpectedly traveling away from home or place of work and being unable to recall one's past

d. characterized by inability to recall important personal information or events; associated with stress, trauma

e. slow, involuntary, uncontrollable movements: rapid twitching of mouth, lips; from use of neuroleptics

f. presence of two or more distinct identities, each with its own pattern of thinking about, relating to world

g. an identifiable gene, or genes, or a specific segment of chromosome directly linked to a trait or disease

h. serious mental disorder with symptoms of delusions, hallucinations, disorganized speech and behavior

i. administration of mild electrical current that passes through the brain and causes a seizure

j. prolonged and disturbed emotional state that affects almost all of a person's thoughts, feelings, and behaviors

Multiple-Choice

_____ 1. Rod Plotnik offers the examples of Chuck Elliot and Michael McCabe to show that
   a. people who have used illegal drugs are more likely to become mentally ill
   b. mood disorders and schizophrenia can be terrifying, crippling disorders
   c. anyone can become mentally ill at almost any time
   d. brilliant, creative people are more likely to become mentally ill

_____ 2. Which one of the following is _not_ a mood disorder?
   a. major depression
   b. bipolar I disorder
   c. antisocial personality disorder
   d. dysthymic disorder

_____ 3. _____ is marked by fluctuations between episodes of depression and mania
   a. bipolar I disorder
   b. major depressive disorder
   c. dysthymic disorder
   d. minor depressive disorder

_____ 4. Science now says the cause of depression is
   a. mainly biological
   b. mainly psychosocial
   c. mainly personal (optimistic versus pessimistic)
   d. both biological and psychosocial

_____ 5. Psychosocial factors putting a person at risk for depression include all of the following _except_
   a. stressful life events
   b. genetic factors
   c. negative cognitive style
   d. personality factors

_____ 6. Antidepressant drugs work by
   a. attacking and destroying depressive memory cells that cause depression
   b. creating feelings of peace and well being similar to the effects of alcohol
   c. preventing neurons from being over stimulated
   d. increasing the levels of neurotransmitters involved in regulating emotions and moods

_____ 7. If you saw the movie _One Flew Over the Cuckoo's Nest_, you may be surprised to learn that
   a. ECT does not in fact cause memory loss
   b. although some doctors use ECT today, it remains a dangerously unsafe treatment
   c. the use of ECT (as a last resort) has increased since 1980
   d. a new use has been found for ECT — the treatment of schizophrenia

_____ 8. ECT is a controversial treatment for depression because it
   a. has serious side effects, such as memory loss
   b. is based on the use of antidepressant drugs
   c. has no effect at all on many patients
   d. is prescribed by psychiatrists but not by clinical psychologists

_____ 9. Which one of the following is *not* a personality disorder?
   a. paranoid personality disorder
   b. histrionic personality disorder
   c. obsessive-compulsive personality disorder
   d. depressive personality disorder

_____ 10. Jeffrey Dahmer represented an extreme case of _____ personality disorder
   a. histrionic
   b. paranoid
   c. antisocial
   d. schizotypical

_____ 11. Psychotherapy has not proved very effective in treating psychopaths (like Dahmer) because
   a. they are fundamentally dishonest and don't see themselves as ill
   b. most therapists are afraid to work with psychopaths, knowing their violent ways
   c. psychopaths result almost entirely from biological factors, which psychotherapy can't touch
   d. this is a genetic, "bad seed" disease, against which talk therapy is helpless

_____ 12. The highest percentages of mental hospital inpatients are there because of
   a. major depression
   b. schizophrenia
   c. antisocial personality disorder
   d. dissociative amnesia

_____ 13. Chances for recovery from schizophrenia are best in patients with
   a. symptoms of dulled emotions, little inclination to speak, and a loss of normal functions
   b. Type II schizophrenia (negative symptoms)
   c. Type I schizophrenia (positive symptoms)
   d. (cases of recovery from schizophrenia are so rare as to be statistically insignificant)

_____ 14. Which one of the following problems is *not* a symptom of schizophrenia?
   a. disorders of thought
   b. disorders of attention
   c. disorders of perception
   d. disorders of moral character

_____ 15. Rod Plotnik tells us about the famous Genain quadruplets to illustrate the fact that
   a. there must be a genetic factor in schizophrenia
   b. science is filled with amazing coincidences
   c. children can "learn" to be schizophrenic from close contact with family members who are ill
   d. schizophrenia strikes in a random, unpredictable fashion

_____ 16. New brain research using MRI and fMRI scans have revealed that schizophrenics show
   a. overactivation of the prefrontal cortex, resulting in disordered thinking
   b. overwired brains, with too many connections to permit rational thinking
   c. excessive neuron development, accounting for the somewhat larger brains of schizophrenics
   d. larger ventricles, fewer brain cells, and fewer connections among neurons

_____ 17. The diathesis-stress theory of schizophrenia says that some people have a/n
   a. overactive dopamine neurotransmitter system
   b. genetic predisposition that interacts with life stressors to cause the disease
   c. atypical neuroleptic tendency in their brains
   d. overactive diathesis in the prefrontal cortex

_____ 18. According to the _____ theory, schizophrenia is caused by the overactivity of neurotransmitters in the brain
   a. dopamine
   b. diathesis stress
   c. genetic marker
   d. tardive dyskinesia

_____ 19. Antipsychotic or neuroleptic drugs work by
   a. increasing levels of the neurotransmitter dopamine
   b. changing levels of neurotransmitters in the brain
   c. increasing levels of the neurotransmitter serotonin
   d. increasing positive symptoms of schizophrenia

_____ 20. What can we conclude about the battle against schizophrenia?
   a. science is on the brink of new drug treatments that will wipe out this disease
   b. drug treatment, considering the high rates of relapse and the dangerous side effects, must be considered a failure
   c. it can be a lifetime problem with a high risk for relapse needing drug treatment, psychotherapy, and social support
   d. it remains too complicated to understand, and may never be conquered by science

_____ 21. The difference between dissociative amnesia and dissociative fugue is that
   a. in the former you stay in contact with reality; in the latter you become schizophrenic
   b. in the former you have memory gaps; in the latter you may wander away and assume a new identity
   c. in the former you forget more than in the latter
   d. these are really two different terms for the same disorder

_____ 22. The case of "Burt Tate," who turned out to be a missing person named Gene Saunders, illustrates
   a. dissociative fugue
   b. dissociative amnesia
   c. dissociative identity disorder
   d. multiple personality disorder

_____ 23. An underlying cause often reported in dissociative identity disorder is
   a. physical trauma, such as a head injury
   b. unstable parents who give their children mixed messages about what they expect
   c. a flighty personality along with a tendency to overdramatize every situation
   d. severe physical or sexual abuse during childhood

_____ 24. According to Aaron Beck's cognitive theory of depression, depressed people
   a. learn depressive habits from other depressed people in their families
   b. have many relatives who also are depressed, suggesting a genetic link
   c. automatically and continually think negative thoughts that they rarely notice
   d. suffer from repressed feelings of guilt and overactive superegos

_____ 25. Which one of the following is *not* good advice if you are trying to overcome mild depression?
   a. improve your social skills
   b. improve your self-esteem
   c. substitute positive thoughts for negative, maladaptive thoughts
   d. learn to accept the fact that your life is really bad

Short Essay

1. Describe the two kinds of factors that cause mood disorders like depression. If you wish, use Sheryl Crow's depression to illustrate your answer.

2. What progress is being made in understanding and treating schizophrenia?

3. Describe the onset, course, and end of dissociative fugue. If you wish, use the case of "Burt Tate" (really Gene Saunders) in your answer.

4. Tell the history of dissociative identity disorder and explain why the diagnosis has been controversial.

5. Why does this textbook of scientific psychology include a discussion of spirit possession? What does spirit possession suggest about how "scientific" our own mental health practices are?

Use School to Learn More about Yourself

On the introductory page for this module I suggested writing a paper on understanding emotional illness. When I give this assignment in my classes, the best papers are often autobiographical. I remember a kindly and understanding English professor I had many years ago who allowed me to write about something painful in my own life. I learned from it, and gained a measure of peace as well. Write (and learn) about yourself.

Answers for Module 23

The Big Picture (explanations provided for incorrect choices)

A   It sometimes seems that way, but consciousness also has allowed the triumph of our species.
B   There is a genetic basis to many illnesses, but even these are preventable and curable.
C   Correct! You see the "big picture" for this Module.
D   This hierarchy does not make sense (see definitions), as well as the many disorders that this statement leaves out.
E   It's just a joke!

True-False (explanations provided for False choices; page numbers given for all choices)

1	T	532	
2	F	532	That describes bipolar I disorder
3	F	534	Major depression is serious — for anyone — and requires long and careful treatment.
4	F	535	ECT is a rarely used treatment of last resort for depression.
5	F	536	People with antisocial personality can be charming and popular with other people.
6	T	538	
7	T	539	
8	T	542	
9	T	544	
10	F	549	There are several steps people can take to combat mild depression.

Flashcards 1

1 b   2 h   3 d   4 j   5 a   6 c   7 f   8 g   9 e   10 i

Flashcards 2

1 a   2 d   3 c   4 f   5 b   6 i   7 g   8 j   9 h   10 e

Multiple-Choice (explanations provided for incorrect choices)

1   a   Illegal drugs are not the main issue here.
    b   Correct! See page 531.
    c   Be assured that this statement is untrue.
    d   The small amount of evidence for the connection does not support this popular belief.

2   a   Major depression is a mood disorder.
    b   Bipolar disorder is a mood disorder.
    c   Correct! See page 532.
    d   Dysthymic disorder is a mood disorder.

3   *a   Correct! See page 532.*
    b   Major depressive disorder does not feature episodes of mania.
    c   Dysthymic disorder does not feature episodes of mania.
    d   There is no disorder with this name.

4   a   Its causes are both biological and psychosocial.
    b   Its causes are both biological and psychosocial.
    c   This statement is untrue (would pessimism alone be enough to cause depression?).
    d   Correct! See page 533.

5   a   This is a psychosocial risk factor for depression.
    b   Correct! See page 533.
    c   This is a psychosocial risk factor for depression.
    d   This is a psychosocial risk factor for depression.

6   a   These drugs do not cause memory loss.
    b   Alcohol is itself a depressant and does not help depressed people.
    c   This is more true of lithium (used for bipolar I disorder)
    d   Correct! See page 534.

7   a   Memory loss is one of the side effects of ECT.
    b   ECT is safer today, and does not cause brain damage or turn people into vegetables.
    c   *Correct! See page 535.*
    d   ECT is still used to treat mood disorders.

8   *a*   *Correct! See page 535.*
    b   ECT is not based on the use of antidepressant drugs.
    c   ECT has an immediate effect on almost all patients receiving it.
    d   This is not a cause of controversy.

9   a   This is one of the personality disorders.
    b   This is one of the personality disorders.
    c   This is one of the personality disorders.
    d   *Correct! See page 536.*

10 a   This personality disorder does not cause a person to harm others.
    b   This personality disorder does not cause a person to harm others.
    c   *Correct! See page 536.*
    d   This personality disorder does not cause a person to harm others.

11 *a*   *Correct! See page 537.*
    b   This might be true in a few, extreme cases, but not for the majority of potential patients.
    c   Psychopaths are caused by both psychosocial and biological factors.
    d   There may be a genetic component, but it accounts for no more than 30-50 percent in an individual.

12 a   Good guess, but another mental illness accounts for a full 30 percent of all inpatients.
    b   *Correct! See page 538.*
    c   Antisocial personality disorder is a rare problem.
    d   Dissociative amnesia does not require hospitalization.

13 a   These are symptoms of Type II schizophrenia, in which chances of recovery are poor.
    b   The negative symptoms and loss of normal functions of Type II schizophrenia make recovery less likely.
    c   *Correct! See page 538.*
    d   Chances of recovery from schizophrenia are fairly good, especially if therapy and support are continued.

14 a   Disorders of thought are important symptoms of schizophrenia.
    b   Disorders of attention are important symptoms of schizophrenia.
    c   Disorders of perception are important symptoms of schizophrenia.
    d   *Correct! See page 538.*

15 *a*   *Correct! See page 539.*
    b   The fact that they were identical (quadruplets) rules out coincidence.
    c   This statement does not fit the case of the Genain quadruplets.
    d   This statement does not fit the case of the Genain quadruplets.

16 a   Just the opposite is true.
    b   Just the opposite is true.
    c   Schizophrenics do not have either too many neurons or larger brains.
    d   *Correct! See page 540.*

17 a   This is the dopamine theory of schizophrenia.
    b   *Correct! See page 540.*
    c   Atypical neuroleptics are antipsychotic drugs used to combat schizophrenia.
    d   Diathesis indicates a genetic predisposition, not a part of the brain.

18 *a*   *Correct! See page 541.*
    b   The diathesis-stress theory involves both brain abnormalities and environmental stress.
    c   A genetic marker is an identifiable link to a trait or disease.
    d   Tardive dyskinesia is a serious side effect of antipsychotic drugs.

19 a   They reduce, not increase, levels of dopamine.
    b   *Correct! See page 542.*
    c   They reduce, not increase, levels of serotonin.
    d   These symptoms must be decreased (back in the direction of normal functioning).

20 a   Too optimistic — there is still vast suffering and no "magic bullet" seems to be on the horizon.
    b   On the contrary, drug treatment offers the most best hope now and may well improve.
    c   Correct! See page 542.
    d   Too pessimistic — with medication, many sufferers can live productive and relatively normal lives.

21 a   Loss of contact with reality does not occur in either disorder.
    b   Correct! See page 544.
    c   The truth is just the opposite.
    d   The two disorders are quite different.

22 *a   Correct! See page 544.*
    b   Think about why he was missing from home.
    c   Dissociative identity disorder was formerly called multiple personality disorder.
    d   Did he manifest more than one personality?

23 a   Head injury is not a factor in dissociative identity disorder.
    b   This is one explanation of schizophrenia.
    c   This is characteristic of certain personality disorders.
    d   Correct! See page 545.

24 a   This would be a behaviorist explanation.
    b   Beck's theory is not based on genetics.
    c   Correct! See page 548.
    d   This would be a psychoanalytic explanation.

25 a   Taking positive action to improve your social skills can help you overcome mild depression.
    b   Giving yourself credit can improve your self-esteem and help you overcome mild depression.
    c   Focusing on positive events can help you overcome mild depression.
    d   Correct! See page 549.

Short Essay (sample answers)

1. Popular singer-songwriter Sheryl Crow illustrates the causes of depression. First, biological risk factors emphasize underlying genetic (Sheryl's family has a history of depression), neurological, chemical (Sheryl knew something was wrong), or physiological components. Second, psychosocial factors, such as personality traits, cognitive styles, social supports, and the ability to deal with stressors (like a world tour and struggling to get a new record contract) interact with predisposing biological factors to put one at risk.

2. Schizophrenia is the most devastating of the mental disorders, but progress is being made. Genetic markers identify persons at risk. Brain scans reveal abnormalities that are involved in the disease. The diathesis-stress theory shows how psychosocial stressors interact with biological risk factors. The main advance is the continuing development of antipsychotic (neuroleptic) drugs that change levels of neurotransmitters and therefore the way the brain works. Harmful side effects like tardive dyskinesia are being reduced.

3. Dissociative disorders are rare mental disorders in which there is a disruption or split in the normally integrated self, consciousness, memory, or sense of identity. In dissociative fugue, a person forgets who he or she is, travels away from home, and may assume a new identity. When "Burt Tate" had a run-in with the law, he could not remember who he was. A missing persons check revealed that he was Gene Saunders, who had been under stress at work, and had disappeared a month before from a city 200 miles away.

4. An epidemic in the 1970s and 1980s of the previously rare "multiple personality disorder," in which two or more distinct identities or personality states take control of the individual's thoughts and behaviors at different times, led to controversy and revision in clinical psychology. The diagnosis, usually in women, was connected to claims of childhood sexual abuse. Some therapists were guilty of encouraging patients to play the roles. Still controversial but less commonly diagnosed, today it is called "dissociative identity disorder."

5. How would you diagnose a person who reports that sometimes a spirit takes possession of her body and mind and makes her do and say things she doesn't always remember? She would be called delusional and abnormal in the United States, but normal in the context of her culture in Northern Sudan. Before you say, "That's crazy!" think about all the disorders diagnosed more often in women in our country! Spirit possession is an example of how cultural factors determine whether symptoms are interpreted as normal or abnormal.

Module 24

Therapies

The Contribution of Psychodynamic Psychology to Therapy

Psychotherapy is one of the great inventions of this century. Whether you consider it an art or a science, it is a young and constantly evolving process. Rod Plotnik discusses four current approaches to psychotherapy, each with numerous varieties and special techniques.

At the heart of most forms of psychotherapy lies a basic assumption and a fundamental process that come from psychodynamic psychology and the work of a great pioneer, good old You-Know-Who. Both the assumption and the technique are inherent in his theory of dreams, about which you read way back in Module 7.

A Model for Understanding Psychotherapy... and Life

The key idea is the distinction between manifest content and latent content. The manifest content of a dream is the story (however bizarre) we remember in the morning. The latent content is the disguised, unconscious wish hidden in the apparently meaningless story of the dream. The challenge to the dreamer, perhaps a patient in psychotherapy, is to gain insight into that latent content because it is a direct line [Our Hero called it the *via regia*, or royal road] to the unconscious. With the help of the therapist, the patient examines thoughts and feelings connected to the dream in the expectation that these associations will suggest an underlying meaning, a meaning that provides insight into the patient's 'dynamics,' or psychological life.

This key idea has broad implications. Freud saw dreams and other unconscious acts (slips of the tongue, losing things, forgetting, accidents) as miniature neuroses, reflecting the larger neuroses of which we all have more than a few. Therefore, we can interpret *any* behavior like a dream. Here's the formula. First, examine the behavior (a comment, an act, even a thought) very carefully. Exactly what happened? That's the manifest content. Next, search the manifest content for clues about what the *latent* content might be. Why did you forget the assignment? Lose your keys? Call your Honey the wrong name? Bingo! Insight into how your unconscious mind works.

This fundamental idea of psychodynamic psychology underlies most forms of therapy, and can be used as a model for understanding almost anything in life from the meaning of Shakespeare's plays to why your roommate is driving you crazy. Just answer two questions: What is the manifest content? What is the latent content?

Effective Student Tip 24

Take Teachers, Not Courses

Take at least a few courses far from your major area of study. Some advisors will urge you to take only courses that fit into your major, but that can be a mistake. One of the purposes of higher education is to broaden your horizons and show you worlds you scarcely know exist. When else will you have the opportunity to investigate ancient history, nutrition, figure drawing, astronomy, women's literature, and other fascinating subjects that aren't required for graduation?

Graduate students, who have been through it all and know all there is to know (just ask them), often say you should "take teachers, not courses." What they mean is that you should sign up for professors with reputations as especially stimulating teachers, without too much regard for how well the interesting courses fit into your official program.

You will come to know quite a bit about the faculty at your school. Some professors will begin to stand out as people you would like to study with and get to know. Try to give yourself at least a few of these experiences. You might learn more from an inspired, creative teacher in an unrequired course than from a dull teacher in the course that fits so neatly into your major.

Your response...

If neither time nor money mattered, what courses would you like to take just for your own interest?

Learning Objectives

1. Understand therapies — putting psychology to work helping troubled people — as the ultimate reason and payoff for all the study and research poured into understanding psychology.

2. Appreciate the historical background of therapy as the groundwork for understanding and evaluating the different forms of treatment... and as a fascinating story in itself!

3. Learn the principles and procedures of the insight therapies of psychoanalysis, client-centered therapy, and cognitive therapy.

4. Learn the principles and procedures of behavior therapy and cognitive-behavior therapy.

5. Understand the basic questions about psychotherapy, including its assumptions, methods, techniques, effectiveness, and common factors.

6. Consider mental healing from a cultural perspective through an example from Bali and evaluate research on a new form of psychotherapy called EMDR.

7. Apply current cognitive-behavior techniques to possible problems you or others in your life may have.

Key Terms

Most of the key terms in this module are closely related to terms you have already learned in other modules.

behavior therapy or behavior modification
client-centered therapy
clinical psychologists
cognitive therapy
cognitive-behavior therapy
common factors
community mental health centers
counseling psychologists
deinstitutionalization

dream interpretation
eclectic approach
eye movement desensitization and reprocessing (EMDR)
free association
insight therapy
intrusive thoughts
medical therapy
meta-analysis
moral therapy
neuroses

phenothiazines
psychiatrists
psychoanalysis
psychotherapy
resistance
short-term dynamic psychotherapy
systematic desensitization
transference

Outline

- *Introduction*
  - ☐ What parts did Anna O and Little Albert play in the history of psychotherapy?
  1. Beginning of psychoanalysis (Anna O.)
  2. Beginning of behavior therapy (Little Albert)

A. Historical Background

1. Definition: **psychotherapy**

2. Early treatments

3. Reform movement: **moral therapy** (Dorothea Dix)

4. **Phenothiazines** and **deinstitutionalization**

   a. Discovery

   b. Homeless

5. **Community mental health centers**

B. Questions about Psychotherapy

1. Do I need professional help?

2. Are there different kinds of therapists?

   a. **Psychiatrists**

   b. **Clinical psychologists**

   c. **Counseling psychologists**

3. Are there different approaches?

   a. **Insight therapy**

   b. **Cognitive-behavior therapy**

   c. **Eclectic approach**

   d. **Medical therapy**

4. How effective is psychotherapy?

   a. **Meta-analysis**

   b. Major findings

C. Insight Therapies

☐ Rod Plotnik quotes from sessions illustrating the three insight therapies. Can you describe the different emphasis and style of each approach?

1. **Psychoanalysis** (Sigmund Freud)

   a. Three major assumptions

      (1) Unconscious conflicts

      (2) Techniques of free association, dream interpretation, and analysis of slips of the tongue

      (3) Transfer strong emotions onto therapist

   b. Therapy session

   c. Role of analyst

      (1) Free association

      (2) Interpretation

      (3) Unconscious conflicts

    d. Techniques to reveal the unconscious: **neuroses**

        (1) Rat man: **free association**

        (2) Wolf-man: **dream interpretation**

        (3) Case studies: Anna O., Rat Man, and Wolf-Man

    e. Problems during therapy

        (1) Rat man: **transference**

        (2) Wolf-man: **resistance**

        (3) **Short-term dynamic psychotherapy**

    f. Psychoanalysis: evaluation

        (1) Decline in popularity

            (a) Lack of research

            (b) Competing therapies

            (c) Psychoactive drugs

        (2) Current status

            (a) Freudian concepts

            (b) Conclusion

  2. **Client-centered therapy** (Carl Rogers)

    a. Therapy session

    b. Therapist's traits

        (1) Empathy

        (2) Positive regard

        (3) Genuineness

    c. Effectiveness

  3. **Cognitive therapy** (Aaron Beck)

    a. Therapy session

    b. Important factors

        (1) Overgeneralization

        (2) Polarized thinking

        (3) Selective attention

    c. Cognitive techniques

    d. Effectiveness

D. *Behavior Therapy*

  1. Definition: **behavior therapy or behavior modification**

  ☐ In what ways is behavior therapy radically different from the insight therapies?

    a. Therapy session

    b. Behavioral approach

     c. Two goals

  2. **Systematic desensitization** (Joseph Wolpe)

     a. Relaxation

     b. Stimulus hierarchy

     c. Exposure

     d. Exposure: imagined or in vivo

  3. **Cognitive-behavior therapy**

     a. Combining therapies

     b. Cognitive-behavior techniques

  4. Kinds of problems

     a. Problem behaviors

     b. Effectiveness

E. *Review: Evaluation of Approaches*

  ☐ Another great Plotnik summary! Can you master the basic elements of each approach?

  1. Assumptions, methods, and techniques

     a. Psychoanalysis

       (1) Background

       (2) Basic assumption

       (3) Techniques

     b. Client-centered therapy

       (1) Background

       (2) Basic assumption

       (3) Techniques

     c. Cognitive therapy

       (1) Background

       (2) Basic assumption

       (3) Techniques

     d. Behavior therapy

       (1) Background

       (2) Basic assumption

       (3) Techniques

  2. Effectiveness of psychotherapy

  3. **Common factors**

F. *Cultural Diversity: Different Healer*

   1. Case study: young woman (Bali)

      a. Western assumptions (depression)

      b. Local healer or balian (witchcraft)

   2. Healer's diagnosis and treatment

   3. Healers versus Western therapists

   ☐ Hmmm… If the balian usually obtains cures, what does that suggest about the successes of Western psychotherapy?

G. *Research Focus: EMDR — New Therapy*

   1. Does EMDR stop traumatic memories?

      a. **Eye Movement Desensitization and Reprocessing (EMDR)**

      b. Francine Shapiro's discovery

   2. Evidence from case studies

   3. Evidence from experiments

      a. Does EMDR work?

      b. How does EMDR work?

      c. Why is EMDR controversial?

H. *Application: Cognitive-Behavior Techniques*

   1. Thought problems

   2. Thought-stopping program: **intrusive thoughts**

      a. Self-monitoring

      b. Thought stopping

      c. Thought substitution

   3. Thought substitution

      a. Irrational thoughts

      b. Rational thoughts

   4. Treatment for insomnia

The Language Workout Marathon

You have learned many new things about the English language. To see how much you remember, try the Language Workout Marathon. You can find it in Module 25!

Language Workout

What's That?

p. 555   developed a terrible **squint** = habit of keeping eyes partly closed
a **gagging** feeling = choking
her **governess**'s dog = woman working as a tutor for a family
an **up-and-coming** behaviorist = young, becoming known
how psychotherapy **came about** = began

p. 556   until they **passed out** = fainted, lost consciousness
a relaxed and **decent** environment = sympathetic
funds became tight = money was hard to find
milled about in a large room = moved without direction or purpose
the **wretched** conditions = terrible, miserable

p. 557   **halfway houses** = rehabilitation centers (halfway between life in an institution and everyday living)

p. 558   a psychiatric **residency** = medical training through working in hospital
an **applied clinical setting** = practical situation in real conditions

p. 560   **comprehensive** theory = complete, explaining everything
laypersons = non-professionals
an **appreciation** of what happens = understanding
Who are you that I should care = Why are you so important

p. 561   made him **pledge** himself = promise, commit
the window opened **of its own accord** = by its own power
their ears **pricked** like dogs = standing up straight

p. 562   called Freud a **"filthy swine"** = dirty pig
the analyst must use **tact** = sensitive understanding
therapy can proceed and **stay on course** = move toward the goal

p. 563   such a question was **unheard of** = never spoken

p. 564   the old **vacuum** = empty feeling

p. 566   gave a real **jump-start** = stimulus, strong push
let people step all over me = allow others to control me
run through some of the situations here = practice
she really wants to **speak her mind** = give her opinion directly

p. 572   periods of **fasting** = not eating food

p. 578   an **evangelical** minister = a Christian group emphasizing the Bible
Witchcraft = the art of doing evil acts
banishing evil demons = driving out, forcing to leave
psychological causes have been **ruled out** = eliminated
Satan's strongholds = places where the devil is powerful
devils were **cast out** = driven out, forced to leave

What's the Difference?

ONCE has more than one meaning.

Once can mean **one time**: Eduardo went to Mexico **once**, but he has never been back.

Once can mean **after**: Once you finish Module 25, you can try the Language Workout Marathon. (NOTE: It follows the Language Workout for Module 25.)

How is **once** used in these examples from the text?

Once you learn different ways to speak your mind, you can try them out in the real world. (p. 566)

Her thinking might have been distorted by selected attention such as forgetting all those activities that she had **once** found pleasurable. (p. 575)

If you think the first example means **after** and the second means **one time**, you're correct!

Flex Your Word Power

Test your way with opposites. Here are some words used in the last few modules. Draw a line from a word on the left to the word that means its <u>opposite</u> on the right:

downplay	moving
causal	dysfunctional
fixed	extraverted
clear-cut	formal
functional	ambiguous
introverted	emphasize

See how you did in the Answers. Look at the next Workout Module for more opposites.

Test Yourself

Try to write the rest of the sentence using **once** to mean **after**.

Once summertime begins, the children _____.

Once _____, we washed the dishes.

Once you finish this module, you _____.

Once _____, the class could start.

Once her visit to the dentist was over, Lydia _____.

Answers

downplay	=	emphasize
causal	=	formal
fixed	=	moving
clear-cut	=	ambiguous
functional	=	dysfunctional
introverted	=	extraverted

Once summertime begins, the children (will not be in school) (will be free to play).
Once (we finished dinner) (dinner ended), we washed the dishes.
Once you finish this module, you (will be almost finished) (can do the next module).
Once (the teacher arrived) (the students were quiet), the class could start.
Once her visit to the dentist was over, Lydia (felt happy) (received a bill).

For psych majors only...

The Story of Psychotherapy: You met many famous and intriguing characters from the history of psychology in this module, people like Anna O., Rat Man, and Little Albert (almost sounds like a circus, doesn't it?). If you were to arrange these names in historical order (as I have done below) and add what each contributed, you could construct a capsule history of the development of modern psychotherapy.

Try it. Match each name to the most appropriate phrase. As you do so, see if you can tell yourself the story of how the four strands of modern psychotherapy emerged, and how they differ from each other.

_____	1. Dorothea Dix	a. reduced hysterical symptoms by talking about them
_____	2. Anna O.	b. publicized the cruel treatment of "lunatics"
_____	3. Sigmund Freud	c. developed cognitive therapy for depressive thoughts
_____	4. Rat Man	d. developed a very positive client-centered therapy
_____	5. Wolf-Man	e. interpretation of his dreams revealed sexual fears
_____	6. John B. Watson	f. worked out a therapy called systematic desensitization
_____	7. Little Albert	g. believed emotional problems are conditioned (learned)
_____	8. Carl Rogers	h. conditioned to fear a rat in a famous experiment
_____	9. Joseph Wolpe	i. free association revealed his repressed memories
_____	10. Aaron Beck	j. developed psychoanalysis — the first psychotherapy

Time to Read

With the end of the term approaching, you will soon have time to read again. One of the paradoxes of education is that just when we should be reading most, we have the least time. This is true for instructors, too. Plan to read a good book you have heard about. Now that you know more psychology, you will find that novels and biographies are more interesting than ever. What will you read over the interim?

Answers to "The Story of Psychotherapy" Quiz

1 b   2 a   3 j   4 i   5 e   6 g   7 h   8 d   9 f   10 c

The Big Picture

Which statement below offers the best summary of the larger significance of this module?

A   A painful truth: psychotherapy is the witchcraft of the modern Western world.
Plotnik's fascinating discussion of a healer or balian in Bali shows why we shouldn't
take psychotherapy too seriously. It's all based on belief and faith.

B   That there are several competing theories of psychotherapy is not so much an
embarrassment as a reflection of the youth and vigor of psychology. The competing
psychotherapies reflect the different approaches to psychology.

C   The crowded field of psychotherapy finally is experiencing what economists call a
shakeout. One by one the old methods are being abandoned, as more and more
psychotherapists adopt EMDR because of its greater effectiveness.

D   Which method of psychotherapy is best? It is mainly a matter of individual
preference. All therapies share the common assumption that problems lie buried in
the unconscious, and must be exhumed and examined.

E   As the famous movie producer Samuel Goldwyn once observed, "Anyone who goes
to a psychiatrist should have his head examined!"

True-False

_____   1. The history of therapeutic effort is a story of continued improvement in the humane treatment of
the mentally ill.

_____   2. Psychotherapists today are more likely to see themselves as eclectic than as adhering to one of the
traditional approaches to psychotherapy.

_____   3. The basic assumption of psychoanalysis is that since maladaptive behaviors are *learned*, they can
be unlearned through training.

_____   4. Transference is the process by which a patient carefully describes his or her problems so the
therapist can analyze and solve them.

_____   5. Although Freud is criticized, psychoanalytic ideas continue to be a force in psychotherapy today.

_____   6. Rod Plotnik quotes from therapy sessions representing the major approaches; the point is that
they all sound pretty much alike.

_____   7. Carl Rogers' client-centered therapy avoids giving directions, advice, or disapproval.

_____   8. Aaron Beck's cognitive therapy assumes that we have automatic negative thoughts that we say to
ourselves without much notice.

_____   9. The systematic desensitization technique is essentially an unlearning experience.

_____   10. Research suggests that the new technique called Eye Movement Desensitization and
Reprocessing (EMDR) will eventually replace all the traditional psychotherapies.

Flashcards 1

_____ 1. behavior therapy or behavior modification	a. a technique that encourages clients to talk about any thoughts or images that enter their heads
_____ 2. client-centered therapy	b. therapy in which client is gradually exposed to feared object while simultaneously practicing relaxation
_____ 3. cognitive therapy	c. core idea is that repressed threatening thoughts in the unconscious cause conflicts and symptoms
_____ 4. dream interpretation	d. uses principles of conditioning to change disruptive behaviors and improve human functioning
_____ 5. free association	e. client's reluctance to work through feelings and to recognize unconscious conflicts and repressed thoughts
_____ 6. intrusive thoughts	f. the process by which a client expresses strong emotions toward therapist, who is a substitute figure
_____ 7. psychoanalysis	g. a search for underlying hidden meanings, symbols providing clues to unconscious thoughts and desires
_____ 8. resistance	h. therapist shows compassion and positive regard in helping client reach full potential, self-actualization
_____ 9. systematic desensitization	i. thoughts that we repeatedly experience, are usually unwanted or disruptive, and are very difficult to stop
_____ 10. transference	j. assumes we have automatic negative thoughts that distort our perceptions, influence feelings, behavior

Flashcards 2

_____ 1. clinical psychologists	a. release of mental patients from hospitals and their return to the community to develop independent lives
_____ 2. common factors	b. go to graduate school of psychology and earn Ph.D., including one year in an applied clinical setting
_____ 3. counseling psychologists	c. basic set of procedures shared by different therapies (supportive relationship, accepting atmosphere, etc.)
_____ 4. deinstitutionalization	d. involves use of various psychoactive drugs to treat mental disorders by changing biological factors
_____ 5. eclectic approach	e. go to medical school, earn MD, take psychiatric residency and additional training in psychotherapy
_____ 6. insight therapy	f. involves therapist and client talking about the client's symptoms, problems, to identify cause of problem
_____ 7. medical therapy	g. involves combining and using techniques and ideas from many different therapeutic approaches
_____ 8. moral therapy	h. the belief that mental patients could be helped to function better by providing humane treatment
_____ 9. phenothiazines	i. block or reduce effects of dopamine, thereby reduce schizophrenic symptoms (delusions, hallucinations)
_____ 10. psychiatrists	j. go to graduate school of psychology or education and earn Ph.D., including work in a counseling setting

Multiple-Choice

_____ 1. Rod Plotnik begins the module with the story of Anna O. to make the point that
    a. Freud had some notable failures as well as famous successes
    b. talking about your problems seems to help
    c. the real credit for inventing psychoanalysis should go to Dr. Breuer
    d. talking won't help unless the client also does something positive

_____ 2. John B. Watson's famous experiment with Little Albert was designed to show that
    a. ethical standards of psychological research are much more stringent today
    b. psychological problems affect babies as well as children and adults
    c. fear of rats is almost natural and may be inborn
    d. emotional problems can be viewed as learned behavior

_____ 3. In the history of the treatment of mental illness, Dorothea Dix is famous for
    a. charging admission to watch the crazy antics of the "lunatics"
    b. inventing early treatment techniques like the strait jacket and bleeding
    c. publicizing the terrible living conditions and poor treatment of the mentally ill
    d. emptying the mental hospitals of almost half of their patients

_____ 4. The effect of the phenothiazines on schizophrenics is to
    a. increase the effects of the neurotransmitter dopamine
    b. reduce symptoms like delusions and hallucinations
    c. promote clearer thinking, but at the cost of longer hospital stays
    d. promote clearer thinking, but at the cost of emotional agitation

_____ 5. The discovery of antipsychotic drugs led directly to
    a. deinstitutionalization
    b. the reform movement
    c. reinstitutionalization
    d. the community mental health center

_____ 6. Deinstitutionalization has led to homelessness, a sad result best explained by a/n
    a. side effect of antipsychotic drugs that makes schizophrenics afraid to be inside
    b. lack of funding and adequate supervision of halfway houses
    c. reluctance of families to allow the "crazies" to come home again
    d. high cost of treatment in community mental health centers

_____ 7. A main reason why many people needing professional help do not seek it is the
    a. social stigma attached to having a mental disorder
    b. high cost per hour of psychiatrists in private practice
    c. requirement of most therapists that new patients spend a period in the hospital first
    d. refusal of insurance companies to cover mental disorders

_____ 8. In order to become a _____ you need a medical degree and a residency with further training in psychopathology and treatment
   a. clinical psychologist
   b. psychiatrist
   c. social worker
   d. counseling psychologist

_____ 9. When asked which approach they use in therapy, a majority of psychologists indicated a preference for the _____ approach
   a. psychodynamic
   b. behavioral
   c. eclectic
   d. cognitive

_____ 10. How effective is psychotherapy? Studies suggest that psychotherapy is
   a. an effective treatment for many mental disorders
   b. no more effective than just waiting
   c. no more effective than doing nothing
   d. an effective treatment, but only if continued for more than a year

_____ 11. The central idea of Freud's psychoanalysis is that each of us has a/n
   a. unconscious part that contains hidden, threatening desires or thoughts
   b. conscious mind containing ideas that can be clarified and made more logical
   c. history of learned behavior patterns that reveals why we act in certain ways
   d. need to grow and develop our full potential as human beings

_____ 12. In a typical therapy session, the role of the analyst illustrates all the following assumptions of psychoanalysis *except*
   a. free association
   b. interpretation
   c. schedules of reinforcement
   d. unconscious conflicts

_____ 13. Free association seems like a great time waster, but Freud insisted on it because
   a. he knew people enjoy talking about themselves, and this would relax them
   b. he was billing patients by the hour, and could not charge high fees like surgeons
   c. patients need encouragement to talk about scary things like rats and wolves
   d. patients have no conscious knowledge of what their unconscious problems are

_____ 14. Freud used dream interpretation because he thought dreams represent
   a. the purest form of free association
   b. sick thinking, which needs to be corrected
   c. nonsensical ideas, which the therapist should expose
   d. the souls of deceased ancestors attempting to speak to us and help us

_____ 15. Transference and resistance are technical terms for what happens in therapy, but perceptive students may also recognize the workings of these processes in their own
   a. thoughts about trying a new school despite their parents' objections
   b. attempts to apply knowledge gained in one course to the next higher course
   c. desires to find and win over a new sweetheart
   d. feelings about their instructors and troubles with some courses

_____ 16. Psychoanalysis has a famous place in psychology, but what is its current status?
   a. it remains as a great story, but few therapists use its odd ideas anymore
   b. its key concepts (unconscious forces and defense mechanisms) are not supported by research
   c. modified forms of psychoanalysis continue to be important in psychotherapy
   d. most psychologists today consider Freud's outlandish ideas a bad joke on psychotherapy

_____ 17. The central assumption of Carl Rogers' client-centered therapy is that
   a. each person has the tendency and capacity to develop his or her full potential
   b. psychotherapy must be freely available in community mental health centers
   c. we must struggle to overcome our basic human selfishness and hostility
   d. therapy should focus on real behavior, not vague thoughts and feelings

_____ 18. Aaron Beck discovered that depressed people tend to interpret the world through
   a. carefully planned negative statements
   b. thoughtless repetitions of what other people believe
   c. secretly hostile beliefs
   d. automatic negative thoughts

_____ 19. In his cognitive therapy, Beck attempts to make clients aware of
   a. the importance of education in the contemporary world
   b. adaptive thought patterns like open-mindedness, acceptance, love, and will power
   c. maladaptive thought patterns like overgeneralization, polarized thinking, and selective attention
   d. how much better they could be if they would just "think about it"

_____ 20. Behavior therapy or behavior modification differs from the insight therapies in that the therapist
   a. encourages the client to free-associate
   b. repeats or reflects what the client says
   c. discusses the client's tendency to automatically think negative thoughts
   d. identifies the specific problem and discusses a program for change

_____ 21. Which one of the following is *not* a step in the systematic desensitization procedure?
   a. relaxation
   b. stimulus hierarchy
   c. stimulus sensitizing
   d. exposure

_____ 22. A popular new therapy that combines learning principles with insight into the mind is called
   a. self-help programming
   b. cognitive-behavior therapy
   c. short-term dynamic psychotherapy
   d. behavior modification

_____ 23. Rod Plotnik's fascinating example of a local healer or balian in Bali suggests that the success of Western psychotherapy
   a. demonstrates the superiority of modern medicine
   b. owes much to what are called common factors in psychotherapy
   c. depends on having intelligent and educated patients
   d. results from its assumption that the problem lies inside the sufferer

_____ 24. Francine Shapiro's new therapy does seem to work, but the question about EMDR is whether the
   a. same results could be obtained on traumatic memories
   b. successes could be achieved without first hypnotizing the patients
   c. eye movements are really important and why
   d. successes are due to the magnetic personality of Francine Shapiro

_____ 25. Which one of the following is *not* a step in the thought substitution procedure?
   a. through self-monitoring, write a list of your irrational thoughts
   b. compose a matching list of rational thoughts
   c. practice substituting rational thoughts whenever you have irrational ones
   d. if you catch yourself thinking irrationally, administer a predetermined punishment, like no TV that night

Short Essay

1. Who was "Anna O." and why is she so famous in the history of psychotherapy?

2. How did the discovery of the drug chlorpromazine revolutionize treatment of the mentally ill?

3. How are the Freudian techniques of free association and dream interpretation linked to the treatment of neuroses?

4. Put yourself on the couch for a moment! Can you find any illustrations of the Freudian concepts of transference or resistance in your struggles as a student?

5. Describe the EMDR treatment and explain why it is controversial.

Answers for Module 24

The Big Picture (explanations provided for incorrect choices)

A Despite common factors, there are real differences between the work of a balian and a Western psychotherapist.
B *Correct! You see the "big picture" for this Module.*
C This is simply not true. Research does not yet support the superior effectiveness of EMDR.
D This assumption belongs to psychoanalysis. Other theories of psychotherapy differ.
E It's just a joke!

True-False (explanations provided for False choices; page numbers given for all choices)

1   F   556   Sadly, the history of psychological treatment also is about inhumane treatment of the mentally ill.
2   T   559
3   F   560   Psychoanalysis is based on insight into the unconscious, not learned behavior.
4   F   562   Transference is projecting feelings about important persons in the patient's life onto the therapist.
5   T   563
6   F   564   Each therapist quoted shows signs of a particular approach to psychotherapy.
7   T   564
8   T   565
9   T   567
10 F   573   The effectiveness of EMDR remains unproved until scientifically compared to other therapies.

Flashcards 1

1 d   2 h   3 j   4 g   5 a   6 i   7 c   8 e   9 b   10 f

Flashcards 2

1 b   2 c   3 j   4 a   5 g   6 f   7 d   8 h   9 i   10 e

Multiple-Choice (explanations provided for incorrect choices)

1   a   Anna O. was Dr. Breuer's patient, not Freud's.
    b   *Correct! See page 555.*
    c   Dr. Breuer treated Anna O., but It was Freud's genius to see the deeper implications of the case.
    d   The point was that just talking about problems can help.

2   a   True, but Plotnik is making a point about psychotherapy.
    b   True, but Plotnik is making a point about psychotherapy.
    c   Little Albert was not afraid of the rat until it was associated with the loud noise.
    d   *Correct! See page 555.*

3   a   Some did this, but not the reformer Dorothea Dix.
    b   This was not the humane reform work of Dorothea Dix.
    c   *Correct! See page 556.*
    d   This did not happen until the invention of antipsychotic drugs in the 1950s.

4   a   They work by blocking or reducing the effects of dopamine.
    b   *Correct! See page 557.*
    c   They do promote clearer thinking, but also lead to shorter hospital stays.
    d   They do promote clearer thinking, and also calm patients down.

5   **a   *Correct! See page 557.***
    b   The reform movement came much earlier, in the previous century.
    c   This is not a term used in psychiatry.
    d   Community mental health centers provide care to people who might not have access to private treatment.

6   a   There is no such side effect with antipsychotic drugs.
    b   *Correct! See page 557.*
    c   Before they can return to their homes, the ex-patients need care and support in good halfway houses.
    d   Community mental health centers offer low-cost assistance, but there are not enough of them.

7   **a**   *Correct! See page 558.*
     b   Some are expensive, but there are many other alternatives at less cost.
     c   There is no such common requirement.
     d   Insurance is a problem, but many employers offer some coverage for mental disorders.

8   a   A clinical psychologist has a Ph.D. and clinical experience.
     b   *Correct! See page 558.*
     c   A social worker has a master's degree and may have special training in psychotherapy.
     d   A counseling psychologist has a Ph.D. and counseling experience.

9   a   Only about 10 percent indicated a preference for the psychodynamic approach.
     b   Only about 7 percent indicated a preference for the behavioral approach.
     c   *Correct! See page 559.*
     d   Only about 10 percent indicated a preference for the cognitive approach.

10   **a**   *Correct! See page 559.*
     b   About two-thirds of all psychotherapy clients experience some improvement.
     c   About two-thirds of all psychotherapy clients experience some improvement.
     d   Many short-term therapies are quite effective.

11   **a**   *Correct! See page 560.*
     b   This would be true of Beck's cognitive therapy.
     c   This would be true of behavior therapy.
     d   This would be true of Rogers's client-centered therapy.

12   a   Free association is the key to how psychoanalysis works.
     b   Interpretation is very important in psychoanalysis.
     c   *Correct! See page 561.*
     d   Unconscious conflicts are very important in psychoanalysis.

13   a   Free association is not always relaxing (try it and you will see that it also can be anxiety provoking).
     b   OK, so now we know you are an anti-Freudian!
     c   In therapy, it is the *unconscious* meaning of rats and wolves that is frightening and needs to be explored.
     d   *Correct! See page 561.*

14   **a**   *Correct! See page 561.*
     b   Freud would not accept the idea of "sick" thinking nor believe mental processes need to be "corrected."
     c   Dreams may appear to be nonsense, but Freud believed they disguised important problems.
     d   This is believed in some cultures, but certainly was not accepted by Freud.

15   a   In psychoanalysis, it is thoughts and feelings, not course credits, that are being transferred.
     b   In psychoanalysis, it is thoughts and feelings, not learnings, that are being transferred.
     c   In psychoanalysis, it is thoughts and feelings, not charm bracelets, that are being transferred.
     d   *Correct! See page 562.*

16   a   Many of Freud's insights, if not his whole theory, continue to influence psychology and treatment.
     b   These two concepts have received research support; others have not.
     c   *Correct! See page 563.*
     d   Some psychologists are very critical, but Freud continues to hold a respected place in psychology.

17   **a**   *Correct! See page 564.*
     b   This statement sounds more like the beliefs of community mental health workers.
     c   This might be more true of psychoanalytic therapy.
     d   This is more true of behavior therapy.

18   a   The negative thought patterns of depressed people are not deliberate or planned.
     b   This is not a characteristic Beck identified in depressed people.
     c   This is not a characteristic Beck identified in depressed people.
     d   *Correct! See page 565.*

19   a   A noble idea, but it has nothing to do with Beck's cognitive therapy.
     b   These are not goals of Beck's cognitive therapy.
     c   *Correct! See page 565.*
     d   This [wrong] answer comes from an old *Saturday Night Live* skit.

20   a   This is what the therapist does in psychoanalysis.
     b   This is what the therapist does in client-centered therapy.
     c   This is what the therapist does in cognitive therapy.
     d   *Correct! See page 566.*

21   a   Relaxation is an essential ingredient in desensitization.
     b   A stimulus hierarchy is an essential ingredient in desensitization.
     c   *Correct! See page 567.*
     d   Exposure is an essential ingredient in desensitization.

22   a   Self-help programs are derived from cognitive-behavior therapy.
     b   *Correct! See page 568.*
     c   Short-term dynamic psychotherapy is a modified version of psychoanalysis.
     d   Behavior modification is a form of behavior therapy, and not cognitive at all.

23   a   People who consult a balian do experience relief from symptoms.
     b   *Correct! See page 572.*
     c   The village people who consult a balian are neither especially intelligent nor highly educated.
     d   The truth *might* be just the opposite.

24   a   Those are precisely the problems it was designed to alleviate.
     b   Hypnosis is not part of the EMDR treatment.
     c   *Correct! See page 573.*
     d   Today EMDR is used by many other therapists as well.

25   a   This is step 1 of the thought substitution procedure.
     b   This is step 2 of the thought substitution procedure.
     c   This is step 3 of the thought substitution procedure.
     d   *Correct! See page 574.*

Short Essay (sample answers)

1. Anna O. was an intelligent young woman who began to experience strange physical symptoms while caring for her seriously ill father. Dr. Joseph Breuer was consulted, but could find no physical causes for her symptoms. So Breuer listened as she talked. Each time she recalled a past, traumatic experience, a physical symptom associated with that trauma would vanish. Breuer discussed the confusing case with his colleague Sigmund Freud, who quickly understood Anna O., and went on to originate psychoanalysis.

2. The accidental discovery in the 1950s that chlorpromazine, one of the phenothiazines, could block or reduce the effects of the neurotransmitter dopamine and reduce schizophrenic symptoms, led to a revolution in psychiatric treatment. Freed of disabling delusions and hallucinations, patients who had been "warehoused" in mental hospitals for years could be discharged. But the triumph of deinstitutionalization was followed by the tragedy of homelessness, as society failed to provide adequate support and treatment on the outside.

3. The psychological problems that Freud called neuroses are maladaptive thoughts and actions that arise from some unconscious thought or conflict and indicate feelings of anxiety. But if the problem is unconscious, how can it be discovered? Freud proposed free association — that the patient say anything that came to mind — as the basic rule of psychoanalytic treatment. Dreams, less consciously controlled and thus the purest form of free association, also can be interpreted. Eventually, the truth will come out.

4. Have you wondered why you like a certain professor so much, or why you seem to be constantly struggling with another professor? Does it seem odd that a subject you could easily master is giving you so much trouble? Could it be that earlier attachments to and interactions with your parents are reflected in your current student life? See if you can discover examples of Freud's provocative concepts of transference and resistance in your academic work. Just lie back, relax, and think about anything that comes to mind!

5. Francine Shapiro's EMDR (Eye Movement Desensitization Reprocessing) involves having the client talk about or imagine a troubling traumatic memory while visually focusing on and following the back-and-forth movement of a therapist's hand. EMDR is controversial because it seems too unusual, too simple, and too quick. Some therapists find it surprisingly effective and others see it as a kind of placebo effect. Research has given some support to the effectiveness of EMDR, but has not solved the mystery of why it works.

Module 25

Social Psychology

The Material That Was Difficult Because It Seemed Easy

Well, not really easy — you'll have to study this module as carefully as the others — but obvious, in a sense. One of the difficulties in studying social psychology is that so many of the facts and ideas it presents seem like things you already know. That makes it hard to get a handle on what to "learn." Here's an idea that may make it easier.

Because you are a human being, you have been a social psychologist all your life. If there is one essential human skill, it is how to live with each other. I don't mean this in a preachy way, but in the sense that our instincts, what few we have, tell us very little about interacting with others. Therefore, we must learn to observe, understand, and predict what other people will do (and what we will do) in any given situation. We soon become experts in human interaction. See? You've been studying this stuff all your life.

The beauty of social psychology is that it can take us outside ourselves and help us see our behavior more objectively, and hence more clearly. Such awareness, which social psychology owes to anthropology and sociology, helps correct the tendency of psychology to focus too much on individual, internal factors. There's a price you pay for this insight, however. Theories in social psychology typically involve fancy names and complicated explanations. Don't be afraid. The social psychologists you'll study are talking about what you do every day. Try to understand it that way. Give yourself credit for understanding what seems obvious. Translate what does not seem clear into the language of your own experience.

The Cross-Cultural Approach to Psychology

If you counted them, you would discover that there are more key terms in this module than almost any other. Another module with almost the same number of key terms is Rod Plotnik's presentation of "The Incredible Nervous System." And that's no accident. Just as Module 4 helped define the psychobiological approach to psychology, Module 25 defines the other end of the spectrum — the cross-cultural approach (some might call it the sociocultural approach). In the earlier module, we were almost off the chart into biology, hence the need for many new terms. Here, we are deep into sociology, and once again need a whole new vocabulary.

One problem sociologists have is that they are talking about things that are utterly familiar, like attitudes, helping, groups, and aggression. Sometimes it almost seems like they invent fancy names for their concepts because what they are describing is so familiar. But they wouldn't do that, would they?

Effective Student Tip 25

Honor Your Need to be Effective

Most of my tips have been quite specific, because I wanted them to be actions you could take immediately. If they worked, you won a victory here and there and perhaps did better in the course. I hope they also contribute to a body of strategies that will make you a stronger student in the courses still to come.

In truth, however, I have an even larger goal in mind. That goal is for you to begin to understand that the need to be effective is the essence of your human motivation. If I am right, you feel a need to be effective not only in your schoolwork but more importantly in everything you do.

My argument is simply this: We humans have almost no instincts to guide us. The only way we can tell whether what we are doing is right is the extent to which it works for us. We know our actions are working when they make the world give back what we want and need. In other words, the extent to which the actions we take are effective becomes the measure of our happiness and satisfaction in life.

Whatever situation you may be in, school or employment or relationship, honor your need to be effective by paying attention to how well your actions are working for you and how good you feel about what you are doing.

Your response...

I am convinced that we all have a constant need to be effective. Do you feel that need in yourself?

Learning Objectives

1. Understand social psychology as a broad field whose goals are to understand and explain how our thoughts, feelings, perceptions, and behaviors are influenced by interacting with others.

2. Learn the basic mechanisms of perceiving others through the social lenses of physical appearance, stereotypes, and schemas.

3. Learn how our thoughts and behaviors are influenced by attributions, attitudes, and social and group influences.

4. Understand the classic experiments and findings of social psychology in conformity, compliance, obedience, helping and prosocial behavior, group dynamics, behavior in crowds, and group decisions.

5. Explore the critical human problem of aggression — its origins in nature and nurture, social and personality factors, situational cues, and sexual harassment and aggression.

6. Appreciate how national attitudes and social behaviors are influenced by cultural differences.

7. Apply the insights and research findings of social psychology to the problems of controlling aggression in children, anger in adults, and sexual coercion.

Key Terms

These terms are especially important because they help define the cross-cultural approach to psychology. There are so many terms because this module summarizes the entire field of social psychology.

actor-observer effect
aggression
altruism
arousal-cost-reward model of
  helping
attitude
attributions
bystander effect
catharsis
central route for persuasion
cognitive dissonance
cognitive miser model
cognitive social psychology
compliance
conformity
consensus
consistency
counterattitudinal behavior
covariation model

crowd
debriefing
decision-stage model of
  helping
deindividuation
diffusion of responsibility
  theory
discrimination
distinctiveness
evaluative function
event schemas or scripts
external attributions
foot-in-the-door technique
frustration-aggression
  hypothesis
fundamental attribution error
group cohesion
group norms
group polarization
groups

groupthink
hazing
informational influence theory
internal attributions
interpreting function
modified frustration-
  aggression hypothesis
obedience
peripheral route for
  persuasion
person perception
person schemas
predisposing function
prejudice
prosocial behavior or helping
rape myths
role schemas
schemas
self schemas

self-perception theory
self-serving bias
social cognitive theory
social comparison theory

social facilitation
social inhibition
social psychology
socially oriented group

stereotypes
task oriented group

Outline

- *Introduction*
    1. Stereotypes (Lawrence Graham)
    ☐ What does "cognitive" social psychology add to traditional social psychology?
        a. Social psychology
        b. **Cognitive social psychology**
    2. Behavior in groups (Violent hazing)
- A. *Perceiving Others*
    1. **Person perception**
        a. Physical appearance
        b. Need to explain
        c. Influence on behavior
        d. Effects of race
    2. Physical appearance
        a. Attractiveness
        b. Advantages
    3. **Stereotypes**
        a. Development of stereotypes
            (1) **Prejudice**
            (2) **Discrimination**
        b. Functions of stereotypes
            (1) Mental standards
            (2) Thought-saving device
    4. **Schemas**
        a. Kinds of schemas
            (1) **Person schemas**
            (2) **Role schemas**
            (3) **Event schemas or scripts**
            (4) **Self schemas**
        b. Advantages and disadvantages

B. *Attributions*

   1. Definition: **attributions**

   2. Internal versus external (Fritz Heider)

     a. **Internal attributions**

     b. **External attributions**

   3. Kelley's model of covariation

     a. **Covariation model** (Harold Kelley)

       (1) **Consensus**

       (2) **Consistency**

       (3) **Distinctiveness**

     b. Applying Kelley's covariation model

   4. Biases and errors

     a. **Cognitive miser model**

     b. Common biases in making attributions

       (1) **Fundamental attribution error**

       (2) **Actor-observer effect**

       (3) **Self-serving bias**

C. *Research Focus: Attributions & Grades*

   1. Can changing attributions change grades?

   2. A study of attributions and grades

     a. Kinds of attributions

     b. Method: changing attributions

     c. Results and conclusions

D. *Attitudes*

   1. Definition: **attitude**

   2. Components of attitudes

     a. Cognitive component

     b. Affective component

     c. Behavioral component

   3. Functions of attitudes

  ☐ What was your attitude toward Shannon Faulkner and her goal?

     a. **Predisposing function**

     b. **Interpreting function**

     c. **Evaluative function**

   4. Attitude change

  ☐ Read the famous 'boring task' experiment several times, until you really understand it.

    a. **Cognitive dissonance** (Leon Festinger)

        (1) Adding or changing beliefs

        (2) **Counterattitudinal behavior**

    b. **Self-perception theory** (Daryl Bem)

  5. Persuasion

  ☐ Can you think of examples for the two routes from current politics?

    a. Two routes to persuasion

        (1) **Central route for persuasion**

        (2) **Peripheral route for persuasion**

    b. Elements of persuasion

        (1) Source

        (2) Message (one versus two-sided messages)

        (3) Audience

E. *Social & Group Influences*

  1. Conformity (Solomon Asch)

    a. **Hazing**

    b. **Conformity**

    c. Asch's experiment

        (1) Procedure

        (2) Results

  2. Compliance

    a. **Compliance**

    b. **Foot-in-the-door technique**

  3. Obedience (Stanley Milgram)

    a. **Obedience**

    b. Milgram's experiment

        (1) The setup

        (2) The conflict

    c. Milgram's results

    d. Why do people obey?

    e. Were Milgram's experiments ethical?

        (1) **Debriefing**

        (2) Experiments today

  4. Helping: prosocial behavior

    a. **Prosocial behavior or helping**

    b. **Altruism**

5. Why people help

   a. Empathy, personal distress, norms, or values

   b. **Decision-stage model of helping**

   c. **Arousal-cost-reward model of helping**

6. Group dynamics: **groups**

   a. Group cohesion and norms

      (1) **Group cohesion**

      (2) **Group norms**

   b. Group membership

      (1) **Social comparison theory**

      (2) **Task oriented group**

      (3) **Socially oriented group**

7. Behavior in crowds: **crowd**

   a. Facilitation and inhibition

      (1) **Social facilitation**

      (2) **Social inhibition**

   b. Deindividuation in crowds

      (1) **Deindividuation**

      (2) Internal standards

   c. The bystander effect

      (1) **Bystander effect**

      (2) **Informational influence theory**

      (3) **Diffusion of responsibility theory**

8. Group decisions

   a. **Group polarization**

      (1) Risky shift

      (2) Polarization

   b. **Groupthink**

      (1) Mindguard, ingroup, outgroup

      (2) Avoiding groupthink (vigilant decision making)

F. *Aggression*

1. Genes and environment: **aggression**

☐ Do you believe that human beings are naturally aggressive?

   a. Genetic influences in animals

   b. Genetic influences in humans

   c. Genes interact with good/bad environments

    d. Genes interact with physical abuse

  2. Social cognitive and personality factors

    a. **Social cognitive theory** (Albert Bandura)

    b. Television/video games

    c. Model of aggression

  3. Situational cues

    a. **Frustration-aggression hypothesis** (road rage)

    b. **Modified frustration-aggression hypothesis** (Leonard Berkowitz)

  4. Sexual harassment and aggression

    a. Characteristics and kinds of rapists

      (1) Power rapist

      (2) Sadistic rapist

      (3) Anger rapist

      (4) Acquaintance or date rapist

    b. **Rape myths**

G. *Cultural Diversity: National Attitudes and Behaviors*

  1. Niger: beauty ideal

  2. Japan: organ transplants

  3. Egypt: women's rights

H. *Application: Controlling Aggression*

  1. Case study (Monster Kody)

  2. Controlling aggression in children

    a. Cognitive-behavioral deficits

    b. Programs to control aggression

      (1) Cognitive problem-solving skills training

      (2) Parent Management Training (PMT)

  3. Controlling anger in adults

    a. **Catharsis**

    b. Cognitive-relaxation program

  4. Controlling sexual coersion

    a. Socialization

    b. Knowing the risk factors

For Psych Majors Only...

Classic Experiments: The classic experiments in social psychology are among the most elegant in psychology, if not in all of science, but they may seem complicated on first reading. Go through the explanations in the textbook more than once, and make sure you understand the logic of each experiment. The research Rod Plotnik writes about is well worth understanding and remembering. These experiments are important building blocks of modern psychology, and you will come across them repeatedly in your further studies.

There is a great irony surrounding these famous experiments: most of them could not be conducted today. Plotnik explains why in his discussion of the ethics of psychological research.

Congratulations!

Here you are, working on the self-tests for the last module. You have worked through a big textbook and a long Study Guide. That means you have done a ton of work this term, and I'm proud of you! Be sure to give yourself the praise you deserve (maybe a reward, too!). You have earned it.

Now that it's over, I would love to know what you thought of your introductory psychology class. Are you glad you took psychology? Did it change you in any way? What was the most important thing you learned? Please tell me by e-mail! **Profenos@aol.com**

Language Workout

What's That?

p. 581   A **posh country club** = a fancy private recreation center
the **exclusive** Greenwich Country Club = limited to rich upper class people
hired to be a **busboy** = waiter's assistant who removes dirty dishes
diction like an educated white person = clear pronunciation
an **associate** in a New York law firm = partner
move up the social ladder = rise to a higher social position
The **touch football game** = a more casual version of football with limited contact
rite of passage = an activity that is connected with moving up a level in rank or age
some minor **hazing** = unpleasant rituals used to join a group
well-to-do Chicago suburb = wealthy
fish guts = the inner organs of a fish

p. 583   **rave parties** = large dance music parties, especially with drug use

p. 584   a **board-certified** neurosurgeon = licensed, officially approved
she was repeatedly **propositioned** = given sexual invitations
primarily **for effect** = to impress others (other men)

p. 585   this **umpire** = judge in baseball games
passed over for promotion = not considered

p. 586   people **of color** = non-white

p. 588   **conventional** medical treatment = commonly practiced

p. 589   having to take **scalding** showers = burning hot

p. 590   an **out-and-out hatemonger** = open, not hidden person who encourages hate

bashed and robbed Japanese tourists = physically attacked
white supremacist = general belief that whites are superior to non-whites

p. 593   used by **telemarketers** = telephone salespersons
drivers who **run** red lights = drive through
an **accomplice** of the experimenter = partner, helper
ask the learner **over an intercom** = using an electrical speaker system

p. 595   60 **onlookers** = people watching, bystanders
do things that **touch our hearts** = give us a good feeling
help **perfect** strangers = complete

p. 597   a runner has a **spotty** history = uneven, inconsistent
arrested for **looting** = stealing during riots

p. 598   the **brink** of nuclear war = edge, border
Watergate cover-up = 1973 scandal concerning illegal actions by president Nixon
Challenger disaster = explosion of U.S. space ship in 1986, killing all the astronauts

p. 600   **drive-by killings** = shootings from a moving car

p. 602   **penal** institutions = punishment (especially prison)
necking and petting = kissing and beginning love-making
things **get out of hand** = go out of control

p. 605   **rant and rave** = complain loudly

p. 608   eager to **set up shop** = start working
opened a **Pandora's box** = source of troubles and hidden problems
values that parents **impart** to children = teach
a **self-fulfilling prophecy** = action that, once predicted, will then happen
because the predictor makes it happen
chiding themselves = criticizing
for **coddling** teen mothers = treating too lightly, not giving discipline

Flex Your Word Power

Here are some more **opposites** from this module and earlier ones. Draw a line connecting each word on the left with its opposite on the right.

prominent	con
reinforce	opponent
hardy	conservative
proponent	weaken
liberal	debilitating
pro	unknown

Do you want to try some more? Here are some from earlier modules:

intrinsic	aversion
novel	deductive
novice	age-old
inductive	terminate
initiate	veteran
attraction	extrinsic

Okay, if you want more opposites, here they are:

implicit	subjective
optimistic	progress
objective	pessimistic
passive	complementary
mutually exclusive	explicit
regress	active

Answers

prominent	=	unknown
reinforce	=	weaken
hardy	=	debilitating
proponent	=	opponent
liberal	=	conservative
pro	=	con
intrinsic	=	extrinsic
novel	=	age-old
novice	=	veteran
inductive	=	deductive
initiate	=	terminate
attraction	=	aversion

implicit	=	explicit
optimistic	=	pessimistic
objective	=	subjective
passive	=	active
mutual exclusive	=	complementary
regress	=	progress

The Language Workout Marathon

Are you ready to test yourself? Try these questions that review the information from the Language Workout and see how much you remember. You can check the Answers, or review the Module for helpful hints.

In the sentences below, write the appropriate form of the word.
Example: The information you **perceive** is your *perception*.

An experience that **affects** many people has a great _____. (Module 2)

An individual who has a **bias** is a _____ person. (Module 2)

If you are **deprived** of sleep, you experience sleep _____. (Module 7)

A person who **abstains** from food is described as _____. (Module 8)

When something is **anticipatory,** it means that people _____ it. (Module 9)

Now let's try some plurals. In the sentences below, write the correct form in the blank.
Example: One **ovum** is normally released, but sometimes two *ova* are released. (Modules 3 and 17)

One **datum** was not enough, so I looked for more _____.

One single **phenomenon** caused many more _____.

If one **stimulus** is not successful, different _____ can be tried.

The first **crisis** was harder than all later _____.

We chose one **criterion** out of many _____.

Read the following sentences and circle the best choice to describe the sentence. (Modules 10 and 14)

The Psychodynamic Theory of Personality was developed by Sigmund Freud.
Is this ACTIVE or PASSIVE?

Sigmund Freud is often called the "Father of Psychoanalysis."
Is this ACTIVE or PASSIVE?

Freud wrote about people like Little Albert and the Rat Man.
Is this ACTIVE or PASSIVE?

The Language Workout Marathon is good practice.
Is this OBJECTIVE or SUBJECTIVE?

There are 25 Modules in the Language Workout.
Is this OBJECTIVE or SUBJECTIVE?

Do you remember our practice in joining sentences with phrases like **to which, some of which, with whom,** and **all of whom**? If not, check Modules 13, 15, 16, and 21 to review. Then see if you can join the sentences below in the same way.

The bank kept control of the money. None of the money could be used for daily expenses.
The _____.

The therapist saw seven patients. Two of patients arrived late.
The _____.

Runners trained six months for the marathon. They participated in this marathon.
The _____.

The professor will arrive soon. All the students are waiting for her.
The _____.

Now let's try some connecting or organizing words. Choose the word that best fits each sentence.

thus *or* **however** (Modules 11 and 18)

The experiment was a success. _____, the scientific evidence was proven.

The operation was a success. _____, the patient will still need another to be healed.

nevertheless *or* **conversely** (Module 18)

He didn't study for the exam. _____, he easily passed the exam.

She is going someplace warm for vacation. _____, her roommate is staying home.

once *or* **while** (Modules 12 and 24)

_____ the research was published, the public reacted.

_____ the research was published, no one read it.

provided *or* **even if** (Module 20)

_____ you finish your vegetables, you can have some chocolate ice cream.

_____ you buy a new engine, your car will never run like a brand new car.

You're almost finished. This last part reviews punctuation that was explained in the **Making Connections** sections in Modules 5, 6, 19, 22, and 23. The sentences below need more punctuation, so you have to decide where to use **commas, colons,** and **semi-colons**.

Americans call the sport soccer conversely the rest of the world calls it football.

Now it is easier to understand the different meanings of the following terms a concept a principle and a theory.

The more she reads the bigger her vocabulary grows.

Seven people were seated at the table one of whom was the murder.

The explanation although it was clear to the professor was quite hazy to the students.

From the first page to the last the book was full of valuable information.

You made it!

Answers

An experience that **affects** many people has a great **effect**.
An individual who has a **bias** is a **biased** person.
If you are **deprived** of sleep, you experience sleep **deprivation**.
A person who **abstains** from food is described as **abstinent**.
When something is **anticipatory**, it means that people **anticipate** it.

One **datum** was not enough, so I looked for more **data**.
One single **phenomenon** caused many more **phenomena**.
If one **stimulus** is not successful, different **stimuli** can be tried.
The first **crisis** was harder than all later **crises**.
We chose one **criterion** out of many **criteria**.

The Psychodynamic Theory of Personality was developed by Sigmund Freud. PASSIVE
Sigmund Freud is often called the "Father of Psychoanalysis." PASSIVE
Freud wrote about people like Little Albert and the Rat Man. ACTIVE
The Language Workout Marathon is good practice. SUBJECTIVE
There are 25 Modules in the Language Workout. OBJECTIVE

The bank kept control of the money, **none of which** could be used for daily expenses.
The therapist saw seven patients, **two of whom** arrived late.
Runners trained six months for the marathon **in which** they participated.
The professor **for whom** all the students are waiting will arrive soon.

The experiment was a success. **Thus**, the scientific evidence was proven.
The operation was a success. **However**, the patient will still need another to be healed.
He didn't study for the exam. **Nevertheless**, he easily passed the exam.
She is going someplace warm for vacation. **Conversely**, her roommate is staying home.
Once the research was published, the public reacted.
While the research was published, no one read it.
Provided you finish your vegetables, you can have some chocolate ice cream.
Even if you buy a new engine, your car will never run like a brand new car.

Americans call the sport soccer; conversely, the rest of the world calls it football.
Now it is easier to understand the different meanings of the following terms: a concept, a principle, and a theory.
The more she reads, **the** bigger her vocabulary grows.
Seven people were seated at the table, one of whom was the murder.
The explanation, **although** it was clear to the professor, was quite hazy to the students.
From the first page to the last, the book was full of valuable information.

The Big Picture

Which statement below offers the best summary of the larger significance of this module?

A   Understanding the behavior of people in group situations involves a complicated mathematics of combining all the individual tendencies to arrive at an average that will determine how the individuals will behave.

B   Rod Plotnik has discussed the famous nature-nurture debate in several modules of this textbook. With his description of the many elegant experiments in social psychology, the answer finally becomes clear: our behavior owes most to nature.

C   No matter how many experiments social psychologists conduct on group influence, the fact remains that we are unique individuals. If we exercise our freedom of choice, no one can make us do anything against our will.

D   We like to think of ourselves as rugged individuals, but social psychology has demonstrated that our behavior, and even our thinking, is highly sensitive to group pressures and the social situations we are in.

E   How many social psychologists does it take to change a light bulb? Three: one to give the order, one to change the bulb, and one to record whether the order was obeyed! [And so we end as we began.]

True-False

_____   1. Prejudice refers to an attitude or belief; discrimination is an act.

_____   2. A schema is an unfair stereotype we apply to a person who is different.

_____   3. Attributions are our attempts to understand and explain people's behavior.

_____   4. An attitude is a tendency to respond to others in a quirky, overly sensitive manner.

_____   5. Cognitive dissonance occurs when an audience hears so many contradictory arguments that they lose sight of the main issue.

_____   6. Advice for all you budding politicians: if the facts are on your side, take the central route to persuasion; if they aren't, take the peripheral route.

_____   7. The famous "electric shock" experiment showed that if you pay people enough they will follow just about any orders.

_____   8. It is the social-psychological phenomenon of deindividuation that can make a crowd dangerous.

_____   9. Because of the pooling of many talents and ideas, group decisions are usually superior to individual decisions.

_____   10. Rape myths are misinformed, false beliefs about women, and these myths are frequently held by rapists.

Flashcards 1

_____ 1. actor-observer effect

_____ 2. cognitive dissonance

_____ 3. event schemas or scripts

_____ 4. external attributions

_____ 5. fundamental attribution error

_____ 6. internal attributions

_____ 7. person schemas

_____ 8. role schemas

_____ 9. self-serving bias

_____ 10. social psychology

a. a state of tension that motivates us to reduce our cognitive inconsistencies by making beliefs consistent

b. tendency to attribute our own behavior to situation, others' to their personality traits or dispositions

c. how our thoughts, feelings, perceptions, and behaviors are influenced by the presence of, or interactions with, others

d. are based on the jobs people perform or the social positions they hold

e. explaining a person by focusing on disposition or personality traits and overlooking the situation

f. attributing our successes to our dispositions and traits, but attributing our failures to the situations

g. explanations of behavior based on the internal characteristics or dispositions of the person

h. include our judgments about the traits that we and others possess

i. explanations of behavior based on the external circumstances or situations; situational attributions

j. contain behaviors that we associate with familiar activities, events, or procedures

Flashcards 2

_____ 1. altruism

_____ 2. bystander effect

_____ 3. central route for persuasion

_____ 4. conformity

_____ 5. deindividuation

_____ 6. foot-in-the-door technique

_____ 7. group cohesion

_____ 8. groupthink

_____ 9. obedience

_____ 10. peripheral route for persuasion

a. any behavior you perform because of group pressure, even though it might not involve direct requests

b. behavior performed in response to an order given by someone in a position of power or authority

c. emphasizes emotional appeal, focuses on personal traits, and generates positive feelings

d. increased tendency for irrational or antisocial behavior when there is less chance of being identified

e. helping, often at a cost or risk, for reasons other than the expectation of a material or social reward

f. says that an individual may feel inhibited from taking some action because of the presence of others

g. presents information with strong arguments, analyses, facts, and logic

h. occurs when group discussions emphasize sticking together and agreement over use of critical thinking

i. increased probability of compliance to a second request if person complies with a small, first request

j. group togetherness, determined by how much group members perceive they share common attributes

Multiple-Choice

_____ 1. Rod Plotnik introduces us to Harvard Law School student Lawrence Graham to make the point that
  a. anyone who has the guts to start at the bottom can work his way up
  b. African-American men are overly sensitive to good natured kidding
  c. how people behave is more significant than what they believe
  d. how we perceive and evaluate others has powerful consequences

_____ 2. Plotnik also gives us an example of violent hazing, to illustrate the idea that
  a. group pressures can cause people to do things they would not normally do
  b. young men in gangs are dangerous when challenged by rival gangs
  c. a strong leader can cause normally peaceful people to take violent actions
  d. prejudices that are normally suppressed can emerge under the influence of alcohol

_____ 3. A discouraging finding about physical appearance and first impressions is captured by the phrase
  a. "Good looks are nice, but who cares about looks?"
  b. "I want a girl just like the girl who married dear old Dad"
  c. "What is beautiful is good"
  d. "Do blondes really have more fun?"

_____ 4. We don't hire any of those people [this is an example of…] because they are too lazy to work hard [this is an example of…]. The correct terms to describe the two parts of this statement in order would be
  a. stereotypes / discrimination
  b. prejudice / discrimination
  c. person perception / person schemas
  d. discrimination / prejudice

_____ 5. When we ask someone, "What do you do?" we are trying to get more information about the person by drawing on our
  a. person schemas
  b. role schemas
  c. event schemas
  d. scripts

_____ 6. In the language of social psychology, _____ means things we point to as the causes of events, other people's behaviors, and our own behaviors
  a. schemas
  b. covariations
  c. attributions
  d. distinctiveness

_____ 7. If I look for the causes of your behavior in your disposition and personality traits, and overlook how the situation influenced that behavior, I am guilty of the
  a. fundamental attribution error
  b. covariation model
  c. actor-observer effect
  d. self-serving bias

_____ 8. "I aced the chem exam because I studied my butt off! The psych exam I flunked? Well, you know he always asks tricky questions." Sounds like the _____ in action, doesn't it?
  a. fundamental attribution error
  b. actor-observer effect
  c. self-serving bias
  d. whiner effect

_____ 9. "Attitude" has been called the most indispensable term in social psychology, because this concept
  a. reveals how feelings are all we need to know in order to understand other people
  b. explains how we think about other people, and beliefs are what count
  c. is just vague enough to be applied to any situation without being challenged
  d. ties together beliefs, feelings, and behavior to explain human social activity

_____ 10. Which one of the following is *not* a component of an attitude?
  a. cognitive
  b. genetic
  c. affective
  d. behavioral

_____ 11. In Leon Festinger's "boring task" experiment, the subjects who were paid only $1 to tell other students it was interesting (a lie) dealt with their cognitive dissonance by
  a. convincing themselves that it was somewhat interesting after all
  b. hoping the students they lied to realized it was just part of the experiment
  c. insisting that they should also be paid $20 for telling the lie
  d. begging Festinger and his assistants not to reveal their names

_____ 12. Daryl Bem (self-perception theory) interprets the above experiment somewhat differently; Bem believes we
  a. consult our attitudes, then adjust our behavior accordingly
  b. observe our behavior, then infer what our attitudes must be, given that behavior
  c. observe our emotional state and adjust our attitudes according to our feelings
  d. govern our behavior according to the kind of person we think we are

_____ 13. Candidate Roberta Reformer, who has an excellent plan for better government, will take the _____ route to persuasion; her opponent Boss Bluster, who plans to label Roberta a hysterical feminist, will take the _____ route
  a. direct / indirect
  b. honest / dishonest
  c. central / peripheral
  d. logical / emotional

_____ 14. When Solomon Asch had his confederates deliberately choose an obviously incorrect matching line, the lone naive subject _____ went along with the group
   a. always
   b. never
   c. often
   d. rarely

_____ 15. But what if subjects in the Asch experiment were just pretending to go along with the group? In that case, their behavior should be labeled
   a. conformity
   b. compliance
   c. obedience
   d. hazing

_____ 16. Tell you what... before you quit just do one more of these questions, O.K.? [I'm using the _____ technique on you in my efforts to get you to do all the questions.]
   a. foot-in-the-door
   b. compliance
   c. conformity
   d. soft-soaping

_____ 17. In Stanley Milgram's electric shock experiment, most subjects continued to give shocks
   a. only up to the point they considered dangerous
   b. even beyond the point they believed was dangerous
   c. only if they had been paid a considerable amount to participate in the experiment
   d. only as long as the shocks seemed to be helping the "learner" do better

_____ 18. Milgram's famous experiment could not be conducted today because
   a. people today are too rational and scientific to obey orders they don't agree with
   b. the experiment has been so widely written about that everyone is in on the secret
   c. few would be fooled by the fake lab, since psychologists are known for deception
   d. a new code of ethics screens experiments for potential harm to the subjects

_____ 19. Sometimes an individual may feel inhibited from taking some action because of the presence of others; this is called
   a. the bystander effect
   b. informational influence theory
   c. diffusion of responsibility theory
   d. deindividuation

_____ 20. Which one of the following political decisions was a classic example of groupthink?
   a. atomic bombing of Japan in World War II
   b. assassination of President Kennedy
   c. Bay of Pigs invasion of Cuba
   d. expulsion of Shannon Faulkner from the Citadel military college

_____ 21. In attempting to explain aggression, social psychology now emphasizes
   a. the frustration that results when our goals are blocked
   b. the interaction of genetic influences with a bad environment
   c. personality factors such as being impulsive, having little empathy, and wanting to dominate
   d. everyday situations like heavy traffic that can lead to "road rage"

_____ 22. Why is rape so common? Researchers point to the fact that
   a. there are other motivations for rape, like aggression, power, and control, that may be more important than sex
   b. women are much bolder today, yet still like to be actively pursued, a situation that leaves men confused about what women really want
   c. Hollywood movies keep our sexual urges in a state of almost constant arousal
   d. unfortunately, rape is as natural as male hormones and female flirtatiousness — but it probably gets reported more often today

_____ 23. A good example of how much culture shapes our attitudes is the
   a. unlikely prospect that a women will ever be elected President of the United States
   b. rapid improvement in sexual, political, and legal rights for Egyptian women
   c. eagerness of the Japanese to obtain organ transplants from brain dead patients
   d. recent change in Nigerian attitudes about female beauty from full to slender

_____ 24. Catharsis is a popular idea for reducing and controlling aggression through
   a. enrolling parents in Parent Management Training (PMT)
   b. learning to "keep the lid on" aggressive impulses instead of expressing them
   c. releasing anger or aggressive energy by expressing or letting out powerful negative emotions
   d. engaging in one of the new cognitive-relaxation programs

_____ 25. An important reason why sexual coercion is so prevalent is that, thanks to the media,
   a. males believe that they need a sexual catharsis more often than women do
   b. abstinence seems like a wimpy or "loser" belief
   c. modern women are afraid to say "No"
   d. sexually coercive males misperceive women as showing interest when they are not interested

Short Essay

1. How does the story of Lawrence Graham, the busboy with a Harvard degree, illustrate the concepts of stereotypes, prejudice, and discrimination?

2. Summarize Leon Festinger's boring task experiment. What did Festinger demonstrate?

3. Summarize Solomon Asch's line judging experiment. What did Asch demonstrate?

4. Summarize Stanley Milgram's electric shock experiment. What did Milgram demonstrate?

5. Rod Plotnik discussed ideals of beauty in Nigeria, organ transplants in Japan, and women's rights in Egypt. What is his point and how does each example support it?

Answers for Module 25

The Big Picture (explanations provided for incorrect choices)

A There is no such mathematics of social behavior.
B Even if you believe that social psychology settles the debate, the answer would be nurture, not nature.
C Experiment after experiment suggests the power of social influence. The truth may be that we are indeed unique individuals, but only within a common shell of cultural and social forces.
D Correct! You see the "big picture" for this Module.
E It's just a joke!

True-False (explanations provided for False choices; page numbers given for all choices)

1	T	583	
2	F	584	Schema refers to a mental explanation of a person, group, or behavior.
3	T	585	
4	F	588	An attitude is an opinion or belief that predisposes one to act in a certain way.
5	F	590	Cognitive dissonance can result from an imbalance between belief and action.
6	T	591	
7	F	593	Subjects were motivated by a tendency to obey authority, not by money (the pay was small).
8	T	597	
9	F	598	Group decisions (groupthink) do not necessarily represent the best thinking of the group members.
10	T	602	

Flashcards 1

1 b   2 a   3 j   4 i   5 e   6 g   7 h   8 d   9 f   10 c

Flashcards 2

1 e   2 f   3 g   4 a   5 d   6 i   7 j   8 h   9 b   10 c

Multiple-Choice (explanations provided for incorrect choices)

1   a   Plotnik's point is about the power of prejudicial attitudes and discriminatory behavior.
    b   The prejudices expressed in this case were neither good natured nor kidding.
    c   You might reasonably say this, but here Plotnik is showing the connection between attitudes and behavior.
    d   Correct! See page 581.

2   *a   Correct! See page 581.*
    b   The high school girls doing the violent hazing were not members of gangs.
    c   The violent hazing was more spontaneous than urged on by a leader.
    d   The senior girls were hazing junior girls just like themselves.

3   a   Research suggests that we do base many initial judgments about a person on looks.
    b   Maybe, but research shows that we are drawn to faces that are averages of many faces.
    c   Correct! See page 582.
    d   This slogan, once used in a famous hair coloring ad, implies sexual attractiveness but not overall goodness.

4   a   This might work if the terms were reversed, but prejudice is a stronger term in this example.
    b   These are the correct terms, but they are reversed (not attached to the right parts of the statement).
    c   These terms are more general, and do not get at the discrimination and prejudice involved.
    d   Correct! See page 583.

5   a   Person schemas include judgments about personal traits.
    b   Correct! See page 584.
    c   Event schemas contain behaviors we associate with familiar activities, events, or procedures.
    d   Event schemas are sometimes called scripts.

6   a   Schemas are mental categories containing knowledge about people, events, and concepts.
    b   Covariation refers to things that vary together in a regular way (if A is present, so is B, etc.).
    c   Correct! See page 585.
    d   Distinctiveness refers to how differently a person behaves in one situation compared to other situations.

7	*a*	*Correct! See page 586.*
	b	The covariation model refers to factors present when the behavior occurs and absent when it does not occur.
	c	The actor-observer effect refers to explaining our own behavior differently from that of others.
	d	The self-serving bias refers to explaining our own successes and failures.

8	a	The fundamental attribution error would only explain half of this situation.
	b	The actor-observer effect refers to explaining our own behavior differently from others.
	c	*Correct! See page 586.*
	d	There is no whiner effect (except maybe on *Saturday Night Live*).

9	a	Feelings are very important, but beliefs and behaviors are also crucial to understanding people.
	b	Beliefs are very important, but feelings and behaviors are also crucial to understanding people.
	c	This answer doesn't show much faith in social psychology to help explain the world!
	d	*Correct! See page 588.*

10	a	Cognition is one of the three components of an attitude.
	b	*Correct! See page 588.*
	c	Affect (emotion) is one of the three components of an attitude.
	d	Behavior is one of the three components of an attitude.

11	*a*	*Correct! See page 590.*
	b	This did not happen in the experiment.
	c	This did not happen in the experiment.
	d	This did not happen in the experiment.

12	a	Just the opposite is true.
	b	*Correct! See page 590.*
	c	Bem's theory is not based on emotions.
	d	This idea is the opposite of Bem's theory.

13	a	Makes sense, but these are not the social-psychological terms used.
	b	Perhaps true, but this is only an opinion.
	c	*Correct! See page 591.*
	d	Makes sense, but these are not the social-psychological terms used.

14	a	This did not happen.
	b	This did not happen.
	c	*Correct! See page 592.*
	d	If this were the correct answer, what would make the experiment significant?

15	a	Conformity would mean that the subject might actually agree with the majority.
	b	*Correct! See page 593.*
	c	Obedience would mean that the subject was ordered by a person in authority to agree.
	d	Hazing refers to parts of a group's initiation ritual that are humiliating and unpleasant or even dangerous.

16	*a*	*Correct! See page 593.*
	b	Compliance is giving in to social pressure but not changing our beliefs.
	c	Conformity is performing some behavior because of group pressure.
	d	This common expression is not a correct technical term in social psychology.

17	a	This statement about Milgram's experiment is untrue.
	b	*Correct! See page 593.*
	c	This statement about Milgram's experiment is untrue.
	d	This statement about Milgram's experiment is untrue.

18	a	Perhaps we are less conformist today, but people still obey orders.
	b	Only a few well-educated people (like you) know about this experiment.
	c	Deception is still successfully used in many experiments.
	d	*Correct! See page 594.*

19	*a*	*Correct! See page 597.*
	b	The informational influence theory says we use the reactions of others to judge the seriousness of a situation.
	c	The diffusion of responsibility theory says people feel less personal responsibility when in a crowd.
	d	Deindividuation refers to the tendency to behave irrationally when there is less chance of being identified.

20 a   The decision to use the atomic bomb was made by President Truman.
    b   The decision to assassinate President Kennedy was made by Lee Harvey Oswald.
    c   *Correct! See page 598.*
    d   Shannon Falkner was not expelled; under great pressure, she decided to withdraw.

21 a   The earlier frustration-aggression hypothesis has been shown to be only a partial explanation.
    b   *Correct! See page 600.*
    c   Personality factors are only one part of a more complicated interaction.
    d   Road rage fits with the frustration-aggression hypothesis, which is only a partial explanation.

22 *a*   *Correct! See page 602.*
    b   If you chose this answer, you've been watching too many talk shows.
    c   Rape is not primarily about sex.
    d   *Down, boy, down!*

23 a   Do the initials H.R.C. mean anything to you? (Just kidding!)
    b   Sadly, very little of this is happening in Egypt.
    c   Most Japanese don't get organ transplants because they define death as the absence of a heartbeat.
    d   *Correct! See page 603.*

24 a   PMT is a program designed to help parents decrease aggressive behavior in the home and at school.
    b   Catharsis is just the opposite — releasing aggressive energy by expressing negative emotions.
    c   *Correct! See page 605.*
    d   The cognitive-relaxation program works by self-monitoring angry thoughts and learning relaxation methods.

25 a   This outdated stereotype wouldn't explain why many men believe sexual coercion is acceptable.
    b   Not all young people believe this, and even if they did it wouldn't justify sexual coercion.
    c   No, they are not, but too many men don't recognize that "No" really means "No."
    d   *Correct! See page 605.*

Short Essay (sample answers)

1. Lawrence Graham, a Harvard Law School graduate who makes $105,000 a year at a New York law firm, could not join a country club. He decided to work for a country club to learn more about it. The best job he could get was busboy. Members were surprised by his diction, but spoke about him as though he was invisible. Lawrence Graham learned firsthand about *stereotypes* based on his appearance, the *prejudice* that members felt towards African Americans, and the *discrimination* that denied him membership.

2. Leon Festinger devised an extremely boring task, then asked participants to lie to new subjects by saying the task was interesting. Some were paid $1 to lie and others $20. The latter, having been well paid, had no problem with lying. But those paid $1 had to justify telling a lie for a small amount. They resolved their cognitive dissonance (what they said versus what they believed) by changing their beliefs, agreeing that the task was interesting after all! Festinger showed that engaging in opposite behaviors could change attitudes.

3. Solomon Asch set up a simple experiment in which participants were asked to judge line lengths. But there was only one real subject; the others were confederates. At some point, all the other participants began agreeing on an obviously wrong answer. What would the real subject do — say what his eyes saw or agree with the others? An astounding 75% of subjects conformed on some trials (although 25% never conformed). Asch's classic experiment was the first to clearly show that group pressures can influence conformity.

4. Stanley Milgram's famous experiment on obedience was based on an elaborate but fake "laboratory" in which subjects playing the role of "teachers" were told to administer electric shocks to "learners." In fact, no shocks were given. According to the labels on the shock machine, the shocks soon became painful, and learners pounded on the wall and protested. But 65% of the subjects kept going until the shocks, if real, would have been lethal. Milgram had demonstrated a frightening level of obedience to authority.

5. Throughout his textbook, Plotnik emphasizes the cross-cultural dimensions of psychology. He offers three examples of how culture shapes our attitudes. In Nigeria, traditional concepts of female beauty put a premium on fullness. But in a recent attitude shift Nigerian young women today aspire to thinness. In Japan, people do not get organ transplants, because dead is defined as having no heartbeat. In Egypt, a long struggle for equal rights for women continues to be frustrated by powerful traditional forces.

TO THE OWNER OF THIS BOOK

May I ask a favor? It would be very helpful to know how well the Study Guide worked for you. I would like to have your reactions to the different features of the guide and your suggestions for making improvements. Please fill out this form, fold and seal it, and drop it in the mail. Thanks!

Matthew Enos

School _____

Instructor's name _____

Used this Study Guide because: Required _____ Optional _____ Comment _____

Did this Study Guide help you with the course? _____

_____

Was this Study Guide interesting and informative? _____

_____

What did you like most about this Study Guide? _____

_____

Please check ☑ the parts of the Study Guide you used and tell me how useful they were:

☐ Module introductions _____

☐ Effective Student Tips _____

☐ Learning Objectives lists _____

☐ Key Terms lists _____

☐ Outlines _____

☐ Language Workout sections (by Eric Bohman) _____

☐ The Big Picture quizzes _____

☐ True-False questions _____

☐ Flashcards matching questions _____

☐ Multiple-Choice questions _____

☐ Short Essay questions _____

☐ For Psych Majors Only… quizzes _____

Additional comments about this Study Guide _____

_____

_____

OPTIONAL

Your name _____ Date _____

May Wadsworth, the publisher, quote you in promotions for the Study Guide or in future publishing ventures?

Yes _____ No _____

Note: You can also send me comments by e-mail! Profenos@aol.com